DISCARD

Emotional Problems of the Student

Second Edition

Emotiona
Problem

Second Editio

APPLETON-CENTURY-CROFTS
EDUCATIONAL DIVISION / MEREDITH CORPORATIO
New York

f the Student

GRAHAM B. BLAINE, JR.
CHARLES C. McARTHUR

Introduction by ERIK H. ERIKSON

Contributors

BABCOCK, HENRY HOLMES, M.D. Consultant (in Psychiatry) to the University Health Services, Harvard University; Associate Psychiatrist, Mount Auburn Hospital, Cambridge, Mass.

BINGER, CARL ALFRED LANNING, M.D. Honorary Psychiatrist to the University Health Services, Harvard University; Honorary Physician, Massachusetts General Hospital, Boston; Editor-in-Chief, Psychosomatic Medicine, Emeritus.

BLAINE, GRAHAM BURT, JR., M.D. Chief of Psychiatry, Harvard University Health Services; Assistant Psychiatrist, Adolescent Unit, Children's Hospital Medical Center, Boston; formerly Consulting Psychiatrist, Williams College, Williamstown, Mass.; Instructor in Psychiatry, Harvard Medical School; Consulting Psychiatrist, Simon's Rock College, Great Barrington, Mass.

BOJAR, SAMUEL, M.D. Assistant Clinical Professor of Psychiatry, Harvard Medical School; Psychiatrist to the University Health Services, Harvard University; Senior Associate in Medicine (Psychiatry), Peter Bent Brigham Hospital, Boston, Mass.

COON, GAYLORD PALMER, M.D. Staff Psychiatrist, University Health Services, University of Massachusetts, Boston, Mass.; formerly, Chief of Psychiatry, University Health Services, Harvard University.

DALRYMPLE, WILLARD, M.D. Director, University Health Services, Princeton University; formerly, Instructor in Medicine, Harvard Medical School, Columbia University College of Physicians and Surgeons; Vice-president for Publications, American College Health Association.

v

DINKLAGE, KENNETH TAYLOR, Ph.D. Psychologist to the University Health Services, Harvard University; Trainee Development Specialist, Peace Corps; formerly Psychologist to the Health Services at Dartmouth College and Cornell University.

ERIKSON, ERIK HOMBURGER. Professor of Human Development, Emeritus, Harvard College.

FARNSWORTH, DANA LYDA, M.D. Henry K. Oliver Professor of Hygiene, Harvard University; Director, University Health Services, Harvard University; Past Director of Health, Williams College, Williamstown, Mass.; formerly, Medical Director, Massachusetts Institute of Technology, Cambridge, Mass.

HODGINS, RODERIC C. Assistant to the Director, Office of Student Affairs, for Counseling, Graduate School of Business Administration, Harvard University; formerly, Assistant Director of the Bureau Study Counsel, Harvard College, Cambridge, Mass.

McARTHUR, CHARLES CAMPBELL, Ph.D. Psychologist to the University Health Services, Harvard University; Sometime lecturer, Department of Social Relations and Graduate School of Education, Harvard University; Management Consultant; Associate Editor, Journal of Counseling Psychology.

MUNTER, PRESTON K., M.D. Assistant Director and Psychiatrist to the University Health Services, Harvard University; Psychiatrist, The Itek Corporation, Lexington, Mass.

NELSON, ROBERT LEROY, M.D. (deceased) At time of death, Consultant in Psychiatry, University Health Services, Harvard University; formerly Instructor in Psychiatry, Rhode Island State Hospitals; Consultant in Psychiatry, Student Health Services, Brown University, Providence; Candidate, Boston Psychoanalytic Institute.

SORENSON, DAVID, Ed.D. Assistant Dean of Students for Health and Counseling and Assistant Professor of Psychology,

Brigham Young University; formerly Psychologist to the University Health Services, Harvard University; formerly Counselor in Winchester, Mass. public schools.

TEMBY, WILLIAM, M.D. Assistant Attending Psychiatrist, McLean Hospital, Belmont, Mass.; Psychiatric Consultant, Pine Manor Junior College, Chestnut Hill, Mass.; formerly, Assistant Psychiatrist to the University Health Services, Harvard University.

WALTERS, PAUL ALLEN, JR., M.D. Psychiatrist to the University Health Services, Harvard University; Director of Training, Post-graduate program, University Health Services, Harvard University; Lecturer in Social Relations, Harvard University; Associate Professor, Clark University; formerly, Consultant to the Peace Corps.

Preface

This edition, like its predecessor, is an attempt to portray the basic nature of the emotional conflicts faced by practically all students at one time or another. In addition, considerable attention is paid to the interaction of personal psychology and the vast social changes now in progress.

Anyone working with college students when the first edition of this book was written would have been greatly surprised if he could have known what would be happening to them in one short decade. All the writers in the first edition were, for the most part, concerned with problems of student psychopathology and the attitudes toward students and their difficulties shown by teachers, administrators, and parents. The vast seething cauldrons of social change were noticeable by their absence. Quiet, rationality, and analysis of problems and plans for meeting them all seemed to be taken for granted.

Then came the great wave of idealism of the Kennedy years, the programs to grant full civil rights to everyone, and to eliminate poverty. Enormous energy was being harnessed toward the realization of what a society could be. The charisma of President Kennedy affected people of all kinds throughout the world, moving them not only to greater action for making a better world, but also to increased expectations that such a goal was an immediate possibility. The assassination in Dallas came as a cruel shock—unbelievable, numbing, impossible.

President Johnson began most auspiciously on the development and passage of legislation of a most progressive sort. Education, medical care, elimination of poverty, granting of full civil rights to Negroes, and increased attention to programs of community mental health all received favorable attention from lawmakers. Then the civil rights movement bogged down in various struggles between students and citizens in the Southern states, the students at Berkeley rebelled, and above all, the Vietnam war intensified. College students were caught in many new personal quandaries, and their frustration and idealism stimulated many perceptive criticisms of the society which they were inheriting. Methods of waging war in Vietnam, research activities sponsored by the Defense Department, environmental pollution, and the neutral attitude toward political issues traditionally held by science and education all came under vigorous attack.

The assassinations of Martin Luther King, Jr., and Robert Kennedy only accentuated the frustration and despair. Many people, especially the young, felt that the society was evil and that violence, or at least strong disruption, was necessary in order to remake it. The colleges and universities became the targets through which society could be attacked—mainly because, as one student stated, they were close at hand. Outbursts of violence and counter-violence at Columbia, Stanford, Harvard, Cornell and many other institutions brought the whole panoply of student concerns into the public eye, while their unorthodox and frequently counterproductive forms of protest aided in a polarization of opinions and attitudes between liberal and conservative factions.

Attitudes toward psychiatry, particularly college psychiatry, changed in various ways. Unrestricted impulse expression increased noticeably during this period and was accompanied by suspicion of the motives and priorities of college health services, even as a common willingness to believe the worst of other people was spreading throughout the society. Attacks on college psychiatry, based on the argument that psychiatrists who work for organizations have a primary responsibility to the institution rather than to the patient, have gained strength even when the opposite point of view has been upheld and practiced by college psychiatrists. Charges that confidentiality is not maintained have gained some credence but this has not attained sufficient proportions to keep many students who need help from seeking it.

The great prominence of student protest movements has created in lay circles a strong opinion that the more ardent and fanatical of the student revolutionaries are sick and should be treated as such. College psychiatrists cannot accept this interpretation, though there is no question that protesting students are no more immune to emotional disability than others. In any case, the college psychiatrist's primary task is to help students and others who come under his care to deal with their inner conflicts effectively, whether or not the traditional causes of psychopathology are reinforced by the use of drugs, involvement in extremely radical forms of protest, or any other forms of expression not in favor at the moment. In brief, the essential task of college psychiatrists is to help the individual deal with his own reactions to events, while college administrators, particularly those concerned with discipline, and local law enforcement officials strive for order in the community.

The tightrope-walking that college psychiatrists (as well as those in industrial organizations) must do is not easy, and occasional mistakes will inevitably be made. But to withdraw from such work in educational institutions because of fear of criticism would be an abdication of responsibility and result in great harm to thousands of students. Fortunately, the great majority of students still respond favorably to the therapeutic efforts of college psychiatrists, despite the efforts of some persons to destroy their confidence. The policy of practicing good psychiatry, with the competence and integrity that that phrase connotes, continues to elicit satisfaction and gratitude from nearly all students.

Dana L. Farnsworth

Cambridge, Massachusetts

Preface to the First Edition

This collection of articles describing the psychiatric problems of students and the manner in which they are dealt with by a University Health Service is presented partly as an answer to the frequently asked question, "Why does a college need a psychiatrist?" In these days when the time of the practicing psychiatrist is so much in demand people wonder why a college like Harvard, supposedly occupied in educating the most promising young men in the country, should need the services of eight full-time psychiatrists. We hope that as the stories of the students described here unfold this question will be adequately answered. The young men who have come to us for help are indeed promising, but despite this and perhaps because of it they are often faced with paralyzing problems which if not dealt with might prevent them from ever realizing their promise. Provided with skillful and appropriate help they have for the most part been able to profit from the educational and social experience of university life at a time in their own development when they can best benefit from challenging work and heterogeneous social companionship.

We feel that with the possible exception of the chapter on the origin of neurosis all the material is presented in language easily understood by educators and teachers irrespective of their knowledge and experience in the fields of psychiatry and psychology. The content of the chapters at the same time should be of value and interest to members of the medical and psychiatric profession, particularly those who deal with students or are interested in them.

We have called our book *Emotional Problems of the Student*, believing that our findings can be taken to be perfectly general. In the past we have found that many readers do not feel comfortable about applying Harvard experience to themselves. Many people seem to have felt that psychological experience with a Harvard population does not count. Somehow we cannot believe that. Our logic is parallel to the most ancient example of the syllogism. We reason:

All human beings show forth the action of the laws of human nature.
Harvard men are human.
Therefore Harvard men show forth action of the laws of human nature.

Some readers may reject the minor in this syllogism. Admittedly, in the absence of this premise the argument falls.

In fact, we are not generalizing from experience limited to one university. All of the contributors to this book have worked in other settings and are presently engaged not only in collegiate but also in general psychiatric practice. Not all case histories offered came from Harvard students; it has seemed as well to specify origins as little as possible for protection of each patient's anonymity. More important than the variety of our individual experiences, however, is the fact that other men in other universities report phenomena similar to the phenomena we have seen. Chassell's description of his caseload sounds familiar, as does Fry's classic text on college mental health problems. So does the volume from Yale, *Psychosocial Problems of College Men.* Talk with other college health staffs has also encouraged us to generalize.

We are especially struck with the fact that Blos, working at a college outside the Ivy League, has had experiences startlingly like our own. For example, his observation that neuroses in early adult life represent adolescent conflicts "kept open indefinitely" is exactly like our follow-up experience to the effect that the "lush Brazilian jungle" of teenage fantasy soon withers and dies in the healthy upperclassman or graduate but continues to flourish in the neurotic men. Again Blos reports the same experience we have had when he "began to realize that he was dealing with case material which was basically different from cases seen in a mental hygiene or child guidance clinic, the difference being that no definite symptom complex had developed." Josselyn, in a non-college setting, seems to have had our experience with the better prognosis of postadolescent neuroses, from which recovery is a good deal more likely than is recovery from an illness of apparently equal severity in other age groups. Vorhaus' picture of the personality types seen in a city-wide clinic for an adolescent group with study problems was clearly replicated by our psychological tests at Harvard. Such parallel experiences make us believe that others may reasonably expect to see in their students the problems we see in students from Harvard.

Not all observers agree with us. Swartz of Boston University, for instance, argues that we underdiagnose, and even if the picture of student neuroses given in this book is accepted, some may challenge our striking assertions about the benign nature of most student psy-choses. Yet we are not alone in this view. The "acute postadolescent identity crisis" that reaches a turmoil state yet soon subsides has been described by Erikson and by others. At McLean Hospital acute post-adolescent turmoils of short duration have been seen in such numbers and follow courses so visibly different from true schizophrenic episodes that the two syndromes are being made the topic of comparative study. The turmoil patients come from all the colleges in Greater Boston and not primarily from Harvard. The clinical pictures recorded at McLean are very like those described in these pages.

Finally, the things we have learned make sense in terms of gen-eral theory. What follows is not just a description of college students; it is a description of how the troubles of college students, while unlike those described in ordinary clinical literature, are good illustrations of modern psychodynamic theory. The syndromes presented here are empirical validations of speculations and concepts offered by Erik Erikson, Irene Josselyn, Florence Kluckhohn, and others. These theories purport to have broad generality. They are part of a new movement in psychiatry that is as yet loosely integrated but might be character-ized as differing from classical psychiatry in being a more "full in-formation" point of view. Not since Anna Freud's *The Psychology of Adolescence* (which deals for the most part with an earlier part of adolescence) has the stage of life just preceding manhood been the subject of any systematic theoretical study. This extension of psycho-dynamic thinking to the special phenomena seen in the twenty-year-old has only recently taken place. If our cases validate such new theory, they also sometimes clarify it and may even add some new ideas to it. In the end, our description of student patients may add up to a new kind of psychodynamic point of view.

Since others have seen what we have seen and since clinical theo-ries as widely honored as those of Erikson and Josselyn are borne out in our data, we are confident that other workers at other colleges will find that their students have the same problems our students have and can be helped with these problems more understandingly from what we feel to be a widely, if not universally, applicable point of view.

The fact that separate chapters on the other graduate schools of Harvard University have not been included should not be taken to mean that there are no psychiatric problems there. The number of students seeking help for emotional problems from the Divinity, Law, Education, and Design schools runs proportionately about the same as from the Graduate School of Arts and Sciences, Medical and Business schools, and the students in the former have problems which are related to the particular field and school in which they are studying. However, until now we have not had an individual psychiatrist assigned to these schools to study the special problems involved in each, and therefore we are not yet ready to report on them separately.

Grateful acknowledgment is made to the *New England Journal of Medicine* for permission to reprint as part of Chapter 19 a large portion from an article appearing in their publication entitled "Short Term Psychotherapy with College Students." Our gratitude is also extended to Miss Virginia Gaylord for her editorial assistance.

We are glad to acknowledge the help of the following people in preparing the second edition of this book: Miss Kathleen Desmond, Miss Carolyn Schatz, Miss Elizabeth Gray, and Mr. Robert Rosen.

Graham B. Blaine, Jr.
Charles C. McArthur

Cambridge, Massachusetts

Contents

CONTRIBUTORS   v

PREFACE   ix

PREFACE TO THE FIRST EDITION   xiii
    DANA L. FARNSWORTH

INTRODUCTION   xix
    ERIK H. ERIKSON

1   THE ROLE OF THE COLLEGE PSYCHIATRIST   1
    DANA L. FARNSWORTH AND PRESTON K. MUNTER

2   FACULTY COUNSELING AND REFERRAL   17
    WILLARD DALRYMPLE

3   THE ROLE OF THE PSYCHOLOGIST IN A COL-
    LEGE HEALTH SERVICE   28
    CHARLES C. McARTHUR AND KENNETH T. DINKLAGE

4   DISTINGUISHING PATTERNS OF STUDENT
    NEUROSES   52
    CHARLES C. McARTHUR

5   ACUTE PSYCHOSIS, DEPRESSION, AND ELA-
    TION (REVISED VERSION)   73
    GAYLORD P. COON

6   BASIC CHARACTER DISORDERS AND HOMO-
    SEXUALITY   94
    GRAHAM B. BLAINE, JR. AND CHARLES C. McARTHUR

7   SUICIDE   109
    WILLIAM D. TEMBY

8   STUDENT APATHY   129
    PAUL A. WALTERS, JR.

9   DRUGS AND ADOLESCENCE: USE AND ABUSE   148
PAUL A. WALTERS, JR.

10   PROBLEMS CONNECTED WITH STUDYING   163
GRAHAM B. BLAINE, JR. AND CHARLES C. McARTHUR

11   INABILITY TO LEARN A FOREIGN LANGUAGE   185
KENNETH T. DINKLAGE

12   THE TEXT IS THE ADVERSARY   207
RODERIC C. HODGINS

13   THE RETURN OF THE COLLEGE DROPOUT   225
DAVID SORENSON

14   THE MOVEMENT   268
CHARLES C. McARTHUR

15   EMOTIONAL DISTURBANCES AMONG COLLEGE WOMEN   306
CARL A. L. BINGER

16   SPECIAL PROBLEMS OF GRADUATE STUDENTS IN THE SCHOOL OF ARTS AND SCIENCES   320
ROBERT L. NELSON

17   SPECIAL PROBLEMS ENCOUNTERED AT THE GRADUATE SCHOOL OF BUSINESS ADMINISTRATION   334
HENRY H. BABCOCK

18   PSYCHIATRIC PROBLEMS OF MEDICAL STUDENTS   350
SAMUEL A. BOJAR

19   THERAPY   364
GRAHAM B. BLAINE, JR.

INDEX   381

Introduction

Erik H. Erikson

1

The keynote of this book is Service. Originating in the Health Services of a large university, it reviews the difficulties and the rewards inherent in day-by-day psychiatric work with students, and offers vital comparative material to all those who are similarly engaged. In this it is eminently instructive and refreshingly frank; it does not hide the fact that college psychiatry—like many of its patients—is still groping for its place in the world of academics and for the concepts most adequate to its daily duties.

I assume that I owe the privilege of having the first word in this book to the fact that my own work with young patients has been representative of what the authors in their preface call a new psychiatric point of view. According to this view there are characteristic emotional disturbances in each stage of life which—although subject to differential diagnosis—are essentially determined by the life-tasks of that stage and are most easily ameliorated during the very period of their emergence. If studied and treated as circumscribed crises of inner growth, which are aggravated by discernible tensions in the sufferer's social condition, these disturbances may be prevented from becoming chronic ailments reinforced by the fatalistic diagnoses which they evoked in the past.

Colleges, of course, are foremost among the institutions which permit the study of comparable inner problems under demonstrable conditions. Students are men and women of the same age-group, who share a certain range of intellectual endowment and a converging set of motivations, and who compete in life-tasks dictated by a known tradition which they have (more or less) freely chosen as a trusted style. Colleges, furthermore, offer young people a sanctioned interim between childhood and adulthood. Such a *moratorium* is often characterized by a combination of prolonged immaturity and pro-voked precocity, which makes colleges not only good study grounds, but—as the surrounding communities always have been most eager to note—breeding grounds for deviant behavior of all kinds, whether such behavior is attributed to the influence of scholastics or human-istics, radicalism, existentialism, or psychoanalysis.

By giving an account of one section of such a college population, namely, the clientele of a psychiatric service, the authors do more than indicate what help can be given to one age-group; for whatever can be learned about the problems in a given kind of institution will eventually contribute to the delineation of problems of other age-groups in other kinds of institutions (of, say, middle age in industry). In the meantime, the authors display a pragmatic and democratic orientation toward emotional problems universal to students—an orien-tation sufficiently backed by data to make clear that if Harvard can-not deny its 10 percent quota of emotional problems, neither can other colleges get away with the assumption that what is described here is essentially (and predictably) typical for Harvard. In fact, com-parative study will make it possible to put aside the competitive question as to how many or how few individuals are troubled in given settings. There are always some, in any setting, who must be steered in their erratic growth or kept from being crushed by a transitory condition. The relevant questions are only what kind of problems re-ceive public recognition and attention; who is appointed to deal with them; and what these caretakers will make of these problems—medi-cally, conceptually, and ideologically.

2

The authors of this book, then, Harvard men dealing with Harvard problems, throw themselves upon the mercy of an inter-professional and intercollegiate orientation. I may be forgiven for using this preface to remind the readers of a few classical formulations concerning mental health, which have come to us from one of the great men of the Harvard past. It is well known that William James, all his life, was preoccupied with what was then called "morbid psychology." He himself suffered in his youth and into his manhood under severe emotional strain, for which he vainly sought the help of a variety of nerve cures. His letters also attested to the fact that he was interested in his friends' crises and that he offered them a kind of passionate advice which betrayed his own struggle for sanity. In the peculiar milieu of Boston, furthermore, which enjoys such blatant contrasts between political dramatics and the immersion of spirit and mind, he was drawn into the argument over the matter of faith-healing. And finally, he was one of the men who played host to the emerging psychiatric schools, among them that of Freud who visited this country in 1907. While Freud himself impressed him as a man obsessed with fixed ideas (he could make nothing in his own case with Freud's dream theories, James said, as have many of the most and of the least intelligent before and after him) he nevertheless expressed the hope that Freud and his pupils would carry their studies on and through. And, indeed, a book like the present one could not have been written, had not Freud and his pupils done just that.

In what follows I will quote a few of James' most outstanding formulations, not from his theoretical treatises but from his more personal confessions in which he gives such vital expression to the *experience* of emotional crises.

William James, as Matthiessen points out "came to maturity extremely slowly."[1] Even at 26, he wrote to Wendell Holmes: "Much would I give for a constructive passion of some kind."[2] This nostalgic complaint we will find, again and again, among the young college men of today; only that in James' life, the doubt and the delay was, according to Matthiessen, due to his father's fanatic insistence on *being,* which made it difficult for most of his children to find what, if anything, they could be *doing* (although at least two of them eventually proceeded to do it extremely well). I point to this, because, today, doubt and delay are so obviously often due to the circumstance that young men and women find themselves involved in a *doing* into which they were forced by a compulsion to excel fast, or by what in

---

[1] F. O. Matthiessen. The James Family, New York, Alfred A. Knopf, 1948, p. 209.
[2] *Ibid.*

these pages again and again is referred to as "parental pressure" before enough of a sense of *being* was secured to give to naked ambition a style of individuality or a compelling communal spirit.

I cannot here go into the personality or the parental habits of the father, Henry James, Sr., who by a combination of infirmity, in-clination, and affluence was permitted to spend his days at home, making his family life a tyranny of liberalism, and a school in utopian-ism, in which every choice was made from the freest and most universal point of view, and, above all, discussed with Father. Nor can I follow here the interesting path by which James' later philosophy became at once a continuation and an abrogation of his father's creed.

What interests us here is the particularly prolonged *identity crisis* which drove William from art school to "Scientific School" to Medical School, and from Cambridge to the Amazon to Europe and back to Cambridge (Mass.). Having suffered severe neurotic dis-comfort in Europe he spent his late twenties a neurotic invalid in his father's home, until at the age of 30 he accepted President Eliot's offer (Eliot had early "spotted" him) to teach anatomy at Harvard. James, however, was an invalidism comparable to that of Darwin, that is, a restriction of activities and associations which left at any given time only a narrow path for interest and activity. And yet, along that nar-row path, such men find, as if with a sleepwalker's surefootedness, their final goal of intellectual and social concentration. In James' case, the path led from artistic observation, through a naturalistic sense of classification and the physiologist's grasp of functioning, to the exile's linguistic perceptiveness, and finally, through the sufferer's self-knowledge and empathy to psychology and to philosophy. As James put it sovereignly: "I originally studied medicine in order to be a physiologist, but I drifted into psychology and philosophy from a sort of fatality. I never had any philosophic instruction, the first lecture on psychology I ever heard being the first I ever gave."[3]

It was not until he wrote, during a period of middle-aged cardiac dismay, his "Varieties of Religious Experience," that James gave an undoubted autobiographic account of a state "of the worst kind of melancholy," purportedly reported to him by a young "French suf-ferer."

---

[3] Matthiessen, *op. cit.*, p. 218.

"Whilst in this state of philosophic pessimism and general de-pression of spirits about my prospects, I went one evening into a dressing-room in the twilight, to procure some article that was there; when suddenly there fell upon me without any warning, just as if it came out of the darkness, a horrible fear of my own existence. . . . It was like a revelation; and although the immediate feelings passed away, the experience has made me sympathetic with the morbid feel-ings of others ever since. . . . I dreaded to be left alone. I remember wondering how other people could live, how I myself had ever lived, so unconscious of that pit of insecurity beneath the surface of life. My mother in particular, a very cheerful person, seemed to me a perfect paradox in her unconsciousness of danger, which you may well believe I was very careful not to disturb by revelations of my own state of mind. I have always thought that this experience of melan-cholia of mine had a religious bearing. . . . I mean that the fear was so invasive and powerful that, if I had not clung to scripture-texts like *The eternal God is my refuge, etc., Came unto me all ye that labor and are heavy-laden, etc., I am the Resurrection and the Life, etc.,* I think I should have grown really insane."[4] To this James added in a footnote a reference to a similar crisis of alienation (and psychiatrists were then called "alienists") which had been experienced and described by his father thus: "One day . . . towards the close of May, having eaten a comfortable dinner, I remained sitting at the table after the family had disappeared, idly gazing at the embers in the grate, think-ing of nothing, and feeling only the exhilaration incident to a good digestion, when suddenly—in a lightning-flash as it were—fear came upon me and trembling, which made all my bones to shake.' "[5]

A comparison of the two attacks leaves the question open, how much conformity with his father's inner life and life style, and how much liberation by way of a revelation may be seen in the experience. One thing is certain: each age has its own forms of alienation (forms often more culture-bound than the individual sense of being utterly "beside onself" would suggest) and the struggle in both father and son concerned the identity of naked and stubborn selfhood so typical

---

[4] The Letters of William James, edited by his son, Henry James, Boston, The Atlantic Monthly Press, 1920, p. 145.
[5] Matthiessen, *op. cit.,* p. 161.

for extreme individualism and the surrender to some higher identity—
be it outer and all-enveloping, or inner and all-pervasive. That the
father (as he further reports), in his moment of distress, finally if
reluctantly turned to his wife, while the son assures us that he did not
wish to disturb his unaccountably cheerful mother, makes one wonder
how much anxiety it took to remind the self-possessed men of that day
of the refuge of woman.

As Henry James, Sr., put it, reviving a bit of agrarian roman-
ticism ". . . time and again while living at this dismal water-cure, and
listening to its endless 'strife of tongues' about diet, and regimen,
and disease, and politics, and parties, and persons, I have said to
myself, The curse of mankind, that which keeps our manhood so little
and so depraved, is its sense of self-hood, and the absurd, abominable
opinionativeness it engenders. How sweet it would be to find oneself
no longer man, but one of those innocent and ignorant sheep pastur-
ing upon that placid hillside, and drinking in eternal dew and fresh-
ness from Nature's lavish bosom!"[6]

Of William James' road to maturity and liberation from such
acute alienation, one important trend is reported by himself, the
other by his father.

"I think that yesterday was a crisis in my life," James wrote to
his father, "I finished the first part of Renouvier's second "Essais"
and see no reason why his definition of Free Will—'the sustaining of
a thought *because I choose to* when I might have other thoughts'—
need be the definition of an illusion. At any rate, I will assume for
the present—until next year—that it is no illusion. My first act of
free will shall be to believe in free will."[7] To this he adds a sentence
which admirably expresses a principle dominant in today's ego-psy-
chology—a psychology governing more or less explicitly a number of
basic assumptions in the book before us: "Hitherto, when I have felt
like taking a free initiative, like daring to act originally, without
carefully waiting for contemplation of the external world to determine
all for me, suicide seemed the most manly form to put my daring into;
now, I will go a step further with my will, not only act with it, but
believe as well; believe in my individual reality and creative power.

---

[6] Matthiessen, *op. cit.*, p. 162.
[7] Letters, *op. cit.*, p. 147.

My belief, to be sure, can't be optimistic—but I will posit life (the real, the good) in the self-governing resistance of the ego of the world. Life shall (be built in) doing and suffering and creating."[8] I am asking a special point of this formulation of a self-governing as well as a resisting aspect of the ego because the term "ego" is used in the book before us with an innocence such as only colleagues can maintain to whom the main concepts in their fields have become a matter of interoffice communication. That other and more popular use of the term "ego" as a kind of egocentric vanity, an exaggerated self-esteem which is both baseless and invulnerable, persists even among otherwise informed people. Yet the psychoanalytic use of the term which speaks of the ego as the central personal core which organizes experience and guides action, only follows scholastic and philosophical usage.

And here is Henry James, Sr.'s report on his son's other great and liberating thought-experience. ". . . (William) came in the other afternoon while I was sitting alone, and after walking the floor in an animated way for a moment, broke out: 'Bless my soul, what a difference between me as I am now and as I was last spring at this time!' . . . He had a great effusion. I was afraid of interfering with it, or possibly checking it, but I ventured to ask what especially in his opinion had produced the change. He said several things . . . but more than anything else, his having given up the notion that all mental disorder requires to have a physical basis. This had become perfectly untrue to him. . . . He has been shaking off his respect for men of mere science as such, and is even more universal and impartial in his mental judgments than I have known him before. . . ."[9] No doubt, old Henry, Sr., suited his son's words a bit to his own style of thought, but this scene is typically James, head and heart participating in a new insight which thus makes a difference. That insight, of course, was progressing in many quarters, not only initiating a liberation of a host of bed-bound, water-treated and leisure-tied patients, but also preparing a new study of the mind through the treatment of those who are most motivated to reveal their true thoughts: mental sufferers. It is clear that the first insight, concerning the self-determination of free will, is related to the second, that is the abandonment of physio-

---

[8] *Letters, op. cit.,* p. 148.
[9] *Letters, op. cit.,* p. 169.

logical factors as fatalistic arguments against a neurotic person's continued self-determination. Together, they are the basis of psycho-therapy, which, no matter how it is described and conceptualized, aims at the restoration of the patient's power of choice.

From here, a variety of paths lead to today's ego-psychological considerations, to which the establishment of a sense of identity in adolescence and young adulthood is central. This, too, is vividly defined in a passage of James' letters.

". . . I have often thought that the best way to define a man's character would be to seek out the particular mental or moral attitude in which, when it came upon him, he felt himself most deeply and intensely active and alive. At such moments there is a voice inside which speaks and says: 'This is the real me!' And afterwards, considering the circumstances in which the man is placed, and noting how some of them are fitted to evoke this attitude, whilst others do not call for it, an outside observer may be able to prophesy where the man may fail, where succeed, where be happy and where miserable. Now as well as I can describe it, this characteristic attitude in me always involves an element of active tension, of holding my own, as it were, and trusting outward things to perform their part so as to make it a full harmony, but without any *guaranty* that they will. Make it a guaranty—and the attitude immediately becomes to my consciousness stagnant and stingless. Take away the guaranty, and I feel (provided I am *uberhaupt* in vigorous condition) a sort of deep enthusiastic bliss, of bitter willingness to do and suffer anything, . . . and which, although it is a mere mood or emotion to which I can give no form in words, authenticates itself to me as the deepest principle of all active and theoretic determination which I possess. . . ."[10]

Without wishing to improve on these formulations by elevating one or the other phrase out of their intrinsic wholeness, I would point to the words "intensely active and alive" and "but without any guaranty" as "authenticating" a state of mental health. For the problem of psychotherapy may well be circumscribed by these words: the patient wishes to feel alive in his activities; he comes to find in therapy a guaranty; yet the therapist, guaranteeing nothing, must try to lead the patient to his authentic self.

William James was one of those passionately twice born, who,

---

[10] Letters, *op. cit.,* p. 199.

in the end, must help themselves, or perish; and who, once they have helped themselves, must think and lead. Maybe there is no other step from a consideration of such men to that of our young patients than the streamlined and easily traveled bridge from inner-directness to other-directedness, and to the popular preoccupation with identity— not as a delineation of individual and deity, or individual and human- ity, but that of individual and man or just plain folks. Yet, inner- directedness in Riesman's original sense keeps a strong hold on our thinking youth, both in the sense of a paralyzing compulsion, and in that of a compelling obligation.

At this point, a question must be faced which many a reader of this book will (and should) ask. I have found it most succinctly expressed by the Chancellor of St. Paul's Cathedral in a book review. "It makes one wonder," he writes, "whether with all our clinics for maladjusted and unhappy children, where psychiatrists put things right, there will be any more geniuses? Does genius arise from the effort to overcome childhood frustration? Take that away and per- haps there will be no more Luthers."[11] But it is not at all certain, and it is, in fact, unlikely that there exists such a simple causal relation between unusual infantile pressures and unusual adult deeds. The child's aggravated conflicts may be the effect rather than the cause of the fact that his, from the beginning, was a precocious mental and moral perceptivity. As far as Luther and other great ideological innovators are concerned, the canon's question could be countered with another one, namely, whether such a man's genius need to be whipped to ferocity by "parental pressures," and, in future history, need be as destructive as such genius has been in the past, and as likely to bring (to its own horror and surprise) the worst out of the people in whom it temporarily elevated the best. Genius as such can neither be explained or treated away; only, at times, its delay and inhibition and its perversion to destructive or self-destructive ends.

3

This book, as any other, offers to each reader his own—his own preference of interest and his own choice as to what he likes to be troubled and provoked by. Most readers will agree on the im-

---

[11] Church of England Newspaper.

portance of two extreme classes among potential health service clients: they will want the psychiatrists to recognize and to keep hands off geniuses; and they will expect them to always spot psychotics and potential suicides.

If the psychiatrists do not say much about genius, it may be that they come to see little of it or to see it in new forms. At any rate, they will find genius as such not easily discouraged, even where its bearer may be depressed and they will be on the side of an individual's passionate search where they can convince themselves that the search is also well-endowed. As to the other extreme, psychotic breakdown or suicidal risk, the psychiatrists describe an encouraging development: they increasingly can and may act decisively to protect an individual and those next to him during periods when youth (with its combination of explosive impulsivity and obsessive introspection) may bring a latent problem to a sudden, turbulent head. For psychiatric enlightenment has progressed to a point where even treatment in a mental hospital need not prejudice a young person's future functioning or standing.

This leaves a "middle-class" of clients. Among these, students with well-established psychoneuroses of long standing can be shown the way to private treatment, if they have not found it, and this particularly in a metropolitan area such as Boston which permits a symbiosis between a well-endowed academic community and a dense concentration of alert psychiatrists. The largest category to whom this book is devoted, then, are students who typically appeal to a health service of the kind described here for relatively short-term help. In regard to these, and the services they receive, I would like, in conclusion, to express a specific interest and, maybe, worry—except that there are matters which need not keep us worrying if we keep a methodical eye on them. I mean the temporarily apathetic and depressed students, and those who "obsess" (as they call it themselves) beyond the call of academic duty. In the accounts of their disturbances a *retrospective* and *introspective* trend is discernible which will arouse in many readers questions as to what these stories are typical for: a section of youth anywhere; American youth; introspective youth; academic youth; youth with too many psychoanalytic paperbacks on bed and shelf and table? Or do these stories reflect the view of the psychiatrists who elicit and report them: psychiatry anywhere; American psychiatry; psychoanalytically oriented psychiatry? It comes, at any rate, as a welcome surprise to hear the authors reflect on the thera-peutic uselessness of the by now stereotyped effort of their clients to "spill" in a formless manner as many childhood data as possible in order to come face to face with some key events which *must* be at the bottom of the disturbance. Here, of course, a universal trend has only found a new form, namely, the wish of the sufferer to believe in a patent medicine of some kind; and psychoanalysis in some brief form offers to many a bottle of sufficiently intellectual coloring.

I do believe, however, that the "natural" selection at work in the encounter of a self-referred or referred section of a population with a branch of the healing arts permits an interesting glimpse into trends of the time. This book offers such a glimpse, first of all, into the motivation to come to the psychiatric service: this varies according to age and chosen specialty. (For one long occupied with the training of psychiatrists, it is good to know that young wives of future physi-cians also come and are seen.) In the largest group of clients it is the *motivation to study* or to *stay in college* which seem to pose the initial questions. Here, it often seems as if the wish to be at Harvard too often springs from the parents' motivation rather than the student's ("pa-rental pressure" is an all too common word in these documents), and where it is the student's, he seems alienated from his own ambition, his motions as well as his emotions being disengaged from his motiva-tion and all three threatening to die down. On the other hand, the psychiatrists speak of the "appreciation" and "increased affection" which many of these students seem to crave above all, as they strive for "good grades." Here, then, one senses the reflection of a competi-tive milieu which strongly tied the children to itself and yet denied them such love as is free of extraneous standards of performance; and which then pushed them into the competitive world of an affluent society and a world of affluence of choices without having prepared in them a strong and eager anticipation of that pull of opportunities (for companionship, competence, and the sharing of ideas) which a good college provides. A key issue in this matter is the psychiatrist's readiness to appreciate the young person's eagerness "to discuss values, ethics, motivations, life, death, suicide, and so forth." This, of course, can be a defense against the consideration of more specific and more specifically embarrassing problems. But it is also important to realize in the eagerness described a search for permission to try to believe in something—a permission which nowadays is sometimes sought from psychiatry, because the psychiatrist, at least, is expected to be free of intellectual illusions and ideological shams; and it is, by the same token, a search for a permission to repudiate strongly (see Doctor Binger's moving words on the recognition of evil) and to repudiate with discrimination. The lives of a not inconsiderable number of college men and women today are not only often marred by a lack of meaningful encounters of a positive kind, but also by a double repudiation of every inner (and past) source of motivation and of any attraction by truly intellectual, spiritual or political issues—a repudiation so stubborn and yet so vague and so general, that it can only end in the self-repudiation of the isolated individual. Such self-repudiation is at the bottom of much of the much decried and yet defiantly maintained "alienation" in college.[12]

One is glad, then, to see the authors speak of the "cognitive map of the universe" which the young individual must gain while in college. What they call cognitive here has two sides: the experience of proven competence in the sense of R. W. White; and the ideological relatedness of such competence to an anticipated world order.

The orientation of the psychiatrist as a healer of motivation who prepares his client for the engulfing movements of his day's techniques and thought, makes him a member of the academic community, which will appreciate him the more, the more his function is delineated. Instead of mutual misunderstandings, one may hope for an optimal degree of healthy and friendly antagonism between the educator's, the administrator's, and the healer's functions, a system of checks and balances which can serve a common educational ideal. What, at the end, youth wants from all three—instruction, education, and treatment —is, again, stated in one of William James' letters when he writes to a friend that he hopes in their friendship to "baptize myself afresh."[13]

---

[12] One is reminded here of another, an international, volume on Student Mental Health in which the ideological engagement of the youth of other countries is discussed. Proceedings of the First International Conference on Student Mental Health, Daniel H. Funkenstein, ed. World Federation for Mental Health and International Association of Universities, 1959.
[13] Matthiessen, *op. cit.,* p. 102.

Emotional Problems of the Student

Second Edition

The Role of the College Psychiatrist

Dana L. Farnsworth AND
Preston K. Munter

The need for psychotherapy is well known and widely accepted, especially in academic communities. But there are other possible functions, and some necessary ones, that the college psychiatrist may undertake. The need for them is not well understood. Indeed, many of them are not yet clearly defined. In this chapter, we will describe some of the corollary activities of the college psychiatrist—ways in which psychiatric thinking and skills can be applied outside the treatment room. Before discussing these, however, we want to make it clear that whatever additional duties a college psychiatrist assumes, his fundamental task is to prevent and treat illness. Indeed, if he is to be effective at all in other activities, he must continue to draw upon his clinical relationships as the primary source of his special knowledge and insight. Furthermore he cannot expect to find broad acceptance throughout the university for his point of view unless he discharges his treatment responsibilities in a skillful fashion.

In *Considerations of Personality Development in College Students, Report* #32, by the Group for the Advancement of Psychiatry, the following statement appears: "The educator seeks to stimulate the development of the student's knowledge and discipline of mind. The educator is also interested in facilitating the development of the student as an individual in our society. Much of the conflict in modern society stems from the efforts to achieve a genuine synthesis of these two goals." The emotional reactions that go on inside and outside the classroom greatly influence the successful attainment of both these goals. We are agreed, educator and psychiatrist alike, that the college should not be turned into a sanitarium. Nevertheless, attention must be paid to the feelings as well as to the intellects of people in education, if the college experience is to count as a major factor in the kind of synthesis cited in this report. During the past twenty-five years or so, we have come to learn that the emotional climate of a school has profound implications for the effectiveness of the education it offers. Among the important determinants of this climate is the emotional status of teacher-student relationships. A student's capacity to accept and integrate information is very much affected by events and relationships which have no obvious connection with the apparent interchange of facts which takes place in the classroom. The student's experiences with the college and its personnel outside the classroom have a very real effect upon how well he learns. The psychiatrist's purpose on the campus in addition to his role as a therapist is to offer professional help in dealing with the emotional determinants of teaching and learning in order to facilitate the educational process for which the institution exists. To do this at all effectively, he must come out of his office and match minds and experience with his academic colleagues. This will involve the psychiatrist in a wide variety of activities which are not therapy, but which, nevertheless, can be turned to excellent purpose, both therapeutic and preventive, as they encourage and foster a healthier emotional climate throughout the college.

One of the broad areas of concern for the psychiatrist in the college is the administration of discipline. Though the psychiatrist should not himself participate in disciplinary procedures, the philosophy underlying discipline and the way this is put into practice by others are his legitimate concerns. If the prevailing relationship between faculty members and students is characterized by the "cops-and-robbers" motif, any attempt by the faculty to alter the behavior of the students will be viewed with considerable disfavor, and it will be considered a sporting event to outwit the faculty in every way possible. If, on the other hand, discipline is represented as a matter of prime importance to the students themselves, and they can be encouraged to develop committees and organizations for the regulation of their own behavior, discipline can become an integral part of the educational process. When faculty and deans take censorious attitudes and impose punitive or arbitrary restrictions, students will react with hostility and rebellion. One can reasonably doubt the educational value as well as the lasting effect of such a system. Contrariwise, attitudes of faculty and administration that support evidences of maturity, and give students an opportunity to maintain self-respect and utilize newly achieved ego strengths, are likely to elicit a positive response. In public and private conversation, the psychiatrist can foster an understanding of individual misbehavior by emphasizing the significance of causes rather than supporting summary punishment for those who break the rules. For example, a probation system which assumes that ethical concerns are the basis for learning how to control oneself responsibly is likely to be more effective than one which enforces conformity by instilling fear in the offending student by imposing strict punishment.

Matters of discipline have special implications for the confidentiality of the doctor-patient relationship in the college. Since this is a delicate and controversial subject, it seems advisable to specify these implications in some detail. Every student seen by the psychiatrist should be fully assured—because it is so—that what transpires between him and the doctor is confidential. That is, the student should understand that he is free to say what he wishes and that none of what is said will be revealed to anyone by the doctor without the previous permission of the student. The administration and faculty should support this covenant with conviction, and the psychiatrist should adhere to it with devotion, despite the many varied and subtle pressures to do otherwise. The psychiatrist should deviate from stringent adherence to this principle of confidentiality only when he considers that there may be danger to the patient or to the community. At such times he may use information obtained in confidence in order to bring about essential action or to warn appropriate persons in order to prevent calamity. When this is properly explained to students, most of them can accept it as reasonable and consistent with the psychiatrist's overall responsibilities. Furthermore, students recognize the protection implicit in such action and find it reassuring.

Problems of a more specific nature are likely to arise when a student is referred to the psychiatrist by a disciplinary officer in contrast with the student who is self-referred and with whom one can establish a confidential relationship as described. The student who is a disciplinary problem should be told by the college officer who refers him to the psychiatrist why he is being referred. This would normally include a statement to the effect that breaking the rules is often a response to emotional pressures and that he is being given an opportunity to investigate his misbehavior from this point of view, with professional help. He should understand that the psychiatrist has no judicial or police authority. It should be further pointed out that the psychiatrist can give his medical opinion to the referring administrative officer without revealing specific details of the student's history or any verbatim communication made by him to the doctor. The student should be informed of the doctor's opinion, in most cases before the doctor forwards it to the administration. That is, the doctor should assume responsibility to the student as well as to the administration for his psychiatric evaluation.

The psychiatrist should not have any authority for discipline. The practice of good treatment is not compatible with legislating, judging, or punishing. The psychiatrist should have the freedom to make recommendations solely on the basis of his professional observations, and these recommendations may or may not be acted upon by the administrative officials, depending upon how these recommendations may be affected by other factors which lie within their knowledge and jurisdiction. If the psychiatrist assumed administrative functions of this kind, his capacity for objectivity would be seriously impaired.

When a student is being treated for an emotional disorder outside the college health services, the college psychiatrist should, of course, support the confidentiality of the relationship between the student and his private doctor. But the psychiatrist is at liberty to request information from the private therapist and from any source available to him in his professional capacity in order to make as reasonable a judgment as he can about a particular student when asked for an evaluation by the college administration. In most cases the college psychiatrist will be able to accept the opinion of the outside physician and make his recommendation accordingly. In those few cases where this is not possible, he will have to depend upon his own information and often will need to request an additional interview with the student to bring his information and impression up to date.

It is important for the college psychiatrist to cooperate with counseling programs. He should be available to faculty counselors for consultation regarding the specific problems of individual students and also to participate actively in discussions on the nature of counseling with groups so that general questions and attitudes may be developed cooperatively. Often a series of seminars focused on matters developing out of counseling situations and related to patterns of personality development, emotional reactions, and maturation can be set up as an in-service program. Programs of this sort provide opportunities for the psychiatrist and the educator to share profitably their special experiences and observations and develop insights into their respective use of language. Accurate and useful concepts of student development, behavior, and needs are derived from such interchange.

During the past few decades a variety of counseling theories and practices has been developed. Most of these encompass some of the basic notions of the dynamic theory of personality development, which, together with the art of critical but unprejudiced interviewing, forms the backbone of most good counseling procedures. Very recently, Erik Erikson's amplification of the dynamic theory, with his emphasis on the adolescent, has proved especially useful. However, each group of counselors and their psychiatric colleagues need to particularize principles and practices to make them appropriate for the special demands and restrictions of the college in which they work. There is no doubt that counseling procedures which tend to support the individual's ego strengths, help him to focus more clearly on realities and to explore their possibilities, encourage thoughtful independence, and do not impose authoritarian decisions upon him are gaining wider acceptance by both faculty and students. The psychiatrist can do much outside his office to teach such points of view and to support them among the faculty members who are already oriented in this direction. It is certainly no surprise that most college psychiatrists find an impressive reservoir of talented and experienced counselors within the faculty. These individuals are usually hungry for professional help in improving their skills and eager to find someone who will be a focus for the counseling program and around whom they can rally. The psychiatrist can readily fulfill such needs.

Students who leave college by choice rather than necessity are proper subjects of psychiatric interest. Both internal and external circumstances impel intellectually competent students to drop out of school for a time. The various circumstances preceding withdrawal from school have been dealt with elsewhere in this book. But the point at which the student *must* withdraw from his studies may be a critical one for his future well-being. Whether his apparent emotional disturbance at this time is severe or moderate, his motivation for learning may well be in jeopardy. This is a peculiarly appropriate time and situation for skillful help by the psychiatrist himself and also by administrators whose attitudes may have been influenced by psychiatric consultation. The separation anxiety which results from leaving college may be especially painful and often is accompanied or succeeded by depressive reactions. The counseling provided throughout this period may prove to be a salient factor in helping the student minimize these adverse reactions, approach his unpleasant situation realistically, and be able to move through the experience with only a modicum of regressive emotional response. "Dropouts" may thus be helped to retreat healthfully in order to reconstitute themselves inwardly as well as outwardly. Good counseling at such times permits motivation for intellectual pursuit to be sustained even though the enforced time away from studies may be spent in quite different activity. Such departing students are more likely to exhibit healthy attitudes toward themselves as well as toward their college after appropriate counseling. When they again take up their studies, they do so without interfering feelings of grievance or hostility.

The manner and method adopted by administrative officers in making official pronouncements will play a significant part in establishing or destroying a good public image of the institution and those who administer it. In the development of better attitudes among administrators, faculty, and students, this image can play a major role. The psychiatrist, therefore, is interested in how the administration represents itself to students. Abrupt notices, for example, tend to invite abrupt responses. This may be illustrated by the experience of a dean of a large college who was overly concerned about the way his students dressed for the evening meal in the dormitories. Most of them wore slacks or blue jeans and sport shirts. Even less reputable attire was noted on some who went to dinner directly from late afternoon laboratories. The dean wanted the students to wear white shirts, ties, and jackets at the dinner table, on the premise that this is the way "gentlemen" dress for meals. Against good psychiatric (and faculty) advice, he issued a fiat directing students to attire themselves in this gentlemanly fashion at least one evening a week, choosing Friday for the occasion. The students responded to this rather arbitrary, and to them unreasonable, order by appearing exactly as directed. But "white shirt" often was a stiff bosomed evening shirt, an eighteen century ruff, or an old-fashioned shirt with a high wing collar; "jackets" varied from red hunting coats to funeral cutaways and everything in between. Since there was nothing in the dean's directive about trousers, many gentlemen appeared in underwear shorts, swimming trunks, riding jodhpurs, or rubber skin-diving leggings. Sneakers, track shoes, flippers, and bare feet put a finishing touch on many an ensemble. Friday night came to be known as Fashion Night publicly, and in private as George's Goof. Simple as it sounds, it is still difficult to persuade some people that reasonable and fully explanatory notices tend to stimulate cooperation. Even fines can be levied with general support from all concerned if the circumstances for their existence and application are appropriate and if these reasons are frankly explained in calm fair-minded language rather than with hysterical threats of punishment.

One of the really important areas of contact for the college psychiatrist outside the treatment room is in his consultation with admissions committees. This is a delicate area for psychiatric participation for many reasons. One of these is the likelihood that the psychiatrist's task will be structured for him as "screening in" those who are well and "screening out" those who have a history of emotional illness. The psychiatrist should be aware of the committee's conscious and unconscious need to polarize his function as an adjuvant selector. He himself should avoid defining his role in this way and avoid also having it so defined by those who would see him merely as an arbiter of troublesome cases. Instead he should specify himself as an expert in a special field offering particular kinds of medical observations as consultant to the admissions committee. The determination as to who is admitted and who refused admission to a college is a complicated one in which the opinion of a physician is rarely decisive.

On the other hand, the psychiatrist may have pertinent and useful opinions to express to those who have to make final choices in the admission procedure. In giving his opinions, the psychiatrist recognizes that there are certain differences between physical and emotional illnesses especially in their direct and indirect effects upon intellectual functioning. However, it is desirable to make as little distinction as possible, philosophically, between a health handicap due to a physical cause and one due to an emotional conflict. In this connection, the language of the application form is of vital importance. The kind of information requested and the manner in which the questions are phrased may significantly affect the accuracy of answers. These questions can promote or disrupt good relations between secondary schools and colleges as well as between colleges and graduate schools. The psychiatrist should be consulted by administrators about such forms and questionnaires in order to help them formulate non-threatening questions to which applicants can respond honestly with the kind of information the school needs without the fear of jeopardizing their chances of admission. What the specific forms and questionnaires should contain and how they should be worded are matters to be decided within each institution. In any case, if a college does request information from prospective students regarding past or current history of emotional disturbance, this information should be sent directly to the college psychiatrist. Appropriate evaluation may possibly include further communication with the student—preferably a personal interview if that is feasible—or with his family or his private physician. The college psychiatrist may then be in a position to make a reasonable judgment in the case and to report this to the admissions committee without revealing any details of the individual's history. In most cases, both the college and the student will benefit from such a procedure. Through the psychiatrist, the college can be aware of those who are so seriously disturbed emotionally at the time of application that they are unlikely to perform adequately. They may be acceptable later, however, when they can give evidence that their difficulties have been modified or overcome. Students with less severe emotional problems which do not handicap them academically find it helpful and reassuring to make contact with a knowledgeable and understanding person whom they can consult after admission for professional advice, help, or treatment, if such is indicated. More and more experience supports the fact that there is not an essential difference between emotional and physical illness which makes it necessary to view emotional illness with special attitudes or to judge applicants with a history of emotional disturbance by separate value criteria. Certain emotional states clearly interfere with intellectual activity and academic responsibilities; others, even severe ones do not interfere. The psychiatrist can make a major contribution to the work of admissions committees if he will distinguish such students as often as he can. But all concerned, including the psychiatrist, should have well in mind the plain fact that a psychiatrist is not capable of predicting very accurately the future behavior of a given individual. His clinical experiences teaches him that there are too many known and unknown variables in human reaction patterns for him to be able to make such predictions. At best he can only make informed guesses. Strengths are less apparent to illness-oriented psychiatrists than are weaknesses. When the psychiatrist is in doubt, he usually recommends in favor of the student. Until psychiatric knowledge and psychological skills improve, there will continue to be great difficulty in distinguishing, except more or less by intuition, from among intellectually qualified people, those who have a reasonably good chance of college success and those who will be seriously handicapped by their emotional problems.

The social setting of an institution gives rise to emotional problems which often come to the psychiatrist's attention, and for this reason he should have a lively interest in the social tensions which characterize a given college. Various sources of tension are found on almost any campus: between majority and minority groups, fraternity and nonfraternity members, residential and commuting students, and among the several social strata of residential students, to name a few.

One of the most dramatic manifestations of tension with its consequent lowering of morale is the student riot. In the college setting morale is a complicated structure related to the expectations of parents, of students, of faculty, and of alumni. It is influenced by the example that faculty and administration set for the community by their behavior as a group and as individuals no less than by the character of the students. Many external factors promote good morale: a successful varsity athletic team, luxurious dormitory accommodations, liberal parietal rules, the quality of food, and the physical beauty of the campus. Of more moment are the personal characteristics of members of the faculty and administration. It does not seem a valid theory that students must develop pent-up energy during the winter and give vent to it in the spring in the form of destructive riots. It is more likely that these demonstrations are an expression of resentment incited by unfair punishments or by arbitrary and poorly explained regulations.

In his formal and informal contacts around the college, the psychiatrist can promote healthy morale by exerting an influence on the side of thoroughly explained rules and regulations, thoughtful and deliberate administrative judgments, and reasonable, appropriate punishments. He should also support academic programs that accommodate the development of individual values at least as much as they emphasize arbitrarily selected facts. In his contacts outside the treatment room, the psychiatrist should underscore the learning process as an intensely personal experience, helping both teacher and student develop respect for the interpersonal relationship that subtends their intellectual endeavors. The prototype of this relationship is a familiar one to the psychiatrist. His knowledge in this area can be of use to the educators as well as to the students in their attempts to develop the kinds of satisfactions from rewarding interpersonal relationships that underlie good group morale. Evidence of these satisfactions is considerably less spectacular than the riots which express dissatisfaction. Yet the mere opportunity to achieve them will often supplant riots.

In any case, social tensions have multiple sources and complicated derivations which make the task of delineating them formidable but necessary if their effects are to be dealt with reasonably. The psychiatrist can probably be most effective in developing community management of these situations if he will organize and motivate an interdisciplinary team of interested experts. Fortunately, most universities harbor at least a few psychologists, sociologists, and anthropologists. Without doubt there are several experts in the liberal arts who have an active interest in community affairs. To these the psychiatrist can contribute his own special knowledge of individual and group reactions and emotions, thus acting as coordinator of a team approach. By meeting with all of the pertinent resources of the community, problems which are usually complex and at times dangerous may be brought to light and then into reasonable and manageable bounds. A group which combines these several disciplines and techniques is in an especially strategic position to educate the community. It can point out the need for resolving generally felt stresses and anxieties and may formulate ways and means for resolution.

It should be added that such cooperative relationships may make it possible for the psychiatrist to practice some preventive medicine. He may be able to use such associations to help allay premonitory evidences of community tensions and hostilities before they become overtly expressed. Such deterrent maneuvers may have significance for the educational process. Such a team of interdisciplinary trouble-shooters helps the college bring what it *does* in line with what it *says*. The attitudes outside the classroom will then be compatible with what is taught inside it, making values seem somewhat more alive and part of daily life and possibly somewhat more attractive.

The psychiatrist should be available for consultation with student government groups, religious, living, and social groups and should be especially responsive to requests for conferences with members of the faculty. They are sometimes in quandaries regarding the behavior of students and spend many hours discussing student problems. Indeed, the phenomenological effects of emotion upon teaching as well as learning occupy a disproportionate share of faculty attention. The psychiatrist can be of great help in such discussion, either by meeting for private consultation with an individual instructor or by working with small groups of faculty through the techniques of group psychodynamics. He can meet with faculty and administration committees as either a customary or invited participant. In some instances college psychiatrists have academic rank, and there is much to be said in favor of this practice, especially if it provides routine contact between the psychiatrist and faculty as they meet to discuss the regular and irregular business of operating an educational institution. To the extent that a particular psychiatrist feels qualified and at ease about it, he should be available to all those who are interested in improving the emotional climate of the institution.

Symptomatic behavior of the so-called acting out kind is also of special interest to the psychiatrist. He sees it in many forms in students but most often in those who have problems of emancipation or maturation and whose overt behavior is flamboyant enough to attract attention and then referral. Some acting out, however, comes to light only under unfavorable circumstances, and no one is aware that a problem exists until the results of the behavior come into public view. Vandalism is this sort of phenomenon and is an especially trying problem for any academic community. Helping some students to develop respectful attitudes toward property is a very difficult task. Probably this is best accomplished by making known to the students the types of vandalism that are being practiced and by setting up a system whereby students share some of the responsibility for the destruction that takes place. Most students are shocked, for example, when they learn from a librarian how much mutilation is perpetrated upon library books. A beginning toward the development of sensitivity and responsibility in such matters can be made in college, however, and the psychiatrist can help in situations of this kind by delineating causes as far as possible and by encouraging the community to deal with the problem in terms of its personal and social significance rather than as a ready focus for punitive attitudes in relation to a single episode.

A college psychiatrist is frequently involved in the management of those persons who converge upon the office of the president and other high places in the university with bizarre ideas and behavior that may seem frightening but usually are only annoying. Such people are likely to be emotionally disturbed and, in some instances, psychotic. It is a very welcome service when the psychiatrist manages to steer these patients into treatment and end the trouble and discomfort they have caused. Almost every college president is the recipient of numerous crank letters. The psychiatrist can help by distinguishing, when he can, which of these may endanger the safety of the president or others and which can be disregarded with impunity.

The psychiatrist has a legitimate concern about the effects of subsidization of students by means of competitive or special scholarships for undergraduate athletes or candidates for advanced degrees in graduate schools. Although this area has been largely neglected and much research needs to be done, it would appear that subsidization practices are clearly related to the emotional health of the community. In terms of their implied and explicit value judgments, they are often inconsistent, even at odds, with values otherwise promulgated on the campus. In addition, such practices tend to exaggerate dependency among students. In this way they effectively diminish the vigor of the maturation process hopefully being encouraged elsewhere in the college. The psychiatrist should also be interested in compulsory course and degree requirements of whatever nature and should be keenly aware of the effects of these requirements upon students. Do they support and promote motivation to learn? Do they have disruptive effects upon students struggling with problems of emancipation?

Most students seek after and eagerly absorb information about the basic principles of the development of a healthy and stable personality. It is important for faculty and administration to take some interest in who learns and how they do it as well as in what is taught. Encouraging educational procedures throughout the college that will enable students, faculty, and staff to learn about personality development is a function of the psychiatrist. He can establish such procedures himself or encourage and assist others to do so, taking as active a part in such programs as his own situation, interest, and skills permit. Curricular cocurricular, and extracurricular means may be used to familiarize the individuals in an educational institution with some fundamental facts about themselves as personalities and emotional beings. This may be done by working with faculty members in courses (not necessarily or exclusively behavioral sciences), by public lectures of a formal or informal nature, by writing, by distribution of reading lists, by active participation in student gatherings, by talking with groups of faculty wives, or by conducting group psychodynamic activities. These programs might include materials dealing with human growth and personality, the understanding of structured human relationships (marriage, family, employer-employee relationships, and so forth), and an awareness of the human and social problems of the college community, its legends, mistakes, and the sources of its conflicts and strengths. Teachers are maximally effective only when they establish good rapport with their students. Sometimes a teacher's own feelings and problems may prevent this or seriously interfere with it. One phase of such activities could include a program to help those teachers who have an interest in discussing their own feelings to do so. It is our experience that, given such an opportunity, many teachers willingly take advantage of it and find that this helps them to make contact with students more easily and to develop these relationships with increased insight. Where this has been tried, as at the Massachusetts Institute of Technology, for

example, the teachers stated that they were able to work more comfortably and with greater satisfaction and that their students learned
more effectively.

Excuse systems have a long and deeply entrenched tradition in
American colleges. By and large, excuses tend to promote irresponsi-
bility and immaturity, since they allow students to avoid obligations
which are clearly specified and understood and, in most instances, are
appropriate. The psychiatrist will want to talk with administrators
and students with a view toward the elimination of such excuses. A
system with formal excuses discourages students from developing and
accepting responsibility for themselves, sick or well. It encourages
them to exaggerate illness and to avoid academic responsibility from
which they should not be released. The elimination of regular excuse
systems permits each case to be judged on its own terms rather than
on the basis of prejudicial rules and regulations and allows all concerned to operate in a more flexible fashion. Students at Harvard are
encouraged to discuss their absences with their professor or instructor
and to arrange for make-up work. The Health Service will confirm
the fact of illness when requested by a faculty member but is rarely
asked to do so.

The development of research activities should be one of the
duties of every college psychiatrist. Sometimes this can be done only
in collaboration with units in the graduate schools of the university
or with other institutions, especially when there is only one psychiatrist in the college. Good programs have been worked out in various
situations, as for example at Vassar, Harvard, Amherst, and the
University of California. Much is understood in a descriptive way
about the nature of the emotional problems of college students, but
college psychiatrists are in a unique position to refine and extend that
understanding in the light of the principles of dynamic psychiatry.
They are also in a position to approach answers to persistent questions
about the effects of recent or old family difficulties upon students'
learning capacities, the problems of adjustment to the college setting,
problems of values, motivation, and sexuality. Other areas of needed
investigation are the effectiveness of short-term psychotherapy and
the frequent responses to treatment which are so surprisingly rapid.
Our vast ignorance about the positive personality resources of college
students must be erased. These resources must be identified and ex-

plored for many obvious reasons, but especially because of the impressive fact that many college students continue in their education, often at high levels of intellectual achievement and uncomplicated social and interpersonal relationships, despite emotional difficulties that one would expect to cripple other people in other settings.

A psychiatrist who works in a college has substantially different problems from one who works in a private hospital or a state hospital or from one who only practices psychotherapy with private patients. He will find it necessary to be a kind of educator himself, even though an indirect one for the most part. Students, as well as faculty members, tend to see the college *in loco parentis*, despite intelligent attempts on the part of many colleges to divest themselves of this role. As has already been suggested, the psychiatrist can, on the one hand, help students to develop healthier states of independence in the college setting. He can also, on the other hand, help colleges to play well the role of good parents. Besides being an indirect educator, a college psychiatrist is, in large measure, a social psychiatrist. Psychiatry, as we now conceive it, is a relatively recent specialty among the medical sciences. Even more recently there has emerged from the parent discipline two new branches: college psychiatry and social psychiatry. These new aspects of psychiatry are expanding rapidly. There are still very few—about forty—psychiatrists working full time in colleges, and they have shared their experiences frequently and in some detail. These experiences have made it clear that college is a place where students are living as well as studying and possibly receiving psychotherapy. The psychiatrist cannot avoid concerning himself with the emotional climate of his institution. It probably would be inadvisable for a psychiatrist to accept an appointment in a college unless he were willing to be so concerned. A college psychiatrist is more a part of his community than a private practitioner or a consulting physician can be of his. The need for this total immersion in the community has led to some concern among psychiatrists generally for what is described as the loss of professional identity. It is feared that when the psychiatrist ventures forth into the community he shatters the time-honored principles and practices which include the maintenance of neutrality and impersonality and the forming of uncritical judgments considered necessary for the establishment of appropriate therapeutic relationships. We believe that in the college setting, psychiatrists should not confine themselves to the treatment of the relatively few people with frank symptomatology. The community will lose a great deal if they do.

In this chapter we have suggested many areas of contact between the psychiatrist and the college community, all of which carry the psychiatrist outside the treatment room. It is our experience that these activities do not obscure the psychiatrist's identity as such but affirm it and define it. Such extratherapeutic contact with both a potential and an actual patient population is consistent with other generally accepted professional practices. Of course, such contacts place stringent requirements upon the psychiatrist, for he must be willing to let his own behavior be measured in the community against the criteria for maturity and healthy emotionality that he espouses in treatment. He is also called upon to express his concepts, ideals, methods, and techniques in nonjargonistic terms and with sufficient clarity and organization to be well understood. Some are reluctant to do this; others find in it an exciting challenge.

Faculty Counseling and Referral

Willard Dalrymple

Dealing with specific emotional problems is not unrelated to the general educational philosophy of a university. An educational insti- tution succeeds to the extent that it creates an atmosphere in which the student learns. One which ignores emotional blocks to learning or treats emotional disorder as primarily a disciplinary matter will make learning difficult for a large segment of its student population.

In the average college population, roughly one out of ten students will encounter emotional disturbance serious enough to give him symptoms or to disturb the efficiency of his life. Where ample psy- chiatric help exists and has been accepted by the community, such students often seek out the psychiatrists. When they do not seek appropriate help or when such help does not exist on the campus, other individuals within the faculty or medical department often find themselves forced to deal with student problems in one way or another. Even when the student is undergoing psychiatric treatment, faculty members must often take cognizance of the student's emo- tional problems.

Whether or not the student presents his difficulty as an emotional one—or whether or not he is aware of difficulty—the dean, the professor, the physician, the laboratory instructor, the dormitory proctor, and even the athletic coach have to deal with students in emotional trouble. Any contact between a faculty member and a student may reveal the presence of the student's emotional illness. It may be behavior in class, blocking on an examination, attitude during an individual conference or social encounter, or performance on the athletic field which makes the disturbance apparent to the teacher. The teacher's attitude toward the student can help him become aware of his needs, and by these means teachers can help students overcome the blocks which prevent learning. For, to the student, the fact that his emotional problems are recognized and accepted as legitimate serves as the first step toward his gaining motivation to do something about them.

The degree of emotional disturbance and incapacity varies widely among students. Natural inclination moves one to try to divide student problems into those needing psychiatric help and those less severe which do not need any help, but this is an artificial attempt to create a line where none exists. Everyone has unconscious feelings, thoughts, and problems; they vary not only in intensity but in their manifestations, in their degree of localization to one area of the personality, and in the amount of incapacity they cause.

Clearly those students need professional help who have an inability to function, whether it be in the social or in the academic area. Those who are in emotional distress but are not incapacitated, and those who are incapacitated only in a nonessential area, can often continue to function as students and to improve their adjustment to life without help. For them, the decision to enter psychotherapy depends on the available facilities, their own desires and motivations, and the effectiveness of the advice and understanding they obtain from the teachers and physicians whom they contact. Competent psychotherapy has never harmed any individual. Nevertheless, indiscriminate psychotherapy is intensely wasteful.

Youth has great resiliency. Many students with marked emotional problems seem to grow out of them. The student's own strength of character and his ability to bring to awareness certain of his unconscious conflicts allow him to handle the problems more adequately. Whether repression, suppression, rationalization, sublimation, or some other psychological process comes into play is not often important to know. What is important is that many such students make improvement by themselves and that nonprofessional help may be as useful as that of a psychiatrist.

The essential duty of the teacher who is attempting to help a student is to be a sympathetic listener. He listens, he understands, he supports without being critical, and when his position as a college officer requires it, he administers discipline while making it clear that he still values the student as a human being. He does not possess the training necessary to lead a student through a maze of insight therapy. Although he may use a quiet, nondirective approach on occasion, he need not concern himself, as the psychiatrist often must, with suppressing his own personality in the relationship or withholding personal opinions and direct advice.

Diagnosis and the understanding of psychodynamics are not necessary prerequisites to helping students with emotional problems. The nonpsychiatric help they receive may be the most important event in improvement—and perhaps it will be the only significant event. For many students, the opportunity to talk to an older person who gives them understanding and acceptance is effective therapy. It can help the immature, the shy, the rebellious, or the insecure to grow into more effective, comfortable human beings. It can help the student precipitated into emotional distress by adversity to strengthen his own resources and complete a college career without a serious interruption. It can accomplish this without the student surrendering any of his responsibility or independence.

At least two explanations for success in this type of counseling exist. First, the student may be in what Erikson calls a "crisis of ego identity." He may be confused about his role in life—what it means to be a student, to become a teacher, a businessman, or a doctor, or merely to be an adult man or woman. The almost universal cause of these crises is lack of a good relationship with one or both parents in childhood. A suitable model for emotional development has not been present. If the relationship was only partially deficient, or if it was supplemented by a good relationship with one or more other adults, then the resulting crisis will tend to be less serious—or even absent. When this crisis does occur, an older person who moves into the breach allows the younger one to proceed successfully once more with his maturation.

Identification is not a process which takes place only when an individual is young or in emotional trouble. It continues throughout life for everyone. For students, teachers of all types are ready objects for identification. While the well-adjusted student may be able to identify easily with a professor without much personal contact, the poorly adjusted student may need a much closer relationship in order to achieve the feeling of identification which allows him to continue his emotional growth. If wise and mature teachers do not allow him this, then he may obtain it from other, less desirable figures either on or off the campus.

Many of these young men and women do not come clamoring at the door asking for help. This is because their lack of identity makes them self-conscious and diffident. They approach only those whose manner suggests that they will not be repelled or ignored. This does not necessarily mean that they will respond only to a hail-fellow-well-met enthusiasm. The serious scholar of limited interests, who does not concern himself with the student's athletics or girl friends, may have obvious desire to impart knowledge that he encourages students' approach and identification on this basis alone.

There is a second way in which contacts with faculty may help the emotionally disturbed student. In these contacts, the student may be able to work out unconscious problems in unconscious ways. When he talks about his difficulties in a history course, or in understanding Kierkegaard, or about his father's health, or his current girl friend, his unconscious mind may be choosing this way of expressing deeper emotions in an oblique way—emotions represented in a vague and unrecognizable fashion in the present situation. The fact that an older person accepts him and his problems makes it possible for his unconscious to bring out otherwise unacceptable emotional feeling in this way. The teacher should not show concern that this sort of double-talk is going on. This is a comfortable way for the unconscious to proceed, without urging or prying. The following interchange between a student and a professor of chemical engineering illustrates the two-level type of conversation which often takes place.

The student was worried, anxious, and disturbed about his academic work. Although well prepared and with adequate intelligence, he was ineffective in his studying. He feared failure in his engineering courses and came to discuss his academic predicament with the professor. When the student had presented this story, the professor remarked, "I was born in England and came to this country when I was eighteen. My first experience here was to flunk a course in chemistry." The two conversed further, and the student was significantly helped. He left feeling greatly encouraged, was able to study efficiently, and his marks rose to respectable levels.

Unconsciously, the student may have been saying to the professor "I am afraid I am a failure and will never be a man. If I do fail, the world, particularly my family, will reject me completely. The very thought of it paralyzes me and makes me unable to do my academic work." And the professor perhaps was replying, "Here I am a professor at your college, a success in your chosen field. And yet I once flunked an elementary course in this subject. Temporary difficulties, even more serious than you have yet experienced, do not prevent eventual success. You can see from my story that you are unjustified in feeling that your momentary academic difficulties mean that you will not gain full maturity as a chemical engineer and as a man." And the student understood and was helped by him without having the mechanics of the therapy explained. Had the teacher attempted to play amateur diagnostician or therapist, by interpreting the unconscious meanings or trying to point out what had happened, he might have set in motion forces with which he was not prepared to contend. A flood of talk, bizarre emotional patterns, or unexplained anxieties might have confronted him.

Friendliness and frequent contact do not mean coddling, lowering of standards, or making exceptions to usual requirements. They do mean that dealings with students are individual rather than stereotyped.

The physician's role may be more definitive than the teacher's. Since his training already has taught him about emotional illness, he is better equipped to diagnose and treat emotional problems. Also, he has the professional standing necessary to assume medical responsibility for illness. The physician's greatest aid in treating emotional problems successfully is the advice of a psychiatrist. With this guidance he may begin to use the specific methods of insight psychotherapy. With periodic discussions about his psychiatric patients with the psychiatrist, he will be able to give effective psychotherapy to patients who would otherwise not receive it.

Psychotherapy by the internist has both advantages and disadvantages. Among the advantages is the fact that the physician may

give the patient needed treatment which he would not accept otherwise because of an irrational fear or distrust of psychiatrists. Secondly, the physician who has seen the patient for an appreciable time
may have already established rapport with him. This may produce a
valuable head start in psychotherapy, especially where only brief
therapy is necessary.

In addition, the physician is able to give support by specific or
nonspecific medical therapy. For example, he may prescribe tincture
of belladonna or another antispasmodic for a patient with cramps due
to emotionally caused "spastic colon" syndrome, or he may prescribe
a sedative for the acutely anxious patient, recognizing that these
therapies are short-term and do not remove underlying causes. This
may increase the patient's trust and facilitate treatment. Furthermore,
if the patient has not been able to accept the fact that his illness is
emotional in origin, the attentions of a medical doctor allow him to
shift gears in his own attitudes from time to time. When psychotherapy touches on an unusually painful spot in his emotional life,
he has more freedom to retreat to the possibility that his illness might
be physical in nature than he would if he were under the care of a
psychiatrist. Such retreats often slow rather than speed therapy, but
if the patient does not fully accept the existence of his emotional
problem, his doctor may be forced to move two steps forward and
one step back for a while. This situation is particularly useful when
the physician is preparing the patient over a period of weeks or
months for more intensive psychotherapy.

The disadvantages of psychotherapy by a physician are two.
First, a psychiatrist will be more skillful in the practice of psychotherapy than a physician who has had less training and experience.
For this reason the physician must choose with care the patients he
is to treat. If the patient's problems are acute and relatively minor,
he may feel comfortable in treating the patient. The transference and
identification which the patient develops with his doctor will be important parts of the treatment, and it may not be necessary for the
patient to work through these feelings for improvement. On the other
hand, if the patient's problems are severe, incapacitating, or chronic,
and if the psychodynamics are intricate and deeply buried, then the
physician must be much more cautious. If the patient recognizes his
problems as emotional rather than physical, and if the services of a

competent psychiatrist are readily available, the physician will give these patients the greatest service by arranging intensive psycho-therapy for them as soon as practicable.

A second disadvantage relates to confidentiality. Some patients speak most freely when addressing a psychiatrist. For such people, the psychiatrist represents a person to whom it is safe and proper to confess any secret and to speak on any subject without danger of censure. These patients are unable or unwilling to attribute the same status to the physician who announces that his position is the same. Often, of course, the patient may be limiting the role of his therapist in order to protect himself from voicing some of his own disquieting thoughts.

Taking into account these advantages and disadvantages, the physician who does not have a formal psychiatric training will be able to render effective psychotherapy to many students. In doing so he will relieve congestion in psychiatric services and improve his methods of medical practice as well. Some of his patients will require but an interview or two, while others will require many months. His supportive psychotherapy will not change basic personality patterns, but it will bring symptomatic relief to many, and for some the effort of many months will convince physician and patient that intensive psychotherapy or analysis should be undertaken.

For physicians and teachers alike, the recognition and evaluation of emotional problems are constant challenges. For some sensitive and perceptive people, the judgment of character and personality seems to come naturally and yet the most intuitive and highly trained psychiatrist on occasion misjudges the nature or severity of emotional disorders. In this area, there can be no set rules—only a few guide-posts.

Essentially, the teacher who finds himself in a counseling relation-ship must assess how well his students are functioning academically, socially, physically, and emotionally. He cannot evaluate their inca-pacity with as much accuracy as a trained psychiatrist perhaps, nor can he diagnose the nature of their disability, but he should attempt to detect the presence of trouble. He should be asking himself these questions: Does this man have the capacity to function at a sub-stantially higher level of efficiency? Is there some problem—of any sort—which is handicapping this man? If the teacher decides that a problem does exist, then he faces the question of what, if anything, to do about it.

To be sure, the teacher who starts to observe students' behavior and thought will soon begin to recognize some of the common psychiatric syndromes described elsewhere in this book. Psychiatric diagnoses, however, are of little use to the average teacher without specialized training. Diagnosis must involve some probing into personal and family background. Some of the feelings, thoughts, and memories elicited by this kind of inquiry are bound to be disturbing and in borderline cases may precipitate or increase symptoms. The nonprofessional will do well not to seek this material.

When and how should one refer a student to a psychiatrist? One answer is easy: Get to know a psychiatrist and ask him if doubt exists. This is more than a glib answer. It is a valued *modus operandi* at many institutions where a psychiatrist is available for consultation.

Beyond that, the decision rests on the acuteness and severity of the student's need and on the interest which the student has or develops in psychotherapy. This is a spectrum, not a limited number of categories. At one extreme is the student who is psychotic or near-psychotic, whose need is obvious and immediate, and on whom considerable pressure must be exerted to get him to a psychiatrist. At the other is the student whose problems are minor, whose symptoms are transitory, and whose need is limited, even though he might benefit from psychotherapy. For the latter type the emotional support of another person is most important. Psychotherapy depends on the student's interest and motivation and on the availability of help.

Occasionally a student's psychotic speech or behavior becomes apparent to a teacher. Situations arising from this may be difficult and disturbing to a person who comes upon them unprepared. Occasionally, there is a method by which to persuade the student that he needs medical attention. Not infrequently, for example, a schizophrenic or depressed patient has a physical symptom or delusion. He may have pain in the abdomen or head, or he may believe that his lungs or intestines are being eaten away. Sometimes the patient himself recognizes that his thoughts are disordered. The teacher may appropriately suggest that there is a medical problem and that with the student's permission he will make the arrangements for prompt medical attention. He may then take the patient to the college doctor or make arrangements by phone, using whatever device he can to transmit privately to the doctor his suspicions about the patient's psychosis.

At other times, the patient does not recognize any part of his situation as a medical problem. This applies particularly to the para-noid individual, who thinks that other people are trying to harm or influence him. If the patient sees no advantage in talking the situation over with a physician, then the only approach is to talk promptly and privately with the college physician (or psychiatrist, if one is available). If the doctor agrees that a diagnosis of a psychosis is likely and that either evaluation or therapy is essential, psychiatric consul-tation must be arranged. The teacher can say that he has been worried about the student's health and therefore has consulted the college physician. He and the physician have agreed that the student should seek medical advice. If the student is reasonably well oriented, he will probably respond to this sort of pressure. If not, the teacher states that as an official of the college he must insist on medical attention, and if necessary inform the student or his parents that he may not continue in college unless he consults the college doctor or psychiatric consultant. Of course, if the student is so severely sick that he is a danger to himself or to others, all these steps must be tele-scoped and emergency measures taken.

Psychotic speech or behavior may be so disturbing to some people that they wish to ignore it and try to lead the student to talk about something else. This does not help. If the student talks about suspi-cions, ask him if other people are seeking to influence him or harm him in some way. If the student volunteers or admits that he is depressed, ask him if life sometimes seems not worth living and if he thinks about suicide. No evidence exists that this will put ideas in his mind, and it serves to acquaint the questioner with important facts about the student's illness.

For less disturbed students, the approach to psychotherapy is apt to take different channels. The student who is anxious for treat-ment and seeks it himself presents no problem, except possibly a financial one. In a different status is the student whose need the teacher recognizes but who resists the idea of psychotherapy or who has not thought of it before. The teacher may use a series of steps in broaching the possibility of therapy. One may traverse them in fifteen minutes with one student, while with another it may take six months. The student may reject one step but accept the next.

First comes the discussion of the problem. With the student who clutches on an exam, for example, there is usually no difficulty in getting him to recognize that he has a problem. One superb teacher, a nationally known scientist, gets such students to seek him out and talk freely about themselves merely by writing on their exam papers, "What's the trouble?" Obviously, the proper approach is not to argue with the student but to encourage the expression of his own thoughts, occasionally quoting him back to himself to emphasize a point.

Secondly, the problem stated and accepted, one tries to find what the student thinks its cause to be. Here the student often volunteers that he has been tired, anxious, or in some upset state of mind. If so, this is a good opportunity for the teacher to remark that it is interesting that the student has noted this correlation and that this is often the case with students who find themselves in such difficulties. If the student does not volunteer such observations, the teacher may remark that sometimes emotional factors are involved in such problems, and he wonders if the student is aware of such a background in himself. This may start the student's thoughts along significant lines.

With the problem stated and accepted as at least in part emotional in origin, one can consider what attention should be given it. Perhaps the student himself will ask for help. If not, one can ask him, "What would you think about getting some help in solving this problem?" If the student is interested, one can discuss the nature and availability of psychotherapy with him. At this point, it is helpful if the teacher is on familiar terms with the psychiatrist to whom he refers patients. Then he will know how soon the psychiatrist can accept the patient for therapy, if he agrees that it is indicated, and give a more personal introduction than would otherwise be possible.

Even if the student accepts the idea of psychotherapy fairly readily, it is well to discuss the process with him at some length. Unless the student goes with eagerness to explore his own feelings and not just to please the teacher, he is unlikely to benefit. Also, lack of understanding may make the start of psychotherapy slow or abortive. A teacher who counsels many students and has high respect for psychotherapy from his own successful personal experiences reports this type of problem among his own student groups. A student whom he has known and with whom he has been on good terms would come to him with a problem—most often one of adjustment to academic work or social life. He would suggest psychotherapy to the student, explaining that many students benefited by such service and that, indeed, he himself had so benefited. The student would accede easily, visit the psychiatrist, but report after two or three appointments that "nothing has happened." This teacher realized that the student had expected the more usual doctor-patient relationship, with the patient presenting his problem and the doctor prescribing a solution. To prevent this impasse, he found it wise to discuss the nature of psychotherapy with the student. He explained that psychotherapy is a way of finding out about oneself in general, and in particular what has caused the current predicament. The main job is the patient's, with the psychiatrist providing the right atmosphere, asking the right questions, and occasionally suggesting possible answers for the patient's consideration. The process is of uncertain length. It may take several interviews to determine how much treatment will be desirable—or even whether treatment actually is necessary. The student must understand, in other words, that the teacher does not mean that psychotherapy will solve the student's problem, but rather that a problem exists for which outside help might be useful and that the next logical step is to see what Dr. So-and-So thinks about it. This approach may lead to the student undertaking psychotherapy under its own ground rules or to his returning to the teacher for further support and advice.

The nonpsychiatrist who deals with students, then, has a wide range of functions in helping them with emotional problems. He should feel equally comfortable in the role of providing the support of an older friend or in suggesting outside consultation. Most important, his own acceptance of emotional problems as honest and involuntary handicaps will allow the students to deal with these problems more effectively, whether this involves psychotherapy or simply facing up to reality and learning to cope by meeting stressful situations head on instead of not talking about them.

3

The Role of the Psychologist
in a College Health Service

Charles C. McArthur AND
Kenneth T. Dinklage

The role of the clinical psychologist is changing very fast. Once he was identified as a mental tester whose armamentarium consisted of a few intelligence tests. Now the practices of the applied clinical psychologist include assessment of intellectual functioning, the assessment of personality, diagnosis, therapy, guidance, and personnel assessment. These functions have usefulness in the college health clinic.

THE TESTING FUNCTIONS

Psychiatric diagnosis and/or personality assessment are the clinical psychologist's traditional practice. This is the part of his practice commonly referred to as testing, but the psychologist who says, "I do testing," is using a very misleading phrase. He does testing in the context of both clinical and history-taking interviews, of the academic records, the aptitude scores in the college folder, and of the story told by the psychiatrist about the referral situation. All these data go to an intellectual product that is not a set of test scores but a picture of "the way this student ticks." Each referral is for a total personality assessment, whether that is formally requested or not, because it is only by summarizing a total assessment that the psychologist reaches the shorthand conclusions he enters as *diagnosis* and *prognosis*.

Typical referrals from the staff psychiatrist may be quoted here:

Name: Roger Sherman
Status: Graduate School
Clinical Abstract: A young man troubled by compulsive eating. Feels himself inadequate, although he has an excellent record.
Information Desired: How severe an ego defect does the eating cover?

Name: Buck King
Status: Fourth Year Theological School
Clinical Abstract: This patient has been subject to the onset of anxiety since he was 17. (He is now 33.) Whenever he got involved with a "good" girl, these attacks would come. He is concerned about his masculinity, apparently in an obsessive way. He is very skittish about this topic.

Information Desired: Suitability for intensive therapy.

Name: Polly Lanier
Status: Undergraduate
Clinical Abstract: This quite young undergraduate has had periods of depression since coming to college. She gives a long history of being a withdrawn, immature girl who has had difficulty with personal relationships. A very talented older brother makes her greatly envious. She has been very close to her rather weak father.
Information Desired: The chief problem seems to be one of adolescent maladjustment but I would like an evaluation of any prominent fixed neurotic trends which may complicate therapy.

These are the common questions addressed to the test psychologist. They may be combined with queries like "How deep is this depression?" or "How serious is the suicide risk?" or "Is the homosexual problem paramount here?"

It may be objected that these are just the questions that the psychiatrist himself has been trained to answer. Why, then, should he refer them to the psychologist? Largely, it is, unhappy to say, because there is never time enough in a college health clinic. The psychiatrist could answer his own questions in six to sixty hours; the psychologist gets answers in one afternoon with no loss of psychiatric time. Psychiatric time, in most college clinics, is very limited. The best manned college health staff in the world offers each patient an average of six psychiatric hours. Under these conditions, it becomes imperative to get answers fast in order to get on with therapy or with diagnosis and disposition. Use of psychological tests in the hands of a clinical psychologist is much more efficient than diagnostic use of precious psychiatric hours.

It is also true that two heads are better than one. A lot more can be learned by exposing the patient to two kinds of observers and two kinds of techniques. The techniques are very different. Psychiatric skills are based to a large degree on free association, psychological skills on a variety of forms of controlled association, when the associative principle is used at all. A number of good psychological tools simply set the person to work on an intellectual task. It is something distinct from the associative hour to watch a man functioning, using his resources and his defenses, while he tries to pass an at first deceptively easy, then catastrophically difficult, block assembly test. There are new things to be learned about the patient in such circumstances. If one hesitates to speak of the times that the psychological test corrects a bad psychiatric diagnosis lest one have also to mention the test reports that were misleading, one has to admit that neither method stands as firmly alone as the two stand together. Nor is it a waste of time when they concur.

Certain referrals are peculiarly and anciently the province of the psychologist:

Name: Roger Thornton
Status: Not enrolled
Clinical Abstract: This young man flunked out as an engineering student. He seems free of emotional illness and quite realistic about his earlier failure's having resulted from doing as he was told rather than what he wished.
Information Desired: He thinks he would make a good liberal arts major (History? Government? Economics?) and then should go on to Business School. Is he right?

This is the psychologist's oldest function and one no one else is qualified to perform.

Again, certain questions of intellectual capacity arise:

Name: McVain Trowbridge, II
Status: Undergraduate
Clinical Abstract: This is the son of three generations of graduates.

He cannot pass his language requirement. He has no neurotic pattern that I can perceive.

Information Desired: Trowbridge went to a local M.D. who diagnosed a language disability. I notice that his College Board scores were very low. Is there a language block here?

A more serious question of intellectual capacity is:

Name: Walter LaPointe
Status: Undergraduate
Clinical Abstract: This boy suffered a severe concussion last summer. He is failing at November Hours.
Information Desired: The electroencephalogram is ambiguous, but we need to know if there is any brain damage.

This is also a situation where only the psychologist can help. Except for a small squib in an out-of-the-way military journal, there seems to be so far no published acknowledgment of the fact that psychological tests of intellectual functioning, especially the standard Wechsler-Bellevue intelligence test, will detect residual brain damage long after the electroencephalogram has returned to normal. There are a great number of tests of intellectual functioning that are very sensitive to small lesions in the brain. Since final examinations also reflect physiological effects not visible to the electroencephalograph, the psychologist's opinion bears most cogently on academic prognosis.

A whole class of referrals deals not only with the content of the illness but with an estimate of the patient's current state of health. Commonest is the referral for evaluation for readmission after a mental illness. In general, it is a good policy to be charitable in such cases; young men have extraordinary powers of recuperation. Yet it is no kindness to readmit a boy who by returning to the stresses he once could not meet is likely to do himself further harm. So the psychologist gets referrals like:

Name: Walter Balen
Status: Not enrolled
Clinical Abstract: This boy had a depression in the fall of his freshman year. He went to a good mental hospital, where he seems to have recovered under a combination of shock treatment and psychotherapy. He was discharged a month ago.
Information Desired: Is he ready to tackle college so soon? What about a reduced schedule? He seems all right to me, in one interview, but I am a little chary of having him return so fast.

The last comment is well taken; one usually likes to see a year of some constructive activity before readmitting someone who has been seriously ill. Nor can one bypass this requirement at the word of the attending physician; most doctors outside the college badly under-estimate the stress of the college environment. The tests, especially the Rorschach Test, will give precise and quite valid statements about the state of the patient's illness at any given time. It is especially useful to retest men who were tested while sick. What usually is seen is the continued presence of all the old conflicts but the development of new ways of coping with them. The presence of these new coping mechanisms and, in general, the health of the system of controls are sufficient grounds to recommend readmission.

Similar test referrals may occur in relation to original admission where there has been a history of mental illness. More of this sort of evaluation probably could be done by most graduate schools to their advantage and that of the students. "Admit" or "don't admit" need not be the only referral questions. A common one is whether the student can wait for his degree before entering therapy or whether he would better continue his studies under therapeutic "cover."

Referral to the health service psychologist normally comes from a physician within the health services, though modally from the psychiatrists. Other personnel in the university may make extensive use of the psychologist, however; referrals may come from the counseling agencies, the preacher to the university, the student place-ment office in the college or business school, the deans, various other members of the university's administration, or even the faculty. Still the modal source of referral is likely to be the college health service psychiatrist. Of course, the most effective way for physician and psychologist to combine know-how is by discussing the referral problem and subsequent report. This is especially useful during the first few referrals by a physician, so that both physician and psycholo-gist may learn what to expect of each other.

Tests Used

A brief description of the tests used may make the type of in-formation obtainable from the referral of a patient to the psychologist more clear. The techniques described below are simply those regularly employed in one college health department. Many others are used occasionally or for special purposes. However, it is relevant to note that there are less than a dozen tests whose validity is really well established. Most clinics use some of the tests described here.

The psychologist picks his own tests. Not only do individual clinicians have their own tastes, but it is also true that no one test is necessarily most relevant to any one problem. Robert White has made this point well in an excellent discussion of the relation of tests to psychiatry. In the book edited by Hoch and Zubin, *The Relation of Psychological Tests to Psychiatry,* White says: "Our problem-solving test will perhaps also be a test of frustration tolerance, a test of control over anxiety, a test of level of aspiration, or a situation that happens to mobilize an infant trauma, and all reports on its results must include as much of this information as can be observed."

The purpose of a test battery is to have the time to observe one person in action under a variety of circumstances, working on a variety of problems, and, whenever possible, for a variety of observers. Such variegated samples of his functioning afford the psychologist the opportunity to contrast and compare, to see what behaviors are more ephemeral, what behaviors more enduring aspects of the person's life style. The tests themselves are a means of varying the situation; the conclusions drawn are the result of logical sifting of the collected evidence. More thinking time must go into each session than the sum of the testing time and the time spent on the clerical work of test scoring. White says it well: "The diagnosis of each personality is a miniature scientific experiment."

All this being so, there is no one test for any one purpose. However, most tests were originally designed for one or more primary purposes, so that some generalizations can be offered. Perhaps it would be useful to describe the battery commonly used in our own psychological service.

The objective tests that measure aptitudes and intelligence are usually selected from four developed by Dr. F. L. Wells, who served as psychologist to Harvard's Department of Hygiene for many years, after a career in which he was established as one of the pioneer designers of objective psychometric tests. Since Harvard students, like students from many selective colleges, normally hit the ceiling on standard intelligence tests, it was necessary to develop these special high-level measures and special Harvard scoring norms. The four tests are:

The Verbal Speed Alpha, which is a multiple choice test of speed and accuracy with simple verbal ideas. A descendant of the famous Army Alpha, this test is a fair measure of verbal intelligence, if by that we mean of the multiple-choice sort. It is also usually an estimate of the man's ceiling; more complex or more emotionally disturbing tests will typically score lower than the Verbal Alpha score, providing an estimate of the loss caused by disturbing elements.
Sample item:
Black is to White as Up is to: In Out Down Between

The Numerical Speed Alpha, which is a similar test of speed and accuracy in handling simple numerical ideas. Like the Verbal Alpha, this test has very short time limits.
Sample item:
Complete this series: 2 4 6 8 —— ——

Work Sample 95, which is a vocabulary test of great difficulty. This test is multiple choice but untimed.
Sample item:
The *ponderosity* of his style: lightness cleverness heaviness thoughtfulness splendor

The Harvard Block Assembly Test, which is a series of eleven problems of the "put-these-pieces-together-they-make-a-block-like-the-model-block" sort. In part, this test measures mechanical aptitude, but in great part it gets at analytic thinking and frustration tolerance. It is a valuable sample of working style. Empirically, one can state that gross oddities in the handling of this task are valid samples of the oddities the patient will show in handling any moderately difficult intellectual challenge—like final examinations.

All four of these tests are customarily scored against local norms, so that the scores are directly comparable with each other and so that the patient being tested can at once be compared with the college as a whole. Scores are usually reported in a standard form, where a score of C represents the local average and the range of scores is from A to E. Thus, if we had a man scoring:

Verbal Alpha	A—
Numerical Alpha	C
Vocabulary	B+
Block Assembly	D

we would see (1) that he is consistently much better on the verbal side than on the thing and number side of the curriculum and (2) that he has verbal skills comparable to those of the best people in the college but thing and number skills average or below average for this school. A premedical program, for instance would be something for him to consider with caution, although he might manage to get by.

The use of such a battery at least partially satisfies the require' ment set by Wells that any assessment of intellectual functioning should triangulate the dimensions of mental speed, power, and range. Meanwhile, the tests yield a great number of unscorable observations about how the boy acts with different examiners, including one male and one female, and how he tackles intellectual problems; in other words, his cognitive style. These interpersonal and stylistic observa' tions are often of as much or more use than the scores.

The only standard intelligence test of any use with bright adults is:

The Wechsler-Bellevue Intelligence Scale, by far the best of the standard individual tests for I.Q. It does not usually extend college men sufficiently but it may be the test of choice when certain questions, especially those of brain disease or of psychopathic personality, are raised. An I.Q. is not usually very relevant at good schools, since students crowd the ceiling of the I.Q., but if for some reason one is desired, this is the test to use. Conversion of Alpha scores into I.Q. is possible and more efficient. The Rorschach also gives an I.Q. estimate. The real advantage of the Wechsler is the opportunity it gives the clinician to watch the patient tackling a dozen different kinds of tasks. Descriptive, nonscorable material from this test is often of great value in diagnosis.

There are a great number of paper and pencil inventories in print. Two of these are best established and practically helpful:

The Strong Vocational Interest Blank, which is the best of the "interest" tests. It contains a large number of items to be marked "Like, Indifferent, or Dislike."

Sample Item:
> Being an actor
> People who chew gum
> LIFE magazine
> Joining a sheriff's posse

The test measures "inventoried interests," which is to say, not the answer to the question, "What are you interested in?" but the answer to the question, "Would your values and attitudes resemble those of men who have fitted well into this or that occupations?" Twenty-year follow-up studies have shown that the test predicts well.

The Minnesota Multiphasic Personality Inventory is an objective test of some diagnostic value. It consists of a long series of items of which the man is to say whether they apply to him or do not apply to him or whether he cannot say.

Sample Item: I break into a sweat before important crises.

The scoring is on a series of scales derived from nosological categories: Hysteria, Psychasthenia, Schizophrenia, Hypomania, etc. Interpretation of the test profiles goes beyond the listing of high and low scores, however. Norms used are from the standardization groups chosen by the test makers.

The two projective tests most often used are the Rorschach and the Thematic Apperception Test.

The Rorschach Test is the inkblot test. "What, with a little imagination, could you see in this blot?" Interpretation of the results goes in two directions: a picture of the cognitive style and a picture of the structural features of the personality. Reporting a Rorschach can be a book-length enterprise; usually, the specific referral question is answered at length, and the rest of the picture, unless something seems urgently important, is briefly lined out. Nosological distinctions can be made very often with the Rorschach, and this is the one test *par excellence* for answering the question, "What are the dynamics?"

The Thematic Apperception Test is the picture-story test. The task is, "Make up a story that this picture could be an illustration from, sketching what might have led up to the scene, what might be happening, and what might come out of it." The series of stories provides a wealth of information about conflicts, values, attitudes, needs, and defenses. In general, this material is analyzable "from the top of the personality down." A lot of it is conscious or preconscious, sometimes conscious but deliberately being held secret. Some deeper unconscious roots become visible, also. For filling in the content of the personality, where the Rorschach had suggested the structure, the TAT is very useful. It lends specificity to the dynamic picture and, very helpfully, offers the chance to see the dynamics as the boy himself sees them. The test shows many sides of the boy's fantasy.

Other tools are used from time to time or as the particular case seems to demand, but the above list contains the core of the battery our department has been employing. The testing sessions take about two and a half hours, varying with the testee and the referral problem.

This half-day testing session is rather shorter than ideal practice. To function at his best, the clinician wants plentiful data. Robert White points out (in the article already cited) that when the testing is for scientific research, where the luxury of an adequate time-budget could be justified for the sake of the pursuit of truth, "an attempt to cut the testing schedule below ten to fifteen hours with each subject is merely a proposal to sabotage the research." However, this fully detailed discernment of the psychodynamics is not usually required for adequate disposition of a clinic case; if long-term therapy is to follow, the dynamics will emerge there. In short-term therapy, prior knowledge of the dynamics might be more useful.

THE TEST REPORT

The test report is a typed memo that first describes the test data collected and then offers some interpretation of the results, both as to how they bear on the specific referral question and as to the personality picture of the patient that seems to fit the facts best. Some attempt to see the boy as a whole is made, so that background information like social origins and family situation may be woven into the test results in order to make sense of them. Indeed, much of the research interest of the psychologist has been in the types of backgrounds within American subcultures and within families that produce the more common personality pictures seen at college. Emphasis must always be placed on the meaning of the scores and even of the psychodynamics within the college scene.

The illustrations below do not include full-length reports, which run from a thousand to five thousand words. The kinds of material contained in such reports are not all represented but may be fairly sampled by these illustrations.

For example, excerpts of the reports on referrals quoted above read:

Roger Sherman

This man gave an MMPI so full of peculiar responses that the MMPI manual says we should doubt its validity. The F scale, a measure of peculiar response attitude toward the test, is much too high. Yet at Amherst, where one quarter of the freshman class showed such an ostensibly invalidating set toward the test, it was learned that a high F score had to be taken seriously, if only as a cry for help.

The psychometric assistant on our staff noted, "I felt some of his choices were just to be different from ordinary people, *épater le bourgeoisie,* or to call attention to how sick he was."

He also gave a very abnormal Rorschach, in which there was no evidence of inner controls available in any section of the profile! Even though his response to the test was clearly resistant, what came through clearly was the utter loss of ego control.

In short, whatever has upset this man has robbed him of all control and inhibitions. He has no defensive strategies. He is just now crippled and helpless before his unruly obsessive thoughts.

That he eats too much and cannot control his behavior is consistent with the general flooding out of his controls by impulsive expression.

(A discussion of the specific nature of his infantile impulses followed.)

Buck King

This man arranged things so that, instead of the usual three hours of testing time, there was only time for a Rorschach test. That may be enough.

The test depicted an essentially normal personality crippled and contaminated by sexual identity conflict. He seems a bit of an introvert, much given to having "his own reasons" for his actions, judging the world by private values, trying to maintain conscious rational control of his world and his impulses. Yet he seems to have not a little anxiety over the sexual conflicts which reduce his ability to think clearly.

The crux of his problem is not his view of men but his view of women. A contaminated response to blot VII expresses his deepest view:

"They look old womanly womanish. The bodies are turned away, look like a couple of dogs. They look as though they have some sort of bundle or shirt. They could be old women."

He goes on to use a number of genital symbols, male and female, yet in the end we always come back to the spider mother.

He needs badly to spill to someone he trusts. He is tough enough to hold together in therapy. He won't like psychoanalysis but will demand more active interpretation to relieve his fears about himself. He could do with some straightforward answers before any referral is attempted.

(A description of the setting of major conflict in the total personality structure followed.)

Polly Lanier

In contrast to the depressions noted on referral, Miss Lanier seemed mostly vulnerable to anxiety attacks of brief duration.

She complained that in high school she had to do little work, but that here "Everybody works so hard!" She had been turned down by all other colleges to which she applied on the basis of her high school grades, and she wonders if she belongs here, where the competition is so stiff. She is generally concerned about competition, particularly with women. It appears that her unconsciously hostile impulses became too strong for her to tolerate.

She is very ambivalent about her femininity and development into womanhood. For instance, these developments awake in her a typical adolescent problem between her inner pressure to establish autonomy and self-expression and her dependent needs and desire to continue to stay protected and cared for.

None of these conflicts seem of overwhelming magnitude. They are the conflicts of someone on the brink of maturity with no deeply established neurotic patterns.

(The results in intellectual activities were then spelled out.)

McVain Trowbridge, II

As you know, we see two very common types of reading or language disability: Type I being the boy whose social status has outraced his I.Q. and Type II being the boy with an obsessive neurosis. Just why obsessives have trouble with language isn't easy to say; one might at first expect them to be good at parsing, etc. At any rate, Trowbridge is not an obsessive. Quite the opposite, he has the typical private school pattern of quality ambition without quantity ambition, of real motivation to be "interested and interesting" but not to "dig very hard." Parsing isn't "interesting" behavior.

Chiefly, however, he seems to fit the Type I syndrome. His College Boards led to our predicting that he would make low-pass grades here; this has been the case. His verbal scholastic aptitude test score is poorer than his numerical mathematics aptitude test score, but he is majoring in a verbal field (Government) and, of course, has the referral problem with language. It seems likely that this trouble is in the greatest part explicable in terms of sheer lack of aptitude for the task. He will buy a passing grade at the cost of much more than the usual amount of work. There is no evidence to suggest that he has tried this cure for his disability.

Walter LaPointe

This very likeable young man shows both a clinical and a test pattern that suggests residual organic lesion. As you know, he still depends somewhat on the little black book in which he schedules himself from day to day, lest he forget where he should be, and which he, with courageous graveyard humor, refers to with a smile as "my brains." His course work shows striking ups and downs in accordance with the principle that concrete examinations about discrete facts are easier for him to pass. This is an improvement, apparently, on his total inability to master any early term quizzes.

His Wechsler showed the sort of profile often associated with brain damage in an intelligent subject: good recall of old learnings, concrete tasks very much higher than abstract, though with apparently conceptual tasks, like the verbal Similarities, scoring well because of the survival of old verbal formulae. What is more critical is the qualitative behavior during Block Design, where grossly "concrete" trial solutions occurred, in the primitive manner that the "concrete" behavior of the brain-injured is described by Goldstein even when later solutions of the same problem were successful.

His Bender-Gestalt figure drawings were generally good but showed some egregious lapses from the smooth performance expected of a boy with the precollege I.Q. that we can infer he possesses. When asked to redraw the figures from memory, he could reproduce only three and one of these imperfectly.

His Rorschach contained some brilliant responses yet descended to the perseveration of some responses where more flexible use of more ideas is normal and to the enumerating of animals' heads, legs, and tails where richer use of the evidence would seem easy to achieve.

All this evidence leaves little doubt that LaPointe still has residual organic difficulties, though they seem to be alleviating. If we take his current Wechsler I.Q. of 115 as a measure of his present operating level, we see that he is in real trouble in respect to doing Ivy League work. Of course, some courses are more possible for him than others.

We would certainly be justified in recommending either a reduced course rate or a leave of absence.

It must be clear that all these reports contain, by inference or open recommendation, practical hints for the strategy either in referral or in short-term therapy.

The report of the psychologist is often of concrete value in such matters. The psychoanalytic rules for inferring therapeutic strategy from free association hours are general enough; the psychologist often has more concrete predictions to make, especially from the evidence of the Thematic Apperception Test. The Rorschach may also help. From the two, a report may conclude as follows:

This boy has excellent ability to form rapport, but he is badly in need of establishing his independence of mind. As a result, he will initially turn to a respected elder for advice but then feel the necessity of "taking the advice from whence it came," which to him means deciding a little aggressively what to believe and what not to believe. He will act out his ambivalent rebellion, but this acting out should not discourage the therapist from continuing in his initial opinion of the good long-term prognosis.

On the other hand, psychological tests often reveal a picture of uncontrolled impulsivity, hypomanic or psychopathic trends that contraindicate the usual kinds of psychoanalytically based therapy and indicate the usefulness of more hardheaded techniques in which the chief function of the therapist is to serve as an external control. Sometimes, too, the therapist will be of most use as a touchstone for the patient's reality testing. The treatment of these problems is discussed in later chapters.

What with this quantity and variety of referrals, the testing function of the health service psychologist is likely to be the one that accounts for most of his professional time unless the ratio of psychologists to psychiatrists is balanced enough to ease the testing load to a point permitting time to be spent in other functions.

VOCATIONAL GUIDANCE

A socially useful skill of the clinical psychologist is his expertise in vocational guidance. This skill may not be very useful in college health services where the college itself maintains a large professional guidance agency. At Harvard, the health service does a good deal of vocational guidance. It may be that the health service in other schools will find itself faced with similar problems where no competent guidance program exists.

When a student chooses his lifetime vocation, he is choosing more than a job. His vocation will carry with it a whole style of life: as a lawyer who runs for local office in a medium-sized city, as a doctor building his world around some great teaching hospital, as a business executive.

To choose a lifetime of one kind of living is a complex task. It involves far more than "aptitudes." Competent vocational advisers are humble in the face of the complexity of the problem; beware of any man who tells his clients that his tests can give the *answer*. All the tests can do is provide concrete facts as a foundation for constructive thinking by the client and the counselor. One might say that the tests can provide a set of odds. "Two out of every three men who had scores like this at this age and have since gone into surgery are successful and happy, while nine out of ten who went into office management are failures." This is relevant data. In the end, however, it is the client's life and it is up to him to decide what odds he wants to buck.

How do the tests lead to statements regarding the odds? Mostly, of course, because the same tests were given to other young men decades ago and these men have been followed up since. For most tests, these validating studies have been done on men in general or college men in general. For a few tests, we know about Harvard men or Yale men or Amherst men who had certain score patterns. We need to learn more about the meaning of tests with respect, for example, to Harvard men and Purdue men as distinct from each other.

What kinds of tests are useful? First of all, individual tests. Almost no tests that are given to large groups of people at the same time are of any value. The chief exception is the Strong Vocational Interest Blank. Yet a good test battery should include many tests that have to be given to one man at a time. The reason seems obvious: the tester is doing something more than grinding out test scores; he is also watching the man operate. It is his individual style that the tester is going to try to understand, in order to suggest its appropriate vocational use. The goal of the psychologist's choice of test battery will be getting to know the student as well as possible in the two to six hours the student spends in his office. In two hours in one office, there are only so many situations that can arise, so the tester has a limited chance to make his subject's acquaintance. He would know him better after six months' intimate acquaintance but he would also have to send a considerably larger bill. So, in the two hours or more, he tends to mix up the situations as much as possible. He sees the man tackling multiple choice problems and open-ended problems, problems with time pressure and problems without time pressure, concrete problems and abstract problems, hard tasks and easy tasks; he watches him handling ideas, numbers, words, and gadgets.

In the end, the tester has a reasonably broad sample of the ways the client works. If there were some characteristic things he did in all these circumstances, the tester feels passably safe in assuming that the student will go right on doing those characteristic things when he works at his future vocation. The question is, "In what jobs will your characteristic style pay off?"

No one test battery is best for everyone. On the other hand, there are only a few psychological tests whose validity for vocational guidance has been proved by follow-up on the careers of people tested decades ago. These few, well-tried instruments ought to be included in the test battery by any competent examiner.

One well-tried instrument is the Strong Vocational Interest Blank. The Strong does not exactly measure interest; if the examiner wants to know what one is interested in, he can ask. (If he is any good, he will.) The Strong measures attitudes or values or *Weltan-schauung*. "Would you easily and naturally talk the language of the group if you went into pharmacy?" The score one gets on Pharmacy is just the extent to which one expresses likes and dislikes that have been expressed by successful and happy pharmacists—and so on, through more than fifty job titles, including Physician, Lawyer, Sales-man, Author, Engineer. If one "talks the language," or shares the point of view of men in a calling, it is an empirical fact that the odds for his becoming happy and successful in that calling are good.

Another interest test often encountered is the Kuder Preference Record. This test is less useful than the Strong. For one thing, it is easier to "fudge" (though why one should want to fool the examiner who has been asked to help is unclear). For another, it is not scored by specific job titles (Doctor, Lawyer), but by broad categories (Literary, Persuasive, Social Service), and offers less direct informa-tion. It is true, however, that a great deal of follow-up study has been done on the Kuder. At the Harvard Office of Tests, for example, one can be told not only one's Kuder scores but also which concen-trators at Harvard have scores that look most like one's own.

The choice of a test of general intelligence for the vocational guidance battery is made difficult by the way college men go through the ceiling of most I.Q. tests. For people in general there are only two really well-validated intelligence tests: the Stanford-Binet and the Wechsler-Bellevue. The Wechsler helps more in vocational testing because it contains many small subtests, each setting the man to work on a different sort of task. Both the Stanford and the Wechsler are individual tests.

No paper and pencil or group-administered test will provide a valid estimate of an I.Q. Sometimes such tests are used for convenience or economy or because they purport to have higher ceilings than standard intelligence tests. That is the reason for use of the Miller Analogies Test by the admissions committee of many graduate schools. Undergraduate schools use the College Board Examinations, which are tests that mix aptitude with educational achievement but are of some use in predicting future accomplishments. The Harvard Health Service uses the Speed Alphas described above.

Thousands of tests claim to measure some special aptitude, such as clerical skill or mechanical aptitude or aesthetic taste. Almost none of these special tests does well what it claims to do. A few might be worth trying, especially if one wanted to know his chances in some highly specialized line of work, but the important point is to remember not to take such aptitude tests too seriously. If the test is a group test and/or a paper and pencil test, one can be almost sure it is worth taking only with a grain of salt.

A more useful kind of test that may be included, and will certainly be included if the tester is at all modern, is the open-ended sort of test called a projective test. These tests do not "measure" anything; they are essay questions carried to their logical end, which is the point at which nothing one says in his essay can be right or wrong. You are given the ball to see where you can carry it. The two best projective tests are the Rorschach ("Here is an ink blot; tell me what you can see in it with some creative imagination on your part") and the Thematic Apperception Test ("Here is a simple little picture; build me a plot this picture could be an illustration from"). With no more help from the instructions than that, and where it is actually true that no answer is right and no answer is wrong, one has to draw on his own ideas a little in meeting the test problem. Unless a man simply clams up, he is bound to reply in his own style. He cannot call what he cannot see. He cannot draw upon internal resources he does not have.

The way one sees things, the private style that is all one's own, may turn out to be a critical difference between two college men. Both may have I.Q.'s of 152, verbal aptitudes, and law interests, yet one may have the flamboyant style of the barrister while another has the pedantic approach of the solicitor, one the common sense of the corporation attorney, another the idealism of the hopeful in international law. Such nuances of personality are most relevant to vocational problems at the level of ability found in college men. In terms of sheer ability, most college men can do anything they badly want to accomplish. The guidance question is not "What can you do?" but "What would come most naturally to you?"

When the tests are completed, the counselor will have a large mass of factual statements about the client. "You are about as good with figures as the average college man." "You have values a lot like those held by architects." The counselor will also have some generalizations about the ways the client was consistent from task to task. "You seem to be the kind of person who tackles things from a common-sense view until it is obvious that more abstruse concepts are required," or "who sets much store by being exact to the third decimal point," or "who builds ivory towers in the air but ignores facts."

Last of all, the counselor will have some odds to quote on success or contentment in various callings. "It's about three to one against your liking to be a doctor, and two to one for your enjoying the law, but you're bright enough to do either, so it's up to you."

It is up to the boy. Tests are no substitute for thinking. If the vocational counselor is at all competent, he will encourage thinking, some of it by the client and him together, more of it by the client alone. The sessions do not end with reading the test scores, nor do they end by reading the crystal ball. "Go and be the third assistant vice-president in the Nylon Division at Dupont" is a sort of crystal-gazing done only by fraudulent advisers.

How can one ensure that the advice a student receives is not fraudulent: The simplest way is by keeping him right in the university. Any number of people at most universities can serve him well. Testing is done at the Health Service, at the Guidance Service, when there is one, or at the Office of Student Placement. Usually there is no charge for these services.

If the student must go elsewhere, he can go to another university or to an established social service agency like the YMCA or a family counseling organization. There he will receive competent treatment and be charged moderately.

Another source of guidance is the private agency, often a management consultant agency. These organizations charge stiff fees.

Apparently, such outfits appeal to a certain type of college man, either because he feels that if the Nth National Bank consults them they must be trustworthy, or because he feels that you have to pay for what you get and you are only getting something worth having if you are getting one-hundred dollar advice. Neither rule holds. Because vocational guidance is a service profession, the rule is more like "The less you pay, the better you get."

The student will receive the best advice and for the least cost in his own university. He will know it is competent advice if it is individual to him, stated conditionally, in the form of data to be considered rather than as conclusions to be accepted, and if he is encouraged to interpret the data in light of his own background and the pressures that are on him alone. It may be that not receiving black and white conclusions will seem unsatisfying to many under-graduates. Another dissatisfying aspect of the tests may be that they "only tell you what you already know." It is to be presumed that intelligent young men are not purblind to their own needs; this confirmation of their insight probably indicates the validity of the tests. At least such conservative advice will do no harm.

What positive aid may vocational tests give? Perhaps just added sureness or clearness about choices that have been made without confidence. Often, however, a new concept of oneself may be opened by the tests. Frequently, a student will learn that he does not have a "block" or a lack of aptitude that he had assumed limited the areas in which he could succeed.

The ability to use data as a means for reaching sound conclusions is supposed to be taught as part of a college education. To use facts *about oneself* wisely and reach sound conclusions from them would seem to be an educational experience within the meaning of education at any good university. Also, within the meaning of "general education," President Conant has emphasized the value of learning to use the experts from specialized sciences outside one's own field. Nor is it a trivial gain to learn to tell the unpretentious but competent professional from the chrome-packaged modern version of the consulting medicine man. One cannot accept the position taken by some members of liberal arts faculties that counseling should be done only by non-specialists, that because tests are technical they are *ipso facto* valueless.

To be able to use the technical findings that bear on one's own fate would seem to be one mark of the educated man.

To offer vocational guidance that is more sophisticated than a profile of test scores, more educational than crystal-ball gazing, more of a shared experience than most students expect it to be, more exemplary of the way an educated man should learn to use a specialist than of the scornful rejection of all specialists now fashionable among some liberal arts faculty members is perhaps a worthy educational goal of the college health service. Vocational guidance conferences often turn out to be quite intellectually respectable think-pieces.

PSYCHOTHERAPY

The winds of controversy that have howled around the issue of whether or not psychotherapy should be the exclusive province of psychiatrists do not erase the observable fact that there are thousands of psychologists being paid by patients, great medical centers, mental hospitals, city, county, state, and federal government agencies, and even private psychiatrists (in group practice) for the practice of psychotherapy. Competent, carefully trained psychotherapists are in short supply; all that are available are needed, and the competent ones are fully employed regardless of whether they hold an M.D. or a Ph.D. in clinical psychology.

Neither degree makes the man a psychotherapist; it is but the foundation on which he builds. Psychotherapy is learned primarily through treatment of cases supervised by a senior psychotherapist. In many centers psychologists and psychiatrists share the same supervisors, but in any case each profession tries to assure the excellence of this training with standards far exceeding the possession of a degree. Just as competent M.D. psychotherapists disparage amateur psychotherapy by physicians, so are Ph.D. psychotherapists embarrassed by the amateur efforts of psychologists not well trained in psychotherapy.

Both groups recognize that the standards of a degree cannot be used to judge all efforts at helping people with problems by talking with them. There is another area called counseling which is not seen as treatment of a neurosis or psychosis but as a warm, understanding, and especially knowledgeable relationship aimed at relieving the client's ordinary human misery or advising him concerning a practical choice. Separating the two is not difficult except at the edges. A couch, hypnosis, or hospitalization is not used in counseling, and career planning, reassuring the homesick, or comforting the spurned rushee is not regarded as treatment of an illness.

At a university, counseling and psychotherapy are sometimes differentiated only by which agency offers the service, but a genuine distinction can be made. The main difference to an outside observer would be that counselors make more phone calls to other officers of the university to consult or recommend concerning the student, and there are more single visits to the counseling office. The reasons for this difference are that the counselor is engaged primarily in assisting in the disentangling of role conflicts, the recognition of which can come without interpreting the transference as is done in intensive psychotherapy, and that the client can make conscious, direct use of the information that is communicated to him by the counselor. This distinction is detailed in a report by Perry.[1] Psychotherapy is seen as primarily concerned with problems in the core personality as opposed to role conflicts and as requiring techniques that can permeate resistance and uncover feelings or issues of which the patient is unaware.

There are many "counseling" clinical psychologists just as there are many research, industrial, and teaching clinical psychologists who have no stake in practicing psychotherapy. But there are thousands of "clinical" psychologists who do have the role of psychotherapist as part of their identity. Their stake in practicing psychotherapy is anchored in many factors, some of which are common to all psychotherapists and need not be discussed and others of which are specific to the psychologist and will be detailed.

A clinical psychologist has training in psychology that can be used to help people with psychological problems. He may contribute to the alleviation of psychological problems through research, through teaching, or through his unique diagnostic skills. But there is no substitute, in a man so motivated, for making the effort directly, for responding with responsibility and involvement to a person in psycho-

---

[1] Perry, W. G., Jr. On the relation of psychotherapy and counseling, Ann. N. Y. Acad. Sci., 63:396—407, 1955.

logical need. A clinical psychologist with this motivation will not feel content with the counseling role. He will not tell the "client" who becomes a "patient" to go along to someone else, because the interviews have moved from the subtleties of role conflict to the subtleties of core personality conflict. If he is not a trained therapist experienced in abnormal psychology, then he should of course make a referral unless he has appropriate supervision. However, if he is a trained therapist with good clinical experience, then he should treat the patient. He is there, he has a relationship, he probably is better for this patient than any other therapist would be; he is trusted, the patient has allowed him into his private concerns. A referral at a point beyond an evaluation period or any time after a commitment to the relationship has been felt by the patient is very delicate.

Referrals are of course commonly made when a counselor and client agree that a deeper or more intensive kind of treatment is necessary; the client does not feel rejected if this is handled correctly; after all the counselor is helping him with wisdom in arranging care that will better suit his needs. Clinical psychologists will also make referrals when the problem appears to be beyond their competence. Cases where legal matters might be important are best handled by a physician, for administrative reasons at least. If hospitalization is necessary, the process will not only be less complicated but will probably work out better therapeutically if commitment is handled by a physician. The process of hospitalization cannot be handled by the psychologist with the dispatch, facility, and force that has proven so beneficial to the course of hospital treatment.

Other cases best treated by psychiatrists, no matter how therapeutically skilled the psychologist, are psychosomatic cases with symptoms that might require medical intervention. Where the psychologist is working in a psychosomatic clinic, this consideration may evaporate because of the specialization in treatment—the psychologist providing psychotherapy and the physician medical therapy during the same visit to the hospital. But in a college clinic, which is specialized only according to age and most diverse regarding disorders, the psychologist, except in very close collaboration with the physician, should probably not be the psychotherapist in cases with physical involvement.

Now that tranquilizers have found such wide use as an adjunctive aid in psychotherapy, certain "medical" issues may arise in cases clearly lying in the middle of the overlap between the provinces of psychiatry and clinical psychology. Clinical psychologists have long been treating people in acute anxiety and providing adequate help simply through psychotherapy. But now the issue is commonly pre- sented of a patient engaged in psychotherapy who does not need the pain of acute anxiety to motivate him into continuous treatment; the intensity of the pain is not serving a constructive purpose; it would be beneficial to take the edge off this pain and perhaps a tranquilizer could help. This is not grounds for transferring a patient to a psy- chiatrist, especially in a college clinic. The psychologist can take up the matter with his medical colleagues, and if such medication seems reasonable, then the patient could be seen by the psychiatrist and given the prescription. Of course, if it is one of the drugs that require checks at intervals for serious side effects, then the patient will have to be followed by a physician, but there should be no need to disturb psychotherapy by the psychologist. In such cases the psychiatrist might well have one of the internists in the clinic handling either the exam- ination or the laboratory checks.

Aside from his service function, the clinical psychologist has considerable stake in practicing psychotherapy as an important learn- ing process. His general clinical acumen is enhanced by therapeutic experience. Self-hatred can be read about; it can show in projective tests with richness of detail; perhaps the projective material may reveal more of the form of the self-hatred than would be discerned by the therapist during months of therapy; but only in therapy can one witness over a period of time the agony of these feelings or study all their ramifications in the life of an individual.

This type of experience is fundamental to a clinician if he is to appreciate fully many of the concepts he uses. Many of the concepts or formulations of dynamic psychology achieve deep significance only after one has experienced being the referent in his own therapy or through empathic experiencing of it with his patients.

Practice of psychotherapy is very important to a psychologist's testing function. Many feel that significant therapy experience is necessary to develop a rich diagnostic sense. For example, it is easy to slip into testing work-ups that take account of only major person- ality features while missing important subtleties that are seen in detail during therapy. The tester who is also psychotherapist will be more sensitive to these nuances. All matters that require sensitive clinical judgment will profit from therapeutic experience. For instance, the development of a feeling for what is intellectually realized but not emotionally felt is greatly aided by the follow-up check on one's judgment that therapy provides.

Prognostic skill benefits even more than diagnostic skill from the knowledge that comes from practicing psychotherapy. The rich collection of clues that results in the clinical "feel" for where a patient is in a particular process (on the horizon, beginning, middle, end) is best acquired in following therapeutically a long-term patient. Psychologists are often asked to "tell from the tests" what kind of therapy someone should have; unless one has been involved in seeing firsthand how a variety of patients respond to one kind of therapy, the bench mark for making specific recommendations about therapy is rather abstract. For a clinic to burden a clinical psychologist with so much diagnostic work that he has no time for psychotherapy is to limit his growth and wisdom as a diagnostician as well as to keep him from an activity for the sake of which he may have entered the profession in the first place. A university health service clinical psychologist whose vocational aim and/or primary function is clinical must engage in psychotherapy if he is to make his optimum contribution.

4

Distinguishing Patterns
of Student Neuroses

Charles C. McArthur

University students' neuroses are basically like anyone else's. To be a Harvard man or a Yale man or a Purdue man confers no exemption from the laws of human nature. Yet the university student is a highly selected person who lives under selected circumstances. For these reasons, his neuroses are not quite like everyone else's. The precipi-tating circumstances that bring him in to the psychiatrist are often the special circumstances of the university environment. The conflict on which his illness focuses will probably be phrased consistently with the phrasing given to all things by the kind of family that encourages —or drives—its son to go to college. His choice of symptom and, in particular, his choice of defense, will be consonant with his self-image as a student. The explosiveness of his problems will largely be a result of the volcanic forces that characterize his, or anyone's, adolescence. It should also be said that youth affects his prognosis favorably. Each of the special factors in his illness deserves our attention: his youth, his background, his college situation.

Sheer youth does not differentiate students from the rest of their generation. We do, however, set students apart by a number of social devices that keep them identified as postadolescents. To prolong ado-lescence in that way may have its uses. Its disadvantage may be that we delay the college men's acceptance of themselves and of their roles in life. This overlong tentative state of mind is fertile soil for the growth of neuroses. If we want to understand these neuroses, we had best begin with some ideas about the psychology of adolescence.

The first challenge comes from the body. The adolescent no longer recognizes himself. "The boy who is five feet three and suddenly, in a relatively few months, becomes six feet tall, does not feel that his body is familiar to him. . . . He does not even know what to do with his feet or his hands. . . . He must learn a new body image, a new physical self. For this reason he can learn to do a breathtakingly graceful swan-dive, only to fall over his feet into a clumsy heap as he leaves the swimming pool."[1] His sense of sureness must often be hurt.

The second challenge to this youngster comes from "changes in body sensations. . . . Feelings that were unknown to the individual, or were experienced in modified form, now strike in all their rawness. The adolescent . . . senses he is different. Again he is alien to himself."[2] Not only has he hormonal changes as a result of sexual growth, but he is also more sensitive to stimuli. He is just at this time very tautly strung.

He cannot express his newly discovered sexual urge freely and so, "he tries to express it in study, in athletic activities, in friendships and in experimental sexual play. All are pallid overt expressions of vivid and confusing feelings."[3] He is limited not only by social rules but by his own conscience and doubts and conflicts. The analytic theory is that he experiences a reopening of the Oedipal conflicts he knew in infancy. The conflicts thus regenerated make very difficult not only his task of coping with sexual maturity but his newly intense relationship to his parents.

There is certainly more involved than Oedipal forces. At least in the middle class, there are cultural imperatives that lead the family to "kick him out of the nest," however reluctantly. We know that "The Future, Doing-oriented family must produce sons reared in the 'achievement mores,' taught to look forward to bypassing or surpass-

---

[1] Josselyn, I. The ego in adolescence. *Amer. J. Orthopsychiat.*, 24:223–237, 1954.
[2] *Ibid.*
[3] *Ibid.*

ing their father's occupational roles. . . . It is these boys who will, after college, be expected to leave their family and make their own way."[4]

Winning freedom is harder when you are not sure who you are. First rejection of the parents, perhaps overdetermined by defensive-ness against longing for their love, can be extreme. Josselyn says, "The adolescent rebel may evaluate his mother as physically unattrac-tive, mentally stupid and emotionally silly; his father as physically a monstrosity, mentally stodgy and emotionally sterile. He may evaluate them quite to the contrary, only to indicate their very virtues to be something to condemn."[5] In particular, the boy's identification with his father, which could be a pillar of strength for him, may become a matter about which he feels turbulent conflict. "To be like the parent is, in adolescence, no longer a source of self-respect and self-confidence but rather a cause for self-depreciation. To be like the parent implies an imitation of the parent and therefore a loss of one's own right as an individual. . . . Proof of individuality is to be different."[6]

This is the function of identification with one's peers. The peer group serves "to a limited degree as a bulwark against losing his identity entirely as he abandons his parents as model. His own age group fails him to a certain extent in this. They are too confused in their self-evaluation."[7]

The conscience he carried with him from childhood is now out of date. Yet he needs a conscience, if only as a form of automation, to get decisions about at least some issues made without prolonged con-flict. When he throws away his childish conscience, often at the time he rebels against his father, the adolescent has to search about for some replacement.

The search for a new pattern is not made easy for him. "How to be a grown-up instead of a child is outlined in our society at best in very intangible terms."[8] The result is, in the less favorable cases, conflict that leads to the neurotic use of defense mechanisms and neurosis itself. The ego has broken down. What is left is regression

---

[4] McArthur, C. Personality differences between middle and upper classes. J. Abnorm. Psychol., 50:207–254, 1955.
[5] Josselyn, op. cit.
[6] Ibid.
[7] Ibid.
[8] Ibid.

to less adequate devices. However, it is important to realize that such devices were seized on *faute de mieux;* when something better offers itself they may be very readily abandoned. That is a critical observation. "The difference between a neurosis in adulthood and normal adolescent behavior is that the adolescent experiments with multiple defenses with an intensity that, in the adult, would result in a crystallized neurosis. In the adolescent the crystallization has not occurred and, therefore, in many instances is subject to spontaneous change or is responsive to limited psychiatric help."[9]

The prognosis is different for adolescent neurotics, not only "because they are young and have resources but, paradoxically, because as is commonly said, their egos are weak. While some adolescents without question do develop a true classical neurosis, such a diagnosis should be offered only after intensive study. A typical adolescent may present a picture today of hysteria while the history indicates that a month ago his behavior appeared typically impulsive. Next month his defenses may be utilized in such a way as to justify a clinical diagnosis of a compulsive neurosis."[10]

It is a young man or a young woman in this fluid state who is, near the end of adolescence, sent off to college.

Perhaps this is the best place to discuss Erik Erikson's theory that the special growth task of late adolescence is to find an identity and the special danger to be reduced to a state of "self-diffusion" or "role diffusion." Erikson quotes Biff's line in *Death of a Salesman*: "I just can't take hold, Mom, I can't take hold of some kind of life."

This phenomenon is prettily demonstrated in White's case of Joseph Kidd. White reports, "This was a peculiarly bad period in his life. . . . Even his girl, on whom he had been leaning for emotional support, demanded that he grow up and behave like a man with a will of his own. . . . The role of the kid was completely played out."[11] At this point the boy himself describes his condition:

I began trying to fit a personality to my make-up. I began acting out personalities and tried observing people and copying them, but I realized what I was doing and so carried that 'how'm I doing attitude,' that is, continually looking at and thinking about what I'd said or done,

---

[9] *Ibid.*
[10] *Ibid.*
[11] White, R. Lives in Progress. New York, The Dryden Press, 1952.

what impression I had made. But these personalities were all short-lived because they pleased some and not others and because they didn't produce that underlying purpose of making people like me; and every time unconsciously I would resort to my childish attitude to make myself noticeable. Examples of these 'personalities' are independence (but I couldn't keep it up); arrogance (but people were only arrogant back at me); big shot in sex (but people weren't so much in love with it as I thought); hatefulness (people paid no attention to me); extreme niceness (people took advantage of it, kidded me about it because I did it to an ultra degree); humorous nature (but I was only being childish, silly); quiet and studious (but people were only passing me by and I kept feeling I was missing something). I became a daydreamer so intensively that up to the present I find I'm daydreaming almost all the time. I became conscious of a person's approach and would become fluttered, flustered, would try to make a friend of him no matter who he was but I overdid it.

As White remarks, "There seemed to be no core to his personality."

This boy differs from many of our student neurotics only in the lucidity of his self-description. It may be argued that he was not a neurotic, that this was a growth crisis. Such an argument is bootless; the protean adjustment problems of the adolescent trying to discover who he is are alike on both sides of the thin line between neurotic and normal.

Two special issues often are seized upon as foci for the boy's diffuse agitation over who on earth he may be. One is his career choice; the other, his maleness.

Requests for guidance in choice of major field or subsequent choice of career are commonly made by both neurotics and normals. At Harvard, at least, the average student makes many choices of major subject and many postcollege choices of career. However, requests for guidance often have deeper implications in terms of the search for identity.

A graduate who had been a "job-jumper" during the years since graduation returned for vocational guidance. His interest test showed several job-families that he might consider: administrative, sales, social service. He had been a salesman, but now felt that a move to junior executive function might be indicated. The social service lead was dismissed as reflecting a personal interest but not a vocational possibility.

A few days later he returned saying that he had been thinking the results over and knew that he really wanted to go into an administrative post in a social service program. He said he had, right up to his previous interview, been carefully "forcing myself to be a businessman." His long-standing interest in social service (including an appropriate undergraduate major) had been suppressed. Asked why, he told a story of conflict with his stepfather who was in that area and identification with his natural father, long dead. His mother also was in social work. (That, being a boy, he did not wish to accept identification with a female model any more than he wanted to accept the loathed stepfather was not said.) He was now married and, at the time of the conference, had a small son. As to social work, "I have had it around the house all these years." As to business, "I realize now that I've been getting farther and farther from the core of the business—out into very special staff functions—so I could avoid facing the fact that I was there to make money. This crass value runs counter to everything my mother and stepfather believe. Given their influence, plus a progressive prep school, plus Harvard, how could I kid myself that I wanted to be a businessman? I was just being stubborn about rejecting him."

Such ultimate closing of adolescent rejections too long kept open is a common pattern among alumni who return for vocational guidance.

The question "Am I male?" can be a very painful corollary of the broader question "Who am I?" The university student is specially vulnerable to this doubt because of his necessary delay in marrying, his past selection for the role of good boy, and the American mores that define study and cultivated tastes as feminine. Often, too, he has been very close to his mother. Usually, such doubts have little basis in fact; reassurance about biological manhood may not relieve the irrational doubts, however. The irrational root of the doubt in the boy's deeply felt unsureness of his masculine identity must be extirpated.

Occasionally, such a fear for one's manliness may sieze upon some slight anomaly as its excuse for being.

A boy who would not meet his swimming requirement had a consistent record of failing even to report to the pool for instruction. This uncooperativeness persisted, though he was otherwise a conscientious student. Psychiatric investigation finally revealed that he was ashamed to show his naked body to other boys because he had rather more than an average (but not abnormal) amount of pigment around his nipples. He was sure that this meant he was homosexual. When educated about this matter, he remained sure that the other boys would call him homosexual. Only after extensive psychiatric work did his underlying fear of "who I may be" become allayed.

One still sees, of course the naïve, old-fashioned fears of being weakened by masturbation. These, too, get well entangled with questions of "Who am I?" (Joseph Kidd felt inadequate because he masturbated.)

One of the few cases of hysteria we have seen was that of a boy with analgesic fingers, who was greatly concerned over his masturbation. His concern was increased by his roommate, who came from a social class where constant fornication was thought to be necessary "to keep healthy." This roommate's attitude to the patient was condescendingly tolerant. "Joe's kinda latent," he would say and tell of his plans to take Joe on sexual adventures. Needless to say, these so-carefully planned charities did Joe's self-confidence and his feeling that he was healthy no good. Extensive psychiatric exploration did not much improve Joe's state; too many converging forces had focused on this apparently simple bit of miseducation about sex. He is still seeking himself by identifying with various ideological movements in the "lunatic fringe."

Finally, one may note the external source of questions about "Who am I?" that are inherent in the college situation. There is often, for the first generation to attend college, a marked discontinuity between hometown and university, parents and selves. "You can't go home again" is a frequent theme.

One boy from a Serbian family came for vocational guidance. "What can I do?" he asked. "I want to be an anthropologist. My family came from another country and another century. They only know four honorific callings: the military, the priesthood, medicine, and the law."

The college setting usually creates the presenting symptom. At Brooklyn College, Blos reports, "The following types of problems were met with regularity: (1) The student who cannot study, who complains of inability. (2) The student who is lonely, who cannot make friends. (3) The student who is unable to speak in class. (4) The student without any purpose or vocational aim. (5) The habitual evader, obstructionist, and complainer. (6) The student in acute conflict with his family. (7) The student with a physical defect. (8) Special problems of veterans."[12] Although Blos was operating a psychological service rather than a psychiatric one, his list sounds very like what our own might be except for the absence of referrals in terms of specifically psychiatric symptoms like anxiety or homosexual panic. At Bennington, Chassel reports, "One-third came for help because of neurotic or psychosomatic symptoms obviously suggesting an emotional basis. . . . A quarter came to ask for advice or support

---

12 Blos, P. Psychological counseling of college students. Amer. J. Orthopsychiat., 16:571–580, 1946.

in the midst of emancipation battles with the family. . . . A sixth appeared because of difficulties in college work, varying from almost total failure to take hold of college tasks in spite of good ability to complaints of dawdling and mind-wandering when papers had to be written. Approximately the same number reported maladjustment in the college community or in personal relations. . . . The remainder consulted the psychiatrist for vocational or other practical perplexities . . . and because of general interest in a personality review."[13] This report is perhaps less weighted with academic referral problems than our experience. However, Chassell remarks in a footnote, "In a college organized around a rather rigid curriculum, the psychiatrist reports many conferences devoted to the wear and tear incident to meeting requirements." Harvard has one difficult requirement for a degree: two years of a foreign language. We have, therefore, all manner of psychiatric disabilities that are presented as "language blocks."

One price of being intelligent is that no one expects less of you when you meet better competition. This is especially a problem for boys who come to Harvard from small and distant public high schools. Their first grades or even their first section meeting, at which they hear other pupils recite, staggers them.

One pupil came in in a panic after his first section meeting in a General Education course. "Those fellows from places like Andover all know who Agamemnon is and they just naturally throw around names like Botticelli!" he exclaimed with wild-eyed panic. "I was accepted at State; do you suppose they'll still let me transfer?"

He survived his "Big League Shock," but others do not. These boys are used to getting A's; their parents expect A's; everyone regards as disgraceful any mark as low as a straight B. Parents and, worse, neighbors cannot be educated to realize that not more than two percent of the college class will get all A's.

One boy, 17, was the first boy from his town to come to Harvard. He had straight A's in high school and his acceptance by Harvard was a community triumph. His November grades were C's. (This was the level we had predicted he would attain, on the basis of his entrance data.) He

[13] Chassell, J. Individual counseling of college students. *J. Consult. Psychol.*, 4:205–209, 1940.

came to the psychiatric service in a reactive depression that was danger-
ously deepened when, returning home for Thanksgiving, he was met at
the train station by the village band!

This boy, like so many, has additional conflict of conscience (and
hence danger of depression) because he is acutely aware of "all my
parents have sacrificed" and he just has to keep his National Scholarship. He finds it difficult to comprehend what we are saying when
we tell him over and over that A's are not necessary for keeping his
scholarship. His whole background, introjected by him as an irrational
conscientiousness, tells him that he ought to be required to get A's in
order to be "deserving" of all his honors. Over and over again we
disabuse him of this notion—to no avail.

Whether this neurosis was institutionally determined and could
have been avoided by proper education of parents and boy before he
came here is an open question. Not all National Scholars react quite
so seriously to "Big League Shock." Most recover after painful experience, either by making a more rational assessment of the requirements and adopting a more realistic level of aspiration, or by "learning
the ropes" by June, when they are already writing final exams as
good—and as full of Harvardmanship—as their classmates. Meanwhile, however, their initial shock will have been the referral symptom
that has brought a number of freshmen to the psychiatric service.

Of almost 600 cases seen by Harvard's psychiatric service in the
academic year 1956-1957, about one quarter were finally diagnosed
as neuroses. One quarter were given other psychiatric labels, mostly
depressions and schizoid states, while a third quarter were given
"Problem Diagnoses" after the system devised for this purpose by
Monks and Heath[14] for labeling cases in which there seemed to be no
identifiable psychiatric ailment. The remaining quarter included a
scattering of administrative problems, "adjustment reactions to adolescence," "adult situational reactions," and requests for information.
These labels are not very valid, especially when applied to the adolescent chameleon. Yet these figures or diagnostic categories indicate
approximate rates.

The presenting symptom tells little of the diagnosis. Sometimes

---

14 Monks, J., and Heath, C. A classification of academic, social and personal
problems for use in a college student health department. Student Medicine,
2:44–62, April 1954.

the presenting problem is the true problem; sometimes it is only the latest outcropping of an old neurosis. Of the neuroses, by far the majority were labeled "anxiety reaction." This label often describes the symptom better than the disease. The next most common label was "compulsive neurosis." Blos had this same experience. "In fact," he reports, "when I tried to classify 387 cases, I was appalled to find that classification would indeed be fitting them into a procrustean bed, for the sake of typology. I began to realize that I was dealing with case material which was basically different from cases seen in a mental hygiene or child guidance clinic, the difference being that no definite symptom complex had developed."[15]

Not only the presenting symptom but the choice of defense may be determined in part by the special circumstances of the student. Choice of defense goes a bit deeper, reflecting not only the values of the college community but those values of the patient's family that led them to encourage him to go to college. Sometimes these values are only the "success mores," but often enough they are expressed in terms of intellectual ambition or purely intellectual goals.

At any rate, a signal fact about the student neurotic is that he is intelligent. This has a structural meaning for the neuroses: he can proliferate symptoms with great flair, but he also can support a good deal of insight therapy. Indeed he often performs prodigious feats of self-analysis, which, however, do not usually have much curative effect. The more important effect of his intelligence, however, is its meaning for his self-image. This varies with the meaning that college has been given in the family and with the state that the student's postadolescent revolt may have reached.

A number of negative meanings are assigned to intellectual achievement. One is that it is dangerous.

For example, a student had been speaking of his "laziness" and his "weak will." He always put things off. He made resolutions and broke them. He had, he said, developed a sense of moral incompetence, of feebleness, shocking to his ideals, but demonstrated by repeated failure. After a long silence, he said, "You know I think I may get a lot out of this laziness, so-called. You know, I think I'm pretty smart, smarter than most people, and I guess it means a lot to me to think I can do a better job at things than them—write A papers and all that. Oh I know I pro-

---

[15] Blos, *op. cit.*

crastinate, and that's a bad habit, but not so bad to me as being dumb or second-rate. And so when I have a paper to write, I think how good it will be and keep putting it off and off until I have to do it in an awful rush and then when I hand it in, I'm *safe*. If it's good, why it just goes to show; but if it's poor, well, I still could have got an A if I'd started on time."

Such a pattern need not be part of a deep neurosis; adolescents are capable of flirting with this sort of defense in isolation from any other. Yet when one tests such a boy with, for instance, the Rorschach, castration imagery is very likely to come through. This is in good part caused by the twin institutions of college and family. As a very wise counselor has commented:

The educator has said nothing about his other hand (because he would like to forget it himself?)—the fist under the table armed with brass knuckles. He has not said, "And while you're at it, young man, you do it *on time, our way*. And if you don't, you'll not only fail to get these wonderful things—you'll be sent shamefully home, *a failure.*" ("My father won't say anything, but I know how he'll look at me when I say anything at dinner.")[16]

This is the student whose Rorschach includes several images of daggers. And not a few of cut-off stumps.

The point is that we can understand studying for what it really is: "*a means of learning and a ritual for the appeasement of authority.*"[17] This has all sorts of corollaries because relationship to authority is "the battle line of adolescence."

One corollary is that there is much secondary gain to be had in nonstudying. Not only can one comfort oneself with fond illusions of what one could have done, but there is also that "triumph in independence and successful effrontery": getting an A without cracking the books! There is, further, the necessity, discussed above, of establishing oneself as different, in order to have a unique self at all.

There is also the desire to avoid identification as a "grind," which is to say, that worst of all negative self-images, "a sissy." The role of the university student may have been attained only by rejecting other roles that are culturally defined as proper for red-blooded

16 Perry, W. Of counselors and college. Harvard Educat. Rev., Winter 1948, pp. 8–34.
17 *Ibid.*

American boys. In the middle class, especially among very "good" families: "It is the hopes of the mother that these sons must realize in order to feel successful. They will have been drawn close to their mother, who so assiduously brought them up, and they will have introjected her precepts." The result is "a danger that the son may doubt his own manhood."[18] This "sissy complex" has been noted by foreign observers. Presumably one reason this possibility is left open is that the family and the sub-culture have so consistently devalued the father. A male identification becomes that much more difficult. Then, too, the mother, in her role as culture bearer, makes demands on the son that increase his difficulty in learning to be a male.

Finally, there is the raw desire to avoid gratifying *Them*. Time and again, a "study block" is phrased in terms of what *They* demand. Often, one feels that *They* have been introjected rather than being "out there." *They* are the personification of the childhood conscience, now being outgrown at the price of conflict and incapacitation. Frequently there is no personal *They*, but only *What One Ought*. The phrase "I know I ought to . . ." runs through many an interview with students who in fact do not do what they ought. Here it is the conscience that is being wrestled quite frankly. Both the archaicness and the introjection of these pressures are suggested by quotation from one of Perry's counselees, "I had a teacher in grammar school who kept nagging me about what I *ought* to do, and now I know what I ought to do, but somehow I don't want to do it."[19]

The common line of defense is, of course, some form of work: ritual notetaking, sitting in front of an open German book six hours without learning any German, or memorizing at the expense of thinking. It is especially with regard to the language requirement (perhaps the subject matter lends itself well to such an approach) that we see many of these ritual ploys used to allay a bad conscience. The ultimate ploy is their inclination to study study methods. These devices are employed by less than neurotic students, particularly with regard to what they consider to be irrationally required courses like languages or to prerequisitely required courses like premedical chemistry. Yet these devices frequently warn of the presence of an obsessive neurosis.

---

[18] McArthur, *op. cit.*
[19] Perry, *op. cit.*

The neurosis most frequently seen and most prolix in development among students is obsession and/or compulsion. Occasionally the first cousin of these, phobia, also appears. Since adolescent neuroses are so protean, all combinations of the three and all sorts of mixtures of the three with anxiety may appear. Such neuroses seem very appropriate to young men of high intelligence. Their social role as intellectuals can be easily perverted as intellectualizing, their culturally determined duty to be self-controlled perverted into repression, and their "egghead" value on seeing myriad shades of grey in every event perverted into compulsive doubt.

Certainly these are the student's commonest choices of defense. Intellectualizing is most pervasive; since use of that defense is so strongly prescribed both by the university culture and the "good" families who sent the boy to the university, one can only be surprised that it is not universal. Where the value of reason is highest (e.g., in the Law School), the neurotic misuse of reason also flourishes. Suppression and repression come next in frequency; the sex life of the "good" student makes these defenses obligatory. The picture most commonly seen, then, is of inwardly turned, impulse-denying neuroses; the acting-out disorders also occur among students but not so frequently. Most students have all kinds of defenses, often, as we have said, by turns. Their symptoms are, indeed, caused by the return of the repressed. It was the "quiet decent neuroses" that so many students had that led us to assign the modal psychiatric label of "anxiety reaction."

The soil in which many of these academic neuroses grow seems to be represented by a particular Rorschach Test pattern. This pattern was first isolated by Pauline Vorhaus in a series of reading clinic cases in New York. Later it turned out to characterize 35 to 40 percent of the psychiatric referrals at Harvard and probably a larger proportion of the neuroses. This pattern is dominated by inanimate movement and color responses, with a large number of accurately seen form responses rounding it out. The interpretation offered by Vorhaus begins with intrapersonal tensions and strains that hamper both free acceptance of instinctual drives and of any sublimated, creative outlets for them. The source of strain is:

. . . that the subject is responsive to affective stimulation; indeed he is responsive to a point where moments of strong feeling occur as often, or almost as often, as do those when a more surface pleasantness is all that is evoked. . . . If this is true, then the actual tension is due to continued experiences of strong feeling, continuing even though, on a conscious level, the subject may have succeeded in repressing recognition that this is so. Since however it *does* persist, it is clear that a mere act of will cannot dissolve it and that it continues on as a threat. It must therefore be modified in such a way as to render it acceptable. This psychological need is accomplished by withdrawing the affect from the environment and directing it against the self.[20]

The ego being in a state of flux or even of collapse, it cannot serve its usual function of mediating between the person and his environment. He is left exposed. The stimuli to which he is exposed must somehow be handled. He may try expressing his emotional responses directly—or indirectly—as in activities, but none of these forms of expression are really adequate. Stimuli still rain in (his own body provides some of them, in addition to those provided by his environment), leaving him no recourse save retreat. The result is an inchoate, self-perpetuating, vaguely agitated mood.

The common diagnosis of these neuroses as "anxiety reactions" does not fit the Rorschach picture. There is sometimes development of the types of shading responses to the blots that are theoretically taken to show the presence of free anxiety. More often, the Rorschach shows (in the inanimate movement responses) a kind of anxious *agitation*. These young people have a private moving picture screen in their heads that plays a continuous feature, but the projector is out of focus. Their problem is to avoid always watching this disturbing, distorted private movie. They are therefore agitated, labile, distressed but unsure as to what distresses them. They try every sort of defense against this return of the repressed, with little effect.

The repressed material is itself inchoate, often little more than body sensations. There is usually a strong sexual tinge to it, as is appropriate to a period of prolonged adolescence. Sexual tension may particularly be associated with classical inanimate movement responses of the sort that attribute movement or emotion to the blot itself.

A girl gave a Rorschach of this type that began with a response attributing dynamic traits to the blot, that was seen to be flowing and somehow dividing. This turned out to be her endopsychic state directly

[20] Vorhaus, P. Rorschach configurations associated with reading disability. J. Project. Techn., 16:3–19, 1952.

projected onto the blot. She was divided between her good and bad self, being a girl or a woman, going home or working away, dropping her boyfriend of long standing or getting engaged and going with him. She had, in English class, been fascinated by and writing a carefully worked-over theme on the topic: *waiting*.

The intellectual defenses are commonly tried by these young people. Typically, they have high formal accuracy in their Rorschach; they are both intelligent and conscientious. They may resort to various projections of their personal problems onto intellectual issues:

The same girl felt that she gained a great deal from *Waiting for Lefty* but resented bitterly her instructor's treatment of *The Plague*. So far as she was concerned, there were certain fragments of *The Plague* that mattered and she resented her teacher's slighting these (to her) emotionally critical aspects.

She liked a composition teacher whose technique was to spot the affect-laden sentences in a fair English theme and warmly encourage development of the ego-involved topic, in what sounded more like Rogerian therapy than formal literary instruction.

On the other hand, these youngsters have not yet found a socially defined role that will channel their chaotic energies. (Rorschachwise, they use color in an uncontrolled way more often than in socialized percepts.) They are prey, then, to impulse and mood.

One such girl complained, "I feel up—up—up," making inchoate gestures to try to convey her meaning, "and then I feel down—down—down!"

She added that she was so uncontrolled at times that even the members of the local theatre group, noted for their unbridled self-expression, could not endure her. She had been sternly lectured by them on the necessity for control!

If we ask how such states came about, we may follow Vorhaus' inferences from the Rorschach:

We again glimpse a . . . 'good' home, the submissive child, and the awareness of pressure. . . . A sense of depreciation again appears to supply the motivation, but in this case it is the affective relationship which seems too precious to surrender. Yet it clearly cannot be continued in its old form. . . . Since the resentment cannot be overcome, the psychological need becomes that of preventing it from being experienced as associated with the environment. This is done by turning the hostility against the self, for the 'guilt' of harboring the resentment. With this accomplished, the subject is made to feel that 'Mother and Father are entirely just in all their demands and expectations. It is *I* who am guilty for not cooperating with them. It is because of my inadequacy and inferiority that their 'good' plans have not worked out.'[21]

Other studies have shown a similar genesis of student problems.

This description well fits our college experience. The student who finds his old love relation to his parent too precious to surrender but knows it cannot continue in its old form is very familiar. Even more familiar is the pathogenic effect of the excessively "good" family, with its unspoken pressures, generating in the child such a desperate awareness of all that he has to do. That he is not punished for failure makes his desperation greater; any text of child psychology will describe the peculiar effectiveness of "psychological punishment."

This agitated, self-blaming, diffusely emotional state is the soil from which adolescent neuroses flower. It produces many varieties. Of fifty students with such Rorschachs, sixteen were diagnosed as having interpersonal problems, ten were diagnosed as depressions (all but one "reactive"), eight as anxiety states, eight as schizoid reactions (many with obsessive elements), three as homosexual disturbances, one as hypomanic, and the rest scattering. This variety may in part reflect the unreliability of psychiatric labels or the unspecificity of the Rorschach syndrome (subtypes of this syndrome with inaccurate form perception could well include psychotics), but mostly may reflect the protean nature of adolescent mental ills. The basic tension finds many expressions. Several cases received three different diagnoses in three different weeks. This may not only reflect the fluidity of psychiatric judgment; it may also reflect the fluidity of the patient's symptoms.

The choice of symptom may often be overdetermined by the special role of the student. His special claim to being intelligent (and the necessity of proving that he is) becomes a focus of infection. When this occurs, association between ability to study and ability to be sexually potent is easily suggested. It may be overdetermined by his family's demand that he produce, since he is so able and had such great potential. This role-determined association of the phallic with the cephalic often overlays the primitive thought-process that Freud called "displacement from below to above." The result may be a

---

[21] Vorhaus, *op. cit.*

series of extraordinary notions about just what is happening in the head.

A student comes in to complain of a "freezing of his brain" just before he gives in to a particularly compulsive impulse. He has great introspective detail to offer, but it turns out that what he is experiencing is the biologically normal mechanism called an autonomic storm, which is the result of the chemical changes in the blood when any of us gets agitated. It turns out that he feels he "ought" to be able to control such impulses by "rational means," since he is, after all, possessed of what has been called "an excellent legal mind."

Overattention to what is going on inside the head and introspective watching of one's own thought processes can sometimes lead these very intelligent young men to independent discoveries of the laws of psychology.

A law student with an extraordinarily proliferated obsessive neurosis and an I.Q. off the top of the scale, even when he is measured against Harvard norms, comes in to complain that his mind is degenerating. We ask him why he thinks so. He reports that he has discovered and repeatedly confirmed, each time with more horror, that he can more easily answer multiple choice questions than open-ended questions covering the same material!

When reassured that he has by introspection rediscovered one of the laws of memory, that recognition is easier than recall, he is not comforted. We point out that this has been true of mankind at least since it was first observed by the great Ebbinghaus around 1880 and that his rediscovery does his powers of observation honor. No comfort does he take! He remains sure that his memory is "as full of holes as a sieve."

He is referred for intensive psychotherapy.

Reading symptoms are legion. Most of them are special cases of this concern with the head, especially the brain, as an overhauled organ and of this extraordinary capacity for introspection.

"I'm reading along," says one obsessive boy, "and I come to a phrase like *de iure* or 'Kangaroo court.' I have to stop. It's almost as if they were foreign words. I have to explore their meaning to the utmost until I've exhusted it. Then, and only then, can I proceed to the next word."

Needless to say, the words chosen as examples turned out to have all manner of private connotations. They were, indeed, near the center of the webs of associated words and ideas that are legitimate referents of that much misused word, "complex." This boy was wrapped up in a course in legal ethics. This turned out to be a fine illustration of the valid generalization that, for most normal students and for all neurotic ones, the assignments that take hold educationally are those which permit the direct projection of the student's central emotional problems. He turned out to have a neurosis of an irrationally developed conscience.

The symbolic substitution of intellectual potency for sexual potency is for many students something very like the story of their life. At any rate, it is encouraged by a whole network of cultural influences that suggest to the "good" student that it would be better to suppress awareness of or devalue his body so as to concentrate on developing his mind. This most private of Mind-Body problems occurs in many students. The success with which they build a psychic Great Wall just at the neckline is amazing. Their Rorschachs frequently emphasize this division, as may their Draw-A-Person Test.

A feature of college neuroses not so far explored is the frequency with which they contain what the psychoanalysts call oral elements. On rereading the psychologist's test reports for our neurotics, we were struck by the large number of oral responses that appeared in the projective tests, even though the psychologist had not been especially interested in this possibility, nor held the opinion that oral problems were to be expected in college students.

The meaning of such imagery may be assumed to be that these students are especially concerned with problems of continuing dependence or are beginning to take aggressively from others. A psychoanalytic formulation would lead us to interpret such a finding as evidence of temporary regression, a refighting of childhood battles, when growth is stymied by the imposing obstacles that confront the adolescent. Another viewpoint might be that orality is scarcely surprising in verbal people like college students; indeed, oral aggression is to be seen in their everyday behavior.

A feature of college neuroses that occasionally shocks the psychiatrist is the starkness with which some boys are able to state feelings that would usually be thoroughly disguised and defended.

At a staff conference, a psychiatrist who works part time in the University and part time in a mental hospital presents a puzzling case. His student patient has in the second interview bared the Oedipal feeling that underlay his symptoms. The doctor is convinced that the boy has not just been reading up on such matters but that this is a solid emotional insight. He is astonished at such naked revelation of primitive and ancient emotions usually uncovered only after months of therapy. The patient, by presenting the doctor with this material, has left him at a loss. His mental hospital experience tells him that only psychotics have so little ability to protect their own ego. Yet he does not believe this boy to be psychotic.

Josselyn notes this phenomenon of adolescent neuroses in these terms: "Because the adolescent, especially one who verbalizes easily, often has not built up strong defenses against his conflicts, he will reveal the nature of his conflicts in a manner that may cause the therapist to wonder if his patient has read all of Freud."[22]

A boy who at first contact was quite depressed and beset by problems of identification but also showed good resources brought into his third therapeutic hour a theme for an undergraduate course in which he quite successfully interpreted a series of his own dreams in terms of their Oedipal meaning. At the same time he discussed the way this infantile complex was related to his current behavior. The pattern he derived was quite valid, if the report from psychological tests can be used as a criterion. The insight was emotionally felt and not merely intellectually slick. Indeed, it was obtained only by an effort at "suspending my disbelief" in the Oedipal theory.

There was, of course, more to be had from interpreting the dreams —e.g., the identification problem—but the boy's interpretations stood up in subsequent therapeutic hours. He continued to make gains. A later crisis precipitated by circumstances calculated to arouse his deepest conflicts was met successfully.

From all these painful conditions the students manage to recover. In estimating the prognosis for a student's mental ills one uses the textbook rules and then adds a large dose of optimism. The optimism is especially called for if treatment is available in the university setting, for the fact is that much can be accomplished by a university psychiatrist even in these apparently deep and proliferated neuroses.

Effective treatment can be undertaken while the student continues his studies. This fact wants emphasizing and reemphasizing. The traditional educator's view is "if he can't work he doesn't belong here," and the traditional educator's remedy is leave of absence—or firing. The traditional psychiatrist's view is "first things first," and the traditional psychiatric remedy is referral outside the university

---

22 Josselyn, *op. cit.*

for intensive therapy. Neither recourse is usually necessary. Referral has to be used if the psychiatric staff is too small. One major Eastern university lists as its "psychiatric service" one doctor who serves 30,000 students; he must make quite a few referrals. Leave of absence may be the only answer where there is no psychiatric service at all, although even then a surprising number of quite neurotic students will, given the chance, somehow muddle through. Where an adequate service exists, the neurotic problems described in this chapter can be alleviated surprisingly often.

What is an adequate service? Our experience suggests that twenty psychiatrists will work very hard to cover the major demands put on them by ten thousand students. This moderate ideal will not be soon realized in many universities, but it may be set as a level of aspiration. Sheer numbers of doctors are perhaps less important than their skill. One point is clear: they must be dynamically oriented. A purely supportive approach to adolescent neuroses is futile and even harmful, since the students who experience a failure with psychotherapy in this crisis of their formative years are not likely to seek adequate treatment later in life or to foster an enlightened attitude toward psychiatry in their community. By dynamic we do not mean psychoanalytic—traditional analysis is a luxury a university health service can hardly offer—but we do mean psychoanalytically sophisticated. We mean a therapy that is sensitive to human feelings, especially the deeper emotions, that gets past the superficial presenting problem, that is aware of and knows how to turn to advantage the unspoken subtleties of the relationship between doctor and patient. The best therapy for college use would seem to be dynamic short-term therapy, as described by Blaine[23] elsewhere. This method is especially useful for treating neuroses, but its use is not limited to neurotic problems.

How much can student neuroses be helped? For the Graduate School of Arts and Sciences in the year 1956–1957, the records of 49 neurotics were reviewed by Dr. Robert Nelson.[24] After therapy, 37 cases showed moderate or marked improvement. These figures seem quite in line with all our staff's clinical experience.

23 Blaine, G. Short-term psychotherapy with college students. New Eng. J. Med., 256:208–211, 1957.
24 See Chapter 11.

Why is the prognosis so good? Partly because treatment is offered quickly and on the spot. One is reminded of the experience of Grinker[25] with war neuroses. Removal from the battle line consolidates symptoms, prevents real life success in coping from happening opportunely as progress starts to be made in the treatment. Mostly, though, credit belongs to the patients. These young people have resources. The goal of the psychiatrist need not be root and branch extirpation of all the neurotic problems but rather freeing the patient's resources so the patient can bring them to bear on his own as yet unresolved problems. Few patients need to be given advice once they are emotionally free to think. A great deal of this freeing of a patient's own curative resources can be done in as few as six interviews. Oftentimes, great strides can be taken by the student patient in twenty.

In the end, the student is free to grow. He has potential maturity. The vicissitudes of the adolescent ego can be weathered. Despite all the painful, complex, agitated conflicts, the maze in which the adolescent has struggled is solved. A student neurosis can become an experience from which the young man can build a mature ego, a mature self-image. He is not untroubled but he is coping. The growth forces are freed.

25 Grinker, R. R., and Spiegel, J. P. Men Under Stress. Philadelphia, The Blakiston Company, 1945.

5

Acute Psychosis, Depression, and Elation

Gaylord P. Coon

Each year at Harvard some twenty or thirty students develop emotional disturbances of such an intense and alarming nature that prompt, definite action by a psychiatrist in their behalf is essential to prevent grave, perhaps calamitous, situations or even death. These are the major psychotic illnesses which are so crippling to the student and so distressing to families and the college community.

Some students, overwhelmed by depression, may become so frozen with melancholy that they are powerless to look after even their simplest needs. A few become impatient of restraint and burst into unbridled mania. The greatest number of students with serious psychotic derangement are those whose illnesses fall into the broad category of schizophrenia.

Schizophrenia has been regarded traditionally as a very ominous disorder tending to pursue a downhill course to an end stage of enduring deterioration and dilapidation. Even those patients whose schizophrenic illness is arrested short of its classical culmination are believed by many clinical observers never to return to a state approximating *restitutio ad integrum*. But such somber prognostication has in most instances simply not applied to the schizophrenic illness encountered in Harvard students. They almost invariably recover completely. Curiously enough, their clinical pictures are strikingly similar.

They seem to be cut from the same cloth, with symptoms, course, and outcome roughly identical.

Characteristically, their trouble starts fairly abruptly, although there are instances in which some weeks of brooding or a short season of mild restlessness marks an incipient phase of the disorder. As often as not there is little indication of earlier instability or notable maladjustment. As the illness gains momentum, these students grow rapidly more restless and sleep poorly. Some may take to drink and at times wander from bar to bar in a peripatetic nocturnal quest for human contact and reassurance. Productive academic activity ceases as the student is possessed more fully by his morbid preoccupations. In his psychotic thinking he distorts the outer world and sees it generally as a rather bewildering place shot through with mysterious forces. Casual, commonplace events, in fact almost all things that happen, seem to be strangely linked and to have a new and special meaning or deep personal significance. Flashing directional lights on passing automobiles, for example, may constitute in the patient's mind some elaborate signaling device spelling out in code a message of vital importance. Or again, casual comments of fellow students or teachers may be construed as queer double-talk, full of innuendoes and cryptic references of a critical or an accusatory nature. The outer world becomes a confusing, hostile place peopled by individuals who point the finger of scorn and seem by their words and actions to indicate their knowledge of the patient's innermost thoughts and secret worries. His twisted view of the world and the mysterious concatenation of strange and highly significant events which happen around him not infrequently lead him to the conviction that some vast plot exists in which he fancies himself to be the central figure. Often the ubiquitous FBI and the Communists will manage to get into the act and contribute their share of imagined persecution.

But side by side with this trend to be an almost passive recipient of persecution, accusation, and exposure, we often witness a parallel drive of diametrically opposite nature. That is, the patient tends to feel that he is in some unusual sense the master of his fate. He may feel a singular surge of power and exaltation. He is likely to speak of a new, uncommon clarity of thought, an ability to penetrate far beyond the barriers of ordinary human thinking and to achieve insights hitherto utterly unattainable or undreamed of. He may, for example, speak of developing a new system of philosophy or of founding a new science. Former indifference or vacillation gives way to clear, forward vision, resolute purpose, and a strong sense of having a mission to perform, often childishly pretentious and sometimes outlandish.

In the course of the disorder there may be short episodes of elation, jocularity, playfulness, punning, misidentification of people, distractibility, and other symptoms characteristic of predominant mania. Auditory hallucinations are sometimes experienced but are seldom a striking manifestation of the clinical picture. Usually the voices are described as comforting rather than threatening and tend to be somewhat prosaic in their content. The voices seem not infrequently to be those of members of the patient's immediate family, perhaps breathing words of encouragement.

Sooner or later there are likely to be various forms of acting out on the patient's part, often at an obscure symbolic level. One patient, for example, rummaged through the inner recesses of a dormitory basement and took up to his room a dilapidated old chair missing its back and one of its legs. He also carted up part of an old bedspring and assorted pieces of metal and broken glass, arranging them carefully in the corner of his room as though they were his most precious possessions. He also purchased a long length of rubber tubing which he wrapped tightly around his middle and refused to remove even when taking a shower. This kind of puzzling dramatic portrayal or queer symbolic acting out may be the first indication to fellow students or college officials that a student is in need of psychiatric attention.

A call was received by the psychiatric service from a worried faculty member about an undergraduate student who had become increasingly restless, excited, and confused over a period of days. He had expressed concern and suspicion about the telephone next door which he thought could pick up sounds from his bathroom. He noted that certain electric bulbs in the corridor of his dormitory were not burning and felt this had some special significance which related to him. When the water in his shower began to run cold, he viewed the incident as part of a plot. His behavior grew increasingly strange.

Late one evening he emptied the contents of his wallet onto a sofa in a school library and left abruptly. This odd behavior was noted by some other students who picked up the money, identification cards, and other contents of the wallet. They trailed the patient to his house, reported the incident to the housemaster, and gave him the discarded articles.

The housemaster called the psychiatric service at once. A psychiatrist and the housemaster went to the patient's room and found him busily engaged in throwing books and other effects out of the door and down the stairway. He was also tearing up paper money and throwing it around the room. He said that the books were propaganda and that the money was materialistic and therefore he would have none of it. He was quite distractible and kept commenting upon casual happenings which he believed had specific reference to him. He talked in an expansive way of a mission he would perform which involved going to a foreign country and delivering it from the grip of Communism. He tended to be somewhat jocular. Fortunately, he recognized in a vague way that he was not well, requested medicine, and then agreed without question to admission to the college infirmary.

Soon afterwards he was admitted to a mental hospital and regressed to an utterly disorganized state in which he would lie on the floor naked, confused, and unable to care for his simplest needs. But he responded favorably to psychotherapy and treatment with tranquilizing drugs and was able to leave the hospital after some three months. He was readmitted to college and is making successful progress toward his degree.

The efforts of the psychiatrist in administering to the immediate needs of the acute schizophrenic student—or any variety of psychotic student for that matter—must be characterized by the utmost resourcefulness, tact, and patience, for the way and manner in which the patient's earliest care and management are conducted often determine not only the future progress of the illness but also the degree of confidence and reassurance relatives feel about the patient and his care.

The plight of the markedly disturbed and disordered student is usually first noted by fellow students or the housemaster. The first step in handling the patient's problem ordinarily consists of the housemaster or his assistant seeking out the sick student promptly, sizing up the situation, and recommending with firmness if need be that he see a physician at once. In almost every case psychotic students are fairly cooperative. Even though their illness may be characterized by confusion, suspiciousness, and lack of insight, nearly always they seem to realize at least vaguely that they are ill and that consultation with a doctor is appropriate. Also, they know the housemaster as a familiar and important figure in their college life, trust his judgment, and respect his authority. Naturally the housemaster, or whoever may have undertaken this first step, will accompany the student at once to the psychiatrist's office. However, if the patient is too confused, excited, or unpredictable, it may be more feasible for the psychiatrist to go directly to the student.

When the initial psychiatric interview is concluded and the patient's need of care in a mental hospital is established, the psychiatrist finds himself called upon to exercise his ingenuity and tact to their utmost, for there are many things to consider in making arrangements to place a student in a mental hospital. First of all, the fundamental question of whether or not the patient is actually sick enough to warrant hospitalization may in itself, especially in certain borderline cases, demand considerable reflection and nicety of judgment. Of primary importance in making this decision is consideration of the danger to the student and to others in having him remain in the environment. Second is the amount of worry and concern he may bring to students and faculty who are already fully involved in their own everyday problems. We have always felt that roommates should not be burdened with responsibility for students who are acutely disturbed or disturbing but that this responsibility should be assumed by the university health service either in its own clinic or hospital or in local hospitals if necessary. Sometimes fellow students and younger faculty members are overzealous in their offers to look out for their emotionally upset friends. We feel it is part of our job to determine carefully when nonmedical people are in danger of being overburdened and to relieve them of their burden before they ask us to.

Before a student can be transferred to a mental hospital a fair amount of spade work is essential. Certainly such a serious and important step should not be undertaken without thorough consultation with responsible relatives. More often than not the parents live at great distance, and although an attempt is made to establish telephonic communication with them at once, they may not be at home or readily available. There have been occasions during our efforts to find relatives when we have had to radio ships at sea or ask for the aid of highway patrolmen in order to flag down parents who were touring across the country.

When contact has been made with the parents, they quite often become deeply perturbed and require gentle reassurance and painstaking explanation of the student's trouble. The student's need of mental hospital care must be tactfully and lucidly presented; the expenses likely to be involved and the issue of private versus public hospitals must be clearly discussed and understood. At times parents will want to hold counsel with their local family physician or psychiatrist before deciding to authorize the hospitalization of the student, and even though relatives live at great distances they may request that action regarding hospital commitment be suspended until they can come on the scene to acquire firsthand knowledge of the situation.

Obviously, all of these deliberations and negotiations are time-consuming, and while they are in progress, adequate supervision must be given the patient. Most college infirmaries are organized to care for the mild illnesses and convalescent states of the members of the student body, but they also can constitute a most provident resource to fall back upon for the interim care of the psychotic student. As a temporary resting place for such a student, the infirmary, of course, leaves much to be desired. It certainly was not planned or equipped as a place to care for students with more or less severe mental disorder; but, in spite of this, it can serve well as a temporary haven which enables the psychiatrist to work out problems in the management and disposition of acutely psychotic patients with a degree of smoothness and expedition otherwise quite unattainable.

These students as a rule voice no particular objection to going to the college infirmary. They usually experience something of a sense of security there because of their vague realization that they are sick and also because they are temporarily tucked away from what appear to them to be disturbing and threatening elements in their usual environment. Sometimes we may want to place them on a ward, but most often a single room is more suitable for their accommodation, especially when its safety is enhanced by simplicity of furnishings, grated windows, and proximity to the nurses' station. We seldom give large measures of sedation to these patients in the daytime for to do so often succeeds only in exciting them and contributing further to their confusion. Frequent, reassuring visits from the nurse often help greatly in allaying their apprehension and perturbation and assist them to some degree in maintaining their tenuous hold on reality.

There are usually no male attendants nor male nurses at a college infirmary to help restrain patients who might show signs of becoming overly active in a violent or destructive way; nor is there ordinarily any way of preventing them from walking out of the building if they have an irrepressible impulse to do so, but usually the patients' former knowledge of and familiarity with their own college hospital and their natural trust of the place tend to sustain them and encourage their cooperation. The fact that it presents on every hand the characteristic appearance of a well-run, orderly general hospital cannot help but serve as a constant reminder even to disturbed and confused individuals that they are patients and should act as such. Probably the very absence of any kind of restraining forces around them engenders greater self-restraint and strengthens their tie with reality. Conversely, if they find themselves locked up in an environment teeming with burly attendants, peopled with distracted fellow patients plucking straw out of their hair, and furnished in general with all the appurtenances traditional in any substantial, duly constituted asylum, they cannot help but take up the challenge and let themselves go like a defective fizz bottle or, chameleon-like, take on all the hues and shades of the confusion and dilapidation which exist around them.

There have been times, of course, when patients awaiting transfer have gotten out of hand. One quite unreasonable and confused patient brushed the nurse aside and walked out to the street while we were awaiting the arrival of his family. The best move in such a case is to call the university police who respond promptly and are always pleased to be of any possible assistance. But in this instance the patient had a head start and was bound to be out of sight before the police could arrive. Someone was immediately dispatched to follow the patient as he walked down the street. Under such circumstances, it is essential to send someone out after a short interval to follow the follower and then a little later someone else to follow him and so on, thus maintaining a chain of communication in which any given member is responsible for keeping the man ahead in sight. On that day a rabbi, an x-ray technician, a nurse, and a willing visitor were pressed into service and formed a stretched-out human chain. Luckily, after some three blocks the patient crossed the street and doubled back. He came along just in time to meet the police car as it approached the infirmary. Recognizing the Harvard constabulary, he instinctively reached out to them for help by flagging them down.

Usually, if we anticipate that a psychotic student is likely to become resistive or unpredictable while awaiting transfer at the infirmary, we call upon the university police to assign one of their members to the infirmary to furnish able-bodied assistance if the patient becomes violent. The policeman simply remains unobtrusively in the background as a kind of reserve force for safety's sake. If he is called upon in his emergency role, he generally has little to do but show himself in order to win the fullest cooperation from the student. There are times when it may be a little too risky or otherwise impractical to use the infirmary as a relay point.

There was an instance in which a physically robust student in a rather bewildered, panicky state felt impelled as part of his delusional system to murder anyone who appeared to rebuff him. He had consulted a private psychiatrist and during the course of their interview had offered to kill the doctor. But, as the patient proceeded to flex his muscles in preparation for his homicidal task, the psychiatrist, who proved to be quite agile, adroitly spun him around and shoved him through the office door into the hall before he was fully aware of what was happening. The student took off into the unsuspecting community and the psychiatrist informed us of what had occurred.

As we had guessed, the student returned to the dormitory where he lived, and with the assistance of various members of the dormitory staff, we quickly got mobilized to deal with the emergency which he presented. He was promptly placed under surveillance. Again we used the system of a chain of observers who could report back to us the student's every movement. He had first been spotted in the library where at one point he gave the man watching him near heart failure when he approached a rather frail, bespectacled youth and asked him if he wanted a fight, but the young man said, "No thank you!" and vanished in a twinkling. The patient next headed for the dining room and lingered alone over his supper.

In the meantime, at our headquarters in the office of the housemaster we were attempting to throw the machinery into gear which would enable us to deal more expeditiously with this very sick student. His parents lived a thousand miles away but fortunately responded to our telephone call, and after some delay while they consulted their local doctor, they authorized us to place the student in a mental hospital in this area. None of us was altogether cheered on learning from the mother that the student had been in a mental institution before and on emerging had made a solemn covenant with himself to commit suicide on the spot if he were ever told he should have to return. Certain officials at the mental hospital we had chosen were at first reluctant to take the patient after we had recounted his symptoms. They enthusiastically and generously recommended another institution, but we finally prevailed upon them and they prepared to receive him. Meanwhile, a limousine with liveried attendants had been summoned and had arrived. Also, two Harvard policemen had quietly joined our organization, so that we now had all the necessary participants assembled. It simply remained for the housemaster to approach the student at the supper table and request him to come to his office. After a half hour's interview the patient was convinced that his interests would be served best by going to a mental hospital. It was explained that from what had been learned earlier his need for care had been anticipated and the necessary arrangements had been made. He simply got up and walked quite willingly through the outer door and into the waiting limousine in which he left with complete aplomb and composure. The police car fell unnoticed into line and followed at a discreet distance. The mission was accomplished without incident.

Things cannot be expected always to go quite so smoothly. In this particular case, we were especially fortunate to have the time to make the arrangements with parents and hospital and to mobilize the forces and equipment needed to meet any eventuality before the student was actually approached. Although the circumstances which govern such cases may not always be as propitious as in the one reported here, it is important to bear in mind the guiding principle of making every effort to lay the plans well and to muster the forces for their implementation before coming directly to grips with the student who requires emergency commitment and in whom violence is likely to flare. Any chess player knows the hazards of premature attack or of bringing the queen into action too soon.

We always try to deal with the patients in as straightforward and frank a manner as possible, letting them know how we feel about their need for hospital care and what we propose to do about it. Deception whenever practiced undermines the patient's confidence and retards his recovery.

Depressive disorders occur relatively frequently in college populations. The kind of depression most often encountered in students is "reactive" in nature. That is, it is an illness which in the main constitutes a special reaction of the student to marked disappointments, frustrations, or other serious difficulties in his life situation.

Such depressions at times may be quite severe and disabling. Gloomy forebodings, a sense of hopelessness, suicidal preoccupations, poor concentration, insomnia, lack of energy, reduction of interest and appetite, as well as certain vague bodily discomforts, more especially headache and indigestion, are some of the commonly encountered symptoms of the disorder. But despite the great despair and hopelessness sometimes suffered by patients with such reactive depressive afflictions, they are usually responsive to sympathetic attention and reassurance. They generally take new heart if some of their burdens are lifted or if environmental difficulties are favorably altered. Certainly in most instances, students with reactive depression can be tided over their period of distress and their academic standing salvaged by timely psychiatric intervention.

There are a few depressed students, however, who do not respond readily to ministrations of any kind and sink steadily deeper into despondency. Often there is little environmental stress to account for their low spirits. Their depression seems principally to spring from obscure inner sources (endogenous depression). Attempts to help or comfort them seem actually at times to worsen their plight and to engender in them deeper feelings of guilt. Self-reproach is one of their outstanding manifestations. They usually exhibit a general slowing down, a retardation of speech, and a marked stickiness of thinking. It may take a very long time for the patient to mobilize his thoughts sufficiently to reply even to very simple questions. His answers are delayed, hesitant, taciturn, and often scarcely audible. The simplest tasks become almost insurmountable for the patient. Feelings of hopelessness, despair, and suicidal urge are almost constant findings. Occasionally the need for help which cannot be expressed directly reaches such proportions that the student resorts to desperate measures, such as dramatic suicidal gestures, in order to force definitive action onto those around him.

For such a student, the altering of the environment proves useless. In fact, any easing up of requirements or special favors increase the guilt and shame already present. Prompt action on the part of administrators or medical personnel is essential. Left alone, the student usually becomes progressively more withdrawn until he reaches such a regressed state that he will not leave his room even for meals. Disordered sleep is almost always present from the earliest stages of the illness. Headaches, constipation, indigestion, lack of appetite, and appalling weight loss are commonly noted. Actually gastrointestinal symptoms constitute the most common bodily complaint in severe depressions. Peptic ulcer is a very frequent occurrence. Such ulcers which are clearly demonstrable in x-ray films recede as the depression improves. In successful electroshock therapy which may clear up a depression often in a few days, beneficial effect on the peptic ulcers may be noted simultaneously.

A senior was brought to the psychiatric clinic by his roommate who told the following story. The patient had always been a moody, somewhat withdrawn boy but had never shown signs of real depression until three weeks previously when he had begun to express pessimistic feelings about passing his final examinations which were to take place in two weeks and also to speak of himself as a "worthless bum who does not deserve to get ahead in the world." He had spent more and more time each day alone in his room with the shades pulled down. At one point he had stated that he was going to remain in his room until May 24, at which time something "definite" would have happened. His roommate had made a determined effort to jolly him out of this mood and succeeded to a limited extent, but the boy continued to be depressed, lethargic, and self-depreciatory.

The night before being brought to us he had suddenly appeared in the living room with a suitcase and upon questioning he said that he was going to a hotel in the city to "sit and think things out." He then walked out of the room, leaving the suitcase behind. His roommates opened the bag and found a length of heavy rope inside. The patient returned late and was heard pacing the floor for the remainder of the night. In the morning, superficial cuts were noted on his wrists and it was decided to bring him to the clinic. The patient put up some resistance to coming, but a firm approach on the part of one roommate proved effective.

The patient appeared tense, rigid, and glassy-eyed. He spoke in a staccato fashion and was on the verge of tears. He felt that because of his inadequacy he had bungled the jobs he had held over the past year and hopelessly neglected his studies. He talked of himself as being "incomplete, clumsy, stupid, dishonest, unworthy." Although somewhat unhappy about the prospects of hospitalization, he begrudgingly agreed and then, after a telephone conversation with his father, he willingly went to a psychiatric sanitarium. He received electric shock treatment followed by supportive psychotherapy. After a year working as a salesman in a retail store, he returned to complete his senior year without further incident.

Inasmuch as suicide is a constant danger in depressions, it is important to discover such illness early and provide prompt psychiatric attention for its victims. When a student begins to be gripped by depression, he tends customarily to shun his fellow students and remain more or less by himself. He may stop attending classes, eat his meals alone at some remote table in the dining hall, or cease to dine there altogether. He may seldom stir from his room and become increasingly untidy, unkempt, unshaved, and unshorn. University officials or others noting such growing isolation on a student's part should be alerted to the possibility that he may be morbidly depressed. Also, the student's general appearance may provide further evidence of a depressed state. Slowing of his movements, grim, unhappy expression, furrowed brow, bowed head, downcast eyes, shoulders drooping as if bearing some heavy burden are characteristics whose presence may further confirm the existence of a markedly depressed state.

Months or years may pass before an endogenous depression lifts spontaneously, but ultimate recovery is the rule. Hospitalization of the patient is essential during the more acute, severe periods of the illness. Electric shock therapy may at times be the only form of treatment which will afford prompt, effective relief, but antidepressive medications, such as nortriptyline hydrochloride or other drugs in the same class, may often prove effective even in very severe depressions. Their only drawback is that they are slow to act and their full beneficial effect may not be felt for a week or two. In patients in whom suicidal risk is great it may be dangerous to temporize till the medication works. Hospitalization and electroshock may have to be instituted at once if the likelihood of suicide seems imminent. Recurrence of endogenous depression may be expected in some 50 percent of the patients. In some instances, attacks of depression may alternate with periods of inordinate upward swing of mood (manic depressive disorder).

There are many instances in which students suffer disabling depressions on the basis of bereavement occasioned by the death of close relatives or friends. Not infrequently the severest depression results not from the death of family members but from the loss of a loved one caused by the breakup of a romance. Such a student may no longer be able to focus on his work. He often feels the future holds nothing and that life is utterly empty. Suicidal thoughts crowd into the mind with insistent force and if the lost object of his affections is in the immediate vicinity, perhaps even attending some of the same classes with him, his agony is compounded. I know a young lady who trudged up twelve flights of stairs to her classes for many months rather than take the elevator and risk the chance of finding herself in painful close quarters with her former lover.

Sometimes grief reactions are delayed. A student, who loses an important figure in his life, may carry on courageously—sometimes even with a kind of bravado—for six months or a year or two seemingly untouched by sorrow and with his effectiveness as a student unimpaired. Then, suddenly, he may lose his zest for everything. He may cease to study or to attend classes. He may become self-reproachful, restless, and have troubled sleep. He displays most of the elements of depression with greater or less intensity. At first he may not connect his condition with his earlier loss but after some self-examination, he may realize that it is only now that he is experiencing the full impact of his loss.

A young lady, a sophomore in college, complained of inability to concentrate on her work. She had lost her interest, was tense and slept poorly. She was failing Spanish. She was discouraged and wanted to withdraw from college. She had been quite successful academically in her freshman year and in the fall of her sophomore year. But in the spring the complexion of things changed; she lost her appetite for everything. She talked to the college psychiatrist about her problem. She recounted that her father had died two years before. He had been a fairly elderly man when he married so in her childhood she remembered him as older than most fathers. As a child she loved him very much and he adored her. They were almost constant companions. But by the time she had reached her teens he had aged a great deal and had become sickly, self-centered, and cantankerous. Their halcyon years together had ended. He was quite ill, helpless, and irascible for several years before his death, and when at last he expired, no one missed him very much. The student herself felt great relief. He had been a trial to her and to everyone else in the family. She pitched into her college work with relish. After about a year and a half of very successful academic effort a valued uncle of hers died and it was not long after that her indisposition described above gripped her. She did not immediately relate her plight to her uncle's death nor yet her father's death which by then seemed quite remote. But it finally dawned on her that for some time her mind had been going back quite regularly to thoughts of her father and those earlier happy years of childhood with him which were so poignant in her memory. She had a wistful, lonely feeling and her eyes would often fill with tears. She would weep quite openly whenever she walked along the street and chanced to see an elderly man walking hand in hand with a child. Her disability seems consistent with a delayed grief reaction to her father's death possibly kindled by the subsequent loss of her uncle.

Another student lost both parents and two favorite grandparents all within the span of three or four months. It was naturally a grievious loss for him but his friends and tutors rallied around, comforted, and encouraged him. He had little heart to carry on with his work but his teachers prevailed upon him to plunge into his studies as the best antidote for his sorrow. He did little else than study for the next two terms. He had no time to contemplate his losses as he pursued his college activities in an almost frenzied manner. At the beginning of his third term he ground to a halt. He had no further drive or interest. He was disconsolate and about all he could do was sit and mull over memories of countless experiences he had shared earlier with his lost relatives. He yearned to withdraw from his hectic college life and retire to some remote place where he might give full reign to his thoughts of his departed family and write their biographies. This would constitute for him "the work of grieving" which was so necessary and so long delayed. He left college on medical leave to grieve.

There is a kind of apathetic state of mind commonly occurring in college students which, though rather different from the depressions described, probably bears some kinship to them. It is not as definitive as the classical depressions nor as dramatic a condition. Nevertheless, in its own unspectacular way this disorder may be quite as disabling and devastating to its victims. Usually those afflicted have been young men of great promise who have made brilliant records in preparatory school and have swept the field of prizes and honors. They have entered college with scholarships and the plaudits of countless well-wishers and proud benefactors.

They have been dutiful students, almost plastically obedient and imbued with a strong sense of obligation not to let their friends and constituents down. They plunge into their work at college with continuing zeal, conscious of their great responsibility. Then, at some point, something begins to go wrong. Perhaps an expected A in an assignment turns out to be a C, or perhaps nothing significant happens at all, but in any case the student suddenly bogs down. All of the virtue seems to have been wrung out of him. He experiences a profound reduction of interest in his work. He no longer has the will to study. He neglects his assignments and often stops going to class. He may thumb idly through magazines and science fiction. He may haunt the movies or sit about listening all day to "hi-fi" or perhaps just languish like Oblomov in the Russian novel of the same name. As uncompleted assignments pile up and academic standing goes glimmering, the student sits unmoved, displaying a kind of *belle indifference* in relation to this gathering tragedy in his life. He seems to have no worry and he is not clearly depressed. If he professes to have any worry at all, it is simply that he worries because he does not worry more in the face of his approaching failure and debacle. Sometimes such a student may experience a vague wistfulness and loneliness. He may seek companionship, participating in nightly bull sessions or indulging in endless pool or poker.

Unfortunately, he seldom seeks any professional help either from teachers, deans, or doctors until his courses have become unsalvage-able. Even if some hope of preserving his scholastic standing still re-mains and remedial measures are taken, he will usually only brighten up briefly and then slump still lower into his morass of indifference and anergia.

Students of this sort usually have little to communicate to the psychiatrist concerning their problems. They generally can point to very little in their life situation which has been disturbing them. They seem to have almost no grudges, antagonisms, or hatreds. Their world seems to be peopled exclusively by individuals, including parents and siblings, for whom they entertain nothing but the finest sentiments. Perhaps their astounding lack of any kind of strong emotion in rela-tion to the important figures in their lives may be the key to the explanation of what is basic in their disorder. It may not be unreason-able to conclude that their surface blandness and paralysis constitute a facade which masks deeply repressed inner turbulence, fear, and hatred too overwhelming to be endured by these proper, dutiful stu-dents. Evidently, at some critical point after long struggle to work for and to please a variety of elders, these obligatively oriented, obedient lads get "fed up" and enter upon a first-class job of demo-lition in which they and their proud benefactors go down together.

A substantial number of these victims of crippling apathy are discovered to have fathers with a forceful and overbearing nature which at times constitutes a serious threat or menace to their sons who may in turn respond quite defensively. They may develop a kind, deferential, ingratiating attitude toward their elders and shy away from any competition with those who wear the badge of authority. Their incentive to make good marks in school may be based on the need to gain approval and approbation of parents and teachers. When such students with their glittering scholastic records enter college, they find themselves all at once in "The Big League" where the de-mands are greater, the stakes higher, and the threats more overwhelm-ing. In such an atmosphere, especially if the student experiences a number of disappointments gradewise or finds himself badly baffled by the complexities of certain courses, and so on, he may abandon every vestige of self-assertion and collapse into a state of abject surrender. This constitutes a kind of protective mechanism in which the boy counts on others to remember the old cliché, "Never kick a man who is down." Young people may feel so ground down by the seeming awesomeness and menace of their fathers and the Establishment in general that they become too constricted and paralyzed to undertake the necessary constructive actions to meet the challenge of their academic assignments. They dare not commit themselves, they dare not act. They find it safer not to do so. Also, in an obscure way they may be taking a kind of revenge on their fathers through their failure.

A student with a superb scholastic and athletic record in secondary school won a scholarship at Harvard mainly, I think, because he was phenomenally fleet of foot and promised to be the white hope of the track team. But he never ran. Wild horses could not drag him to the Field House. Running in "The Big League," so to speak, seemingly posed too much of a threat. He did fairly well in his studies for a year but usually made a poor showing on examinations.

In his second year he developed a typical apathy syndrome as described above. All efforts to revive him failed. A number of interviews with him revealed that he had strong feelings of loyalty toward his father, a preacher, who ministered to a small flock of devout, religiously conservative, underprivileged people. The father was a righteous man whose rectitude, sternness and potential for wrath rivaled that of Jehovah himself. He ruled his son with an iron hand, insisted that he play the organ at all services, conduct the choir, and carry out a variety of other ecclesiastical duties which cut deeply into his precious time.

When the student started talking about his problems, it was extremely difficult to fathom what he was trying to say and it took a great deal of patience to listen to him. He would begin a sentence and with much hesitation get about half way through, then stop abruptly and start the sentence all over again. After five or six false starts, he would shift his ground, couch his sentence in somewhat different form, and finally bring it to completion. It took some amount of time to realize just what was going on. At last it became apparent that he made repeated futile attempts to communicate in a simple, straightforward, declarative manner using the pronoun, "I," and speaking in the active voice but this proved too threatening to him so he invariably had to switch to the use of the passive voice before he could finish his sentence. He dared not display the assertiveness inherent in the employment of the active voice.

Usually, after such a defeat, students with the apathy syndrome who have been dismissed from college are likely either to find a simple job or enter military service. Their interest and zeal begin to revive with or without psychiatric help, and after a year or so they may return to their studies with new vigor. But usually this time they come to college on an independent status and on their own terms. They now work to please themselves instead of their benefactors. Their orientation and attitude are different, their motivation is sounder, and their continuing success more likely.

Manic disorder is observed much more rarely than depression in the college student body. The symptom picture of mania is almost diametrically opposite to that of depression. The manic possesses an elated, merry mood. He is very lively and quick in his thoughts and actions. His thoughts may flow with such facility and rapidity that his thinking takes on a flighty quality. He is exceedingly alert and especially quick to note everything going on around him. It is quite characteristic of the manic to comment in an unreserved, often im- pertinent way concerning the appearance of those about him and to note the minutest details of their dress and demeanor. The manic, is, in fact, greatly distracted by the many casual sights and sounds in his environment and flits in his comments from one observation to another in quick succession, never apparently being able to keep his attention focused long. His quick perception, ability to take every- thing in at a glance, and his quick-witted facility to see and to be impressed by countless associations and similarities in relation to what he hears and observes, explain his usual propensity for making playful misidentifications of people and his tendency to rhyme and pun.

These patients are constantly "on the go" and exhibit marked press of speech. They are likely to keep up a continual chatter not uncommonly punctuated with profanity as well as various merry quips and jokes. They seem to have an inexhaustible store of energy. They sleep little. They are enterprising and full of all kinds of pro- motional schemes, but they are so carried away that their judgment is likely to be seriously impaired.

The infectious good humor and jocularity which they usually display may quickly change to irritability and anger if they are thwarted in any way. They then become quarrelsome and domineering and engage in fights and fracases with little provocation. They are likely to be very extravagant, and if given an opportunity, they may rapidly sink a fortune in ill-judged ventures or pile up appalling debts. They are intemperate in all things, more especially in the use of alcohol. The manic with his impatience of restraint may indulge in many unbridled, disorderly acts. Profanity, assault and battery, trespassing, fornication, evasion of taxi fare, breaking glass, and drunkenness are a few of the familiar gaucheries which may land the madcap manic in the toils of the constabulary.

We may speculate that the manic's illness with its manifestations of elation, overactivity, and distractibility constitutes a special adaptive device by means of which he forces himself to avoid painful personal memories and problems. By being uncommonly alert to and distracted by a myriad of casual experiences and situations outside himself and by pursuing relentlessly a host of schemes and enterprises, the manic permits himself no time for reflection and self-analysis, thereby succeeding in keeping away from the anguish of unbearable inner personal conflict. His elation and gaiety may be a facade covering internal travail and troublesome moods. Attempts to pin the manic down with questions concerning his personal life almost invariably cause him to become inordinately tense, angry, wretched, and tearful, for deep depression lies close beneath the surface in all students suffering from this illness.

Obviously, the acute manic must be hospitalized promptly for his own protection and that of others. Fortunately, acute mania is rare in college settings. There are a fair number of patients encountered among college students, however, who suffer from mania of a somewhat milder form than the acute, severe disorder already described. This milder disturbance, called hypomania, is a borderline psychotic condition which may mark an incipient phase of a more severe, full-fledged mania to come, or it may remain mild and run a protracted course without gathering momentum.

Each year we run upon certain students who arouse growing concern in administrators and faculty members as reports keep drifting in from various quarters regarding their conduct. Officials may learn, for example, of an unpleasant incident created by a given student in which he had been rude to a secretary. Shortly afterward, perhaps, word comes of a senseless brawl the student provoked while in the cafeteria line. There may be accounts, also, of loud arguments in the dining hall in which the student was the chief participant. Next, officials may be appalled to hear that he threatened to punch an instructor in the nose. When the psychiatrist sees the student in consultation, he is impressed with the kind of impudence or "fresh-

ness" he displays as well as a propensity to ask decidedly inappropriate personal questions of the doctor. In the course of the interview
it may develop that the student has many irons in the fire, so to speak.
He has taken a selling job on the side; he is writing a novel; also he
has been competing for a special part in a play; and at the same time
he is campaigning for a particular office in his class. When inquiry
is made relative to his course work, it is learned that he has not done
a tap of studying in six weeks and he has seldom found time to attend
classes. He is domineering and talkative, there is a glint in his eye;
he speaks of sleeping little. It is also discovered that he is heavily in
debt to local merchants and his club.

In such a case, we would have little doubt of the student's hypomanic state. Several just like him may be discovered in the college
each year. There are some hypomanics, however, whose clinical picture
is a bit more obscure and likely to be confused with the familiar
acting out behavior of students in a state of adolescent turmoil. In
such cases, the hypomanic diagnosis may not become altogether
clearly apparent until it is more definitely confirmed by the subsequent
development of serious depression in the patient or the discovery in
his history of an earlier season of despondency.

There was a student who spent about half his time underground
exploring the extensive maze of tunnels which connect the various buildings throughout the large domain of the University. These subterranean
passages, which contain steam pipes and cables and in places are barely
passable, are not open to the public but are sealed by a series of locked
doors. This student, however, had little difficulty in breeching these
barriers.

Whenever he emerged from the ground, he created very serious
problems. He bullied and frightened his roommates. He had a twenty-
two revolver with shells tipped with wax bullets which he would let off
about the room with prankish abandon. His New Guinea blowgun was
a more lethal plaything. He would often sit moodily in a corner and let
his darts fly in a desultory fashion with such incredible velocity that they
would split a door panel. But for his roommates, his most terrifying
instrument was his trusty gasoline stove which he would place in the
middle of the room, ignite, and then vigorously pump up air pressure
until the flames roared up to the ceiling. When his roommates would
not bend to his will, he would threaten to bring out his gasoline stove.
They would cower, pull their jackets up over their ears and plead, "No,
no, not the stove," and capitulate forthwith to his demands.

Outside of his room he continued his unbridled harassment. Once
he threatened to punch his botany teacher in the nose. He frequently
went to a nearby church where funeral services were held almost every

morning. He continually disconcerted the funeral directors by snooping around the hearses and peering inside. But his most shameful performance would occur in the evening when it was the habit of a priest dressed in clerical robe to leave his dwelling and stroll down the sidewalk for quiet meditation in the cool of the twilight. At such a time the student would collect rocks and bowl them down the sidewalk. He seemed to take exquisite delight in watching this man of God gather up his skirts and leap high in the air.

His cumulative gaucheries finally caught up with him and he was dismissed from the College for disciplinary reasons. He was given various labels by the administrators who dealt with him, some of which I am reluctant to put in print, but neither administrators nor physicians managed to put their fingers on the real springs of action in his case.

After leaving the College he succeeded in getting a job as a tree surgeon and he revelled in his arborial acrobatics. But one day he came down from the trees, passed in his surgical instruments, retired to his room and stayed there, brooding and unhappy. He began to ruminate on the evanescence of life, the imminence of death, and the destructive power of the atomic bomb. He had the gloomiest of forebodings. He was profoundly depressed. The true nature of his behavior at College which should have been recognized at least by some of us was no doubt the hypomanic manifestation of a manic-depressive cyclic disorder.

It is our experience that early recognition of hypomanic disorder in students and concentrated psychotherapeutic efforts in their behalf actually, in some instances, bring about a dissipation of the gathering storm of their illness. Naturally, we may fail in our therapeutic efforts, but at times hypomanic students can be prevented from "taking off the launching pad" into a full-blown manic excitement and kept at their academic work by being given intensive psychiatric help. Their treatment sometimes requires daily interviews. They must be apprised again and again of the nature of their disorder and the practical problems and pitfalls which their mental state repeatedly engenders. The persistent efforts of the psychiatrist to confront the hypomanic patient with the facts of his ill-judged, unbridled actions and to admonish him forcefully during frequent interviews to order his life with greater sobriety and restraint seem often to modify the patient's behavior, check the advance of his illness, and save his academic standing.

It is well known that drug treatment may be helpful in controlling manic excitement, but in the author's opinion the drugs of election—such as Thorazine—in order to be effective usually must be given in doses too large to make it altogether safe to risk their administration outside of a hospital setting. Also, these students usually are quite unwilling to admit to being ill and cannot be persuaded to take medication regularly.

Something approaching a breakthrough may be in progress in the treatment of mania. Excellent results have been recently reported following the administration of lithium carbonate. This form of treatment, however, is still being studied and appraised before releasing the drug for general use.

6

Basic Character Disorders
and Homosexuality

Graham B. Blaine, Jr., AND
Charles C. McArthur

In every class there are a number of boys who seem to pride themselves on being different. They frequently enjoy playing pranks on
the administration and cause concern to the faculty. the deans, and
also often to their contemporaries. The question always arises as to
how much of their behavior is due to sickness and how much to plain
orneriness. Also, since the trouble they get into often verges on the
violent or destructive, it is important to know how much of a danger
these students are to the community as a whole. Not very many of
these students come voluntarily to the psychiatrist, but questions about
their management are recived frequently by the psychiatric clinic
from deans and members of the faculty.

Because our contact with these unruly students is so brief, it is
difficult for us to gain a complete picture of their personality structure
or come to any real understanding of why they behave the way they
do, but they seem to be genetically different and can be diagnosed as
suffering from a basic character disorder. In general, they present a
picture of diffuse and changing symptoms, appearing to have difficulty
in more areas than the dropout or underachiever groups. These students seldom come to the clinic of their own choice, not because they
feel they should go it alone, as the dropout students so often do, but
rather because they do not believe that their difficulties are a result

of emotional conflicts. Many of those who do come on their own do so to seek a favor or for support in their efforts to manipulate the authorities. The majority reach the psychiatrist only after considerable pressure from tutors, housemasters, or professors. Occasionally they come only after an ultimatum from the university administration.

Initially, many of these students present themselves in an open, defiant fashion. They reject the notion that their difficulties might be the outward manifestation of internal distress. They reject the sug-gestion of therapy, also, feeling it to be a superficial type of relation-ship aimed at depriving them of their individuality. This fear of loss of individuality as a result of psychotherapy is a common theme and gives a clue to the general process that so often appears to underlie these behavior disorders. Many of these students, reacting to a sense of inner uncertainty and confusion, attempt to force the establishment of a sense of identity by resorting to some form of colorful, bizarre, and often self-defeating behavior. In order to prove their manhood, their uniqueness, and their conviction, all of which they deeply doubt, they grow beards, scale buildings, get in fights, provoke and defy authorities, or race about on motorcycles.

One boy given to breaking speed laws on his motorcycle finally explained to the dean his desperate need to continue this activity. "I have to every so often," he pleaded. "When I get on my bike and kick her into high, the environment on all sides gets blurry. There's nothing left in focus except me and my machine. It's such a relief, it's the best psycho-therapy for me!"

We suspect that very often it is important to these boys to be able, by controlling a few levers, to cause the world around them to "go blur." The implied control over their world may also be important to them. This group also includes the Bohemian segment: students who cultivate the bizarre and deviant as much as possible, often engaging in activities which afford them little pleasure, in the vague hope of displacing their sense of loneliness and inadequacy.

In their assets as well as their liabilities these students seem to suffer an embarrassment of riches. Their aspirations are numerous, conflicting, and evanescent. They believe intellectual accomplishment of the standard sort to be of relatively little value, although they often do very well despite distracting symptoms. Many of them are troublemakers to the university administration or their fellow students. They are the most demanding of changes in administrative practices, courses, or regulations. They often are in trouble for breaking rules. Some steal or cheat on exams and others are picked up by the police for misdemeanors, which may be manifestations of severe mental illness.

Characteristically, these students prove reluctant to engage in a therapeutic relationship. They do not want to come to the clinic and they tend to deny their difficulties or blame them upon the environment, the university, the police, or their parents. They show little willingness to assume responsibility for their own behavior. Their symptoms appear to be more the function of a disturbed personality development than the expression of specific unconscious conflicts. Such disturbed function may be of a relatively mild nature as in the youthful prankster or it may reflect a severe character disorder in the student who repeatedly steals with little guilt or anxiety. Typically, the clinical picture is a changing one, reflecting the fluid state of their personality structure. On top of the world one moment, they are furious at it the next, and such swings in mood are often accompanied by corresponding changes in plans, behavior, and friendships.

For example, one student who was ordinarily a prince among men became fascinated by monkeys in biology. Asked why, he replied, and meant it, "Because I've developed a scunner against homo sapiens." Another common expression of the same theme is avid reading of flying saucer literature "which proves that somewhere in the universe there's a race that is intellectually way ahead of ours." One boy, much given to alternating between sociophilia and misogyny, used to join and leave the boxing team several times a season. He also won or lost bouts according to the rhythm of his buffeting by alternating sadistic and masochistic feelings.

The classic case of this syndrome in our experience was nicknamed "The Sultan." This boy was the product of an old Main Line family. His great-uncle was a notorious Victorian character whose estate is still an architectural wonderment in the region.

The Sultan did well enough in his Harvard courses without ever doing much work, though he always contrived to include one D or E among his B and C grades. He elected only advanced courses in his freshman year.

His expectation about Harvard was, "Harvard men were known to be complete intellectuals and complete dopes." To his amazement, "The ones I've met have been colorful!" He spent most of his time in the Club, where he succeeded in irritating the membership by his ability to luck out impossible situations at billiards. This was for him more fun than winning by orthodox skill of which he possessed an abundance. At home, the family played "devilish" bridge.

In the science laboratories, he could devise the most ingenious and entertaining experiments with real scientific flair. He never did his assignments. The Sultan was soon on probation for a string of minor breaches of discipline. He became a regular, and rather welcome, visitor to the offices of various deans. He was a big, warm fellow whose boyish appeal reached the paternalistic side of the administrators' hearts. Unhappily, none felt moved to abrogate the rules. Unhappily, too, the Sultan displayed a massive dose of what one psychiatrist dubbed "traumatophilia" (a liking for hard knocks). It is not clear that he really wanted the warmhearted reaction he evoked from all. At one point he was able to say that he realized that he had an irrational feeling that study was degrading. To open a book was "cheating." Also, he knew that he "wanted to be scared" and that we "wouldn't oblige."

He came to the psychiatric service by a fluke; ordinarily, this sort of boy does not come in to us unless sent. We were also warmly on his side but, loath to alter reality until it is no longer recognizable, we refused to keep the Sultan in good standing by asking for special dispensations on his behalf.

His creative genius was unexcelled. When not driving his motorcycle into a Harvard Square store, he was organizing an expedition to climb the Memorial Hall tower. He was intoxicated on most weekends and one Monday morning appeared in the waiting room, drooped, teeth loosened, eyes black, head aching. Sympathetic inquiry revealed that he had attempted to fly! Since he lived in a second floor room and his flight was powered only by whisky, the results were pathetic to see.

And so it went. At one point, he was going to enter the service before being fired; somehow that fell through. At another, he managed to get his parents interested enough to come to Cambridge to negotiate his case, but by then it was much too late.

He was dismissed from college.

Since leaving, the Sultan has held a succession of jobs, briefly and spectacularly. As a freight clerk he moved pianos onto freight cars unaided; then he became vice-president of a sales agency. Then he decided to return to another school, where he made a straight A record for a term and quit while he was ahead.

In the end, he settled in Hollywood, living on an allowance, going to studio parties, and doing bit parts off and on. He is universally acknowledged—even in the gossip columns—to be a genius at gin rummy.

He applies for readmission to Harvard semiannually but, on being told the procedure to follow, never quite follows it.

Early in this story, the Sultan received psychological testing. His Rorschach was clearly neurotic. Very much in touch with reality, he had decided not to face it. He was a fine instance of someone impinged on the first horn of Erikson's dilemma: avoiding the "autocracy of conscience" by submitting to the "anarchy of impulse." His anarchic impulses were his retreat from the unhappy features of the world of everyday living.

Why he needed such a dodge became clear at once when he began his Thematic Apperception Test. To the initial picture, a child looking sadly at a violin, he said assuredly, "But this is purely obvious! The child made the mistake of showing interest in a violin and lo and behold he gets stuck with a violin. At present he's trying to think of something like putting pennies in the violin and seeing how they'll distort the noise."

We could call that "creative resistance."

Later, in the same TAT story, the hero's fate is described. "All through his life, he's going to be pushed. By this time his family has decided he's a potential genius. He may be somewhat proud of that."

The Sultan was, in objective fact, a genius. Like so many of these students with character disorders, he suffered from a plethora of assets which he never geared to productive use.

Later on, his TAT stories revealed a specific and usual neurotic sexual conflict, whose repressed aspects had stimulated the boy's guilt, which in turn was atoned for by generating trials and tribulations which he seemed to enjoy so much.

The boy fled from therapy, as his kind usually do. For this, we all felt sorry.

If we wish to speculate on the psychiatric meaning of this syndrome, we may think that it is a mixed one, which includes the constitutional psychopath, but the bulk of this group of cases is best labeled character disorder. In the development of adolescent character there is a dilemma phrased by Erikson as a conflict between "the anarchy of impulse" and "the autocracy of conscience." These students have submitted to the anarchy of impulse. After a while their submission becomes worship. They now make impulse their fetish.

These boys are somehow provocative to both the administration's and the doctor's conscience. The very term character disorder has come to have a pejorative overtone. Neutrally, it means illness in which the symptoms are not felt by the patient to be alien, and hence he does not report that he suffers or thinks of himself as possessing an illness. These are the so-called acting out neuroses, in which an irrationally overdetermined behavior pattern of a personally unhelpful and socially undesirable sort is the chief sign of the disease, but there is no isolated symptom. The character disorder may show no tics, no anxiety states, no physical symptoms, no compulsive rituals. What he does, in his sickness, he feels to be simply his personal decision. He does not easily find out that his decisions were not determined in quite the same way as anyone else's. Hence, he is hard to cure. He is even hard to get into therapy in the first place. Probably the psychiatrist uses character disorder in a slightly pejorative sense because he feels so frustratedly helpless.

Perhaps the administrator takes a pejorative view of these cases for more moral reasons. These students break rules so blithely that they are continually spoiling that ideal administrative situation: a state of No Trouble. They seem too "unsocialized" for the college community, which much prefers the more decent neurotics who are hung up on the other horn of the adolescent dilemma: the autocracy of conscience. If a student with a character disorder is not fired punitively for conduct beyond the pale, he is likely to be suspended charitably so that he can have time to mature. It is rarely understood that he is just plain sick.

Unhappily, he does not often mature. Chronologically older, he usually has not done any work on his problems after a year or two of sheer rustication. It is in the nature of his disease that he probably has not even seen that he has a problem.

When he returns to college, he is still a misfit. At Yale,[1] followup on readmissions has shown that it is the character problems who have the worst prognosis. This is our clinical experience. These boys never learn.

Of course, it could be argued that the college does not readily make room for them. One can understand their not fitting in at Yale, and they meet only moderate tolerance even at individualistic Harvard. The university ideal of encouraging a variety of personal pathways to truth does not, rightly or wrongly, include the pathway of perpetuated childhood. Nor is there any point in encouraging an adjustment that continues from day to day and year to year a total lack of intellectual production. Few of these students do much work of any nature either assigned by professors or emotionally generated on their own. Theirs is not just nonconformity; it is nonconformity that is unproductive.

Such a solution to the adolescent dilemma is less than mature. On the other hand, it can be made to work passably well, especially among a special clique of one's own kind, other children who have, permanently or temporarily, moved into the same half-way house to

[1] Harrison, R. W. M. S. Leaving college because of emotional problems. Student Med., 4:49–60, April 1956.

maturity. This type of student is often very likable and usually very colorful. He may be the idol of the pool-playing clique, or he may organize and edit an unintelligible student publication. Not rarely, he starts an esoteric student club, which may or may not be able to gain the blessing of the dean. Frequently, he is well liked by all the members of the administrative board who vote to fire him.

The sicker ones, especially the prepsychotics, sometimes become minor martyrs of the intelligentsia. The less sick ones take themselves and are taken less seriously. Yet their failure to find themselves in college or out of it constitutes a sizable loss of potentially able members of the educated community.

In general, the student in this category who does appear for treatment or counseling should be seen for several interviews over a period of weeks, with an eye to the changing nature of his symptoms. In rare cases, this diagnostic period reveals disturbances in personality development sufficient to warrant more extensive therapy. These students can then be offered explicit long-range treatment in the clinic or be referred to private therapists or out-patient clinics.

In cases where the symptoms appear to be the expression of less severe personality defects, the psychiatrist is justified in intervening appropriately in the student's environment, recommending a different dormitory or a change in curriculum. Except for cases where the student has been caught by a coincidence of stresses, it should seldom be recommended that he be excused from any academic demands. Ordinarily there is little justification for altering the rules to fit individual needs. On the contrary, many of these students seem to profit from a sympathetic but firm restatement and clarification of the rules rather than relaxation of them or special consideration. Often there is a history of inconsistency and weakness in earlier relationships, and the student has now found it necessary to test all situations in order to define their limits of tolerance. We have found it most helpful to maintain an active contact with all the officials of the university in the management of this group of patients where consistency is so often crucial.

The appraisal of results with this group is difficult; many go on to graduate despite the fact that they are still clearly disturbed. Others may drop out of college to continue elsewhere with considerable growth. The immediate goal is to provide the student with some relief from the pressure that drives him into self-defeating behavior. Thus far, an understanding relationship that provides clarification of the environment and insight into the student's own problem and how they relate to his misbehavior seems to be our most effective technique.

Sexual deviation may also be classified along with persistent self-defeating rebellious behavior as a basic character disorder. Its real roots are not known but its consistent nature, early appearance, and resistance to therapy make it appear to belong to this category. Deviations other than homosexuality are so rare among college students that it does not seem worthwhile to discuss them here. Also, their nature and treatment do not differ from that with adults.

According to Kinsey, over 27 percent of the young men in America between the ages of 17 and 25, who have reached the college level in education, have had at least one homosexual experience. This represents a significantly smaller number than those of the same age in the total population who have had a similar experience (36.3 percent) and seems to be generally consistent with what our experience would lead us to believe to be the prevalence of homosexuality at Harvard.

Making a statistical study of the prevalence of homosexuality, however, is complicated by the vagueness of the concept. Kinsey, in his work, defined a homosexual experience as a relationship between people of the same sex which leads to orgasm. While this would seem to be a relatively sharp distinction, it does not really tell us very much about the amount of homsexuality which is actually present in a community. Many students have strong homosexual inclinations which they are able to keep so completely under control that they do not engage in any homosexual acts. Other students engage in one homosexual act more or less experimentally, and this one isolated experience serves to solidify their feelings against homosexuality and enable them to put it out of their minds for the rest of their lives. These two types of students obviously distort any kind of statistical analysis of the total situation. The former is often preoccupied so much with thoughts about homosexuality that he should be classified in the homosexual category, while the latter is so briefly concerned with the subject that he does not deserve to be included, and yet, because of his one experience, he would be labeled in Kinsey's statistics as homosexual.

We are a long way from a real understanding of homosexuality.

We do not have any clear-cut conclusions to offer about the origin or the causes of this type of deviation. Most psychiatrists and psychoanalysts today seem to feel that a combination of constitutional and environmental factors is involved. There seems to be fairly complete acceptance of the fact that everyone has some degree of homosexuality in his make-up and that there is a variation in amount from one person to another. This variation extends from the rare experiencing of a homosexual dream or a homosexual yearning all the way to the living of a homosexual life with heterosexual desire nonexistent. Although we feel that some people are born with a stronger homosexual instinct than others, we also believe that certain factors in the growth and development of an individual are responsible for the reinforcement or the repression of these instincts.

These factors are, for the most part, concerned with parental characteristics and attitudes. Parents who dress and treat a child of one sex as though he had been born another, even during the earliest stages of the child's development, can have an effect on the sexual orientation of the child during later years. This relatively uncommon treatment of a child is not the only environmental factor, however, which is important. In order for a boy to develop into an independently functioning, normally aggressive man he must be able to identify to a considerable extent with his father, and this can be accomplished only if he is able to enjoy a relationship with his father in which there is a substantial degree of warmth and closeness. If this cannot be achieved during childhood, it often is sought during adolescence, and it is at this time that substitutes for a cold and rejecting father are sought out. Since adolescence is also a time when sexual impulses are most strongly felt, it is not surprising that the seeking out of a close relationship at this age should be contaminated by some sexual needfulness. It is thought that much of the temporary and sporadic quality of the relationship between homosexuals is due to the fact that each is seeking the gratification of impossible needs—the need of a child for a father—and because of this each homosexual partner in turn is bound to be a disappointment.

The mother, too, plays an important role and can influence her son's future sexual orientation adversely in two strikingly different ways. If she is an overly aggressive, frightening kind of woman who depreciates and humiliates the father, she contributes to the growing boy's picture of all womankind as frightening and dangerous. He then often will feel safer with those of his own sex and grow up preferring their company to that of girls who are associated in his own mind with the dominating and destructive qualities of his mother's personality. On the other hand, we have seen many cases where an overly feminine, seductive type of mother seems to have contributed to the development of homosexuality inclinations in her son later in life. This seems to be due in large part to the fact that any introduction of sexuality into the mother-son relationship is felt as threatening and dangerous by the son because of his instinctual feelings of revulsion toward incest. Heterosexual relationships then are associated later in life with these same feelings of disgust in such a way that the burgeoning sexual desires of the adolescent are channeled away from the opposite sex and toward individuals of the same sex instead.

Because adolescence is the time when the first strong outwardly directed sexual impulses are experienced there is a good deal of confusion in the minds of college boys as to what sort of outlet is most healthy and appropriate. Sexual feeling is at its strongest at this period also, so that whatever degree of homosexuality one may have inherently or as a result of environmental influences is felt more powerfully and urgently during these years. Many students feel and do things at this time which they never repeat again during their adult life. Many students believe, and some physicians agree with them, that this is a time when young men pass through a critical period of choice—a time when their actions and behavior may determine in the period of a few weeks or months their sexual orientation for the entire remaining period of their lives. It is our opinion that this is not a voluntary choice but something which has been predetermined many years before and, for the most part, remains uninfluenced by the ordinary occurrences and encounters during college years. We often see students who feel strongly tempted to experiment with a homosexual experience but fear that doing so will bring about the release of powerful forces within them over which they would then have no control. Their feeling is that they are constantly walking on the brink of the pit of homosexuality and that one misstep will plunge them in forever. Often, however, after they have achieved a more enlightened view of homosexuality, they are able to experiment; and after profiting from the experience by learning more about the details of homosexuality and their own disinclination to pursue it, they can proceed to develop a fulfilling heterosexual life for themselves.

Another manifestation of this fear that homosexuality is lurking deep within and waiting to pounce is the kind of acute panic reaction often seen in students who have suddenly experienced a homosexual dream or a transitory homosexual yearning for a classmate. These students often appear at the clinic in states of extreme anxiety and tension, stating that they have never before been aware of any kind of homosexual feeling and, quite the contrary, have been extremely interested in girls and have had many satisfying heterosexual experiences. They are at a loss to explain the sudden appearance of these obviously homosexual feelings in themselves and are filled with disgust and terror. They are almost always quickly relieved of this anxiety when it is explained to them that there are elements of homosexuality in everyone and that while they are more than offset by stronger heterosexual elements in most of us, occasionally the homosexual constituent comes into consciousness undiluted and causes a homosexual dream or impulse to flash across the mind.

Many boys come to the service each year for help with the resolution of problems which do not appear, at first, to be associated with homosexuality. Sometimes these center around difficulty in accepting a mode of behavior which may be protecting the individual against the expression of homosexual wishes. This behavior sometimes is not accepted as being appropriate and yet when it is understood that it serves as a replacement for much less socially acceptable activities, it can be tolerated by the student without causing him concern.

A student in the Divinity School came to the psychiatric clinic because he was worried about the fact that he preferred to take boy scouts on camping trips to going out on dates with girls. He was disappointed in himself because of this, feeling that it singled him out as different from others. It also made him feel discouraged about the possibility of eventually getting married. In the course of a few interviews he was able to see that he had never felt any sexual desire for girls, in fact, had no real interest in them at all as individuals, although the general concept of being married appealed to him. He was naturally a very conservative individual and considered that getting married was one of those things which every normal person does. He recalled having had a number of very close emotional relationships with contemporaries during college and told of some homosexual fantasies which he remembered having had at that time. His need for unusually close emotional relationships with men, as well as his fantasies, had been absent since he had been in the

Divinity School and had taken so much interest in the boy scouts and other youth activities. As a result of therapy he came to understand that, while he had no sexual interest in the work he was doing with boys, still it was somehow satisfying to him. By associating with members of the male sex in a helpful and altruistic manner he was utilizing a defense mechanism in an effective way and by means of it he was gaining a gratification through companionship with boys which satisfied him to such an extent that his homosexual fantasies were entirely eliminated. This understanding about what was going on within him relieved this student of his anxiety completely.

Another outward manifestation of inner sexual turmoil may be depression. Often a homosexually inclined student who has an un-usually fastidious nature and who may have had a very strict and moral upbringing will completely repress his homosexual feelings so that he has no sexual outlet whatever. The result often is a slowing up in all areas of activity with a consequent falling off in achieve-ment, discouragement, and depression.

A graduate student in philosophy came to the psychiatric clinic com-plaining that he had suddenly lost interest in his work. He felt so dis-couraged about the future that he was seriously contemplating suicide.

This student came from a Midwestern city where his father held an executive position in a bank and his mother worked as office manager, nurse, and financial adviser to the most prominent physician in town. This student's father was a mild-mannered, vague, fairly neutral person who expected that his son would be the aggressive, athletic, exceedingly male person which he, the father, had always wanted to be. Early in the boy's life his father saw that this ideal was not going to be realized. After that he completely lost interest in the boy and coldly rejected him. The mother, on the other hand, enthusiastically took over her only child. She praised and complimented him for every small achievement and gave him the feeling that he was a very special child with fabulous intellectual endowment and a quite extraordinary future ahead of him. This embar-rassed and upset him so that he came to both fear and dislike her. He remembers with particular distaste a time when she forced him to appear on a "Quiz Kids" program on the local television station.

This boy was sent from the Midwest to an Eastern preparatory school where, despite his rather different background, he made an instant success as a result of his charm and intelligence. It was here that he had his first homosexual experience. When he moved on to become an under-graduate at Harvard, his popularity among his contemporaries continued, but along with it came increasing homosexual activity.

When this boy came to graduate school he made a conscious decision to give up all homosexual contacts. He did this because he felt that these relationships were complicating his life and he wished to con-centrate on his studies. He claimed that he felt no guilt about his homosexuality and that his renunciation of it was motivated entirely by factors other than conscience. He held to this opinion through several months of therapy despite the occurrence of many dreams as well as day to day occurrences which corroborated the therapist's feeling that this boy actually felt tremendously guilty about his homosexuality and that this was contributing to his depression.

One night this student attended a little known play of Shakespeare, *Titus Andronicus*. The play portrayed the revenge taken by a queen upon another royal family. At one point the two sons of the queen, whom the patient found very attractive, asked the queen if they might have one of the ladies of the royal family for a few days before the queen put her to death in order that they might "enjoy" her. When this woman appeared on the stage, the patient immediately identified with her, feeling that he would like very much to be "enjoyed" by these two attractive men. As the play went on, the two princes took the lady behind the scenes, and a few moments later she returned disheveled with her tongue partly cut out and hanging out of one corner of her mouth and both hands cut off so that her arms were stumps dripping blood. When the patient saw this he felt immediately nauseated, thought he was going to vomit on the spot, and had to rush from the theatre. When he was seen a day and a half later he was still pale and trembling but extremely curious as to why he had found this such a shattering experience. During the course of this hour he was able to realize that he had felt, through his identification with the injured woman, justifiably punished for wanting to sexually "be enjoyed" by the two men. After this he was able to talk for the first time about his strong guilt feelings about being homosexually inclined and, interestingly enough, shortly afterwards was able to participate in a discreet homosexual relationship for the first time in many years. Also, his depression was completely relieved.

There are some students for whom the relative strength of heterosexual and homosexual impulse is so close to being equal that they feel continually pulled in both directions. For them, there does not seem to be any possible, complete commitment either to men or to women and they feel constantly disloyal to one or the other. Such students often profit from a series of interviews over a fairly long period of time which are directed toward the achievement of insight into the causes of the conflicting impulses as well as toward the ways in which the student himself can help to resolve specific conflicts when they arise.

A law student came to the clinic for help in overcoming a strong homosexual attachment which he felt toward a fellow student. The patient was married and the father of five children and he felt that his "crush" on another boy was interfering with the full expression of affection which he felt should be directed toward his wife and children.

He gave a history of having had a number of close emotional attachments to other boys, most of which had not resulted in any sexual relationship. His interest in girls had been comparatively less, but six years previous to his beginning treatment he had fallen deeply in love with a girl who was in many ways quite masculine. They had married and had a continuing strong bond between them which had resulted in a very satisfying and healthy family relationship. There had been some sexual difficulties during the early months of the marriage but these had been entirely overcome. Sporadically, however, over the past six years the patient had found himself involved emotionally and sexually with other men, and it was in hopes of eliminating this need that he was seeking therapy.

Early interviews were spent in a discussion of what had been going on in other areas of his life at the times when he had experienced these surges of homosexual feeling. Gradually a pattern emerged which indicated that these sporadic periods of homosexual feeling came at times when he was either separated from his wife, or else at times when he was unable to have intercourse with her because she was late in her pregnancy or immediately following pregnancy. He also traced out a relationship between his feeling frustrated in his work at the Law School or in his outside job and the times when he sought the companionship of another man. Previously, he had not connected any of these events with his homosexual feelings. Now, being able to correlate them in this way helped him both in his understanding of what was happening within him and also, to some degree, in being able to foresee times when he might be tempted by homosexuality. Now he was able to take steps to prevent the predisposing factors from coming into play.

Something else, however, seemed to be extremely important in helping this student. As therapy progressed he talked more and more about his early childhood relationships, and it became clear that his relationship with his father had always been an unusually strained one. The patient's mother died when he was one year old and his father had remarried almost immediately. His stepmother was a dour, mechanical, efficient woman who served more as a housekeeper than as a wife or mother. His father was a school teacher and seemed entirely wrapped up in his work. He maintained a distance from the patient which was hard to understand. One day the patient recalled that his father had told him many times that he bore a striking resemblance to his mother. Gradually an interesting picture began to be sketched in. It appeared that this boy's father had substituted his son into the place of his wife, treating him with the deference and respect which he had shown toward his first wife when she was alive. Thus, in subtle ways he had encouraged effeminacy in the boy and been pleased by every trait which the boy showed which was similar to his mother. Shortly after the discussions about these attitudes on his father's part, the patient was able to give up his close dependence on his classmate and reported that his homosexual yearnings and preoccupation were noticeably less strong.

Psychotherapy can play a significant role in helping students with homosexual problems. Perhaps as important, however, is the help which the psychiatrist can give to deans and faculty members in their dealings with the student who has problems in this area. In general, the attitude of college authorities toward homosexuality is one of horrified denial. Usually they will say that this problem does not exist in their particular college or university and that if such a thing should be called to their attention, they would see that it was immediately investigated and eliminated. Closer examination of the facts, however, usually reveals that there has been ample evidence brought to the attention of the authorities that homosexuality exists, that there are some problems regarding it, and that his evidence has been either discreetly ignored or just plain not seen. Actually, this appears to be a very good way to treat the problem, that is, by not treating it, but it seems too bad that there cannot be some frank appreciation of what is happening and some communication among administrators about their attitudes.

Students of college level who have homosexual inclinations behave almost without exception in a discreet and inoffensive manner. They do not attempt to seduce other students; nor do they blatantly proclaim their difference from the average student. They do not constitute a menace and they often come from the most creative and academically productive contingent. The psychiatrist can often allay the fears of administrative officers in this respect. We had one housemaster at Harvard who was fond of belligerently stating that if he found a single shred of evidence of homosexuality in any one of his students he would have him out of the house and out of the university within two hours. Yet the psychiatric clinic knows that this housemaster did not once act upon this threat in any individual case despite the fact that he had often gathered incontrovertible evidence. Each time he discussed the student with one of the psychiatric staff and found good reason not to carry out the threat. This is usually the way it works out. Of course, rarely there are cases in which the personality structure of the student, above and beyond his sexual deviation, makes him the cause of concern and discomfort for those around him and it is imperative that he leave the community. Here again, the psychiatrist's opinion in regard to the total personality picture is important in making the right disposition.

7

Suicide

William D. Temby

The first conclusion that emerges from a review of the suicides at Harvard is that, short of clinical depression, open expressions of despair, or actual mention of suicide, there is nothing easily recognizable about the student who is going to commit suicide. There is no "suicidal personality."

At the time of admission to the college or a graduate school, each student fills out a complete medical inventory. Included are several questions designed to cover psychological matters. After this has been completed by the student, he is given a physical examination by a specialist in internal medicine. From a perusal of what the student has written and from impressions gained from examining and talking with him, the examiner writes a very brief summary. Included in this is usually a rough prediction of how the student will fare both academically and psychologically. In a few of our cases of suicide these evaluations were made only a few weeks before the act, yet what the physician wrote is seen to run the descriptive gamut.

For example, an entering freshman impressed the examiner as being mature with many interests, and the conclusion was drawn that he should do well in his studies and in either of his possible selections of major field, social relations or medicine. Three months later he was found in his automobile dead of carbon monoxide inhalation poisoning. A graduate student was described as "intelligent and well-adjusted" at the time of admission. Six months later, in the midst of a depression, he shot himself. A student who killed himself

109

two months after entering college had impressed the examining physician as an "easygoing, moderately extroverted, pleasant fellow who is rather sure of himself in an inoffensive way. . . ." On the other hand, a student who committed suicide in his freshman year had been characterized as "emotional worried type." Another was "tense and dreamy." "Mild occasional depression" was noted but "no difficulties anticipated" by the examiner. Another was described as "full of repression, hypersensitivities, and introspective conflicts."

Even the wisdom of hindsight does not produce from the impressions of the examiners generalizations as to who might have been identified as likely to commit suicide. Even where abnormality was detected, there were no telltale suicidal signs.

Of the 25 suicides from 1946 on, when more medical staff time was available and even more careful examinations conducted, there were only 6 in which psychological abnormality was noted at admission that could be described in any more specific terms than, say, "shy" or "overactive." In 4 of these 6 cases, the students had actually made mention of difficulty in the medical inventory which the examiner reviews before seeing the student. Two of them specifically listed depression. None of the 25 had said anything about considering suicide. Two had listed emotional difficulty, but nothing in their examination struck the eye of the physician. Premonitory acts, symptoms, or personality changes were noticed by friends, family, or teachers shortly before the suicidal act in 15 cases. In 6, no psychological difficulty except something as general and unqualified as "immaturity" was commented on by anyone, including the student himself. It is possible that in many more of the cases signs would have been noticed immediately before the suicide, but our study indicates that there are no enduring signs or stigmas which would offer any hope of prediction in the course of routine work-ups at the time of admission.

The question as to whether a psychiatrically trained person might have been able to make the kind of observations at the time of admission that might reveal common characteristics which would be useful cannot be definitely answered. It is interesting, however, that among our cases 3 had been referred previously to the psychiatric clinic for evaluation for reasons having nothing directly to do with self-destructive tendencies. In none was there anything that indicated to the psychiatrist that suicide might be the outcome.

The college administration received a letter from a member of a student's family suggesting that he be seen by a psychiatrist because "he seems to take his mind a little too seriously." The student was interviewed and judged to be all right "except for worry about finances." Two months later he killed himself. Friends recalled afterwards that he had seemed "often morose and discouraged" and had mentioned on the day before the suicidal act that he was "tired of fighting so hard; I've been fighting all my life." Either he had not seen fit to confide his innermost concerns to the psychiatrist who saw him two months earlier or he did not have such thoughts at that time.

A college student was referred to a university psychiatrist because of an increase in his stuttering. The student was only seen once, at which time no suicidal inclination was detected. Soon afterward he began discussing suicide with friends, even showed them capsules and a revolver which he had secreted in his room, and six months after his visit to the psychiatric department, he was a victim of self-inflicted cyanide poisoning. Word later reached the director of the hygiene department that during the previous year he had attempted to anesthetize himself with ether. Here the trend had been obviously present for some time but was not detected at the time of the psychiatric visit.

A college senior was referred by the medical clinic to the psychiatric department in his sophomore year because of numerous complaints, such as fainting, gastroenteritis, colds, right lower quadrant pain, and pain in the shoulder, for which adequate organic cause could not be found. He had been discharged from the service the year before because of anxiety attacks. When he was examined he was found to be symptom-free and was not seen again. Soon occasional frank depressions were observed by his friends and finally he killed himself.

Even in those cases in which the student was referred to the psychiatric department for actual depression, suicidal thoughts could not always be elicited. One student was seen, at the insistence of his mother, for weight loss, tension, poor appetite, fatigue, and feeling fed up with school. Nothing about suicide is mentioned in the record of that interview and the boy denied feeling depressed. In fact, he said that he had just decided to withdraw from school and felt relieved and more relaxed now that the pressure was off. Two weeks after leaving college he committed suicide.

Although there may not be such a thing as a suicidal personality or even a general type of personality prone to suicide, it is nevertheless agreed that there are suicidal trends *within* personalities. These may manifest themselves in various ways, and there are events, situations, and surroundings which may potentiate, or even activate, these trends. It is to these factors that we next turn our attention.

We shall discuss briefly what may be called the environmental aspects of suicides at Harvard. The suicide rate at Harvard is approximately 1.5 for every 10,000 students per year. This is about 50 percent higher than that of the American population at large. Some investigators with a sociological frame of reference have indicated that suicide is strongly related statistically to social disorganization, to absence of stable institutions and organizations, customs, ideals, and group ties sufficient to give the individual both outlets for his needs and interests and controls for his behavior. One does hear the complaint that Harvard is an impersonal, apathetic environment where no one cares what happens to the student and he is likely to meet his faculty advisor only at a cocktail party or, at any rate, more by accident than by design. The medical and psychiatric records of our cases mention no such complaints and therefore throw no light on the matter. Perhaps these particular students were not the kind who are able successfully to verbalize the sources of their discontent.

It is literally true that for the student the transition to college represents a sudden breakdown in the life he is used to, a loss of the traditions, controls, and ties of family life. This is especially difficult because it occurs in late adolescence when the tension between the struggle for independence and identity on the one hand and the need to find guidance and group affiliations on the other is often so great. However, there was no disproportion in the number of suicides occurring in the freshman year, the period when the greatest change in milieu might be supposed to occur. Of 22 undergraduate suicides, 7 were freshmen, and of these only 4 committed suicide within three months after they entered school. Of 12 graduate students only 2 took their lives within the first three months of their move to new surroundings.

The difficulty with such ecological generalizations is, of course, that they are incomplete. They yield little information as to why a particular individual should be so profoundly disturbed as to take his own life. Where social disorganization exists, not only suicide, but crime, mental illness, and other desperate and deviant patterns are present. It does not explain suicide as a specific outcome.

Religious affiliation would not appear to be an important factor in these suicides. Of our 34 cases, 12 declared themselves to be Protestant, 6 Catholic, 3 Jewish, and 1 Greek Orthodox. One stated that he had no religion. Eleven made no mention of religion on their medical inventory forms, in most cases because it was not asked for. The percentages, then, of those in which it is known are: 52 percent Protestant, 26 percent Catholic, 13 percent Jewish, 4 percent Greek Orthodox, and 4 percent no religion. The approximate religious affiliation of all Harvard undergraduates has been unofficially estimated to be 41 percent Protestant, 14 percent Catholic, 25 percent Jewish, 9 percent "other," and 11 percent no religion. Although there seems to be a reversal of the proportion of Catholic and Jewish among suicides as compared with the university at large, the relation observed between all religious affiliations and suicide could have occurred by chance. (Chi square test suggests p greater than 0.10). Perhaps a correlation more interesting than that between suicide and stated religious affiliations, where the individual is asked to choose among a few stereotyped alternatives, would be that between suicide and demonstrated devoutness. People asked to designate a religion will perhaps oblige more often than not, and while there is no doubt that the choice has significance, it tells little about what role religion plays in the current emotional life of each individual. Unfortunately, we were unable to obtain such detailed information in our cases.

In 7 of our 34 cases there was a known recent or impending loss of a person who had emotional significance to the student. Two had broken up with girl friends. One had lost a father. The father of one was leaving for a foreign country. The best friend of another was soon to marry. One was turned over by his psychiatrist to another physician to receive electric shock treatment. One was separated at Christmas time from his wife and children on another continent. Three of these 7 students are known to have suffered previous parental losses by divorce, death, or "nervous breakdown." In the other students in whom suicide was preceded by such occurrences as academic failure, worry over finances, or a visit with a mentally ill mother, about one-half had suffered the loss of a parent in childhood from death or divorce. Presumably the recent loss or trauma revived older emotions in these cases.

In the total group of 34, the parents were known to be divorced in 3 cases. In 9, one parent had died. In one, both parents had died. In one, a parent, the mother, was known to have committed suicide. In 2 cases the home was broken up, and in 4 there was known mental illness in one parent. In one of these a maternal aunt had a diagnosis of manic-depressive psychosis. Comparison with figures for a group of 200 randomly chosen Harvard graduate students shows that the incidence of mental illness is higher (4 of 34 cases as opposed to 10 of 200) but not to a statistically significant degree. The incidence of divorce is higher (3 of 34 as opposed to 13 of 200) but also not significantly so. The incidence of death of a parent is higher (10 of 34 as opposed to 30 of 200) and this is statistically significant. (The value of p is less than 0.02.) The correlation between suicide and death of a parent is the most impressive of these traumatic influences.

The methods employed in suicidal acts have fascinated both physicians and laymen. The method is known in a total of 31 of our cases. Shooting occurred in 13. Ingestion of poison or drugs was chosen by 5, including cyanide in 2, barbiturates in 2, and a combination of agents in 1. There was asphyxiation by gas in 5, the agent being carbon monoxide from automobile exhaust in 4 and illuminating gas in 1. One hanged himself. One slashed his wrists and then leaped from a hotel window. Three others leaped from hotel windows and another from the window of his room at college. One jumped from a cliff. One ran into a whirling airplane propeller.

In one case more than one method of suicide was employed. In 2 others there is evidence that more than one method was strongly contemplated. One of the students who leaped from a window also had both poison and a knife with him in the room, the knife wedged into the bed springs with the point upward. One, who elected to take cyanide, had been known also to have had a revolver, two kinds of poison, and capsules of unknown description in his room at college. Review of their records suggests that 2, and possibly 3, of these students had been among the most seriously disturbed among our cases. One seems definitely to have been psychotically depressed. All are among those known to have ruminated for some time about suicide. A fourth student, who did not choose different routes of suicide but did take two different kinds of poison, had also talked repeatedly of suicide. This seems to indicate that choice of more than one method is correlated with severity of disturbance, possibly with depth of the wish to die, and possibly with psychosis.

In 2 or 3 cases there seems to have been an element of contagion. A student was found in his room dead of a self-inflicted gunshot wound in the head. That morning there had been an article on the front page of the college newspaper describing how another student in the same class committed suicide by the same method. This sort of suggestion may have been a factor in the case of the student who ran into a propeller at an airport in his home city. One day previously the local newspaper had carried an article about a man who had been seriously injured when he was struck by a whirling propeller at a nearby airport in the same city. Of course, in each case it is only presumed that the student had read of the other suicide. Nothing more can be said except that these incidents could have had an influence upon the timing and method of the suicidal act.

A feature of one of the suicides is interesting enough to deserve mention. A student had often said jokingly to a good friend that he wanted to die in white tie and tails. One evening he called the friend to his room, and there he sat in a tuxedo. He produced a suicide note and, before anything could be done, drank a fatal dose of poison. Several authors have made reference to suicides among primitive peoples in which the individuals dress up in ceremonial clothing. It had been noted that what is embodied in the customary conscious thought of primitive people, and also in the rites of organized religions, is found individually in the unconscious minds of "civilized" people. The connection between death and ceremonial dress is perhaps expressed in our Western expressions, "dressed fit to kill" and "I wouldn't be caught dead in those clothes." What significance it had in the mental life of this particular student must remain a mystery. However, it is known that he was soon to have been best man at the wedding of the friend whom he summoned to witness the act. Possibly they were to have dressed in tails for the wedding.

The most common location chosen for the suicidal act was the college. Thirteen died in or near their rooms or en route to the hospital. These comprise 45 percent of the 29 cases in which the location is recorded. Six died in their homes or home towns. Four others chose hotels, one an airport, one a lonely road, one the Charles River, one a faraway cliff, one a garage near college, and one a town near home.

The seasonal occurrence of suicide is another aspect of the subject which has interested many investigators. Our finding is that 28 out of 34 occurred during seven of the school months, October through April. This runs counter to the observation that suicide attempts in the Northern Hemisphere are most frequent in May and June. Only one in our series was in May and none occurred in June. An interesting fact is that of 29 students who committed suicide while registered in the University, all did so either while in actual physical attendance or while on a short vacation during the academic year. Of the 3 who died during the summer, 2 had withdrawn because of academic failure and the other had only recently received his undergraduate degree.

One finding which is in line with others' observations is that the suicide rate was lower during wartime. In the four years the United States was at war there was only one recorded suicide. By comparison, there were 5 during the four years which preceded the war and 8 during the four years which followed it. During wartime there is a ready-made enemy against whom to direct one's aggression rather than toward oneself. Also, a student who has a suicidal impulse has the possibility before him that he may be killed at war.

A variable which might be expected to be important is academic standing. In the 25 cases in which standing at the time of the suicidal act is known with any accuracy, 4 had above average or high grades, 13 were average, 4 were below average, and 4 were failing or close to failure. No particular correlation is suggested. However, the importance of academic standing to the individual might be expected not to be reflected fully in rough statistics. It is relative to such things as goals, expectations, and fragility of self-esteem. In many of our cases there was evident concentration of all hope of success in one area. Many showed a lack of interest and of proficiency in any other sphere except studies. This may help explain why even slight or imagined academic failure could be enough to induce deep concern.

Two of the students had just withdrawn from college because of academic failure. Another had failed his freshman year. One had received a notice in the morning mail that he had failed a course. One student had been brooding over a mediocre grade in a mid-semester examination. Another had received three D's at mid-years and was known to be worried about his studies. One had been given a D in his first freshman English composition. In the cases of 2 who were worried over studies it is not known that they were actually doing badly at all. One of these was afraid of flunking out of college and having to go into the army (it was during the war), where he was convinced he would be a failure. One student who was very worried over coming examinations had high academic standing. One had told a physician in the medical clinic the year before how much he had hoped to make the Dean's list and had not. He was an average student. Two of the suicides were premedical students; one, although his grades were good, obtained his lowest grade in a premedical sub' ject and had changed from the premedical course. He had expressed a strong desire to be a doctor. The other also had made good grades, but he had reached midterm of his senior year and was depressed at not having heard from medical school. The cases in which a direct connection between concern over studies and suicide is definite or suggested total 14, or 41 percent.

Many correlations such as the above might be attempted. One is not sure, however, when such facts are gathered, what they all mean and how they can be put to use. The orientation of the clinical psychiatrist, especially one involved in day to day therapeutic work with students, has to do less with the sociological or academic situation of the student, which he can seldom do anything about than with the factors in the individual personality which contribute to the choice of suicide as a solution. Our review of records of successful suicides, conducted from the standpoint of discovering the deeper, private factors and motives, unfortunately leads us down a virtual blind alley. Ten of thirty-four had been seen by the psychiatric service, and of these only three had done so on their own initiative. Only two had taken advantage of psychotherapy of a continuing and searching kind. Six are known to have left suicidal notes, which might be expected to give clues, direct or indirect, as to the state of mind and motive oper' ant at the time of the act. One of these was written while poison was taking its effect and is thus incoherent. Four others were addressed to members of the family and are not included in the records. More potentially productive sources are the accounts of people with serious suicidal intentions who come to therapy for help.

One of the frequently mentioned sources of the self-destructive impulse is an unconscious, hostile wish against someone else turned against the self or, symbolically, killing another person whom one has taken into one's self. This kind of motive or process is usually not an easily demonstrable one. There is one case in which it is suggested. The student was observed to be arguing heatedly with his father at an airport before he suddenly leaped over a barrier, rushed into the path of an airplane, and was killed. Here and there in other cases this mechanism is hinted at.

The suicidal act in the male may represent a killing of what is seen as the inadequate, weak, or feminine part of one's self. At least three students had expressed conscious worries about homosexual tendencies. One of these had been unable, because of medical illness, to engage in athletics. This may have been interpreted by them as meaning that they could not get along adequately as men or reinforced previous convictions to this effect.

The statistical significance of recent personal loss was cited earlier in this chapter. Several of the students had experienced one or more deaths in the immediate family. Some dynamics of this correlation are suggested by our cases.

Both parents of one student had died, one of suicide, when he was 21. He was discharged from the service after a psychotic illness which had been precipitated by knowledge that Americans were committing war atrocities, such as pushing Japanese out of planes. Several years later, in graduate college, he became preoccupied with the idea of failing in his studies and in discharging his responsibilities to his wife and children. He had the fear that he would jump from a high place. He did indeed jump to his death, from the window of a hotel in a nearby city.

Another boy appeared to have been strongly identified with his physician father who died when he was seven. He wanted very much to be a physician and died at his own hand after having become depressed in January of his senior year over not having heard from any of the medical schools to which he had applied.

Identification with a dead family member as an influence toward suicide has been mentioned in the literature. It can be prominent in boys whose fathers have died, especially if combined with despair at not living up to the image, often exaggerated, of what the father accomplished when he lived. It might well have been present in this and others of our 7 cases whose fathers had died.

Another possible compelling motive or factor, perhaps related to the above, is an unconscious sense of guilt. This seems well exemplified in the case of a graduate student who shot himself a few days after the death of his father-in-law, toward whom he felt at times quite antagonistic. Such guilt and self-punishment are also known to play a part in suicides committed when the individual has reached a new plateau of success. One of the students, who committed suicide in the middle of his senior year, ranked very high in his class academically. He had just received a valued senior prize and been informed that he was about to be the recipient of a scholarship to study abroad. It may be that he felt these honors were undeserved and the winning of them only increased his basic feelings of guilt and unworthiness.

One of the questions prompted by our review of cases is: What is the significance of the observation that only 10 of 34, or 29 percent, of those who committed suicide had consulted the psychiatric service? Two were known to have been in treatment with psychiatrists outside the university. Yet, over the academic years 1952–1957, when treatment facilities had increased substantially, only 2 of the 10 suicides, or 20 percent, had utilized the services of the psychiatric clinic. In addition, most of those who did visit the service did not continue for one reason or another. Two withdrew from school and 5 were seen, but nothing was done directly about preventing suicide because suicidal impulses, if present, were not expressed. Another left school suddenly and did not resume psychiatric treatment when he returned. In this case the suicidal danger had been known. He expressed to a member of his family dissatisfaction with the psychiatrist who had seen him and used this as an explanation for not resuming treatment. In all but a few, therefore, obstacles of some kind prevented entering intensive treatment.

In 6 of the cases a kind of improvement in mood was noticeable to observers just prior to the suicidal act; 4 of them follow.

One boy had been quietly studious and somewhat hypochondriacal as a freshman. When he returned to school for his sophomore year he began to drink, went to parties quite frequently, and slept often until noon. Six weeks after the fall term began he was found dead, a presumed suicide. His roommate had noted no signs of depression before the act. In fact, he had noticed "rather the opposite."

A student with problems serious enough to have prompted him to consult a university psychiatrist and also to disappear mysteriously from school in the middle of his junior year had been observed by friends to have been moody for a long time. On the day of the suicidal act he had received notice that he had failed a course. However, these same friends commented afterward that he had seemed "in good spirits" that day.

A student had been depressed for some time and was seen to be acutely disturbed a few days before ending his life. His mother afterward reported that on the morning of that day he seemed to be in good spirits.

After a graduate student swallowed poison, one of his friends was questioned and commented that, shortly before the suicidal act, "if anything, he had seemed to be in a better mood than usual."

To the extent that disturbances of mood are related to unresolved underlying conflict and a feeling that one's situation is intolerable, the change of mood in these cases may be assumed to reflect the fact that a solution has been found. Perhaps, once seriously adopting suicide as a solution, an individual will not take kindly to anything which might undermine this solution and require him to experience again the tension or depression he was seeking to avoid in the first place.

Another reason for not seeking help is that suicide, like psychosis, is not only a solution but a retreat from solution or, putting it another way, a regressive attempt at solution. To the extent that retreat has obsessed the personality, the taking of responsibility for oneself involved in psychotherapy, aimed as it is at understanding one's conflicts and learning to regulate one's life more effectively, seems not only unattractive but impossible.

Another possible element in the avoidance of psychiatric help in our cases might be related to depression. Depression may be looked at from one point of view as a state designed to appease one's conscience through suffering. Involved are self-recriminations, feelings of worthlessness, and often grand ideas of culpability for all of the world's sins and outrages. In such a condition it is understandable that the idea of psychotherapy as doing something for oneself, potentially leading to increased self-esteem and happiness, can only be resisted.

In 24 of the 34 suicides some evidence of preexisting emotional illness, usually depression, was found. One had made an abortive suicide attempt the year before; another had told a friend that he had attempted suicide several years previously; and in two more cases suicide is known to have reached consciousness, in one as a definite intention and in the other as a fear that he might jump out the window (which he later did). Five had been observed by a member of the medical staff to be chronically or subacutely depressed but without expressed suicidal ideas. Three had had serious psychiatric difficulties without evident mention of suicide but necessitating, in one case, discharge from the armed services and, in the other two, withdrawals on two separate occasions from college. Eleven more were reported afterward by friends or others to have been upset, brooding, or depressed. Of these, three were reported to have engaged in repeated, seemingly detached or philosophical, discussions about suicide, and one wrote an English theme balancing the will to live and the temptation to die. Another was known to have been emotionally disturbed and under private psychiatric care.

In the 10 remaining, there seems to have been nothing pointing to a suicidal outcome. However, 2 of these had numerous somatic symptoms of the type that could have reflected considerable depression. Also, included with the 24 who had preexisting emotional illness are 6 who had visited the medical clinic numerous times or had a known history of psychosomatic illness. Another perhaps betrayed his desperation in scattered actions which, taken separately, would not have been thought to indicate anything seriously wrong. This student had previously withdrawn after one month of his freshman year to enter military service. As he began his freshman year for the second time, he broke up with his girl friend, went to the Bureau of Study Counsel for help with his studies, and, finally, visited the medical clinic for a mild upper respiratory infection. The same morning he suddenly left school for home. Two days later, he committed suicide by carbon monoxide poisoning. Another student seemed to have been quite involved in the subject of accidents.

He was a sophomore who had undergone a splenectomy following abdominal trauma at the age of 14. He also had a history of repeated sprains and contusions of the right knee and had been forbidden to take part in athletics. Because of poor vision he had been rejected for military service before entering college. In his freshman year he wrote an article for the college paper about the subject of athletic injuries. After he committed suicide the only recent entry in his medical record was dated 16 days before: "Contusion right foot, playing basketball."

Such an interest in injury may represent an attempt to deal with self-destructive impulses that have not yet reached consciousness.

The death of one student was considered a complete mystery, and it was thought at first that it could only have been an accident.

A note to parents and friends was finally found in his pocket, indicating that it had been planned. Another committed suicide also without apparent warning but did leave a note. Two, in whom there was no indication of any kind that suicide was in the offing, had mentioned in their medical inventory at the time of admission a tendency to become depressed and moody. In 2 others only their mothers were later found to have had forewarning of personality difficulty. In the 1 case remaining of the 10 without history of previous illness nothing out of the way had been remarked upon by the student or anyone else. He had recently left college, after being fired for academic reasons, when he hurled himself over a cliff. In this case there is a theoretical possibility that the academic failure itself was a result, more than a cause, of the self-destructive tendency which ended in actual death.

A few of the students, although not reporting or being observed to have psychological difficulties, had visited the medical clinic for physical ailments minor and major. In 4 of the cases psychosomatic problems had been the chief manifestation of difficulty. In 6 others they were known to be present. One of these 6 presented complaints of somatic symptoms, such as tiredness, at a time when others observed him to be tense, harried, and depressed. Another did not make mention of his mood but had numerous acute disorders, such as grippe, upper respiratory infections, and enteritis, and repeatedly spoke of fatiguing easily. The note describing the suicide of one graduate student comes as an isolated and stark entry in his medical record amid those describing numerous inflammatory reactions and infections of short duration involving many organ systems. Another student had often discussed and joked openly about suicide with a friend, but the only thing he had listed on his medical inventory was "very bad allergic stomach upsets." He came to the medical clinic only to receive the shots that his home town physician had prescribed for inducing active immunity to his hay fever and asthma.

Three of the 34 cases had bronchial asthma. In each of them, psychological symptoms were noticed by friends, but it was only or chiefly the asthma that the student chose to complain of to the University medical staff. What the relation was in these particular cases between the asthma and psycholocial factors cannot be established. The idea that they were depressed and committed suicide because they had asthma is inadequate at best. In none of the cases had it been a disabling condition in recent years.

Represented in the 10 cases mentioned above as having psy-chosomatic problems are several ways in which the body may play a role. There were repeated somatic problems, acute or chronic, often involving numerous organ systems, with or without depression. There were bodily symptoms conforming to a pattern that is known to be related to clinical depression yet occurring completely without self-recriminatory ideas—tiredness, sluggishness, slowing of bowel func-tion, decreased appetite. Or there was a combination of these mani-festations.

In three cases, the suicide occurred during a period of success in the medical or surgical treatment of an organic condition or after such treatment had been completed.

A college student had had rheumatic fever with minimal residual structural heart disease and recurrent osteomyelitis of the right tibia. Beginning at the same time of his entrance physical examination, he had a host of somatic complaints such as shortness of breath on slight exer-tion, gastrointestinal symptoms, and minor diseases such as colds and a wry-neck. In his sophomore year he developed a recurrence of the osteomyelitis. During the five months this was being treated none of the above symptoms were complained of. Finally the osteomyelitis was operated upon and he did well. At the beginning of his junior year he left a suicide note and ended his life.

Somatic symptoms, even those with an obvious and considerable infectious or allergic component or origin, can be utilized by the personality to mask underlying emotional disturbance. The psychic element may or may not be in consciousness. The fact is that the somatic side of things may be the only one seen by the physician but not the only one present. To be unaware of this is to be un-prepared for what can ensue as the somatic condition is successfully treated.

In two cases, the last visit of the student to the medical clinic was with some minor complaint for which many people ordinarily might not consult a physician or clinic. One of them reported with an upper respiratory infection, left school that afternoon, and killed himself two days later. The possibility exists that, in each of these cases and in others, the student himself was aware that this was not the chief or exclusive reason for his visit and, in a way, hoped that his psychological state would be noticed and something done about it. Several ruminated to friends about suicide, including one who actually showed poisons, capsules, and a revolver to friends. One wrote a thesis about despair and death, emphasizing how thin the thread was that held him alive. In these cases communication of despairing thoughts had a purpose which might have betrayed their suicidal content, namely, a plea to be rescued from extremity and from self-destructive tendencies.

In summary, 13 (38 percent) had a definite history, recent or remote, of gross psychological symptomology. Taking reports of friends and medical staff together, 15 could be said to have been depressed. Conscious thoughts of suicide are known to have been present in 7 of the cases, or 21 percent. In only two was it known beforehand by medical authorities to have been in the student's mind. Actual warning was not present in most of the cases, but in practically all some psychological or emotional difficulty appears to have been present. The impression of suddenness must be tempered by the awareness that on closer examination an element of latency was usually present, so that suicide was the last step in a process rather than merely an isolated act. Of none of the cases could it confidently be said that a healthy personality suddenly became sick and destroyed itself.

Sociological and epidemiological explanations of suicide are inadequate, but the milieu of the student is extremely significant. For example, athletics are necessary outlets for agression and provide reassurance concerning developing masculinity, self-mastery, and feeling of intactness. A wide variety of facilities, serving as outlets for every kind of energy and fostering the development of interests and self-confidence, is a worthwhile accompaniment of the academic process. It is especially important that an interested person, someone who knows about adolescents and their crises, be available. A consultation between each entering student and his advisor sometime in midautumn, with one of its main purposes being to discuss the results of the first examinations, should be built into the custom of university life. At that time the individual's college experiences, including grades, could be put in perspective and his adjustment to his new life sized up. Such an evaluation may be most useful when inadvertent and unobtrusive. In a few of our cases, although nothing alarming was present or detectable at the time of arrival at the college scene, suicide occurred soon after. Five freshmen and four first-year graduate students committed suicide late in their first term without warning to the administration or medical staff. Such a midautumn consultation might have succeeded in providing needed encouragement and advice. The university psychiatrists should be available as consultants to advisors. If simple, common-sense measures and interest on the part of the advisor do not suffice, efforts should be made to refer the student to a psychiatrist.

In discussions with depressed students it is vitally important that what the student says be taken seriously, often not only in spirit but in letter. The ruminations of suicide, usually abstract and often of a joking nature, which preceded suicide in five of our cases, illustrate this point. Communication of suicidal thoughts often reflects a wish to be rescued from a tragic dilemma. This is especially true in the case of administrative officials and faculty members, who are in a real sense *in loco parentis* and who may therefore fairly suspect that what a student tells them is partly intended to invoke a parental type of response, such as advice or help in controlling impulses. It is important to avoid showing that one is offended or shocked at the student's expression of an intention or temptation to do away with himself.

One student wrote in one of his early freshman English compositions of his temptation to commit suicide and of the meager hold his religion had on him as a deterrent. His instructor wrote at the end of the paper that if he seriously entertained such thoughts he should get over them quickly. He called the theme to the attention of a freshman dean and thence it came to the attention of the medical department. Several times the student was sent for, without the precise reason being mentioned. He did not keep his appointments and finally committed suicide. It is possible that the indignation of the instructor might have led him to respond in a way which destroyed the confidence of the student, whose expression of desperation might have represented a turning for help to the first adult in the community with whom he was in real contact. He might not have avoided seeking medical help if he had been told in the first place that the instructor had informed the administration and the medical service out of a sincere interest in his welfare. Often a bitter and depressed person will say something to someone, including mention of suicide, to bait him, inspire anger and rejection, and by this means obtain justification for his attitude that the world is not a good place to live in.

If a suicidal attempt or threat of suicide has been made, there is an excuse for calling someone, policeman or doctor, who can arrange to have the person taken where he can be treated or hospitalized immediately. But short of an actual attempt or threat, the course may have to be one of watchful and tactful waiting. Often a dean or instructor may have to await the moment when he senses that the relationship between him and the student is such that medical help can be suggested without offense. When suicidal thoughts are only suspected the situation is especially delicate. Suicide is a solution which offers relief from tension and despair, and the possibility of having it prevented may represent a threat, but the delicacy of the situation does not need to inspire a passive, fearful approach in the teacher or official attempting to help. A blunt and forceful way of intervening may, if accomplished at the right time, be responded to favorably. The student may sense a firmness and interest in his welfare that he has lost in himself and desperately needs to find in others.

There are occasions that call for prompt and definite action. If there has been a threat of or an attempt at suicide, the student may be deemed a danger to himself and hospitalized. This may be because he is considered a suicidal risk even if he has not expressed suicidal thoughts. It should not be the responsibility of a layman to decide whether or not a depression is serious or a suicidal preoccupation significant. This is the doctor's job, one for which the psychiatrist is specifically trained, and he should be consulted freely when this sort of problem arises.

Depression itself is not always easy to identify. Self-recriminatory ideas that prove to be more than transient appeals for support and are not swayed by argument are signs of it, as are repeated expressions of worthlessness, despair, or hopelessness. Sleeplessness, diminished appetite, and slowed bowel function may be complained of or noticed by others. There may be prolonged lassitude, lack of enthusiasm for or even interest in customary pursuits, and a disappearance of any humor save the most sardonic and bitter kind. There may be agitation, handwringing, and a kind of desperate restlessness. The more of these signs one sees, the more serious and dangerous the depression.

After the student has been referred to the psychiatrist he may have to be hospitalized immediately. But the psychiatrist's job may also involve watchful waiting. He may have to establish a relationship with the patient and watch him closely by means of frequent, short visits, rather than coming to grips immediately with the strong underlying emotions. To do the latter might drive the patient back to the edge of the cliff or the hotel window.

The psychiatrist may make his first contact with a suicidal patient while he is in the hospital. If the referral has been made without the compliance of the student, as is sometimes necessary, there will be difficulties in the way of psychotherapy. Paradoxically enough, the more serious the suicidal intent, the more reticent the student may be about admitting it to the doctor. The doctor may represent someone who might hospitalize him and cut off this possible route of escape from pain, or he might recommend his removal from school when school may be the only thing left with any meaning. The university psychiatrist has first to establish that he is primarily interested in the student's welfare and not in prying information from him that might be used in administrative action. Only a continuing relationship and genuine tact and interest on the part of the psychiatrist can convince the student that it is in his best interest to be frank. Only if the student realizes that his position will not be compromised by confiding will he bring up for discussion serious problems, such as suicidal thoughts.

One of the important things the psychiatrist can do about preventing suicide is to stay informed about ill students in the university in general. It is important that staff members communicate with one another. One psychiatrist on the staff might make suicide one of his subfields of interest, being responsible for compiling statistics and conducting investigations of all suicides. Cases in which suicidal attempts and threats occur should be studied carefully insofar as is possible. The psychiatrist with this as one of his responsibilities can share experiences with the other members who are working with potentially suicidal patients, noting their approaches and the important predisposing factors which are uncovered. Some of the elements involved in suicide are deeply unconscious impulses and primitive fantasies.

These are often not revealed or more than hinted at in short-term work. Even in intensive, analytically oriented therapy the emphasis is more apt to be on current difficulties and their antecedents. As the patient improves, suicide may not remain long in focus and therefore not be thoroughly studied, despite the interest of the therapist. Continuous investigation of this distressing consequence of illness should be an important concern of the psychiatric service of any university.

8

Student Apathy

Paul A. Walters, Jr.

The title of this chapter suggests immediately the whole student population at one time or another during the college career. Fortunately for most students disintrest or apathy is a transitory state which is precipitated by concern over a course, career choice, an uneven romance, or other realistic difficulties. There is, however, another group of students, inevitably men and usually lower classmen, whose disinterest cannot be attributed to such realistic causes. These students usually come to the attention of the faculty when their survival at college is threatened by a total disinclination to study. Expecting to see an agitated and apprehensive student, the college official is often surprised when the student presents himself as either indifferent, languid, indolent, lethargic, dulled, or apathetic. Any or all of these adjectives may be applicable. What they briefly indicate can be more fully described as a state of reduced emotional lability, preoccupation with current work difficulties to the exclusion of past experiences and future expectations, and an inability, in spite of constant effort, to study effectively. The students themselves describe a state of affectlessness or emptiness combined with physical lethargy and intellectual impotence. In some colleges this reaction is frequent enough to be referred to as the sophomore slump. In others it evidently attracts less attention. But in every college, indeed in any aggregation of late adolescents, there can be found individuals who have become apathetic.

One might be tempted to dismiss these young men as scholastically inadequate or just naturally lazy except that close examination of their records frequently reveals notable past academic performance and enviable aptitude. Further comfort might be derived from con-vincing oneself that the student is in the wrong major, has unsuitable roommates, or just does not know what he wants to do. In many cases this will be true and is certainly the most realistic and practical area to explore first. But after these avenues have been exhausted the educator will often find himself confronted by the inability of the student, despite all his best intentions, to do anything about himself. At this point the educator might be tempted to replace interest by exasperation and thereby wash his hands of the whole affair. Before he does this, however, it should cross his mind that he may be ex-asperated more at his own inability to aid this puzzling young man than at the young man himself. Undoubtedly it was the student's sincere plea for help and the teacher's obvious good intention to be of all possible help in his recovery that led the educator to believe direct intervention would be effective. After this has failed it does not mean that the educator has been betrayed or that the student is inadequate, but rather that there are psychological instead of purely realistic prob-lems. The major premise of this chapter is that apathy is a frequent psychological defense which a particular type of late-adolescent boy employs as protection against a specific set of circumstances either real or imagined.

The earliest clear example of the existence of this reaction is to be found in the Russian novel, *Oblomov*,[1] first published in 1836. Oblomov is a young man of almost unbelievable indolence and leth-argy who spends most of his time in the comfort and warmth of his bed idly dreaming of opulent sustenance and comfort furnished by a frankly maternal woman. After initial disappointment in a more potentially mature relationship with a desirable woman, Oblomov turns to a motherly woman but is inevitably disappointed and gradu-ally wastes away. The striking thing about this book is how per-ceptively the author depicts the emptiness and constriction of Oblomov's apathy. The humdrum trivia of Oblomov's life are eloquently con-trasted with the richness of his fantasy life which is full of warmth, love, happiness, fullness, and peace. In modern psychodynamic terms

---

[1] Yoncharov. Ivan's Oblomov. New York, E. P. Dutton & Co., Inc., Everyman Paperback, April 1960.

these are conditions clearly relating to that satisfaction found by the very young child with his mother. Thus, in fiction, at least, apathy represents a wish for maternal love and is aggressive in nature. But before the reader objects that practically any psychological motivation can be ascribed to a fictional character, let us turn from what seems fictional license in *Oblomov* to what is startling reality in modern times.

In 1949 Greenson[2] wrote of apathy in World War II support troops who were subjected to boredom, emotional deprivation, and constant humiliation over a long period of time. Strassman[3] and Lifton[4] described similar reactions in returning Korean War prisoners who had been subjected to continual political indoctrination combined with attacks upon previous emotional ties. In the early days of the war when physical deprivation, mental harassment, and humiliation were extreme, many prisoners became completely apathetic and died unless they had a "buddy" who would "nurse" them. This reaction has an earlier analogue in abandoned three- to six-month-old babies who show signs of anaclitic depression or marasmus. These babies become lethargic and anorexic unless a mother-substitute whom they come to know and expect at times of need can be found. In all of these examples the apathetic reaction was held onto until the external environment had changed, and then was gradually relinquished. In such cases apathy is a primitive psychological defense against physical and emotional deprivation combined with constant humiliation and defeat. The rest of this chapter will try to demonstrate, first by cases and then by discussion, that in middle and late adolescence apathy is a reaction to expected humiliation and defeat in the task of forming a mature and effective masculine identity.

The first case shows long-standing apathy pervasively extending to inhibit social as well as academic life, fantasy as well as rational thought, and physical as well as emotional motility.

---

[2] Greenson, R. R. The psychology of apathy. Psychoanal. Quart., 18:290–302, 1949.

[3] Strassman, H. D., Thaler, M. B., and Schum, E. H. A prisoner of war syndrome: Apathy as a reaction to service stress. Amer. J. Psychiat., 112:998–1003, 1956.

[4] Lifton, R. J. Home by ship: Reaction patterns of American prisoners of war repatriated from North Korea. Amer. J. Psychiat., 110:732–739, 1953–1954.

A locally distinguished lawyer in a large Western city made an appointment for his twenty-year-old son who had decided to drop out of a small but excellent college in the middle of his junior year. The father was willing to underwrite any plan of treatment that was recommended, but this seemed more motivated by professional courtesy than by personal conviction. The patient was a soft-spoken, polite, almost gentle young man who appeared genuinely disturbed about his inability to "get interested in anything worthwhile." His manner throughout the first few interviews would have been called obeisant but for a slight smile, ironical in nature, gently provocative in intent, which constantly played about his mouth as he spoke. The patient first became aware of his difficulties at age 16 during his junior year in high school when he began to feel purposeless and disinterested. Throughout adolescence he had had difficulty in studying, but that year he did little or no work. His parents reacted to this critically, stating he would never get into a "good" college. The patient seemed to feel they were totally unfair and ununderstanding in their criticism, and at best his attitude toward them became one of distant, almost derisive forbearance. This attitude extended into his daily life where he was known among his fellow students as the "most casual guy in town." The patient overtly enjoyed the attention this gained but covertly felt isolated, lonely, and unwanted. During the next four years his attitude changed little. Upon going to college he achieved marginal grades and could not make a career choice. He wanted a professional career in either social work or medicine, but realistic concepts of these fields were vague and uncertain. His social life, while active and seemingly successful, contained little satisfaction. He made a few close male friends, but his relationship with girls was marked by sexual aggressiveness, lack of respect, and distrust of the girls' esteem for him which prevented any real closeness or warmth. The summer preceding his junior year in college he worked in a settlement house in a large city where he was successful with "kids who didn't have much to look forward to." He wanted to continue this work, but his parents insisted that he return to college. He did little or no work that fall and finally decided to leave at midterm.

The patient stated that in his childhood he was known as a happy, contented baby, and grew into an even-tempered but not submissive child. This was in marked contrast to his sister several years his senior, who was aggressive, demanding, and unquestionably bright. She seemed to get her way by temper tantrums; the patient gained his ends by being pleasant. The sister continued this pattern, growing into a temperamental, often quarrelsome girl who openly rebelled and defied the parents. This was evidently permissible only because she was extremely capable scholastically, making honors throughout her school career. The patient always felt her to be a spoiled, unreasonable person and was covertly resentful of the respect and affection accorded her. With his family, however, the patient acted as if it did not matter and denied his own feelings of inadequacy by pretending that he could do as well if he tried. That this denial had not worked in the past as well as the present is illustrated by the following memory. In kindergarten the patient was enrolled in a private school where his sister previously had done well. Because he seemed distant and somewhat lackadaisical in his efforts he was psychologically tested. From this he gained the impression that he was inferior, although actually the tests showed ability to do the work adequately if not brilliantly. His later work improved but never approximated his sister's record.

He consistently believed that although his parents wished him to be successful, if only to protect the family name, they were convinced he would do nothing really well. Another early memory seemed to indicate that this conviction began around four or five. He built a fire in his room one day and asked his mother to call the fire engines. His mother ran upstairs and put out the fire. Instead of becoming angry she chided him for thinking the fire was large enough for fire engines. Although later memories seem to show the mother in a more understanding and sympathetic light, the patient never seemed able to overcome the feeling that his mother could tolerate his failures more easily than she could believe in his success. He saw little of his father during his childhood and felt him to be distant and formidable. As the patient became older he admired his father for the drive and ambition which had led him to become one of the more respected and successful members of his profession. The patient secretly desired to be a man like his father, but continually found himself overshadowed in the family as well as in school by his more aggressive and capable sister. Early in adolescence when he was beginning to express openly the resentment he had carried so long, the patient's father became disabled by vascular disease and was forced to retire from practice. Within a few short months he changed from an active and assertive man into a semi-invalid and often querulous patient. The son then felt unable to fight the father's criticism openly lest he precipitate heart failure, and he became more evasive with his family and indifferent about his future hopes and plans.

Although he seemed disinterested in future accomplishment at home, he continued to be more assertive and aggressive away from home but always in a way that would not attract attention. Soon after the onset of his father's illness, he took up the trumpet and became quite proficient at this. The patient spoke of this interest in personal terms. Through his playing he could express all his feelings of anger and loneliness in a way that was acceptable and well received. Upon first studying the trumpet he made rapid strides, achieving semiprofessional proficiency within three years. In the summer he worked hard at part-time jobs at which he felt capable and adequate. In these jobs he was competitive and aggressive, particularly with superiors, and this was tolerated because of his superior performance. But around 16 three events seemed to precipitate a marked emotional and intellectual withdrawal.

The first of these occurred during the summer between his sophomore and junior years in high school. He was working as an office boy trying to identify himself as a future lawyer. In his work he came across the estate settlement of a former boss of his at a local meat packing plant. This man had been autocratic and critical. He and the patient had clashed frequently. They respected each other, however, for each did his work well. The patient remembered that this man had complained frequently of stomach upset, but that instead of being concerned, this patient had remarked to himself that it was probably a hangover. From the estate papers he learned that this man within a few months had died of carcinoma of the stomach. The patient felt both guilty and frightened when he discovered this.

The second event occurred the same summer. For some time his sister had considered going into law. The patient had hoped she would change her mind and withdraw from competition with him, but that summer she was accepted by one of the better law schools for the coming fall. The patient felt that this by far overshadowed his efforts in the law office and withdrew into discouragement and despair. He still had the trumpet to sustain his self-esteem and he channeled his aggressiveness into acceptable competitiveness, but a third event occurred in his junior year and ended this.

He had done well enough to be considered for captaincy of the band in his junior year and was appointed soloist for the final concert as a prelude to this. During this period he had carefully maintained his air of casualness, much to the irritation of the bandmaster. During a rehearsal when he was studying between trumpet passages, the bandmaster caught him and berated him for his indifference before the band. The patient answered this with a "go to hell" for which the bandmaster knocked the trumpet from his hand. What concerned the patient most was the damage to his new trumpet. After this incident the patient lost the solo part, the captaincy, and the respect of his teacher.

This marked the patient's last efforts at competitiveness and rebellion. The attitude of bland indifference became habitual. He spent less time on his school and college work and more time playing the trumpet professionally. His social life comprised a great deal of "partying" and promiscuous sexual activity with girls socially inferior to him. He dated girls of his own background but would never let himself become involved. Underneath his casual exterior he felt increasingly frightened, frustrated, and empty as he became aware that he had never been successful at anything or in his own words, "I loused up everything I ever tried. It's an old pattern, I guess." He decided to seek help, talked to the dean about his problem, and was advised to seek psychiatric treatment. At the same time he decided to drop out of school because of inability to make definite career plans and a lack of interest in his studies.

This case has been presented in detail because it demonstrates specifically the particular life events which culminated in apathy. Readers without clinical experience in medical psychology might look at the significant events presented here and be tempted to assume a directly causal relationship. For instance, it would be naïve to assume that the fire incident with mother produced the patient's feeling that she thought him inadequate. Rather this recollection must be looked upon as a screen memory, a relatively painless memory of a childhood experience which screens a more painful event. This memory often expresses in an acceptable way a whole series of painful memories, fantasies, and events centering around a specific theme, in this case inadequacy with women.

With the warning about causality firmly in mind let us proceed with a dynamic formulation of this case. The most obvious theme is this young man's constant necessity to present himself as weak and inadequate. This would be more understandable if there were definite past instances of failure due to lack of ability, but what is seen instead is a definite reluctance to allow success to arrive. Whenever success was possible he retreated instead of carrying through. Unwillingness to commit himself to any action which would have a definite end in either success or failure is characteristic of the apathetic patient. Of paramount importance in the genesis of this patient's apathy was his brilliant, aggressive older sister, who by her constant success pre-empted the position of esteem and encouragement usually reserved for the oldest or only son. To exceed or even equal this sister's accomplishment would be a formidable task. Not only did this patient feel that he had to surpass the sister to get his father's love and respect but also that he had to surpass the father to get the mother's respect; and by the same token the affection and acceptance of the woman in the future, the wife, could only be obtained by successfully meeting impossibly difficult challenges later on in life.

Still another patient's reluctance to allow himself any direct commitment to action because of a belief that he would have to surpass past family accomplishment to gain acceptance as a man is demonstrated by the following case:

> An undergraduate presented himself, complaining of profound disinterest and lethargy of about four years' duration. He had had a mediocre record until the present when he found himself in serious academic difficulty with survival doubtful. He stated that he had come to college hoping that finally there would be someone or something that would encourage him to do the great things of which he was capable. He stressed the fact that he had been told repeatedly throughout his life that he had great potential. In the last couple of years, however, he had resorted to a device used in earlier years, namely, that of charm and wit to gain his ends. He prided himself on his ability to manipulate people and was both delighted and chagrined at his ability to hand in papers late without penalty, in getting excuses for make-up exams, and in convincing friends and teachers that he had infinite capability without producing the grades to prove it. Behind all of this, however, was the conviction that he would finally be found out and recognized as inadequate. It was this fear that made him hang back in actual accomplishment. An early memory illustrated this.

When the patient was from three to seven years old, his father was making an enviable combat record in World War II, just as others in the family before him had done in earlier wars. During this time patient, mother, and young brother shared a small apartment. The patient was justly proud of his father and had an image of a strong, powerful fighting man whom he longed to emulate. His mother encouraged him in these ambitions, and he rather fancied himself as her "little man." When he was about six, the patient, younger brother, and mother had to share a room for a short time. The patient wanted to share her bed because he was too big for the crib which had been allotted him. He was filled with rage and disappointment when this was denied him. This was complicated by the return of the "powerful" father within a short time. Not only was the patient replaced as "man of the house" by him, but within a short time mother's affection was further diluted by a pregnancy. Discouraged by the giants of the past and present whose accomplishments seemed far beyond the grasp of a little boy, the patient withdrew from competition by direct effort and instead relied on wit and charm (like mother) to gain his end.

He was seen weekly over a period of 18 months, and in the course of therapy he became convinced of the fact that his apathy was indeed a defense against his fears of being overly aggressive toward men whom he saw as powerful like his father and therefore potentially dangerous. During this time his grades improved, he made a career choice, and he fell in love. As he improved, his latent rage became apparent and did not threaten him. His papers became means of expressing his dissatisfaction with courses, deans, teachers, and the like. In short, he dropped his apathy when aggressive action became no longer threatening.

But why did rebellion fail with the first young man? He, too, had begun to assert his rights, but a series of events discouraged him. The striking thing about two of these events was that a strong man was injured—first father and then the foreman. This was a prominent theme. Men were always pictured as strong, ruthless, cold, and aggressive. In their efforts to "get ahead" they "cut people down" and were therefore hated and lonely. Because of their aggressiveness men were always "under fire," and frequently were injured, like the father, or killed, like the foreman. Thus for this patient manhood was equated with aggression and injury. An outlet for his competitiveness and ambition was found for a time in the trumpet, but this was ended by the final disappointment, the attack of the bandmaster. A solution for this young man would have been to identify with the mother and become a weak, passive, feminine man. While in many ways he seemed ostensibly to do this, he still retained the wish to be a strong man but was unable to be open about this because of fear of hurting or being hurt.

The preceding cases emphasized the most frequently unsettled questions of adolescence, namely, the effects of competitiveness. Most high school students have the picture of a man as being able to challenge and presumably defeat anyone who gets in the way of his rise to success which, of course, should be greater than anyone in the family before him. All the characteristics of phallic male genitality are valued; those of femininity are devalued and unacceptable. Thus he cannot make either choice totally but must first find his limits. Secondary schools seek to aid the student in this task by emphasizing competitiveness in sports, social life, clubs, and so forth where it is "in fun." This means that there has been no harm done by losing or winning. This is also carried over into the classroom where mediocre work will suffice as long as aptitude or potential is higher than actual achievement. Thus it can be rationalized by the student that he can do well if he wants to. This is effective for the secondary school student, but it is not enough in college. Within the first two years the student begins to recognize that "promise" is not rewarded for itself alone. It must be accompanied by performance. Thus aptitude, the scholastic equivalent of the ego ideal, must now begin to approximate achievement, the equivalent of the self-image, thus bringing fantasy and reality closer together.

To act purposefully upon a chosen plan of work without guilt, fear, or loss of self-esteem, the student must in the first place be reasonably comfortable about the effects of aggressiveness and competitiveness, and secondly must have made a realistic appraisal of himself so that what he wants to do and what he can do begin to approximate.

Unfortunately, the latter cannot be achieved until the student begins to discover through competitive action what his limits are. Mastery of aggressive and competitive impulses, therefore, is one of the most formidable tasks of the late adolescent. Equally important is the acceptance of the antithesis of aggressiveness, namely, tenderness, without feeling that this signifies "sissiness," weakness, or inadequacy.

In the first two cases fear of being hurt or the fantasy of having been hurt was most prominent, but in addition there was also the fear that someone would be hurt by the patient's aggressive action. The first boy was frightened that as a result of an argument with him his father would die; the second referred to himself in contact sports, where he was the smallest, as a giant killer. In the apathetic patient the rage that the patient feels at his own helplessness is projected onto the important figures in the family, thus making them more formidable so that action is further inhibited. But in all cases there is still a residual fear that the patient himself either has hurt, or might hurt, someone close to him. It is usually this fear that brings the patient to treatment and then paradoxically may cause him to leave it. This it illustrated by the following case.

A freshman was asked to go to the psychiatric clinic by a dean because of poor grades, cutting classes, and failure to meet physical education requirements. The patient stated he began to lose interest in his studies in his senior year in prep school. He had been sent away to boarding school for preparation for a "name" college by his father, a self-educated executive in a large company, who wished his son to have the "best" education, the success of which the father could measure only by achievement. The patient hated to leave home where he felt secure among friends and family but after much argument acceded to the wishes of his father and the pleas of his mother. Soon after his arrival at school he learned that his mother had had her first attack of a gradually debilitating, ultimately fatal, disease. The patient consciously felt that arguments associated with persuading him to go away to school plus the strain of moving to another city the year before (because of father's promotion to an executive position) were responsible for her illness. Psychological testing showed that this belief covered the more basic belief that something mysterious, probably of a sexually aggressive nature, had been committed against the mother in the past as a result of which she had been injured. Further history revealed that there had been frequent arguments among the five children, between the patient and the mother, and between the mother and the father. Mother frequently complained that the constant argument and "care" of five children was "wearing" her out. The patient made it clear that he shared with the father the responsibility for this injury, but that due to his complete lack of action and argumentativeness he could no longer be held responsible for further injury. He also used the apathetic defense as a means of punishing himself by failing his courses, and punishing his father by failing to satisfy his father's own vicarious pleasure in his son's education.

It should now be clear that apathy has multiple uses as a defense. It protects the patient or those close to him from being hurt; through it the patient lives out the fantasy that he is deficient; and, by masochistic means, it prevents the patient from dealing with the effects of his own aggressiveness. But the fantasies of the apathetic patient are filled with rage and potential destruction. How does this rage remain repressed? Some of it is repressed by projecting the anger onto other men, and there it becomes even more threatening and inhibiting. Some is turned inward and produces guilt at "failure." The rest is turned outward. This is the provocative aspect of apathy. By promising success and then turning near success into failure the young man torments and tantalizes his would-be rescuers, finally reducing them to a state of helplessness approximating that of the patient. The following clinical example clarifies the provocative nature of apathy.

A 21-year-old college junior was referred for therapy because of the conviction that he was intellectually inferior to his friends because something (either heredity or a disease) had impaired his memory. He was a potentially bright, innately warm young man who had long substituted these gifts with uneven, mediocre performance and a defensively reserved manner. Like the first patient he too was aggressive, but only in projects in gunsmithing and automobile mechanics where his considerable talents were well hidden from his outgoing and popular older brother and his eminently successful father with whom he was in passive competition. In therapy he soon worked through his feelings of intellectual inferiority and allowed himself academic success. He social defenses, however, proved more formidable. His innate warmth and compassion seemed to be sensed by fellow students and over his protests he was included in the usual social activities. In contrast, his view of this was that his friends only felt sorry for him; and he would cite their inevitable exasperation that his passivity would ultimately produce as examples of their untrustworthiness. A turning point in therapy, however, began with his insight into the following incident: The patient was playing hockey with friends. The score was close and competitive spirit was high. The patient, however, reacted to this by a completely lackadaisical attitude. When the puck was passed to him, he would make a grossly ineffectual stab at it, miss it, and then slowly, even indolently, skate out of bounds to retrieve it. Quite naturally this soon reduced both sides into railing at the patient for his lack of spirit. The patient, quite predictably, assumed that they were angry and intolerant of his inadequacy. By clarifying this example, the therapist was able to point out how the patient had made both sides feel defeated, and thus was using "passive resistance" as a way of satisfying his own aggressive urges. By rationalizing this into inadequacy he protected himself from seeing the aggressive nature of his action.

The fact that apathy not only protects the patient from the effects of his aggressiveness but also satisfies his own aggressive impulses by reducing those interested in him to helplessness makes it both a blessing and a curse to the therapist. Apathy is a blessing because enough anger is turned outward to remove suicide as a real danger.

This is an important consideration, for these young men are filled with despair and hopelessness and may indeed speak of suicide with seeming seriousness. At this point the patient is both letting the therapist know that he too can be defeated and that he, the patient, wants reassurance that the therapist really cares about him. This is different from the depressed patient who is primarily preoccupied with his own guilt and loss of self-esteem and cannot let himself see the hostile or revengeful aspects of his threat, and the rage, therefore, is inaccessible to immediate interpretation. This is not so with the apathetic patient. This threat is usually a near conscious desire to get even with the therapist (really father as shown by the first case) by reducing him to helplessness. The therapist at this time must help the patient to see the transference aspects of his threat in simple and direct terms, letting the patient know that there might be other ways of handling the rage he understandably feels. The therapist must allow the patient to see that he (the therapist) is concerned that the patient is so uncomfortable and offer to see him promptly when the thought of suicide makes the patient anxious. Then, the therapist is allowing the patient to see that the despair is a part of treatment that will be worked through and, in addition, that the therapist will not react to the patient's hostility by exasperation or withdrawal but by continued interest. Apathy is a curse to the therapist because it is an extraordinarily stubborn defense and will undoubtedly cause strong countertransference feelings of exasperation and helplessness on the part of the therapist. The therapist must recognize these and work through them if therepy is to be successful.

There may be many readers, particularly among psychiatric colleagues, who object to the term apathy being used as a diagnostic category. They might state that the predominant theme is that of depression, as shown by the feeling of emptiness, and the preoccupation with past failures, and that for this reason a diagnosis of neurotic depressive reaction would be more appropriate. Depression is a frequent visitor to the apathetic patient but it is not the predominant affect. Mendelson[5] in a recent article has objected to the indiscriminate use of the term depression to embrace any form of mental illness

---

[5] Mendelson, M. Depression: The use and meaning of the term. Brit. J. Med. Psychol., 32:185–192, 1959.

where retardation, low self-esteem, emptiness, or sadness is out-standing. It would be more precise to restrict the diagnostic term, depression, to describe an affective state where prolonged grief, sad-ness, rage, and guilt are predominant. Whereas these feelings are transiently present in these patients as they are in any adolescent, the word depression does not classically describe the feelings of emptiness, despair, and emotional withdrawal that are more out-standing. Also, these patients in their emptiness are not trying to wrest love from the outside world like depressed patients but, instead, have renounced the outside world as not containing what they need. They have retired from the competitive arena, so to speak, and will return only when love, encouragement, and something to make them feel adequate are furnished. Another reader may object that the with-drawal and paucity of feeling suggest a schizoid disorder, a socially disabling disorder characterized chiefly by passivity, aloofness, and a deep distrust of human warmth because of early and chronically repeated disappointment. None of those patients could be described as having the deep distrust and coldness of a schizoid patient. The passivity and seeming imperturbability of the apathetic patient are defenses against predicted defeat, not character solutions to continued frustration in love relationships. Thus, these patients suggest reserve and caution, not aloofness and complete disbelief. Educational col-leagues may state that the goals of these patients are beyond their capabilities. To me, the problem for the present is that these patients have never allowed themselves to formulate goals; they are committed to nothing. Many will call them underachievers, but a negative defi-nition never adequately forecasts the future. For those who say these students are poor protoplasm or just lazy, this type of approach will cause too many difficulties.

At this point I would like to suggest that the primary clinical picture of apathetic patients is that of adolescence. Not only is ado-lescence a social term but it is also a diagnostic term, representing a variety of defenses and solutions which are more characteristic of this stage of life than any other. The lack of masculine identity, failure to effect separation from parents, vague career plans, and lack of real efforts at forming a mature love relationship with a woman are char-acteristic of this period. Also characteristic of late adolescence is the type of defense used. According to Anna Freud,[6] the defenses of adolescence are chiefly characterized either by total gratification of all instincts or by equally total renunciation. The emotional withdrawal, the lack of competitiveness, the lack of commitment, the inhibition of social activity, and the emptiness are characteristic of the completeness of adolescent withdrawal, and this state is best described by the term apathy. The real diagnostic and descriptive term, therefore would be: apathy prolonging late adolescence because of an unresolved conflict centering around the formation of a masculine identity.

The preceding four cases are representative of other cases seen in a college psychiatric practice. While each of these cases is distinct, the patients have common characteristics which make their identification easier. First of all, they usually present themselves at times of academic stress (exams, term papers, and the like) and at times of decision (definite commitment to field of concentration or to career) or are called in because of deficiencies in these areas. The student usually opens the interview with, "I don't know what has happened but I can't seem to get interested in my work," or "I can't seem to get anything out of my work," or an equivalent statement expressing the idea that something has happened to him whereby he has lost interest in the active pursuit of learning. Secondly, he is usually a freshman, sophomore, or a first semester junior, and almost invariably is male. For reasons which are not completely clear, women usually become depressed, anxious, or agitated rather than apathetic. Lastly, if the student is questioned further, the interviewer will usually find that the disinterest extends into other areas of the student's life. He has either become more seclusive or else busies himself with meaningless social activity. Sports no longer hold a challenge for him, and formal social activities, such as dating, clubs, and parties, have become less gratifying. Frequently, this state will have begun during the last two years of high school. If this is the case, the prognosis for immediate improvement in the college community is questionable. On the other hand, if the disinterest is confined solely to studies, the necessity for an interruption of education is less likely.

After having established the diagnosis of apathy, the educator is

---

[6] Freud, A. The Ego and the Mechanisms of Defense. New York, International Universities Press, 1946.

then confronted with a student who is firmly convinced that something has deprived him of the opportunity for success. Even though he tends to be pessimistic about the educator's ability to set things right again, he nevertheless expects a definite recommendation which will rescue him from his difficulty. Obviously, in a situation that is as psychologically complicated as this, long-term planning must be substituted for immediate action.

It must be remembered that apathy is a normal psychological reaction to expected defeat, humiliation, or deprivation. Examples of this are to be found in prisoner-of-war camps, prisons, and to a large extent in the American public's reaction to the threat of nuclear attacks. In cases such as this when the threat disappears, so does the apathy. The student who becomes apathetic is also reacting to defeat, deprivation, or humiliation, but the threat in these cases is psychological rather than realistic. Thus it cannot be removed by realistic or practical means. Rather the educator should remember that these students feel deprived in regard to the esteem they receive from others and in the self-esteem which is based on accomplishment. They are humiliated and resentful of their inability to complete and seek mastery over these feelings by projecting the blame outward. They are convinced that action or commitment to action leads to injury or that previous injury is responsible for lack of action. In short, these students hold the conviction that action leads to further failure or harm, and they are determined to avoid this. Since the reasons for this belief are based on the past, not the present, immediate reassurance will not have sustained effect. Instead, the student must avail himself of the opportunity to work this out in his own way over a longer period of time.

The educator, therefore, should make clear to the student that what has occurred is not a result of congenital inferiority, laziness, worthlessness, or inability but, on the other hand, represents a period of inactivity which prevents the student from defining his own ability and worth. This encourages the student by introducing the concept that his present state will pass and by recognizing his potential worth but at the same time does not demand the immediate commitment which these patients are unable to make.

These students have constricted the measure of their worth to include only academic achievement. Ancillary accomplishments in athletics, journalistic endeavor, student government, and the like, traditionally as important in American education, are discounted. The apathetic student represents an exaggeration of the widespread belief among present-day college students that the sole measure of success in college education is based on numerical academic achievement. A general debate upon the merits of this is beyond the scope of the clinical or therapeutic approach discussed in this chapter. Specifically, however, emphasis on academic achievement is harmful to the apathetic student. It must be remembered that to these students activity means competitiveness, and competition leads to injury. Competition in the academic area has more tangible and immediate rewards or deprivations in regard to fellow students than the extracurricular areas of the student's life. Admission to graduate schools, selection for preferred jobs, scholarship aid, and so forth are clearly seen as dependent on scholastic rank or as "beating out other students." These students have temporarily retreated from such activity because they temporarily confuse aggressiveness with aggression. In time, however, if given the opportunity to amalgamate his own natural male aggressiveness with his individual expression of feminine tenderness into a more mature definition of his ability, the student will return to the classroom stressing curiosity and originality rather than academic competitiveness.

The educator, therefore, may find it best to refrain from passing judgment on this student's academic average. The potential C student is not prepared to hear that he should be doing average work. He hopes for more and would accept this assessment as confirming his own worst fears. Likewise, the potential honor student undoubtedly knows he should be doing better, and reminding him of this further increases his guilt and resentment. The immediate necessity for these students is the opportunity to define their own ability and expectations under less pressing circumstances. If the apathy is confined to studies alone, often this opportunity can be accomplished by course reduction, make-up exams, or paper extensions. Frequently, also, permission for a change of field is indicated. If the apathy extends back into high school and/or extends into extra-academic areas of a student's life, a leave of absence may become necessary. In such an event the educator should tell the student that this is not yet a failure, merely a temporary interruption, pointing out that a successful educational career does not have to be orderly at all times. At the same time he should make clear to the student that readmission will depend on how much help his time away has been to him not on how much time has passed. Also, that a successful job record and recommendations are fully as important as personal evaluation when the time comes to consider readmission. This tends to limit the student's trend toward inactivity while at the same time allowing him to achieve some success under less pressing circumstances. More often than not, this same explanation should be repeated to the parents so that they do not indulge in what is so often the natural tendency of parents to treat an interruption of education as quitting or as a failure. Psychiatric evaluation and subsequent treatment are often indicated, if such help is available.

Not only is this of great help to the student in making future plans, but it will also be helpful to the college from the standpoint of prognosis and future reassessment. If no such help is immediately available, it can be suggested to the student that if he notes no improvement in six months, psychiatric consultation might be helpful to him. In any event, the educator should not attempt treatment, he should counsel the student in trying to extricate himself from the immediate difficulty by helping him with realistic plans.

While psychiatric evaluation is helpful in all cases of apathy, psychotherapy is not inevitably indicated. As stated before, disinterest is a normal human response to the threat of certain defeat or humiliation; once this crisis is past, the individual resumes his former interest in activity. Thus, the student who is reacting with disinterest to a specific set of circumstances of recent origin may be expected to resume his former efficiency once these have been solved. The apathetic patient, on the other hand, who is reacting with profound, generalized disinterest over a longer period of time to less defined and often obscure circumstances, frequently hangs on to his disinterest until academic indolence results in his withdrawal or severance from college. Many of these patients recover spontaneously in the workaday world. Others do not. Fortunately however, apathy like depression is a state from which there will be eventual recovery. At this point it is not possible to predict with reliability the duration of the state or to estimate with accuracy the extent of the character defect signified by the presence of severe apathy. It does not herald the approach of psychosis but it may herald the approach of neurotic symptoms. Long-term follow-up is needed to evaluate this further. (More is known, however, about the psychological dynamics of this state, but discussion of this sort is helpful only to psychiatrists and will be reserved for later publication.)

Some general comments, however, might be helpful to those undertaking psychotherapy with apathetic adolescents. The psychiatrist must avoid letting the patient make the assumption that he, the psychiatrist, has a gift which will fill the patient's emptiness. This encourages oral passive dependency and makes regression more attractive. Instead, the therapist must continually confront the patient with "What action are you avoiding by lack of action?" This is a confrontation aimed at the competitive active level from which these patients have regressed. Another way to forestall further regression is to insist that the patient pay for part of therapy from savings, earnings, or a loan from parents. Naturally, if he is out of school, a job is a preliminary requirement for therapy. Although the therapist makes clear that he will not encourage or gratify the patient's oral dependent needs, he must be careful not to demand success or competitiveness. This arouses premature fears of injury or humiliation. A beginning in this direction can be made early in treatment by the statement, "It is not pertinent to what we are doing here whether or not you remain in (or return to) college—this is not our task. Rather, it is to help you understand what you want and are able to do. That may or may not include further education." This disengages the psychiatrist from the college administration and from parental goals. In most cases he should also make this clear to the parents whom it is best to see early in treatment. The psychiatrist should be firm and consistent in these early requirements, particularly that regarding a job.

Depression frequently is a cause for concern but is usually not of sufficient depth to require hospitalization because of the threat of suicide. As these patients will become very provocative toward their parents, living away from home is often best. Other than these initial ground rules, therapy will proceed with these patients in the manner predicted by the past history and character structure of the patient. The prognosis is good if the therapist is not impatient, easily provoked, or too ambitious for his patient.

In this chapter the author has tried to point out that among

late adolescents disinterest is either a reaction to realistically impending defeat or a symptom of psychological difficulty centering around
real confusion over the difference between competitiveness and injury,
aggressiveness and aggression. It is not laziness, worthlessness, or
weakness. With proper handling most of these students will resume
their former interest with renewed curiosity and imaginativeness.

9

Drugs and Adolescence:
Use and Abuse

Paul A. Walters, Jr.

It has become popular to speak of the drug problem, whereas what we really mean is the marijuana problem and the LSD problem and the amphetamine problem. In lumping them all together, we fail to recognize that there are very important differences between them. As of the late sixties, the use of marijuana has become commonplace among college students and some urban high school students. In contrast, the use of LSD has remained fairly constant at a level from 5 to 15 percent of young adolescent college students.

The hallucinogenic drug phenomenon was popularized by Doctors Timothy Leary and Richard Alpert in the late 1950s and the early 1960s when they advocated the use of LSD and marijuana to "turn on, tune in, and drop out." Their message was that modern life had become sterile and meaningless and that young people could appreciate and expand the meaning of life and love by the use of "consciousness expanding" drugs. Their message attracted many disaffected young people looking for a quick solution to emptiness, and they became the popular antiheroes of the early sixties. With our growing commitment in the Vietnam war, the political activists became the more popular antiheroes as the decade progressed, and the "hippie revolution" remained the province of a small but constant group of more passively alienated youth.

Marijuana, on the other hand, continued to grow in popularity and may well continue to do so. Surveys done by Blum[1] among five colleges in 1966, and King[2] in an Ivy League college in 1967, showed that 15 to 25 percent had used marijuana. In contrast, by 1968, marijuana usage in a college similar to King's had risen to approximately 66 percent in two independent studies.[3] LSD usage had remained fairly constant.

It is also clear that marijuana use is a general phenomenon among late adolescents and middle adolescents not only in colleges but also in high schools and in the military. In short, marijuana use has become a national phenomenon associated with youth who do not belong to any one category such as hippie, beat, etc., and who from all appearances are leading otherwise "straight" lives. It seems clear to me from this that we must try to understand the use of marijuana as a distinct problem which is only related in some ways to the use of LSD among those who are very alienated and who use marijuana heavily. Furthermore, it seems likely that the use of marijuana does not portend the degeneration of modern youth of the present middle class. It indicates, however, that modern middle-class youth is disillusioned by achievement orientation in American culture and is disaffected by materialism. This was clearly and somewhat whimsically stated by Hunter Thompson[4] in his book *Hell's Angels* when he stated that if Horatio Alger had been born near a field of loco weed, his story would have been different. Years later he'd have been found standing there, saying with a smile on his face, "Don't bug me baby, you'll never know." It seems likely that, in part, marijuana use represents a protest against these issues, as well as against the hypocrisy of the adult generation and the condemnation of a drug about which little is known and whose danger seems to be grossly exaggerated.

The medical and educational community was unprepared for the rapid explosion of drug use among the younger generation. It seems likely that many of us were quick to condemn the younger generation

[1] Blum, J. Students and Drugs. San Francisco, Jossey-Bass, Inc., Publishers, Vol. II, 1969.
[2] King, F. W. Marijuana and LSD use among male college students. Psychiatry, 32:265–276, 1969.
[3] Goethals, G. W., Walters, P. A., Jr., and Pope, H. G. The relationship of drug use to alienation among undergraduates, and Zofnass, P. J. Marijuana use by Harvard seniors. Cambridge Senior Honors Thesis, 1969 (to be published).
[4] Thompson, H. Hell's Angels. New York, Ballantine Books, Inc. 1967.

for the use of drugs which we were not familiar with, while supporting the use of more familiar tranquilizing drugs, some of whose long-term effects are still in question. Furthermore, youth feels we have been too slow to recognize the outright addictive qualities of tobacco and the socially destructive effects of alcohol addiction. In our bafflement, all too frequently we have characterized drug-takers as long-haired, dirty revolutionaries who have rejected outright the whole warp and woof of middle-class American life. What is obvious from this is that drugs have furnished an excuse for condemning young people whose social style many of us are not in agreement with. Drug use represents most clearly the alienation between the young and the old, and each acts as though drugs justify their alienation when drugs are only the symptom of it.

In retrospect, it seems fairly obvious that the rootlessness of the Beat Generation represented by Kerouac in the middle and late fifties was really a prelude to the use of drugs and extreme political activism, but that was not clear at the time. The first response of the caretaking adult community was traditional. We tried to fall back on the traditional ways of thinking, ways which have proved to be ineffective. Our first refuge was that of pharmacology. Marijuana was variously lumped with narcotics and then with the heavy hallucinogens such as LSD. Young people were warned that the use of marijuana leads to the use of addictive narcotics. This tactic was not successful in the early 1960s even though it had gained limited success in the late 1930s when this controversy first began. It was clear to the young people that these two problems were dissimilar. It was equally clear to a number of medical investigators, notably Vaillant[5] that narcotic addiction represents a defense against chronic depression, and that the addict is essentially a depressed and potentially suicidal person. This means that narcotic addiction is a chronic debilitating illness, and is the result of a complicated series of socio-economic, developmental, and character problems. From this I think we can safely conclude that narcotic addiction is a problem for a highly selected group of young individuals who very occasionally may be college students, but in no way is a major

---

[5] Vaillant, G. E. A twelve year study of New York narcotic addicts. II The natural history of a chronic disease. New Eng. J. Med., 275:1282–1288.

danger among the majority of college drug users of this decade. In addition, marijuana is in no way similar to the narcotic drugs since it is
neither addicting nor habituating in most individuals. Pharmacologically,
it seems a relatively safe drug with few side effects, no increase of tolerance, and a considerable latitude of safety in its use.

Marijuana has likewise been inappropriately included in the
same category as the other heavier hallucinogens, such as LSD. Some
of the effects that are part of the LSD experience, such as the added
dimensions of sensory perception and the feeling of timelessness, also
belong to the marijuana experience. But the LSD hallucinogenic experience is more profound, more static, lasts over a longer period of
time, and the feeling of being let down after the use of the drug is
much greater.

It seems to me that youth once again have been caught in a
paradox. From one side, they represent the so-called psychological
generation. It has been said to them that insight into a person's
mental life is of great value, and self-knowledge is equated with
virtue. Furthermore, psychoanalytic doctrine, as interpreted popularly,
promises understanding and acceptance of the protean recesses of
the human experience and an entrée to individual freedom. LSD
allegedly reveals protean recesses by imposing on the individual a varied
emotional and cognitive experience which in some circumstances
may be enlightening, and in others frightening and self-destructive.
Unfortunately, it is difficult to predict which will occur. In any event,
the experience is profound and moving, giving the subject glimpses
into areas of experience only hinted at in his dreams. This is the
paradox. The young person has learned that self-knowledge is good
and LSD is "revealing," but the fact is that, without guidance, LSD
does not furnish the wisdom it promises. The reality it reveals is too
elusive. After exposure to such magic, the young person feels we are
being frankly paternalistic when we say that the use of LSD under
all circumstances is dangerous. We may be, but, danger or no danger,
outgrowing the dependence on magic is one goal of maturity. There
is evidence that LSD causes profound changes in the individual, particularly in the area of reasoning, affect, and goal-oriented behavior.
It is also clear that with some individuals an LSD experience is
profoundly destructive psychologically. For all these reasons, it seems

abundantly clear that we cannot include marijuana and LSD together, and colloquially refer to "the drug problem." *LSD use is a problem. Marijuana use is at this point an unexplained phenomenon.*

To look at drugs strictly from a pharmacological point of view is a very limiting experience for physicians, counselors, and educators. One does need, however, the pharmacological point of reference in discussing drugs. To me, the clearest classification of drug use is a somewhat colloquial one found in Hinckle's article[6], *The Social History of the Hippies.* Drugs here were divided into the "head drugs," such as the hallucinogens or the amphetamines (speed), and into the "body drugs," such as heroin, cocaine, the barbiturates, etc. It seems clear that the aim of those taking the first group was pleasure through heightened, albeit distorted, perception, and those taking the second, oblivion. Marijuana falls within the classification of hallucinogenic drugs but it is a mild hallucinogenic drug.

One of the penalties of the Sputnik revolution has been a very knowledgeable group of young chemists who have quickly become aware that LSD has its dangers and have been looking for more effective and less dangerous drugs. They have come up with a variety of drugs such as synthetic mescaline, psilocybin (which is from the mushroom), DMT, MDA, and TMA, which are similar to LSD 25. Each of these drugs is said to have rather specific effects; for example, MDA increases the empathy and affect while TMA has greater visual effects and at higher doses euphoria turns to hostility and paranoia. What I have tried to indicate in this section on pharmacology is that, first of all, the pharmacology about which we are concerned is that of the hallucinogenic drugs; secondly, the hallucinogenic drugs about which we should be most concerned are LSD, mescaline, psilocybin, MDA, and TMA. Thirdly, marijuana is a mild hallucinogen and as such poses different problems in understanding its widespread use than we encounter when we try to understand use of the heavier hallucinogens by a selected group of more alienated and disaffected youth.

The second traditional bastion upon which we tried to fall back in our attempt to stem the growing use of drugs was limits set by legal

---

6 Hinckle, W. The social history of the hippies. Ramparts, 5:5–26, March 1967.

means. For reasons which have become less and less clear, the treatment of illegal drug use has largely fallen within the province of the
law-enforcing agencies. What is quite clear is that for the most part
this has been an ineffective approach. Narcotic addiction in this
country has been growing and the effectiveness of treatment has not
been at all augmented by having the responsibility relegated to the
court. Furthermore, no effective way has been found to control the
importing of heavy drugs or, indeed, the manufacturing of the
hallucinogenic drugs. As for marijuana, it seems patently absurd to
believe that it can be controlled legally. It is a drug easily grown
in most temperate climates in the world, is easily transported and is
too widely distributed to come under the exclusive control of any one
criminal group, as is the case with the opiates. Furthermore, it is quite
clear that the marijuana laws represent an anachronism. These laws
are unjust. Marijuana use under no circumstances should have been
called a felony. In fact, there is considerable doubt as to whether
users should be prosecuted by the courts at all. Once again a paradox
arises. It is clear that the marijuana user does not deserve the severe
treatment that he can get at the hands of the law. But, on the other
hand, marijuana should not be legalized, since not enough is known
about the long-term effects of chronic use of this drug to be at all
certain that it is a completely safe substance. It is certain that intermittent and occasional use of marijuana is not destructive. Frequent
use, however, results in a "gentle confusion" in which development is
retarded and realistic life goals diffused.

One student put this quite well:

> The old drug problem is as much a spiritual as a medical problem
> (and certainly should never have become a legal problem). . . . Getting
> back to drugs, the area is full of walking drug casualties and every drug
> known to man is readily available on the streets. But I feel no temptation
> to go back to that world again. My decision to stop using drugs wasn't
> made in the spirit of a New Year's resolution, but was more of a quiet
> realization that I had carried the whole drug trip to its logical conclusion
> and that insights on drugs remain just that—insights on drugs. But it's no
> good telling someone to stop taking drugs—the decision must be personal.
> The more intense experiences approach the realm of religion and thus fill
> a great void in the personalities of some of my friends. If anyone tells you
> that grass has no long-term effects, I can see in retrospect that it brings a
> sort of gentle confusion to the mental processes after a period of several
> months of heavy use, but happily this confusion wears off.

Thus, there are many students who become embroiled in a world of gentle confusion for varying periods of time. This is a spiritual world, a world of crisis in ideas rather than in deeds and action. These are young people who fill a void in their life, whether it is a void in a relationship or a void in a meaningful ideal, by experimentation with drugs. They cannot be classified as patients, or diagnosed as "mentally ill," or its more invidious alternative, "emotionally disturbed." Some are confused and looking for spiritual sustenance in a world which they see as alien, hypocritical, and unjust. I think it is to the credit of many of them that they choose a quiet confusion. It is my hope that we could bring to their gentle confusion a quiet wisdom, gained from the teachings of Freud, Sullivan, and other great interpersonal humanists, rather than the moralizing of many approaches to the use of drugs.

I have suggested in this section that all of us were unprepared for the rapid, almost epidemic rise of drug use among adolescents of the middle and late sixties. We have tried the traditional means, namely drug control through medical warning, legal prosecution, and control of imports. These have not been effective. To me, the next step is to try to understand the phenomenon of drug use, particularly marijuana use, as a social phenomenon which says something about the culture of the sixties, and as a developmental problem in that it has particular attractions for young people and therefore seems to be related to their attempts at solutions of certain developmental problems.

To understand the use of drugs is to understand the whole of behavioral psychology in that the habit's origins lie within the fields of social psychology, neuropharmacology, developmental psychology, and clinical psychiatry. Information must be forthcoming from all these fields before this phenomenon is understood fully.

The drug problem has interested me for a number of years as a problem of adolescent development. In the previous edition of *Emotional Problems of the Student*[7], I focussed on apathy as a reaction to "realistically impending defeat or as a symptom of a psychological difficulty centering around real confusion over the

---

[7] Walters, P. A., Jr. Student apathy. *In* Blaine, G. B., Jr., and McArthur, C. C., eds., Emotional Problems of the Student. New York, Appleton-Century-Crofts, 1961, pp. 153–171.

difference between competitiveness and injury, aggressiveness and aggression." My emphasis in that discussion was on impulse control in adolescence and on the defensive aspects of a state which pro-longed late adolescence, delaying the formation of masculine identity by the use of ego constriction and impulse control. Now, over a decade later, I feel this formulation emphasizes too much the impor-tance of defense in adolescent development at the expense of a con-sideration of other adaptive devices that are used in maturation. It seems clearer now that identity formation depends more on the ability to respond to most internal and external demands as opportunities for adaptation. Rather than focussing on drugs as a defensive device against internal problems in an individual, I would rather discuss drug use in relation to areas of adaptation with which it may or may not interfere. Clinical observation leads me to believe that adolescents are attracted to the use of marijuana because of its effects on object relations, on cognition, and finally, its effect on internal structures, namely the self-image and ego ideal. I would like to consider each of these in some detail.

It seems obvious now that the hallucinogenic drug phenomenon was introduced in the 1960s through the popularization in the press of the psychedelic philosophy of Richard Alpert and Timothy Leary. The core of their psychedelic philosophy suggests that Western Man in his technical culture is separate and imprisoned because of his quest for individuality. In a talk given at Haverford College in 1966, Dr. Alpert[8] suggests:

. . . most of us have grown up as reasonably isolated people. Our likelihood of making a genuine contact outside of ourselves, that is, transcending the subject-object barrier, was reasonably slim in 1966 in the United States. One of the fascinating characteristics of the psyche-delic business is that it seems to break through that subject-object barrier. When you feel at one with the universe, it is as if you've taken your chronological self and expanded it until it encompassed the universe.

Here he states that those who are empty and isolated return to an objectless state where fusion in the primitive sense is the goal. Unfortunately, periods of emptiness, isolation, and lack of positive affect are characteristic of all young men and young women, par-

---

[8] Alpert, R. Talk given at Haverford College. Haverford College Horizons, 8:11, 1966.

ticularly at various times in adolescence. Dr. Alpert suggests that the solution to difficulties with object relationships is a return to the concept of fusion, or a solution by the defenses of oral narcissism.

Carstairs[9] has wondered if youth in the United States has become a generation of "lotus eaters" unable to tolerate the stress and unhappiness of modern life. He feels that many young people, rather than viewing unhappiness as an impetus to dealing actively with the outside world, look upon it as something to rid oneself of in passive ways, such as fantasy formation, symptom formation, or retreat into the cognitive analgesia of the hallucinogenic world. During adolescence, temporary retreats are needed and occasional use of marijuana may furnish them. That tactic may be adaptive but, if habitual, it becomes defensive and may lead to general inability or unwillingness to tolerate frustration.

In a penetrating study, Zetzel[10] points out that depression must be mastered by the developing adolescent without undue regression into primitive means of defense. To do this, the adolescent must first accept his inability to modify a painful existing reality, a reality which in adolescence usually involves the recognition of important goals and ambitions which may not be available to him. The second step he must take involves a shift from unadaptive responses to these unobtainable goals to other, available, means of gratification, such as obtainable ambitions or closer intimate relationships. It would seem that the heavier hallucinogenic drugs, particularly LSD, bypass both of these growth tasks through the modification of existing painful reality by the narcissistic means of creating one's own reality.

To most adolescents, the psychedelic philosophy of Alpert[11] and Leary after a time provides an empty tune. A few choose to drop further and further out of straight middle-class society into deeper involvement in drugs in the context of a way of life which is a collective narcissism. The young people who choose this solution are most often those individuals who would be classified as "borderline" personalities by psychiatrists. This category is best defined by Grinker

9 Carstairs, G. M. A land of lotus eaters? Amer. J. Psychiat., 125:1576–1580, 1969.
10 Zetzel, E. R. Depression and the capacity to bear it. In Drives, Affects and Behavior. New York, International Universities Press, Vol. II, 1965.
11 Alpert, op. cit. p. 175.

et al.[12] as individuals whose main affect is anger or protest, who have serious defects in affectional relationships, who have a poorly defined self-identity and whose predominant attitude toward the outside world is that of depressive loneliness and despair. The psychedelic philosophy pays tribute to their anger and gratifies them with a promise of better things to come and the sense of specialness in a group of people unified against the unjustness and deprivations of the modern world. For these people, it can be said that hallucinogenic drugs are adaptive and the psychedelic philosophy sustaining. For most users, however, it is but a temporary way station as a reaction to an insurmountable crisis at one point or another in their development.

Obviously, not all people who use hallucinogenic drugs, particularly marijuana, have serious problems in terms of object relationships. With the new morality, with the so-called sexual revolution, there has been an increasing demand for more and more sexual intimacy at an earlier and earlier age. Many young people are willing to accept the sexual act long before they are able to accept the responsibilities of the sexual relationship. Most young people are struggling not only with isolation and emptiness but also with maintaining object ties in the presence of feelings of ambivalence and competitiveness. Women, during this period, are trying to surmount their fear of loss, with its concomitant absence of security and with its inconsistencies in the level of self-esteem. To many adolescent young men the hallucinogenic drug represents a glorification of the physical aspects of the relationship while it undermines the importance of the commitment and responsibility to the partner. For many adolescent young women, on the other hand, the hallucinogenic drug experience provides an outlet for the emotional love without any sexual anxiety. Many drug groups feel quite certain in their manifestations of love for each other and in their absence of differentiation between members of the group. In this way, individual ties are diluted and the real goal of intimacy, namely a commitment to and responsibility for one other person, is avoided. Thus, for many young people, marijuana can be temporarily adaptive by helping them avoid the responsibility of intimacy through the creation of a seemingly intimate group, in which narcissism is a

---

[12] Grinker, R., Sr., et al. The Borderline Syndrome. New York, Basic Books, Inc., 1968.

unifying aim. If used temporarily, this device is not likely to interfere with the development of object relationships. If used as a solution
to concerns and anxieties about object relationships, it can delay the
process of maturation. If heavier drugs such as LSD are used ha-
bitually in an attempt to solve these problems, they can permanently
impair the development of intimacy as a cornerstone of human security and happiness.

Bieberman[13] has summarized this well in discussing the Alpert-
Leary psychedelic scene. She describes the mushroom people as an
indissoluble family, brave and wise, destined to offer the "kingdoms"
to the believers. Five years later she is lamenting the dissolution of
the movement into a bizarre, popular caricature. The possibility of
trust has been lost: "Do our interpersonal relationships have to be
so shallow and short-lived? Must the movement leaders deliberately
foster distrust between age groups? Do cheating and stealing have to
be the rule among acid dealers?" She ends wondering how Utopia of
1962 was so bad by 1967. A movement is only as permanent as the
ties of its members and LSD fosters shallowness and egoism in relationships.

Kenniston[14] has suggested that there is a group of young people
who use drugs who can best be classified as "seekers." These are young
people who are searching for a deeper meaning to life than is found
in the contemporary values of the traditional middle-class society. This
search is described by a Harvard senior:[15]

> Last year at one point I used it 'too' much to relieve tensions, i.e.,
> I did become slightly psychologically dependent on it. Now I try to use
> it only to get closer to things, not to escape from problems. Some people
> might use it to escape and that's bad. For others it might show them the
> world in a fresh way and that is good. If you like to be high, you will
> continue to smoke. If, in addition, you have some reason not to face
> reality, being stoned most of the time is an easy and self-perpetuating out.
> I found myself in this position for the earlier part of my sophomore year.

These young people are on a philosophical or religious quest.
They illustrate how the idealism of the forties was followed by the

13 Bieberman, L. Cambridge, Bulletin, Psychedelic Information Center, No. 12,
1967.
14 Kenniston, K. Heads and seekers: Student drug users. Speech at Divisional
Meeting of the Amer. Psychiat. Assoc., New York, November 17, 1967.
15 Zofnas, op. cit.

apathy of the fifties and in turn superseded by the discontent of the sixties. Their discontent is both active and passive. The active side of the discontent is a search for new political philosophies and struc' tures which will promise the individuals equal freedom and oppor' tunity. The passive quest is that related to a search for new moral values and religious doctrines which will be of greater meaning than the perceived hypocrisy of the Judeo-Christian doctrine. For these young people, drugs provide an important outlet. Their heroes are found in Aldous Huxley and *The Teachings of Don Juan*.[16]

Here the children of the psychoanalytic era have become stu' dents of the nonrational mind. One student comments nicely in a final examination paper:

In defiance of the predictability of an identity-crisis, drug-taking promises an irrational solution. It is a rebellion against the logical, goal-oriented, achievement-based secondary process thinking which has been constantly demanded throughout a young person's development. Through hallucinogenic drugs, the late adolescent reestablished contact with the childhood self, that self who is creative, omnipotent, narcissistic, and part of a world made for himself, by himself.

It is refuge from the demands for cognitive realism which are con' stantly made in the educational community. If it becomes a temporary refuge, perhaps it is adaptive. But if a drug user attempts a permanent solution through magically oriented hallucinogenic thought as a substitute for reality, and rebels against using thought as a prelude to action, thought becomes for him an end in itself and so is defensive rather than adaptive.

I indicated above that drugs also may have an effect on internal structures, namely the ego ideal and the self-concept. One of the principal goals of late adolescence is a devaluation of the ego ideal in order to allow a closer approximation between that ideal and the self-concept. Most adolescents alternate between the idealization of their abilities, in which they feel omnipotent, with unlimited potential, and a poor self-concept, in which they feel despair and a lack of competence. Many young people pass through adolescence in this affluent society without ever having had to develop competence at

---

[16] Castaneda, C. The Teachings of Don Juan: a Yaqui Way of Knowledge. San Francisco, University of California Press, 1968.

any manual skill or even having to experience work in the day-to-day world taking care of themselves through the sweat of their brow. It is as if with a great many of these young people cognition has been glorified at the expense of competence in the day-to-day world. They feel that competence is based entirely on intellectual accomplishment and so they seek an intellectual solution for the terrors of the realistic world. They are different from the "seekers" in that they are not looking for a philosophical solution; they are looking for a solution whereby their self-esteem can remain high. What is then devaluated, as in the apathetic patient, is the ego ideal. These young people say that achievement is not worth the effort, and they offer a number of rationalizations for this. In other words, internal structure is preserved by alienation from the outside world, and it is the outside world that becomes defective while the inside world is glorified. To maintain this stance, one must expose oneself to new experiences which are not readily explainable or understood. This is accomplished with drugs, particularly LSD, which change reality into a subjective experience where the goal is not communication but rather personal revelation. This represents a triumph of wish-fulfillment over the secondary process and is thus regressive in nature. It substitutes a fantasy of invulnerability for a self-concept based on realistic worth.

With many young men, drug-taking also becomes regressive in nature in that it represents a fear of their own competence and their own great sense of entitlement and specialness. LSD creats a special fantasy in which the person is invulnerable, with special powers which harm no one. This is one of the most frequent statements about drug-taking: that it is a peaceful solution. One can therefore say that for many young people drug use represents a peaceful rebellion against fear of their own aggressive impulses, and as such is adaptive.

If, however, this becomes a total way of dealing with the demands of reality, it can be thought of as defense and finally as symptom formation. As one student said, while under LSD.

I looked at myself in the mirror. I was surprised at how masculine I appeared. Although I felt somewhat childish and weak, I nevertheless seemed to present an aggressive, almost brutish figure. But I returned to the room where the lights were flashing and I felt like a child who was in the process of mastering a toy of which he was afraid.

This young man was caught between a great need of feeling masculine and being frightened by this masculinity, feeling that the child had become a brute and so feared his own impulses. Here drug-taking created a special fantasy in which he was invulnerable but then became frightened of his power. In this instance, drug-taking was a peaceful glimpse of a frightening fantasy which this student was able to integrate, and as such the insight gained by it was adaptive. For someone else, with an ego weakened by crisis, it might not have been so good.

To summarize, the psychedelic experience in many young people represents the preference, either temporary or constant, of wish fulfillment over realistic thought as a means of dealing with reality. To some, the psychedelic experience provides the illusion of intimacy while maintaining separateness and discharging aggressive and sexual impulses inward through fantasy formation. For others, the experience maintains self-esteem by creating a childlike world in which the subject is king of a world made by himself. For still others, the experience represents a narcissistic enlargement of the ego ideal until the young person can construct a new ego ideal more personal and in harmony with his individual aims. If used temporarily, and infrequently, the hallucinogenic drug experience, even that with LSD, can be adaptive for the young person. However, if it is used as an escape from the demands of reality in the push towards maturation, it represents a narcissistic and regressive solution and is antidevelopmental.

In conclusion, I have tried to elucidate the meaning of the drug experience in terms of individual adolescent development. I have tried to treat it from the standpoint of adaptation, and to point out that it is an individual problem, even a symptom, not a disease entity, in most of the youth who are "hung up with drugs." If that is so, a legislative approach will be ineffective. If that is so, it is clear that drug use is a problem belonging to the educational and medical communities. Many of us are unprepared for that challenge because of our misconceptions about "illegal drugs" and our inability to deal with the paradoxes and ambiguities raised by them. It is clear that a great many young people who use drugs have dropped out of the traditional middle-class society. Nonetheless, they do not deserve our censure or our prosecution, only our help, even our wisdom, if we have it.

It is equally clear that there is another group of college students, a majority perhaps, who use marijuana intermittently and socially without any effects at all on their adaptation in college. A recent survey by Goethals, Pope, Zofnass, and Walters[17] suggested that as many as 66 percent of college students have tried marijuana. There was no way to distinguish these users from the nonusers in terms of their grades or their participation in the life of the college community.

What drug use indicates is alienation from the current values by which young people are surrounded. Drug use represents a refuge which is halfway between the narcissism of childhood and the adult's mastery of reality. For many young people, the drug experience is an important prelude to maturation. For others, it represents a prolongation of childhood. All of this does not suggest making hallucinogenic drugs, or even marijuana, legal, but neither does it offer an excuse for the legal prosecution of those young people whose social style of protest is not traditionally middle-class. It is clear that both generations must have tolerance for each other's differing styles of adaptation without the surrender of older values nor subjugation to the new. All of us must participate in all aspects of each other's problems. Moralizing about drugs represents a paternalistic attitude which further alienates already alienated youth. We elders must help them with their fright in a world they never made and not censure them because of it.

---

17 Goethals, Walters, and Pope, op. cit., and Zofnass, op. cit.

10

Problems Connected with Studying

Graham B. Blaine, Jr., AND
Charles C. McArthur

The most frequent complaint with which the college student comes to a psychiatrist or counselor is that of difficulty with studying. If we add to this specific complaint those of tension, anxiety, and depression, which are directly related to obtaining poor grades or fear of doing badly in course work, we find that over 50 percent of the students who come to us fall within the category of study problems of one kind or another. For the most part, these students are "under-achievers," by which we mean students whose actual performance falls considerably below the intellectual potential indicated by College Board scores and tests of innate intelligence.

The severity of the problems which are presented varies all the way from a fairly mild degree of procrastination to what we have come to term "a complete study block." In the latter type of case we find that fairly intensive treatment can be helpful, but even this does not always succeed in breaking up the stubborn pattern of resistance to doing assigned work of any kind—resistance which usually is unconsciously motivated and strongly denied by the student both in his own mind and in his discussions with the therapist. It is a strange paradox that these boys, whose intellectual endowment is high and whose motivation to utilize this endowment seems on the surface to be strong, in actual performance achieve so little. The forces at work in the unconscious which are sabotaging the conscientious efforts of the student are multiple in most cases, but usually one can isolate one or two which predominate. Once these have been delineated and brought to the surface their sabotaging effect is often eliminated or ameliorated and far more effective and productive studying can be accomplished.

It is not always unconscious forces which are preventing the utilization of a strong potential. Sometimes the student is consciously aware of feelings of dislike toward the course he is studying and with full awareness makes a decision to do as little work as possible in order to skim by, or else he has decided that he will enjoy the non-academic pleasures of college until such time as he is forcibly removed from the environment. These obvious "slackers" rarely come to the psychiatric or counseling services for advice. Occasionally, however, they seek a medical excuse for their laziness, hoping for a chance to continue on at the university on the pretense that they are sick and in need of treatment rather than be fired because of conscious lack of effort. These dissimulating students are usually easy to spot, and it is important that we do identify them. The administration of a university is often concerned about the number of excuses which counselors and psychiatrists give on behalf of students. They sometimes feel that physicians defend poor performance on the basis of illness. It is important that the doctor make clear to them that the medical department physician understands the existence of the lazy student, the "goof-off," and the blatant dilettante, and that when they speak of a student being unable to study because of emotional problems, they are careful to distinguish him in their own minds from the one who is consciously making a mockery of education and does not sincerely want to be helped.

There is one cause for academic failure which seems to have both an organic and a psychological origin. This consists of an inability to learn a foreign language and also includes spelling and writing difficulties. Letter and syllable reversals occur, both in speaking and in writing, and ability to spell is shockingly below average for chronological age and grade. There is usually a family history of this disability appearing for many generations back. This provides the strongest evidence for the presence of an organic factor. However, the embarrassment and feeling of inferiority which accompany this disability result in psychological ill-effects which may be severely incapacitating.

It is rare for an individual with specific language disability to pass the admission requirements for college, but it does happen; and this often results in puzzling crises at the time of graduation when a student brilliant in every other field is unable to pass his language requirements. Specific language disability is often associated with confusion about being right-handed or left-handed. Its most important characteristic, however, is that with the proper kind of speech and reading training, it can be successfully treated and significantly improved. The chances of real improvement are much greater if this training is started during the early school years.

A college senior came to the psychiatric service seeking our help in getting him relieved from the language requirement so that he could graduate from college. He gave a history of having had difficulty with spelling and reading in elementary school and of finding it impossible to get a passing grade in any foreign language since his early days in high school.

His family history revealed that he had relatives on both his father's and mother's side who had been poor spellers and had never learned to speak a foreign language. In addition to his spelling difficulties, he had a tendency to make reversals in his letters, writing B's as D's, and also to do some things with his right and others with his left extremity. For instance, he used his right hand when he held a tennis racket or threw a baseball, but he always held his water glass in his left hand when drinking and also used his left hand to unscrew nuts from bolts. In other areas he was ambidextrous. He was a switch batter in baseball, and in the testing of his eyes it was found that neither eye was dominant. In boxing, he had difficulty in putting his left foot forward as he felt strongly inclined to lead with his right and this also confused him in his marching in ROTC exercises.

His first difficulty with languages was in Spanish during his first year in high school. He became so frustrated over his inability to learn the language that he lost his appetite and became nauseated at meal times. He also became seriously depressed and lost twenty pounds. Because of this, he was allowed to discontinue languages in high school and was well until he began taking French in his freshman year at college. At that time he again became depressed and told his tutor, "If I had a gun and the guts, I would shoot myself." He was excused from further language courses until his senior year when he was told that he would have to pass one secondary level course in order to fulfill the special requirement for a degree.

His work in all other courses was excellent as had been his general adjustment in college. He had been an outstanding athlete, the captain of one of the major sport teams, a member of the Student Council, and an enthusiastic participant in many other extracurricular activities. His language problem had been very much on his mind and he had attended summer school in hopes that being able to devote his entire energy to one language course would enable him to pass it. He worked assiduously eight hours a day throughout the summer and again was plagued by nausea and vomiting as well as severe depression. Despite this he continued working but still was unable to obtain a passing grade. Another summer he went abroad in hopes that speaking French in France would help him overcome his difficulty. This, too, was ineffective.

At the time he came to the psychiatric service, he was not in a disturbed state but simply anxious to obtain information about the nature of his difficulty. He stated sincerely that he did not wish any special favors in regard to getting a degree, but because his acceptance into the military service was dependent upon his graduating he felt that he should leave no stone unturned in his attempts to fulfill the requirements.

This boy was sent to a physician specializing in speech and language disturbances and was subjected to a number of special tests. It was found that on the Wechsler-Bellevue his full-scale I.Q. was 127, his Verbal 132, and his Performance 115. On a special reading test (the Nelson Denny Test) his total score was at the 93rd percentile for college students. On the spelling tests, however, his grades were shockingly low. On the Stanford Written Spelling Test and the Lincoln Diagnostic Spelling Test his scores put him at the eighth grade level. These test findings were consistent with the diagnosis of specific language disability. He was immediately started on special speech and language training with the hope that he would be able to take a language course during the summer following the June during which he would have graduated and that his improvement would have been enough by then to enable him to pass the necessary language course.

It is unusual for a boy with this degree of disability to gain admission to college, but when there are as many compensatory factors as are present in this case, it is understandable. Early detection of his difficulty and subsequent treatment would have saved this boy a great deal of unnecessary emotional turmoil.

Often students complain of uncontrollable tension and restlessness coming upon them as soon as they try to study assigned work. As long as they are engaged in less clearly structured activities around the university they feel relaxed and are able to behave in an efficient and productive manner. As soon as they sit down to write a paper or do a reading assignment, however, they become filled with anxiety and have to break off almost before they get started. This severe restlessness is often the result of some anxiety about a pressing problem which is not directly related to the student's academic life. Such things as financial stress, a frustrating or disappointing love affair, or the illness of some close member of the family may be the source of considerable concern to the student, and this concern may be divert- ing his energy and handicapping his powers of concentration to such an extent that he is unable to do any consistent studying. Frequently, he will say that although he recognizes the presence of the "other problem" he is not worrying about it and feels sure that his difficulty in concentration is directly related to the material he is trying to study, or else is a manifestation of a serious emotional disturbance which is crippling his intellectual ability. The therapist, by concen- trating in his discussions with the student on the conflict and the uncertainty which surrounds it, can often help him bring about a resolution of the problem itself or at least express his underlying feelings about it with the result that anxiety is decreased to a point where once again he can study consistently.

A boy was sent by his dean because of a sudden falling off in his grades and demonstrated effort at the time of the midyear examinations in his freshman year. The boy had had a brilliant record in a city high school whose standards were very high.

During the early months of his first year of college he had continued to perform well and his midsemester grades placed him in the upper tenth of the freshman class. Beginning in November, however, his professors had noted that he had begun to cut classes and that he seemed unprepared at the ones which he did attend. Several papers were handed in late and done sloppily. His midyear grades placed him in the lower half of the class. The boy himself was at a loss to explain the deterioration which had occurred in his study habits and willingly came to the psychiatric service in hopes that he could come to some understanding of what had happened to him and why.

When first interviewed this student wished to talk entirely about his difficulties in terms of the courses which he was studying, saying that he felt the work was more difficult than it had been in high school and that the material was presented differently. He felt that this might be contributing to his inability to maintain a good record. Also he was planning to go to medical school and wanted to complete college in three years. He felt that the extra pressure imposed upon him by competing for admission to medical school and the extra courses which he had to take in order to complete his requirements for a degree a year earlier might also have something to do with his problem in studying. When asked if he had any other problems unrelated to his academic work, he stated that some people might consider that he had, but he was able to push them out of his mind and he was sure that he did not worry about them. When pressed further he discussed them in some detail. A most unusual story emerged.

He was the only son of Albanian parents who had come to this coun- try shortly before his birth. His father had managed a restaurant in New

York City and had suddenly died of the complications of alcoholism when the patient was ten, leaving very little money for the family to survive on. The mother, who spoke no English and actually had stirred from her apartment hardly at all during the time she had been in this country, did not wish to seek employment, and the patient, who was strong and mature for his years, worked as a delivery boy for various grocery stores after school and at night helped in the cleaning of office buildings. During the summers he worked full time as a messenger for one of his uncles. (The whole story had a definite Dickensian ring to it!) When it came time for the boy to go to college his mother obtained a factory job which actually was a fairly good one and paid her considerably more than a living wage for herself alone. She did this begrudgingly, however, and with the expression of considerable resentment.

The boy himself felt that he was perfectly justified in going to college, despite the fact that it meant some sacrifice on the part of his mother. His own feeling was that a college education and a medical degree would enable him eventually to support his mother in much better fashion that he would be able to if he went to work immediately after high school. His uncle, however, and other members of his mother's family who were living in this country carried with them the cultural tradition of Albania and impressed upon the boy at every opportunity their feeling that his obligation was to go to work immediately, support his mother, live with her until she died, and remain unmarried. The patient felt inwardly torn between the strong family pressures and those of his American contemporaries to whom such slavish devotion seemed absurd. Natural internal pressures towards independence and self-reliance were also strong.

Therapy allowed this boy to express the feeling surrounding this conflict and to examine and give vent to his strong feelings of resentment against his mother for demanding so much from him. Gradually he was able to feel more completely justified in his own stand. He moved away from home and into one of the freshman dormitories for the last month of his freshman year. His ability to utilize his intellectual powers gradually increased so that at the time of his final examinations he was able to bring his grades up to within a few points of his initial achievement during the fall.

This is a good example of the necessity for looking behind the smoke screen of the immediate presenting complaints to find the anxiety-producing problems in the background. This boy had been so accustomed to pushing aside his feelings of being imposed upon by his mother during all the early years of supporting her that it became exceedingly difficult to see for himself the importance of those feelings when he came to college. The cultural tradition of unswerving loyalty and devotion to one's parents contributed also to his reluctance to allow into consciousness the irritation and annoyance that he felt. These feelings were so strong and so close to the surface that a few months' work with a therapist, who was able to keep the content of the interview focused on the significant area, produced remarkable results. The student needed further support off and on during his college career, but these occasional interviews were more in the nature of direct advice with the therapist functioning as a father surrogate than of the more interpretive and ventilative type necessary at the start.

Few people can work hard at anything if they do not feel that a reward of some kind, whether it be material or emotional, is going to be attained. For many college students emotional reward in the form of appreciation and increased affection from others forms the principal reward for which they are striving. Often, they are not aware of this and feel that they should be satisfied with their own inner feelings of gratification which result from the attainment of good grades. While the proverb, "Virtue is its own reward," may apply to some students, it appears that most require a more tangible and realistic expression of appreciation from those who are important to them.

The student who feels that his parents are so concerned with their own problems that they have no emotion left over to be invested in their child's career tends to develop a feeling that he is working in a vacuum and his own interest in his studies diminishes. Sometimes as simple a thing as geographic separation will contribute to this. A dramatic case came to our attention a few years ago.

A sophomore came to the clinic in an extremely tense and anxious state of mind. He reported that his midyear examinations were to take place in two weeks, and for the past week he had been virtually unable to study. He had been troubled by nightmares and insomnia and was haunted by a feeling of impending disaster which he could not shake despite the fact that he realized it was quite irrational. He had always achieved good marks and never experienced anything similar to this panic at any time previously in his life. So far as he could tell this upsetting state of mind had descended upon him for no reason at all. Because of his mounting anxiety he was seen daily, and early in the treatment it was learned that his parents, who had been living in Arizona for several years, were in the process of moving their home to the East. In the course of the move they had planned to tour the United States, stopping off at various places of interest whenever they wished and staying for as long as they liked. For a period of eight weeks or so, they would be incommunicado for their itinerary was completely unpredictable. The student was unable to write to them or to contact them by telephone. It had been within two days of their leaving Arizona that his symptoms had begun.

Discussion of this as being the possible cause of his anxiety was dismissed by the student as completely impossible.

During the first week of therapy he became progressively more disturbed and began to be delusional. Because of this we contacted his parents with the help of the State Police, and he was able to speak to them on the telephone. Immediately after this conversation with them he began to feel better, his delusions left him, and his anxiety started to decrease. His parents came immediately to visit him and took up residence nearby. The boy experienced no further difficulty during college until late in his senior year. At this time he had applied to several graduate schools and had not been accepted by any of them. Although it was by no means too late to expect an acceptance from one of them, he again became exceedingly anxious and sought help from his former therapist. It was pointed out that the feelings about being unsupported and at loose ends, which had caused him trouble when his parents were traveling, might be in the process of reactivation by the uncertainty and the lack of "acceptance" from the various graduate schools. Some of his symptoms were alleviated, but he remained quite disturbed and unable to concentrate on his studies until acceptance from one of the better schools, to which he had applied, came through. Immediately after this he lost all anxiety and was able to pursue his studies without symptoms.

It is clear from this boy's reaction to the physical remoteness of his parents and the fancied rejection by the graduate schools that he desperately needed a strong and tangible feeling of being appreciated and accepted. Denied these buoying influences, his ability to study deteriorated almost completely.

Another interesting example of this sort of need for support was told to me by the dean of a small college.

A sophomore, who had been doing little or no work during his second year at college, came to see the dean in order to resign from the college. Previously he had been a good student, but during the summer following his freshman year his father had died. The boy had tried to continue to do his studying conscientiously, but he had begun procrastinating and gradually the mountain of work became too great and he had decided to withdraw from college and planned to tour throughout the West, doing odd jobs on the way. The dean told him that it was perfectly all right for him to withdraw and added that he would like very much to hear from the student as he traveled about the country and hoped that he would send postcards back regularly. He offered to write the boy from time to time if he would give him addresses to which mail could be sent. The student showed great surprise at this interest on the dean's part, tears came to his eyes, and he said, "I did not know that you cared that much about me." He left the college that afternoon but traveled only about a hundred miles before he changed his mind and returned. There were some stormy periods between then and the time he graduated, but he never asked to withdraw again.

It seems hard for those who have not worked with upset students to believe that a boy who comes asking for help in overcoming his inability to study might actually want very much to fail. On a conscious level, of course, he wants to do just the opposite, but despite all his efforts to succeed and excel scholastically he finds that he simply cannot put out the effort to achieve passing grades. Some unconscious force must be sabotaging his efforts. Often in the course of therapy the nature of this unconscious force can be brought to the surface and into awareness. It is then that the paradox of "high intelligence and good intentions but no results" can be understood.

There seem to be two main unconscious drives which undermine achievement in students. One of these is an unwillingness to be what someone else wants him to be and instead an insistence on individual performance according to his own personal standards even if this means loosing prestige in everyone's eyes except his own. The second drive is a rebellious one and represents a retaliation against parents who are unconsciously resented.

A freshman was referred to the psychiatric department by the freshman dean because his performance academically had been shockingly bad despite extremely high College Board scores and a brilliant preparatory school record. Many members of the faculty were distressed about him because they sensed from their contacts with him that he was a truly brilliant and outstanding person, but none of them had been able to inspire him to do even the simplest assignments. The student would indicate to each of these teachers that this man alone among all the rest really understood him and could help him out of this despondent paralyzed state, but the more each one of these did for him, the less the student did. He seemed to have learned how to bring attention to himself by disappointing people rather than pleasing them.

During the course of his treatment he revealed that his father was a writer for a well-known magazine and his mother was an executive secretary in a publishing office. He was their only child and they had made great plans for him. His intelligence tests revealed a high aptitude in mathematics and a career in this field had been outlined for him, but since he also had some talent in creative writing they had made plans for him in this field also. His future success in both these fields was constantly talked about when he was at home. He told his therapist that anything which he accomplished was always hailed by his parents as being evidence that he was doing just what they had always expected that he would do. He said that he felt that there was nothing which he could do and feel was his alone. Everything had been preempted from him by his parents and immediately became part of what they had planned for him. The only thing left to him which he could do and feel was his own private performance was to fail miserably.

With boys like this, to whom encouragement and support are only intrusions upon their independence, therapy is seldom effective. In this particular boy's case, even insight into the mechanism which lay behind his work paralysis failed to bring about any change. Later, after more than a year away from college working in a menial and unpleasant job, he decided that he wanted to continue his education for his own reasons and to achieve his own goals.

Students are sometimes driven toward failure as a means of striking out against parents toward whom they may feel, unconsciously, strongly resentful or antagonistic. Some students, who are unwilling or unable to oppose their parents directly through argument or disobedience, may find expression for their suppressed rebellion in the form of academic failure. To many parents, the humiliation and hurt involved in having a child flunk out of school are far greater than any that come from open defiance. This can be unconsciously sensed by a student and his subsequent retaliation may come in this irrational form. It is irrational, of course, because it hurts the student in the long run much more than it does his parents and is not the form of rebellion he would choose of his own free will.

A freshman at a small college came to the psychiatric clinic complaining of a newly acquired need to procrastinate, difficulties in concentration, and an inability to keep himself from cutting classes. The result of this behavior had been a sharp decline in his academic standing. He had been brought up in a very strict, religious home. His father had insisted that there be no smoking, drinking, or card playing in the household and was a man who felt that any kind of fun was wicked. He believed in hard work, both physical and mental, and insisted that his son live up to the kind of standards which he set for himself. The student, thrown into the comparative gaiety and relaxed living of a college environment, felt sorely tempted and also rather out of things because of the difference between his standards and those of his contemporaries.

During his early interviews he talked with high praise about his father, describing him "as the most perfect father a boy could have." As treatment went on, however, he gradually became aware of feelings which had previously been locked up in his unconscious, feelings of antagonism and resentment against his father for insisting that he continue to live according to his rigid standards even though he was away at college where such self-denial was unheard of. He spoke with considerable anger about his father, and as these feelings flowed into consciousness he began studying more efficiently. He never communicated this anger directly to his father, either through letters or later when he returned home. Expressing it in his therapy alone was sufficiently satisfying to allow him to use his powers of concentration again and not be forced to express his antagonism towards his father by doing badly at college.

It is not always possible to limit the expression of repressed antagonism against parents to the therapeutic situation. Often, a good deal of intrafamilial friction has to be endured before there is sufficient release of repressed resentment to break up the pattern of scholastic failure. This kind of friction, however, is usually much better tolerated in the long run than continued failure, and it certainly is far less damaging to the future career of the student himself.

Many students have a deeply set feeling of inferiority which lies just below the surface and which is stubbornly resistant to the assaults of logic. Students who have done exceedingly well on intelligence tests and have been told of the results still may have a feeling of inadequacy. This can be an unconscious feeling which manifests itself only by an unwillingness on the part of the student to make a total effort. Although he may seem to be working very hard, he never does a complete job and his final grades are usually far below his potential achievement level. He seems to need to have an excuse handy at all times should the anticipated failure occur. As long as he can say that he did not try, then no one can accuse him of not having the ability. He prefers to be called lazy rather than stupid. It is often hard to help a student come to grips with these unreasonable feelings of inadequacy and to overcome them. Their origins usually are found in parental attitudes during early childhood which result in a feeling of being innately deficient in some way and less capable than one's contemporaries.

A junior sought help from a college psychiatric clinic because he found himself having increasing difficulty with his work. He was a premedical student and his problems seemed to begin with the courses which he was required to take for admission to medical school. He had had an average record at preparatory school and during his first two years in college, but recently he had begun to put off doing his assignments until the last minute and then to turn in sloppy work. He found it hard to take notes at his lectures and was certain that he was going to fail most of his courses at the time of the midyear examinations.

In the course of therapy it was learned that his father had died when he was ten and that he had two older brothers, both of whom were teachers in universities. The boy himself had a high intelligence and knew it. He was entirely at a loss to explain his present difficulties.

Deeper probing turned up memories of merciless childhood teasing by his father and his brothers. He had been a clumsy child and considerably overweight. He had been ridiculed for both these characteristics as well as being tricked into many situations in which he was made to look stupid or foolish. Shortly after his father's death he determined to become a doctor despite the fact that his brothers tried to discourage him, at first on the basis that he was not sufficiently intelligent and later because they felt the expense of putting him through medical school would be too great for the family to bear.

As the boy talked about these various influences in his background, he was able to call to mind the feelings of weakness and inadequacy which plagued him during those early years. He also gradually came to see that many of these feelings were still present on an unconscious level and that the challenge of actually getting into medical school was very frightening to him. After several months of fairly intensive therapy, which included supportive as well as interpretive treatment, he began to feel a new kind of self-assurance and to take more interest in his studies. Soon he was getting results which were in keeping with his basic intelligence.

Studying is often equated with aggressiveness by students, and those who may have some doubts about their ability to control their destructive impulses may find themselves inhibited as far as studying is concerned. Throwing one's self into writing a paper or absorbing an entire book requires a commitment of energy and an emotional involvement which can be compared with the energy expended in participation in a physical enterprise. For those of us who have confidence in our control mechanisms there is no problem in becoming enthusiastic about almost anything we do, but for people who have fears of losing control, spontaneous or enthusiastic participation feels dangerous.

A student came to the psychiatric service for help in overcoming a "laziness" in regard to school work which had completely paralyzed his study efforts and was now jeopardizing his college career.

The boy's mother was an alcoholic and his father a man who lost his temper violently and frequently. He was constantly at odds with the world, expressing his resentment against his fellow workers, the government, and his family in angry terms. Because of this, his son spent his childhood afraid to express himself in any way for fear that it would bring an explosion from his father. He recalled sitting often at the table with his fists clenched and his eyes closed tightly, holding in his feelings while his father and mother were fighting.

He had no trouble at college until one afternoon in his sophomore year, following a party at which he had become fairly intoxicated. He was trying to open a bottle with an ice pick when a friend of his came up behind him to give some advice. This boy suddenly became furious and turned on him in such a way that the ice pick pierced his chest. His friend was seriously ill as a result but recovered. The boy who had caused the injury was required to withdraw from college for a year because of this incident. When he returned he began having difficulty with his studying.

Early in therapy he was able to see that he had always been afraid of becoming angry in the kind of explosive way which his father did. He said that the ice pick incident had been a demonstration of just this kind of powerful anger. Previously to that his controls had always been good enough to keep him from exploding, but after this episode he had had to exert tighter and tighter control over himself and this had extended into the area of his studying.

Therapy with this young man had to be fairly long-term and intensive. Eventually he was able to get over the fear which he had had of his own impulses and to throw himself into relationships with his contemporaries, athletics, and also his studies.

Boys who are afraid of their aggressive impulses and feel them to be destructive and in danger of getting out of control need help in gaining an understanding of the control mechanisms which are available within the human personality. This gives them reassurance and helps them to trust themselves to a greater extent. They need to gain a greater knowledge of the nature of their impulses. Although they may seem frighteningly powerful, the student must learn that they can be channeled into effective and productive areas without causing pain or destruction to the individual himself or to others.

In addition to the underachiever there is another category of students who present academic problems. They do not have the dogged determination seen in those already described but are students who decide that they are not getting all they should out of college and feel that they would be better off taking a year or two away from study to follow their own pursuits. For many of them this is a difficult decision to make, and they often come or are sent to a psychiatrist or counselor for help in making up their minds. Sometimes it takes a number of interviews and quite an interval of time for it to become clear to them that this is the best course to take. For many it turns out to have been a good decision, and they are grateful for having been helped to make it.

These students have as a distinguishing feature an extreme reluctance to seek or accept any help for the basic problems underlying their academic difficulty. That is why they come to the attention of the psychiatric clinic only when they are on the verge of dropping out of college and often on direct referral from the dean's office or a faculty member. Characteristically, this dropout group has no other sign of difficulty. They are not pranksters; nor do they violate official rules. Often they may appear somewhat isolated and introverted with a paucity of social activity. They frequently have had little hetero-sexual contact. Upon clinical interview they usually relate well, often with the expression of considerable gratitude for the opportunity of discussing their difficulties—an opportunity in the case of many stu-dents which they could not request themselves.

One finds a surprising willingness, almost an eagerness, on the part of these students to accept the university recommendation that they take a leave of absence. So striking is this that one is forced to conclude that they sense their lack of maturity and consciously force the university to grant them the moratorium that their parents' aspir-ations would not allow.

Characteristically these students place a high value on intellectual accomplishment. They come from families of professional or intellec-tual prominence, or from families of low achievement but high aspira-tion for their children. The students themselves have had records of high grades and great promise at high school. They have many ob-sessive-compulsive features in their personalities and are subject to frequent depressive moods. They appear also to suffer considerable anxiety, much of which is not only related to work but also to feel-ings of sexual inadequacy. However, they seem to have a fairly high tolerance for enduring anxiety. They have a rather overambitious set of goals, and it is extremely difficult for them to entertain consciously the possibility of altering them in accordance with their actual ability.

The dropouts as a group ultimately do quite well if properly handled. We attempt to establish a relationship, however brief or tenuous, with these students, not so much to prevent their leaving school, but rather in the hope of giving them some insight into the determinants of their difficulties so that their dropping out can be ultimately converted into a meaningful constructive experience instead of mere failure. Specifically, we attempt to point up the way in which their demands for independence preclude their seeking help from others toward the resolution of their conflicts. It should be emphasized that these students, promising in their prospects, usually go on to do

well in college if given the time and opportunity to solve their problems during a period of time away from academic life.

A 20-year-old freshman was referred to the psychiatric clinic by the
Bureau of Study Counsel. His tutor had referred him to the Bureau when
it had become obvious that his grades were consistently unsatisfactory.
Several of his instructors had previously suggested that he seek assistance,
but he had not done so.

He acknowledged an almost complete inability to study, describing
hours spent at his desk, fiddling, reading magazines, polishing his shoes,
and doing any number of things except study. His first exams had been
most creditable with three B's and one C, but his grades had steadily
declined to the point where he was almost certain to fail out of school.

The patient was the oldest son of a prominent physician in a Midwestern city. His father had attended a small college but had come on
to do his medical work at Harvard. His mother was also a college graduate, active in civic affairs. He had an older sister, married to an architect,
and a younger brother in high school. He had done poorly in junior
high school, having lost considerable time because of repeated respiratory
infections. During his last two years before college, spent at a preparatory
school, he seemed to blossom. He was successful socially, captain of the
school hockey team, and a straight A student his senior year. Harvard
was his first choice and he was very gratified at his admission here. He
planned to take a premedical course.

Almost immediately after his arrival he found himself to be restless.
He roomed with two boys from his home community and found them to
be compatible enough. He had few complaints about the University and
was greatly perplexed as to the source of his study difficulties inasmuch
as he felt his courses were interesting and his instruction good. He had
gone out for hockey but quit because he felt he could not afford the time
away from his studies. Aside from a few dates with a girl he had met at
a college dance, he had little social life. He went to the movies once a
week and played the pinball machine every evening for fifteen minutes
after supper. He attended all his classes but found that he could not
maintain his attention on the material. On one occasion he became so
exasperated at his inability to concentrate that he threw a bottle through
a windowpane. He stated that it looked as though he were going to fail
and there was nothing he could do about it. When it was suggested to him
that his problem was not of an unusual nature and one that was often
helped by therapy at the clinic, he appeared somewhat relieved but
dubious.

The patient was seen at weekly intervals for four weeks. He was
prompt and expressed a desire to come but showed very little concern
at his plight. When it was suggested that he might have some inner need
to fail he responded with interest, venturing the fact that he had felt
compelled to go to Harvard College because his father had been unable
to for financial reasons. Nevertheless, he had often thought of going to
a Midwestern university instead.

His father came to the clinic to discuss his son's position and during this visit spoke to the boy at some length, deflating the exaggerated image his son had obviously held of him and pointing out his own weaknesses and failures, specifically telling of his experiences in having been dependent on others. The patient seemed considerably relieved by this conversation with his father, saying that he now felt closer to him than ever before. He began to be able to work and on one exam did very well. However, his grades were generally so poor that it was suggested to him that he take a leave of absence. He greeted this eagerly, stating that it was almost as though that was what he had wanted all along.

This student was readmitted one year later. He had gone home and spent two months hanging around doing little. Then he obtained a rather responsible job in the laboratory of the local hospital. He saved some money and spent the summer traveling abroad where he developed an interest in architecture.

Upon his return to the University he appeared physically healthier and more robust. He was less certain about his goals, expressing some conflict between medicine and architecture. He arranged a curriculum that would prepare him for either, and after two follow-up visits to the clinic was discharged. His grades have been perfectly satisfactory, though not outstanding, and he has a much more active social life.

The actual number of boys who decide on their own initiative to drop out is considerable. According to a survey made of the class of 1956 at Harvard, it was found that almost 15 percent decided voluntarily to withdraw from college at some time during their four years. It would seem desirable to find some way to predict which students would require this sort of moratorium and screen them out at the time of admission. In hopes of doing this a study was conducted in which the admission questionnaires of 44 men who withdrew from college were matched agains 44 students, picked at random, who completed their four years without interruption. Such factors as College Board scores, previous symptoms of emotional instability, history of divorce or separation in the family, and types of secondary schools attended were carefully compared, and no statistically significant difference was noted between the dropouts and the stayins. It would seem difficult, therefore, by ordinary standards to find a way in which to screen out those who are not ready to complete four years of college.

While studying dropouts, we ran a brief series of them through psychological testing. The dropouts did not show the dramatic Rorschach picture that lay beneath so many student neuroses. Rather, the opposite was the case. The dropouts tended to give barren performances, devoid of feeling. All they wanted was the facts!

Such emotional constriction might explain their dropping out in terms of their lack of ability to get emotionally involved in any activity, including college, or it might possibly have been a result of their being tested just before dropping out, when they had already emotionally shaken the dust of Cambridge from their feet. The latter effect seemed unlikely, since the Rorschach usually taps more enduring aspects of the person, but if it was the cause, our results were mere artifacts. We, therefore, compared a short series of men who were tested in their freshman year and who later dropped out of college with a control group tested in their freshman year who stayed in school. This comparison was run within the cases of the Health Service so that we were comparing dropouts and stayins within the admittedly unhappy subgroup of students.

The striking result was that the stayins gave an average of 50 responses per test while the dropouts gave an average of 30. (This difference is statistically significant with a probability of less than 0.001.) The stayins presented a wide variety of patterns, so many that we were forced to conclude that "almost anyone can stay in," at least anyone who has managed to be admitted. Many stayins displayed the typical agitated neurotic pattern. These records tended to raise the number of responses on stayin tests. The dropouts average of 30 responses per test is not, of course, low by ordinary standards. It is, however, on the low side for people with the intellectual and personal resources usually found in university students. Furthermore, this tendency to be unresponsive was backed up by a tendency to respond in unresponsive ways.

The freshmen who later dropped out also gave emotionally constricted performances. They were not as severely constricted as the boys tested when leaving, which might indicate that a change takes place in the boy himself or in his attitude to the test or in both by the time that his decision to leave crystallizes.

This lack of emotion and dry interest in the facts is an attitude known to psychologists as anti-intraception. These boys who drop out do not see into themselves. In addition, the dropouts do not seem to be able to attach their feelings to any external goal. They are often just happily indifferent; they live self-sufficient lives.

All this is consistent with the experience of Farnsworth and Funkenstein in tracing the fate of dropouts from the Early Admission Program of the Fund for the Advancement of Education.[1] Whenever they talked to roommates of boys in the program who had quit school, they would be told, "Oh yes, I remember him, he was the best roommate I ever had, he was always so sunny!" Flunking never disturbed these boys' sunny natures.

Obviously such imperturbable students can let go of college with a small sense of loss. Apparently they also feel little guilt or sense of failure. They just go.

A theory that suggests itself is that these students' real interests are involved elsewhere. College just may not be "where they live." It is certainly true that they are not devoid of resources. Their behavior at school suggests what is not so, that they are emotional and intellectual ciphers. Where *do* they live?

Sometimes, perhaps, they live at home. It is certainly true that college demands a new self. The role of "college man" may be incompatible with an earlier cherished role in the family or in the home town. Perhaps the gap is too wide to be spanned. Farnsworth and Funkenstein learned, for example, that at state universities one great class of dropout is the boy from a lower-class background who understands only the necessity of learning a trade and to whom the role of "getting an education" is incomprehensible.

More often, however, the clinical and projective test pictures suggest that the boy is more concerned with an urgent growth task of adolescence: getting his place in the universe straight. This task has two halves. One half is the matter of personal identity, to develop an adult self out of the welter of possibilties that present themselves to the postadolescent. This is Erikson's problem of "identity crisis." The other half is defining a cognitive map of the universe so that the self, when devolped, will have a place to stand. This part of the problem generates the adolescent's brooding interest in abstractions and absolutes. God, Communism, creativity, right, wrong, evolution, relativity, and a host of other ideas are somehow personally important to the boy. By sorting them out, he sorts his self out. This aspect of his growth task is little emphasized in psychodynamic literature; psychiatrists and psychologists both often tend to overvalue human relations

[1] They Went to College Early, Evaluation Report Number 2. Published by the Fund for the Advancement of Education, 1957.

and understate the importance of purely cognitive understanding of the nature of things.

By chance, we have had opportunity to observe a dropout from another university at the time of his leaving and subsequently to see something of "where he did live" when, to the authorities of his own school and to his family, he turned the bland, uninvolved face we are so often shown by our own dropouts.

Lonnie was tested a month before he left State. The psychometric picture would have offered little guidance. His I.Q. was more than adequate for State work. His Strong Vocational Interest Blank emphasized the sciences and gave its highest score for Physicist; he was a physics major.

His "official" account of his behavior at State, that is to say, the account he gave readily to all questioners, whether family, deans, or counselors, was, "It wasn't that I couldn't; I just didn't." He said he spent lots of time just mooning, a lot listening to music, but most of his time "just sitting around my room." Occasionally, he bestirred himself enough to play at "some goofy experiments" in physics with his roommate's assistance. And he had read *The Trial* by Kafka. That had been an inchoate but hilltop experience.

As to his leaving school, "It bothers them more than it does me. People ask, 'And what is Lonnie doing now?'; and what can my mother say?" He thought very little and very vaguely about where he would go. He'd like to go back to a summer job just to make some money, but then he would also like to go to Colorado to climb a few mountains.

In his personality test responses he presented himself as a totally constricted person with little awareness of his problems. He felt that others thought little of him. He tended to project his own feelings of inferiority in this way. His Rorschach was an extreme instance of the dropout pattern. He gave only 16 responses. His "experience balance," that is, the ratio of response showing emotions from within to responses showing emotions from without was 0:0. All he had to offer were formal, intellectual responses, reporting accurately on the shapes of the blots. He had a high index of stereotypy and saw all the popular images. He saw no human figures at all. (On one occasion he did go so far as to perceive a "mask.")

In short, Lonnie was the very prototype of the dropout.

In follow-up interviews, we went after information about what he might have been thinking during all those hours he spent mooning in his room. Our hunch, supported by some leads in his Thematic Apperception Test, was that he had no time to think about studies or social life or dates with girls because his mind had prior business elsewhere. It happened that by the time of our follow-up Lonnie had shaken the dust of State from his feet and was immediately relieved of much of his involvement with what had been his problem there. We have suspected that our boys show similar improvement as soon as they leave Harvard but, of course, we cannot document our hunch, since it is part of the psychology of the dropout to be as totally unavailable as he can to his own past. This sense of distance enabled Lonnie to discuss his past thoughts rather more lucidly then he could at the time of testing.

It turned out that he had been fighting the private battle of choosing his *Weltanschauung*. He and his best friend had spent endless hours in bull sessions over the nature of the universe. If they had been able to structure their cosmos, the ancillary, moral issues should have fallen into their corollary places. Of course, the matter did not work out so simply. And so the conversations went round and round. The friend decided to become a social worker, but for Lonnie that solution was not workable. It all seems a little silly to Lonnie now. "I remember telling him fervently how much I admired the courage of his intellectual convictions," he says with a wry face at his former immaturity.

Of course, it turns out to be his own inner perplexity that he has projected onto the cosmos as a screen. To such a nonintraceptive boy, this fact could never become apparent. His projective tests, however, make clear the insistence with which his unconscious demands that he solve the riddle of things. His dream of glory is scientific discovery, hedged enough so that he envisages a scientific hero who "is not making a real brilliant earth-shaking discovery, just something small and slightly significant he's been working on for a while."

Lonnie's been "working on it" for a while, too. He did no college assignments. His mind had business with a higher priority: finding a satisfying philosophy of life.

He tells us his own prognosis in response to a picture on the Thematic Apperception Test.

He is a college student. He woke up real early one morning. He was just thinking. He had just entered a mixed-up stage of his life. He liked to look older, to be alone, to listen to records of good music, and to contemplate various things. He'll lose it all pretty soon. He'll look back on it and think how silly it was.

By means of this story he tells us that the whole problem will be sealed over. He will go on being a constricted person but he will have no higher priority business than daily chores. He will be able to function again.

There seems to be little doubt that for many boys like Lonnie a year away from college, whether it is working at a menial type of job or simply traveling about the country, is maturing and therapeutic. It results in the student's being able to return to college with a different attitude and an ability to apply himself which formerly had been absent. It is hard to describe accurately what happens internally to these individuals, but sometimes the students themselves can put into words better than the physician what has transpired in the interim. A junior who took a year and a half away from academic work described in his application for readmission what his feelings were before, after, and during this moratorium period.

In describing his feelings at the time of withdrawal he writes as follows:

I wanted a general, liberal education, which to me was a chance to study *great* books and discover (or create) and expand upon a coherent, integrated *Weltanschauung*. President Pusey's statement that the end of liberal education is greatness was not a truism to me—it was a meaningful, precise statement which I believed (and still do believe) literally. Because if the end of education is not the same as the end of life, if they do not both "navigate by the great stars," then they are both meaningless.

It was when I began to feel that I was not getting what I wanted from some of my courses that I began to neglect those courses in order to get what I wanted on my own. More specifically, what dissatisfied me with some of the courses I was taking was that there are so many works of literature and science, philosophy and religion, which are indisputably great that one could not hope to gain a very profound mastery of more than a few of them during the four years of college even if one studied nothing else; and to understand all of them as well as I wanted to would require, I knew, living with them for a lifetime. That is why it was so frustrating to have to waste irretrievable time on less inspired authors, simply for a grade, when there was not even enough time for the best.

It was just that once the first compromise had been made, once I felt that I had been working for grades instead of for what I conceived an education to be, and felt a conflict between the two, I ever thereafter dissociated the idea of "courses" and "school" from the idea of "great books" and "education." I began to feel that school was interfering with my education, and I almost felt guilty for reading many of the assigned books.

The biggest problem of all during this period began to be myself, however, when I realized that I was beginning to spend far too little time on the books which I supposedly was neglecting my courses for. One reason for this, I think, was that I was caught in a fairly simple dilemma: I constantly felt so guilty about neglecting to work for grades that I would automatically have an inhibition against reading a "great" book which would have taken time away from courses; but the courses themselves had lost enough of their meaning for me that I often would not pick up the books which they assigned. So I wound up in the middle with nothing.

So the problem became one of choosing between a life of suffering and self-sacrifice and a life of pleasure and self-indulgence; for while the latter had its own obvious attraction, the former had a curiously strong power. But there was no basis on which to make a choice. Both morality and immorality were without rational foundations. If behavior was without rational foundations it was absurd, arbitrary, a matter of whim, completely without significance. Therefore either choice was as valid as the other, since they were both completely arbitrary anyway.

After a year and a half spent working on a railroad in the Far West and reading voraciously of the classics in public libraries throughout the country, he summarizes what he learned as follows:

I realized that my former alternatives had been, by definition, invitations to the *dis*integration of the personality, or at least to the deadening, anesthetizing, of parts of one's sensitivity to life; and I can no longer see any reason for *not* deepening and unfolding your sensitivities to the highest degree possible on all levels of your being.

Whereas last year I had run into a dead end, this year I am at least going in a direction which permits of almost unlimited expansion. Last year I was in a position where there was no answer possible; this year, while there is no single "answer," there is at least the possibility of progressively richer and more fruitful answers."

Not all those who drop out have such a rewarding experience, but most of them return and try again to obtain their degree. According to our survey, 76 of the 160 students from the class of 1956 who withdrew had returned by the spring of 1957. Of these, 60 were in good standing and well on their way toward graduating. These figures would seem to indicate that voluntary withdrawal is both a frequent and a generally valuable occurrence for the individual.

11

Inability to Learn
a Foreign Language

Kenneth T. Dinklage

There are people all over the country who failed to get their college degrees simply because they could not meet the undergraduate language requirement. Though they were good students in all other respects, their repeated efforts to pass elementary foreign language courses were fruitless.

At Harvard University the number of such students from each class has been small but constant over the years. They were heartbreaking cases. Their enjoyment of the whole educational experience was corroded and spoiled. An indeterminate but significant number of dropouts could be attributed to the language problem. The educational and psychological waste caused by the hours of conflict with their language barrier was overwhelming for many students and their anguish was shared by teachers, tutors, deans, and counselors who were trying to help. There are people who have survived this ordeal and gone on to achieve eminence in their careers, even fame; but others seem to be permanently scarred by the humiliation of their experience or embittered by their frustration.

The notion that one cannot be a truly educated man without being accomplished in a second language (or perhaps more) has many powerful arguments to support it. This is not the place to pursue the philosophy behind a language requirement in college, but it is obvious that the study of a second language has purposes beyond its utilitarian function in certain scholarly disciplines. At the very least it seems to make language salient, to sharpen one's awareness of word usage in his native tongue. Particularly with students for whom their own language was never a special object of interest or concern, the study of a second language opens up the process of verbal communication to analysis. The penetration into another culture afforded by the learning of a second language has also been regarded as an essential part of a liberal education. One could develop consensus on a long list of the values of learning a second language. However, when one moves from these generalizations down into the rationale for a college-wide requirement to learn a second language, the reasons are fewer and debate begins.

In spite of mounting numbers of faculty members who question the wisdom of a college-wide foreign language requirement, the policy still holds in most liberal arts colleges. But what to do about those students, otherwise gifted, for whom no amount of hard work seems to enable them to pass muster with regard to the requirement?

At Harvard the policy has varied cyclically. During World War II it was so strict that even a legally blind student who could only see two or three letters of print at a time in the field that a tripod magnifies was not exempted from having to take the reading courses in languages that were then being offered. In the fifties, a humane dean encouraged consideration of hardship cases by the administrative years, Dr. Gaylord Coon noted the history of many students unable to learn languages. Dr. Charles McArthur tested these men with the tools then available, of which the most useful turned out to be the Wechsler-Bellevue Intelligence Scale and the Wechsler Memory Scale. The stigmata that appeared in the clearest "language cases" were concreteness of cognitive process, difficulty with new concepts, and especially new symbolic connections. (The Digit Symbol Test was rich in cues.) Reversals were sometimes seen. The classical Wechsler signs of anxiety often appeared; whether as a cause or an effect of the student's problems could not be discerned. Towards the end of this period Professor Carroll made an early form of his Modern Language Aptitude Test available to us.

Most of the language cases were seen by an outside consultant; this did not work out well. The resulting communication gap, changes of administration and of senior tutors, and a deterioration of face to face conferences between tutors and doctors led to a hardening of the line on the academic requirement.

The line was held until about eight years ago when one or two students who had tried long enough and hard enough and so impressed the administrative board with their superior intelligence that they were granted exemptions from the language requirement. The first such case was that of one of the most literate students ever to go to Harvard. He had published a novel and was generally so gifted academically that it simply made no educational sense to deny him his degree even though his years of trying to pass the required foreign language courses (or test at the required level) had been fruitless. The anguish generated by this student's futile struggle in the context of spectacular success in other educational areas wore down the board's adamant policy stand.

For four or five years after this, one of the essential ingredients to any exemption from the language requirement was that the student had experienced an inordinate amount of trying and failing. It was almost as though a certain "suffering quotient" had to be achieved before the student could become a candidate for a waiver of the language requirement. This is not as cynical as it sounds; granting so few exemptions necessitated no diminution in faculty support of the language requirement. It was felt to be as important as always. The conservative way of knowing whether a student could not, by virtue of some limitation specific to this one subject, meet the requirement was to see him put in great effort and diligence only to fail repeatedly. One student collected six E's in full year courses (two of them were in summer school) before he was finally taken off the hook; not counting these grades he had a B average, which is fantastic considering the fact that each year he spent as much time studying his foreign language as he did on all of his other courses combined. Some weaker students of course could not pull this off; their other subjects suffered to a point where they were lost from the system before a sufficiently self-explanatory record could be compiled.

Once the idea of granting waivers from the requirement was established, there was an obvious need to determine by means other than trial by fire which students had this specific handicap in learning a foreign language. Understanding of the problem began to emerge when detailed educational and life histories of the students were once again taken. Not only did they now have trouble learning foreign languages, most of them had experienced serious difficulties in learning to read English in the early grades. Such problems varied in intensity from those where only a year or two of remedial tutoring had solved the deficiency to cases where the student had not learned to read for any practical purposes until the seventh grade. A number of such students had repeated one of the first three grades in school because of their reading problems; some of these Harvard men had even been labeled as retarded by some perplexed school teachers. (A nonreader might indeed appear so from his score on a group administered I.Q. test.) These men had, however, overcome their reading problem in English by virtue of remedial work, their high intelligence, or simply the effect of years of living and working in the language. Once these students got over the hump, as it were, many of them seemed to compensate for their late start and became voracious readers. Others remained rather plodding readers but their intelligence and diligence still brought them to college. These college students for whom no amount of hard work would yield mastery of a foreign language in spite of their having demonstrated capacities in all other academic areas seemed to have had a similar problem in learning to read their native tongue.

While there is little information in the literature about inability to learn foreign languages, there is a great deal written in the medical, educational, and psychological fields about reading problems. It is not a particularly inviting literature, abounding as it does in a weird variety of diagnostic labels: congenital word-blindness, strephosymbolia, dyslexia (this one comes in three flavors: specific, developmental, and specific developmental), specific reading disability, etc. To make matters worse, there are competing definitions of the problems and wide variation in hypotheses concerning causality, each one propounded with religious fervor and inspiring "cures," some of which seem worse than the "disease." However, when one gets by the most fervently doctrinaire of the writings which try to explain all reading problems by one hypothesis, some sense emerges. There seem to be three main sources of difficulties in learning to read: poor teaching, emotional conflicts in the personality of the student, and constitutional limitations of the student. By focussing upon the inability to learn a

foreign language we can avoid entering the debate between protago-
nists of these various hypotheses about reading. (That debate, by the
way, seems to prove that the territorial imperative operates as strongly
in professional fields as it does in the geographical claims of baboons.)

When one looks at college students failing foreign language
courses who also have had a past reading problem, one finds that most
of them have a cluster of other problems which seem to go together
in the manner of a syndrome. In the beginning of their schooling they
were not only poor readers but poor spellers as well; furthermore, in
contrast to their having overcome the reading problem, they continue
to be atrocious spellers. An instructor in a freshman expository writing course asked such a student if English was his native language.
Another student, when asked if he had any trouble with spelling,
answered, "None at all. I have all my term papers typed by my
father's secretary; she can usually tell what the word is supposed to
be." Others use roommates for proofreaders and of course there are
some slaves to the dictionary who compensate for their limitation by
extraordinary diligence.

The spelling errors are not random but seem to show a tendency
towards reversal of syllables or letters or omission of letters extraneous
to the pronunciation of the word. These students often make gross
reversal errors in reading aloud, reversing word sequences, or reading
a word backwards (such as "was" for "saw") or misperceiving letters
in a mirror-image way ("b" for "d," "p" for "q," etc.) The more
striking reversal errors do not seem to persist into the college years
but are commonly reported by those students with past reading problems to have been a serious problem in their school days.

Another observation about these students is a high frequency of
right-left confusion. They get their right and their left mixed up.
Some will report failing a driver's test because they several times
turned the opposite way from the directions of their examiner. One
very good quarterback frequently wiped out his own backfield when
he ran the opposite way from the play he himself had called.
Mnemonic devices are often used by such students to keep things
straight. ("That's left because I have a ring on my left hand," was
one boy's mnemonic. Another carried the mental picture of his
grammar school classroom, remembering that the flag next to the

windows was to his left.) By college level this problem has usually been solved one way or another although for some it is still bother-some.

There also seems to be manifestation of this cluster of findings in other members of the student's family. The father may have been unable to pass the college language requirement, a younger brother might be repeating third grade because he has not learned to read. A Harvard student who did a senior honors thesis on the subject found evidence of reading disabilities spotted throughout his extended family.[1]

We find that these students unable to learn a foreign language who have this particular cluster of findings (poor reading, poor spelling, tendency to make reversals, right-left confusion, occurrence of the problem elsewhere in the family) have been observed before. This particular form of reading disability is beautifully described by Macdonald Critchley[2] who draws upon findings from a host of in-vestigators: Samuel T. Orton and Katrina de Hirsch are notable contributors. The reader is referred to the books listed at the end of this chapter for good, well-balanced technical discussions of this problem. Critchley calls it developmental dyslexia; more of the American investigators prefer the terms specific reading disability or specific language disability.

This latter designation has a great deal of appeal because of its descriptive clarity, but it is perhaps too general a label for what I believe is only one of several causes for a person to be specifically unable to learn a foreign language. "Dyslexia" would be fine if everyone had read Critchley but the word seems to cause near riots at PTA meetings and endless controversy among professionals. We will use Orton's term strephosymbolia to designate the form of language disability just described. I don't like this large word much, either, but we certainly do not need still another new label for the same cluster of observations.

One other part of the syndrome has not yet been mentioned;

1 Brewer, W. Specific Language Disability: Review of the Literature and Family Study (unpublished). Department of Social Relations, Harvard University, Cambridge, Mass., 1963.
2 Critchley, M. Developmental Dyslexia. London, William Heinemann Medical Books Ltd., 1964.

in a high number of the cases there is evidence of poorly established cerebral dominance. Orton considers this an essential part of the syndrome but there are serious questions about that view, questions which Critchley lucidly discusses. I find that most college students with the other features of strephosymbolia do have some mixed laterality, but not all of them, and there are certainly lots of people with mixed dominance that never have any language problems. The diagnosis of strephosymbolia does not depend upon this factor.

While none of the investigators carry their discussions of this type of language disability on to the matter of learning a foreign language, it is not difficult to see how it might operate. The grammar school student with strephosymbolia eventually overcomes the problem more or less. He speaks the language already, gets remedial help in learning to read it, and of course practices it all the time by total immersion in an English speaking culture. Some students have such a crippling degree of this problem that they never do well enough academically to get to a good college. But those who are very bright or who have a less severe form of the problem or who get very good remedial training may go on to a college that has a foreign language requirement, in which case there is a booby trap waiting for them just when they think they are coming down the academic home stretch.

Some of these students encounter problems with foreign language courses in high school but it is amazing how many go through two or three of these courses learning little but getting wafted along by sympathetic teachers. Some of them get by in high school language courses by feats of memorization, others make up an otherwise failing performance by writing extra papers in English about the country whose language they are studying. At Harvard we encounter students who never got anything but an A in any school course; language teachers in high school sometimes are intimidated by this; they don't want to be the only teacher to spoil the record. The student may feel that he has great difficulty with foreign languages but often his high school record shows no sign of this.

In college this student will almost certainly not be able to pass a high caliber foreign language course. Those handicaps that are part of strephosymbolia will show up again in the learning of a second language and this time the student will not have going for him nearly what he did in his efforts to read English. He does not, of course, start entirely from scratch, but even so, mastering a second language through the medium of an ordinary college course is, for all practical purposes, impossible, if he has the strephosymbolic type of handicap to a significant degree.

The figures that have been accumulated at Harvard on the incidence of such cases probably have little general applicability beyond our particular population of students. We have found somewhere between 1 and 2 percent of a class to have past reading disorders traceable to strephosymbolia and by virtue of this to be unable to pass foreign language courses in college. As alluded to before, the relationship between strephosymbolia and being unable to learn a foreign language under normal classroom conditions, at least to the level required in college, has been thoroughly put to test. Before exemptions were given such students were repeatedly hurled (by themselves as well as by the college) against a brick wall that did not budge. Occasionally one of these students might pass an elementary course on the second or third go around but they could never get through a second year language course.

The identification of this problem made it possible to diagnose students who would, for all practical purposes, be unable to meet the language requirement, but who were otherwise deserving of a college degree. The model for this action was rather like that followed when the medical service of the college would recommend someone for a waiver of the physical training or swimming requirement. A physically crippled student would be exempted. So too would one with the constitutional specific language disability known as strephosymbolia warrant a waiver of the college requirement in the special area of his handicap.

At first these cases were very strictly screened. Not only did the diagnosis of strephosymbolia have to be made but additionally the student had to demonstrate his disability for all to see by trying and failing a course or two. There had to be clear-cut evidence of his having given it the old college try; but if he failed in repeated efforts, and if he had strephosymbolia, he was exempted from the language requirement.

In order to be more quickly responsive to suspected cases of difficulty, and to have consultants available for discussions with teachers and deans, the diagnostic function was taken over by doctors in the University Health Service, especially psychiatrist Gaylord Coon and psychologist Kenneth Dinklage. The strephosymbolia cases were easy to spot and posed little problem either for diagnosis or for the administrative board.

A typical case of this sort was seen when I examined a freshman who had squeaked through the fall term of the elementary German course with a D but was flunking dramatically in the spring term. His teacher at first thought he was simply not working hard enough; how else to explain that he knew some things but not others and was getting hopelessly behind in the class? He seemed so dramatically inept that he stood out like a sore thumb in the group. The notion that he was not working hard enough was bolstered by the fact that he began to cut some classes but when this point was pursued it turned out that he was spending 25 hours a week outside of class on his German and cut the classes he did out of embarrassment over his poor showing. He had been an all A student in his Midwestern public school; and the unaccustomed humiliation of being exposed as an academic failure in front of a group of his peers day in and day out, was more than he could bear.

In my examination of him I found him to be extremely discouraged and perplexed by his performance. He did not want an exemption from the language requirement because he needed the German for graduate school purposes. (He was a chemistry major.) Also he hated to be defeated by a school subject of any kind. His SAT scores were 620 in the Verbal section and 760 on the Math section, and, as we have seen, he had all A's in high school. Besides being desperate about his futile efforts in German, he was worried about his other courses which were suffering from the disproportionate time spent with German. His much anticipated experience at Harvard was turning into a nightmare.

His trouble with German was not altogether unanticipated. He had taken two years of German in high school but he knew he had not really learned much German. The 348 he had scored on the Harvard Placement Exam confirmed this. (This test is comparable to College Board Achievement Tests except that part of it is given orally). He got A's nonetheless in those high school German courses partly because the teacher could not bear to be the only one to break his golden record of all A's and sympathetically allowed him to write a lot of extra credit essays in English (book reviews of Thomas Mann and Herman Hesse in translation). Whenever the class got around to the language *per se* he had had little to show except some diligently memorized rules of grammar and vocabulary lists.

This was not his first difficulty with language, however. He had had considerable difficulty through the first three grades with learning to read and to spell. The school had wanted to hold him back in the second grade but when the school psychologist tested him he was found to have an I.Q. of 135 and it was decided that the trouble lay specifically with reading. He had lots of remedial tutoring on the side and in about three years was sailing along fine. Almost as if to compensate for lost time he became a voracious reader. He nevertheless remained a poor speller. His reading problem had been highlighted by reversal errors, a misreading even of simple words, and even a tendency to inject novel words with no correlate in the text at all into his "reading" of a sentence. He also had atrocious penmanship. All of his difficulties save spelling were surmounted eventually because of his high I.Q. and massive remedial help.

It was also noted in the history taking that he had a younger brother with the same problem. Additionally there was evidence of mixed dominance. Father was right-handed, mother left. My subject was right-handed but his younger brother was left-handed. My subject's left eye was dominant and he reported that he preferred to kick a ball with his left foot. He reported a tendency to mix up his right and left, mentioning anecdotally his difficulty in learning complicated routines when he was a high school cheerleader; once he socked his female partner in the eye when told to spin right and he had spun left with arms outstretched.

This clear-cut case of strephosymbolia was judged worthy of a waiver of the language requirement. If there had been time and facilities for a massive effort in special education aimed at teaching him a second language in spite of this handicap, then he probably could have overcome the difficulty as he had done in learning English. In the absence of such facilities an exemption from the requirement is humane and makes sense educationally.

There were other cases, however, that were not so clear-cut. Until seven or eight years ago there were elementary language courses at Harvard geared strictly to learning to read and write the language; then these were abandoned in favor of the audiolingual method of teaching. The old reading courses were considered by the language departments to be inferior ways of learning a language, as indeed they perhaps were. However, with total reliance on high powered audiolingual courses a door was closed that had been the salvation of a certain group of students. It turned out that there was a fair number of students who could pass a reading course but who could not get to first base with the audiolingual method. This was a more or less separate group from those with strephosymbolia for whom both types of courses were impossible.

This other group did not have a history of an old reading disability; they could spell all right; they did not make reversal errors, have right-left confusion or reading disorders in their family. They could keep up with the written side of learning a language but in the oral and aural part they were completely lost. One such student remarked how much he loved the sound of French, "It is like music—exactly like music. I can't tell the difference between the words. It all just flows together—it's beautiful." Teachers spot these students in class when they give dictations in the language. The student simply has to write down the sentences that the teacher dictates, but even though these sentences may be drawn from the previous night's homework that he studied diligently, he cannot do this simple exercise adequately. Such students are often asked to spend more time in the language laboratory plugged into a tape recorder. They report that this is of little help since they are completely lost once they stop following the book. The problem, upon closer inspection, turns out to be in the specific area of auditory discrimination. They are handicapped in telling the difference between similar but different sounds. Those with strephosymbolia often have this difficulty too, but there seems to be another group for whom the deficit in auditory discrimination is the only observable language problem. For some it exists to such a degree as to constitute a disability specific to the matter of learning a foreign language.

We know that the more familiar one is with anything, the greater one is able to discriminate between small differences. In English these students can discriminate sufficiently well the familiar sounds of their native tongue although even here such students sometimes betray their limitation; however, when it comes to discriminating novel auditory inputs, these men are so seriously handicapped that an audiolingual course is extraordinarily difficult.

Fairly demanding audiolingual courses are given in many secondary schools now. One student reporting on his six years of French courses in private school before coming to Harvard told how he either flunked the course or got a D when he repeated it, except for one summer when he took a French course given in public school by the old reading method and did quite well. There is a placement examination in particular languages given to students once they arrive at Harvard. Part of this is in written form similar to college board achievement tests and the other half is oral. The students with auditory discrimination difficulties do on the written part whatever one would expect from their prior study of the language, but as so many report, they are utterly baffled on the oral part.

There is a related difficulty that would require some systematic research to understand better, but which can be described as poor memory for novel auditory inputs of a symbolic nature. From students' reports of their own difficulties, from teachers who are sensitive clinical observers in the classroom, and from psychological test findings, there seem to be some students in foreign language courses who can remember what they see but not what they hear in the foreign tongue and who have such a tentative hold on the auditory material that they cannot rearrange it in their mind. Teacher, student, and psychologist all find evidence of a sort of auditory scrambling. The student may know all the words involved, could define them on a list, is familiar with the rules of grammar but when the same words are thrown at him too quickly in spoken sentence form or in sentences that are different from the dialogues he memorized, he cannot comprehend. Or if he manages to get the point and tries to respond to the question put to him with a declarative sentence, he is lost; he may inject stray words, sometimes neologisms, or he may simply shuffle the words together in rather random combinations. This is more than just being weak in grammar. The student could handle the exercise fine on paper but not in the oral-aural mode. In extreme cases this can be observed even in his handling of verbal arithmetic problems where he comes up with laughable answers or attacks on the problem even though he can do superior work with numbers given a piece of paper.

Not all students who are significantly handicapped in the area of auditory discrimination have this other problem with memory for auditory symbolic material, but many do. Whether these are discrete problems or only points along some continuum concerned with talent for the oral-aural tasks involved in audiolingual language learning will require further study. Many investigators see these auditory deficiencies as part of the strephosymbolia syndrome, as indeed they seem to be from the perspective of the college years. However, many college students show these limitations and seem to have none of the other features present or past of strephosymbolia. As far as disposition of such cases is concerned, they rate a separate category.

A case combining both of these elements of audiolingual difficulty was that of a boy from a good Eastern prep school who during freshman year at college was referred for evaluation by his French teacher. The teacher observed that while he could do well with written translation he seemed to be hopelessly lost in the oral interchange that constituted the bulk of the classroom work. Except with familiar material he could not seem to differentiate similar French words. His pronunciation did not seem to improve and his comprehension of spoken French did not improve in spite of his considerable study outside of class. He was learning what could be learned from a book, but getting nowhere with the audiolingual techniques that were the backbone of the course.

My examination revealed no reading, spelling, or mixed dominance problems but showed he had encountered his aural problem before, when his three years of French classes in prep school had been taught by the audiolingual method. While an honor student in other subjects he had gotten D's in French and had flunked the second year French course. That summer, however, he had taken at his local municipal college a second level French course taught by the old-fashioned reading approach and had done extremely well. On the basis of this performance, his school allowed him to go on to French 3 where he again floundered badly with the audiolingual approach. This difference between his learning in the two types of courses was also shown by the fact that he had excelled in the traditional Latin courses he took in 7th, 8th, and 9th grade before embarking upon audiolingual French.

He was so worried about his difficulty with the spoken language that he thought there must be something wrong with his hearing. An audiometer test ordered by his physician revealed no hearing loss in any frequency range.

On the Modern Language Aptitude Test he scored well on all but one of the subtests, that which is essentially a test of auditory discrimination. He also showed a marked discrepancy on the two parts of the Harvard Placement Exam in French, i.e., he did well with the written material and "only guessed" on that part of the exam involving spoken French.

With an individually administered intelligence test (Wechsler Adult Intelligence Scale) he did generally outstanding work except that on the arithmetic subtest, which consists of orally administered arithmetic problems to be worked out in one's head, he made some peculiar errors that amounted almost to random scrambling of the ingredients of the problem. This same boy earned a 700 SAT Math score and in our office was doing magnificently on a series of printed arithmetic tests that were much more difficult! The problem was simply that he could not hold symbolic material he had heard long enough in his mind to rearrange it in order to do the problem. His difficulties with verbal arithmetic seemed to be an exact parallel with the problems he had in the classroom which were described by his French teacher.

Through a variety of techniques it became apparent that he had a distinct handicap in the area of auditory discrimination and memory for novel auditory material of a symbolic nature. These findings, coupled with solid evidence of the boy's hard work, and the teacher's observations in class yielded a judgment that as far as audiolingual courses were concerned, he had a specific language disability.

This group raises sticky policy questions. Even where all other major departments have gone to the audiolingual method, Latin courses are still primarily focused upon reading and written translation. For a while, students unable to pass elementary courses in French, German, or Spanish because of this oral-aural difficulty were shunted into Latin and spent a good part of their junior and senior years in this pursuit when all concerned would have preferred that they be focussing upon the subjects relevant to their academic concentration. The Latin teachers were of course not very delighted to have this captured audience; no one was happy about it. What had been a language requirement offering the student a wide range of choice from which he could pick the language he had pursued in the past or a new one relevant to his interests, had for this desperate group, become a Latin requirement simply because of the teaching methods employed.

Another question that this group raises concerns the amount of effort one is going to require to pass an elementary language course. Even if one is very poor at auditory discrimination it is possible to get familiar enough with a new language to make the necessary discriminations. If one had this problem and had had enough high school French he could probably pass an elementary college French course if he put in excessive effort. The effort required in French would hurt his performance in his other subjects and might only yield a D in the course. If he did not have very good instruction in French before coming to college he would probably flunk the course even with compensatory effort. In all likelihood, however, he could pass the course if he repeated it next year. The question for the policy maker is whether this sort of exercise makes any educational sense. It seems that in these instances, holding the student to a requirement designed to improve his education is significantly detracting from it.

The administrative board at Harvard has seen fit to grant exemptions in these cases. Another college faced with this proposition has reinstituted some of the old style reading oriented courses in modern languages, thus allowing themselves to hold all to the language requirement except those with the strephosymbolia type of disorder. There are arguments in favor of having a few such courses in the larger modern language departments quite aside from the matter of the requirement; many students who cannot pass an audiolingual course with any sort of reasonable effort nevertheless want to have a reading knowledge for graduate school purposes. This is obviously a decision that belongs to language departments and faculty committees on educational policy. In the absence of such course offerings, however, it makes good sense educationally to exempt students with this deficiency in auditory discrimination or memory for auditory inputs where their limitation is of such a degree as to constitute a significant disability specific to learning a language by the audiolingual method.

Before turning to a discussion of the university apparatus by which such a policy of exemptions could be administered, some remarks should be made concerning other possible reasons for a specific inability to learn a foreign language. The students who have had years of humiliation in foreign language classes usually react rather emotionally to the experience. It was commonly observed of students long locked in this ordeal that they became nauseous in their language class or simply when thinking about it. A fair number of cases have been accumulated where the student would throw up each morning on his way to language class, usually right outside the building. A considerable variety of anxiety reactions were shown by students engaged in futile efforts to learn a language while getting honor grades in all other subjects or on the other hand, perhaps seeing their excessive effort with language study ruin them academically. It was easy to suspect that their problem might be emotional in origin but psychotherapy never cured them and thorough diagnostic efforts yielded evidence of the type of disabilities outlined above.

A few cases have been found at Harvard, however, where an emotional disorder was the cause rather than effect of the problem. We are talking here only of specific language disabilities, not of general limitations that might also affect language learning. For instance, a student might have such a serious depression that he cannot do any of his schoolwork. That would, of course, not be an exemption case, if the depression was too serious to be treated in the context of going to college one would recommend a leave of absence until such time as he is recovered. Such cases might first come to the attention of the language department because in many other subjects the fact that one is not working does not become apparent in class. Few courses involve daily performance based on daily assignments the way a language class does. It is also possible to get by in lecture courses, particularly in one's own field, on the basis of old knowledge and not have the absence of new learning so immediately apparent.

It is possible to have serious psychological conflicts that are specific to the learning of a foreign language. Only two or three have been found in the hundreds of "language cases" screened in recent years. The cases are too rare to discuss even generally without betraying confidentiality, but suffice it to say that they were cases of very serious emotional disorder specifically explaining why the student could not learn a foreign language even though he had spent many years in the effort and actually had a high aptitude in the area, as measured by the Modern Language Aptitude Test. If these cases had been identified earlier in their college careers, psychotherapy might have solved the problem, but they were caught so late in the game that an exemption was the only thing that made any sense. Such cases would always involve a good deal of judgment concerning their disposition; who would be eligible for an exemption would depend upon how strict the policy was. Even with a fairly hard-line policy there might be an occasional case of a student with psychological conflicts more or less specifically disabling to foreign language learning (specific at least as far as not affecting other courses) who might warrant a waiver of the requirement. Such cases have been rare in my experience.

This focus on new learning of entirely novel material also makes language classes the place where a student with a recent brain injury is sometimes first spotted. A graduate student in the English Department, who spoke two foreign languages, had suffered an injury to his cortex over the summer. Upon his return to school he managed to do well with his literature courses but could not pass his course in Old English. A withdrawal from school was indicated to give him more time for recovery.

Administration of an Exemption Policy

A large Midwestern university recently put up for adoption the following policy statement. It seems particularly clear and appropriate:

A mechanism should be established to identify otherwise competent students who have such a severe language learning disability that they should not be held even to the minimum requirement of foreign language proficiency. Students whose experience reflects such basic psychological or physical disability should be tested and interviewed by appropriate specialists. Recommendations for waiving the requirement should then be acted upon by a college committee which may ask for the advice of staff psychologists, language instructors, or others with special competence in the area.

The principle of exemption should be extended, wherever practical, to admissions procedures (especially preadmission testing) to the end that no student, otherwise admissible, should be denied on the grounds of such a severe disability as that described above.

The procedures for implementation of such a policy will obviously be shaped in large measure by the nature of the college but some guidelines of general relevance can be suggested.

Obviously the understanding and cooperation of the heads of the various language departments in the college will be part of the initial policy construction but that is by no means the end of it. All of the language teachers, particularly those responsible for elementary courses, need to be made familiar with the sort of disabilities that may prevent an otherwise gifted student from learning a foreign language. Without their cooperation, the problem of detection and diagnosis of such cases is much more difficult.

I have found in my talks with language teachers at various colleges that many of these teachers operate on the assumption that anyone able to learn his native tongue can learn a foreign language. This is probably true in the theoretical sense that if one were to give the student with a specific language disability the same amount of time, massive pedagogical effort, and total cultural immersion that it took for him to learn English, he would learn a second language. None of those resources are available to the student trying to learn a second language as only a part of his academic program.

If a really deep commitment were made to the notion that a second language is essential to an educated man it would be possible to teach those with the strephosymbolia type of handicap. This is apparently done in Denmark where several languages are learned by all students. They have special schools for youngsters with specific language disabilities; the staff is trained in specialized techniques and they are able to overcome not only the problems with the native language but also to teach concurrently a couple of foreign languages. Thus the teacher who says that anyone smart enough to learn his native language can learn another language is right; but for handicapped students this will entail allocation of a lot of the college's pedagogical resources to that undertaking and require investment for a while of nearly all of a student's time. Most American colleges do not have these resources to offer the student nor feel that language should be studied to the exclusion of other disciplines.

Another assumption commonly held about the inept language student is that he simply is not trying hard enough. This might in fact be true of some and that is why the cases for exemption must be carefully screened if the requirement is to be administered justly. Assessing negligence requires some knowledge of the student by teachers, deans, advisors, dormitory residents, etc. The time involved in making this assessment is worthwhile, however, if one is not going to rely upon the transcript for a measure of diligence. It might take two or three years of failed courses before the hapless student's effort, conscientious, albeit futile, is demonstrated in his record. It is considerably better to observe the student carefully and listen to what he has to say about his experience. The motivational factor in the equation is rarely an issue with the college student who has a history of strephosymbolia; he made it to where he is by such pluck and diligence that in all likelihood he has more academic motivation and capaicty for hard work than most of his classmates.

A third assumption that language teachers commonly make is that the poor language student is simply stupid. Sometimes this is true but it does not explain the cases with which we are concerned here.

Most resistance to the notion of a specific language disability melts away when one gets down to particular cases. Indeed, language instructors seem to welcome an explanation for their "failures" in teaching. One French teacher in a group to whom I was explaining this problem told what a great relief it was for him to hear about this. He had spent the previous summer teaching French to a group of new State Department people and there were two members of the class who did not get anywhere with the language and were not able to take the jobs for which they were in training. The teacher knew that all members of the group were bright and highly motivated (their jobs depended upon learning French) and he had felt guilty for a year about his "failure" as a teacher. He assumed that college students in a required course who did not learn were not trying hard enough; but he knew these State Department trainees were trying and concluded that he simply was a poor teacher. As the type of difficulties associated with strephosymbolia were described he recalled seeing all the signs in his two failures. What a relief to learn that someone might be unable to develop a specific skill and have it be no one's fault!

Language instructors familiar with this problem can be excellent "case finders." Often the disorder can be apparent in the first two weeks of class; other times it takes longer. The time it will take for the problem to show up in class will be a function of the student's prior training in the language, the degree of his handicap and the observational acumen of the teacher.

Whenever a student is thought by his teacher to have a specific language disability he might be reviewed by the chairman of the department or someone the chairman designates and, if the conclusion remains, a referral can be made to the psychologist or other professional responsible for making a thorough diagnostic evaluation. A battery of psychological tests can furnish diagnostic data in conjunction with a careful history taking and educational review. If warranted, the diagnostician can communicate his relevant findings and recommendations to the appropriate administrative committee. If a waiver of the requirement is not thought to be justified perhaps recommendations can be made to the student, his teacher, or advisors to help with whatever the problem seems to be.

This method of finding students with a specific language disability has the great advantage of collecting as part of the diagnostic process a significant sample of the student's functioning in the classroom. Discerning the presence or absence of some degree of language disability is easy, but assessing whether or not it is of a degree that prohibits the student from meeting the language requirement is not so easy except in the clear-cut instances of strephosymbolia. Those with only a deficit in auditory discrimination and memory for symbolic auditory material are harder to assess concerning degree of disability without benefit of a closely observed "trial run" as it were. The diagnostician is on increasingly shaky ground the less of a "track record" he has to go on.

Nevertheless there are strong arguments for trying to spot those who are specifically disabled in regard to language learning before they waste a semester or two in a course.

To meet this need at Harvard, the Office of Tests administers the Carroll-Sapon Modern Language Aptitude Test[3] to all freshmen who score below a certain level on their placement exam in a foreign language. A brief questionnaire administered with the MLAT allows students to notify us of past reading or foreign language difficulties. All of this takes place as part of the massive testing and sectioning process that makes Freshman week the horrendous proposition it is at most colleges. Machine scoring techniques and utilization of computers speed the process to allow for a contingency testing program. Another school that had no prior data in this area might simply have to give the MLAT to the entire class.

Actually, a fairly detailed questionnaire might do this screening job just as well. It might not be a bad idea to send such a questionnaire to the student's home before he arrives and allow his parents who may be more aware of early school difficulties to participate in answering it.

Whatever procedure is followed, the yield will simply be a number of suspected cases who then should be seen individually by the diagnostician for an evaluation. It is quite important that whoever does this evaluation have a good feel for the degree of stringency in the exemption policy. Will only those with the strephosymbolia type of problem be exempted? How much compensatory effort will be required of those with a deficit in the audiolingual area? What if one of these latter students could pass an elementary language course because of his four years of prior study but in all likelihood could not pass a second level course? The diagnostician needs a fair amount of exposure to these cases before he can make accurate appraisals of degree of disability, but if he is to be used for screening purposes he needs to have a very clear idea of what he is trying to predict.

---

[3] Carroll, J. B., and Sapon, S. M. Modern Language Aptitude Test. New York, The Psychological Corporation, 1959.

The policy makers define the target. In short, there needs to be quite sensitive and particularistic communication between the diagnostician and the administrative committee. The decision regarding the exemption belongs to the committee but if the diagnostician does not understand all the parameters of the decision he does not know fully what to assess or how to make his findings relevant to the issues.

As difficult as the procedure is for finding candidates for exemption before college begins, before they fall out naturally from the educational process, it is perhaps an effort worth making. The advantage of a very tight screening process afforded by the amassing of classroom evidence of a disability is perhaps offset by the cost of this method to the student (financially, educationally, and emotionally), to his language instructor, and the others in his language class.

The granting of waivers of the language requirement to those with a specific language disability does represent a retreat from the sanctity of the requirement. A hard-liner could still say that students with a disability in this area should go to a college that has no language requirement. Such a position, however, will deny to that college the student who they would on all other grounds have invited to their campus. Among these rejects would be some of the most gifted and creative students to come through the doors of any university. Actually, a sensible and humanely administered exemption policy can operate to preserve the undergraduate language requirement by avoiding the faculty and student antagonism engendered by the frustrating, wasteful, and agonizing consequences of a rigid rule.

BIBLIOGRAPHY

The books listed below contain excellent reviews of the literature on reading disabilities with exhaustive references and are themselves good primary sources. The Natchez book contains 44 articles by different writers. None of these authors, however, address themselves to difficulties in learning a second language.

Critchley, M. *Developmental Dyslexia.* London, William Heinemann Medical Books Ltd., 1964.

Natchez, G., ed. *Children with Reading Problems.* New York, Basic Books, Inc., 1968.

Thompson, L. J. *Reading Disability.* Springfield, Ill., Charles C Thomas, Publisher, 1966.

Vernon, M. D. *Backwardness in Reading. A Study of its Nature and Origin.* Cambridge, Cambridge University Press, 1957.

12

The Text is the
Adversary

Roderic C. Hodgins

A student walking through Harvard Yard in the autumn of his freshman year can hardly overlook Widener Library, standing like a fortress in the middle of his apprehensions. If learning is a battle to be won, surely this is the ultimate stronghold of the enemy. It is garrisoned by some two million books, many of them worthy opponents for the stoutest-hearted student.

If, unhinged by the magnitude of this challenge, the student decided to read them all, he would do well to prepare himself by taking a course in speed reading. If he does, and learns to read at the rate of six thousand words per minute, reads sixteen hours a day, takes neither holidays nor coffee breaks, he might expect to finish his colossal task in a bit more than a hundred years.

The siege of a library, even a small one, is likely to be long and bitter. Frontal assault is even more hopeless than the figures above suggest. Widener is growing at a rate which will double its size in a generation, and many of its books are written in Old Church Slavonic, or bristle with mathematical notation. Nor is the task of the student merely to read the books, but to understand, criticize, compare, and put to use the ideas in them. The idea of attacking a body of knowledge by speeding up one's reading leads quickly to a quantitative fallacy. Nevertheless, the idea has its attractions.

Reading is the scholar's most basic skill. The scope of human learning insures that it can never be done well enough. For that reason, for more than a quarter of a century, Harvard has offered a course for the improvement of students' reading under the auspices of the Bureau of Study Counsel, an office which is part of the regular advisory program of the faculty. The aim of this course is to teach students who are already superior readers[1] how to apply their skills and courage to the task of learning at Harvard. The course is ungraded and does not receive academic credit. Each year it is taken by some six hundred students, mostly freshmen, with an admixture of upperclassmen, graduate students, and occasional faculty members.

Serious attempts at this kind of instruction began in 1938 when the Harvard faculty noted with some irritation that not all undergraduates read as skillfully as they should. When irritated, Harvard imitates the oyster. Around the original irritation, successive instructors at Harvard (of whom the writer was one) have deposited layers of something, not necessarily pearl, to keep the irritation tolerable, and the ideas of the course have grown by a process of accretion. The approach of each instructor will be determined by the location and intensity of the irritation as he feels it, and as the remarks of his students help him to refine his perception. A historical cross section through the course reveals what different instructors seem to have thought important at various stages of its development.

In 1938, Walter F. Dearborn, professor at Harvard's Graduate School of Education, developed the first set of Harvard Reading Films, which showed the reader a page of text in a series of jumps, in mimickry of the action of the eye. After a student had read one of these films, he was given a comprehension check, and then a "transfer selection" to read. This was a short essay in printed form, presented in the hope that students would transfer their skills from the movie screen onto the printed page. Students would be quizzed on their comprehension of this "transfer selection" by a short multiple-choice test.

---

[1] If we use the Scholastic Aptitude Tests, verbal section, a splendid measure of reading ability, the average student accepted at Harvard is in the 99th percentile of high school seniors in the United States.

The original ideas were far from perfect, but they did serve a valuable purpose, and a "remedial" course making use of them was offered every year to some thirty student volunteers who had been identified through tests as the thirty least able readers in the Harvard freshman class.

In 1946, the original materials of the course, films, "transfer selections," etc., had been worn to tatters, and the Bureau of Study Counsel took over its instruction. When William G. Perry, Jr. and Charles Whitlock took charge of the thirty lost souls who had been identified as the uttermost dregs of reading ability in Harvard's freshman class, they found that every one of them could score better on a standardized test of reading than 85 percent of the college freshmen in the country. This threw grave doubts on the "remedial" nature of the course and the entire emphasis was shifted from the polishing of bricks to the gilding of lilies. New reading films and "transfer selections" were produced at a higher level of difficulty. The doors of a new course were opened and 800 students crowded in, including 400 freshmen, 150 upperclassmen, 230 graduate students, and 2 professors—from the Law School.

By this time, it had become increasingly clear that the original emphasis of the course was not nearly broad enough. To be sure, students needed to increase speed, but speed in reading, as in war, is primarily defensive, to prevent a quick encirclement and defeat of the student at exam time. Taking the offensive requires that the student have a notion of the rules of the contest and of the adversary's favorite strategems and weak points. The adversary here, of course, is the subject matter, not the professor, although confusion on this point is common.

To supplement the tactical virtue of speed with strategic planning of longer-term objectives has been a major effort for instructors of the reading course since 1948. This goal has had many consequences. Among them was the construction of a reading test for incoming freshmen which attempts to discover how many of fifteen hundred extremely bright young people will look at the end of a lengthy and tedious chapter of history to discover a paragraph headed "Recapitulation" which gives the whole weary game away in a dozen sentences. Each year, less than 10 percent of them do. To the other 90 percent of the incoming class, the test is used to suggest that such use of one's wits is appropriate in reading done around Harvard Yard.

Since 1948, the instructor of the Harvard Reading Course has always been a trained counselor at the Bureau of Study Counsel. He will need all of his training, for the problems his students will experience in the course will be subtle and sometimes painful to them, and he will spend a great deal of his time outside the classroom listening as they try to make sense of what the reading process means to them. The approach of each instructor will be modified in both classroom and consultation hour as the remarks of his students help him to refine his perception of their difficulties, and his own.

In a time when great stress is placed on sheer speed of reading, the student and teacher will need to consider this variable, though it is not necessarily the one of paramount importance. Some figures follow on this dimension, although, for reasons to be discussed, they should be taken with a grain of salt.

On the average, students entering the Harvard Reading Course read at a speed of about 275 words per minute, with about 70 percent comprehension of what they have read. After the course, the class average will usually be somewhere over 700 words per minute, with the same scores on comprehension tests. This comes to the same comprehension in less than half the time. These figures, to be sure, are only averages. Some students have achieved factor-of-ten speed increases while improving their comprehension. Others have protested that the course damaged their reading and have been able to produce test scores to prove it. Fortunately, these have been few.

If these figures seem low in comparison to the claim often made about speed reading, it should be remembered that "words per minute" is incomplete by itself as a measure of speed. Words per minute of *what*? Nor can speed be divorced from comprehension. Should a Harvard student say "I read *War and Peace* this morning. It was about Russia," he will find the laughter of his instructor appropriately hollow.

Some books are appropriately read at six thousand words per minute, perhaps by holding their pages to a strong light so that both sides can be scanned simultaneously. Any book the reader feels is worthless should be read faster still—by dropping it in the wastebasket. Such a decision cannot be made lightly, especially where the book has been "assigned"—but "assignment" of a book represents the teacher's assessment of the worth of the book to the class as a whole. An individual student may obtain more benefit from using his time to read something else.

Further considerations affecting the speed of reading, such as the reader's I.Q., his previous knowledge of the subject matter and his interest in it, make quantitative measures of reading speed next to meaningless without a great deal of supplementary information.

If measurement of speed reading in words per minute is misleading, the measurement of comprehension as "number right" on a multiple-choice comprehension test is not much more satisfactory. Consider a multiple-choice test of ten items, each with four alternative answers. A group of students guessing at random should average a score of 2.5 having read neither the material nor the questions. If we let the student read the questions but not the material, the student may be able to score 80 percent on the basis of prior information, test sophistication, and the use of his wits. Finding a test's true "zero point" is therefore difficult to do for a group to obtain norms for the test, and impossible to do for an individual, for showing a student a test on material before he reads it "spoils" his naïveté. (Note: This type of "spoiling" forms a central part of the instruction of the reading course. See, for example, the section on exam-taking.)

Measurement of comprehension by multiple-choice tests has two further drawbacks. First, this type of measurement may encourage the student to think that the teacher wants him to obtain objectively measurable "facts" from his reading, which is often not the teacher's intent. Second, such measurement leads the student to suppose that speed and comprehension are separate variables, whereas the whole idea is speed *of* comprehension.

Both "words per minute" and "number right" are used in the Harvard Reading Course, but are presented to the class as first approximations only, to be viewed with grave suspicion. At the level of reading skill in the Harvard population, the best criteria are probably the subjective impressions of the reader himself, which do not lend themselves to expression in numbers. A measure of comprehension which students are encouraged to adopt at the present time is a brief summary written by the reader, which he can compare with summaries prepared by the instructor. The loss in quantitative precision with this method is compensated for by its qualitative advantage of requiring active thought, not passive response, in understanding what was read.

To abandon numerical measures of reading capacity is to step into deep waters, but the step is eventually necessary for the reading instructor at Harvard and for his students. For both parties, it requires consideration of a great deal more than the mechanics of reading, and involves consideration of the reader as a person with purposes of his own. A book, any book, may be read by students with wildly differing intents: to pass a course, to pass the time, to form a new and more complex view of the universe, to justify one's actions, to serve as an ornament for a cocktail party, to solve a problem. Each of these intentions will produce a different mode of reading in the student, and the appropriateness of this mode, or the inappropriateness, is a complex thing. Dissatisfaction arises in a student when his intentions are thwarted by his methods. If the student, in all his complexity, brings his discontent to an instructor in hopes of an off-the-rack solution, his chances for satisfaction are small. In the very nature of things, the most effective solutions must arise from the student himself.

Wherever he comes from, the freshman at Harvard is likely to be jarred by the challenges he faces here. Even if he has been a "good" reader in his previous academic experience, the change in the quantity of reading is nowhere near as shocking as the change in the quality and direction required. What was formerly a "good" strategy of reading is now not simply inefficient—it is obsolescent and off the point. Reading to discover the dates of the major battles of the Civil War is an entirely different matter from reading in order to discover how the leaders of the 1860s were acting on social principles which still may not be wholly clear. Discontent with the inapplicability of old techniques to new problems is no new notion to the psychologist working with college students, nor is the idea that nonneurotic students may need help with it.

In this sense, the resemblance of reading instruction at the college level to counseling is strong. Introspection must be encouraged and supported by the teacher. The student, who is attempting to modify his basic assumptions, will inevitably experience anxiety. Few direct suggestions can be made with profit by the teacher, for, as in therapy, they can be followed in minute detail, only to backfire. The verb "to teach" in reading, does not seem to take a direct object. One does not so much instruct as make learning possible (hopefully) by providing students with material on which to practice, urging them to be high-hearted, and getting the hell out of their way. Perhaps the most useful thing the instructor can do is to consider with them the proper uses of reading at college. When the student finds the classroom experience in the reading course inadequate by itself, he may wish to consult his instructor-counselor at the Bureau of Study Counsel.

Parallels to psychotherapy in reading instruction can also be misleading: for one thing, there is rarely anything pathological in the reading processes of Harvard students. By any usual measure, they are superb readers. They are well-motivated, although sometimes a bit desperate about their work, and they usually approach dissatisfaction with their reading with sanity and good humor. Nevertheless, the anxiety involved in changing reading procedures may involve exchanges between student and teacher as profound as any in a therapist-patient relationship. It is the custom of instructors in the Harvard Reading Course to ask students for their comments at the end of each day's class, and to read them all aloud and attempt to respond to them on the following day. One such comment, scribbled in fury by a Radcliffe girl on the back of her answer sheet, read as follows:

"I wish I were a teacher of speed reading. It seems to involve no talent whatever. In fact, I am sure you have none! When are you going to stop pranking around in the front of the room and teach us to read faster? You are a sonofabitch!"

With these words, battle was joined. For the instructor, whose feathers were ruffled, the temptation to dismiss his student's feelings as an instance of "negative transference" was very strong. To do so, however, would miss a real issue the student raised. The instructor was, in point of fact, powerless to change the student's reading. He could not come out into the auditorium and wiggle her eyes for her, and still less could he alter what she was doing with her mind as she read. He decided to read her comment aloud to the class without naming or singling out the author, and ask them what a student can do after it becomes clear that the instructor is hopelessly incompetent. When the class was thrown open for a discussion of this question, the consensus of student opinion was that while *total* incompetence was rare in Harvard instructors, the discovery of such a thing would still leave the burden of learning on the student, and to ignore that fact was to run grave risks. To begin with, in a graded course, one would almost certainly flunk. . . .

Not many of the students' comments are as angry (or as peda-gogically useful) as this one. The instructor is often handsomely thanked for the improvement he has wrought in the student's read-ing. Responding to comments such as these can be even more awk-ward. Without being ungracious he must respond in a fashion which says, "Thank you, but I didn't do it, *you* did it! Good for you! Now go do it some more." To decline responsibility for the student's failure correspondingly means granting him full honors for his vic-tory. Teachers cannot have it both ways.

The particular content of a day in the reading class depends a great deal on the instructor, but certain features are standard. The class begins each day with a reading film. The films begin slightly below the average speed of the class and increase in speed each day, until by the end of the course the films are shown at approximately 800 words per minute. At this speed, reading mechanically is an exercise in pursuit. One student commented that during this exercise his eyeballs were rattling in their sockets and his tears were turning to steam.

After the film, students are urged to summarize what they have seen in their own words, and then to take a multiple-choice test con-cerning the material. Following this, students will do various skim-ming exercises during the class, and each day ends with the reading of a brief essay from a booklet in which the student is timed and on which he is tested. Students are encouraged to keep a log of their progress and to write comments and questions to the instructor each day about their progress or the lack of it. These techniques are de-signed to improve the student's reading on a tactical level, and most of the time they are effective to some extent.

The more important work of the course, however, is strategic in its intent, concerned not with how a page is read word-by-word, but how a book is read idea-by-idea, how two books are compared, and how reading is put to use in papers, discussion, and examinations.

Strategic approaches to reading are touchy subjects. Students and faculty frequently see in them something perilously close to a cynical "examsmanship" which can be used to pass courses with little true knowledge of subject matter. The question of whether or not they really constitute a form of intellectual cheating depends more on the student's intent than on what he does. As Perry[2] has pointed out, the structure of an answer to an exam written as a bluff to conceal ignorance (the politer of the two common terms is "snow job") is likely to be the same as the structure of the genuine "A" essay. Both involve thought, but one is devoid of content.

Reading done immediately prior to exams is often done in desperation, and is called "cramming." It is widely decried by educators, who feel that it is an admission of indolence by the student during the term, and unlikely to produce results of lasting value, even though it may temporarily serve for getting by. The truth of the matter is more complex: cramming is often a highly efficient method of study, and students who have been plagued by an inability to "concentrate" often find their powers at towering heights on the night before the examination. The trouble with cramming is not that it is done at all, but that it is done at the wrong time. At the end of a term, its results are small. Done in the beginning of a term, in an attempt to gain an admittedly superficial overview of an entire course, it can be strikingly productive. With this overview, the student need not be so concerned about losing the forest of the course for the trees of his daily assignments, and can tackle topics of interest using his own informed judgment about their relative importance.

For that reason, it was decided to introduce cramming techniques into the Harvard Reading Course a few years ago, with the idea of urging students to "read" and compare two entire books in slightly more than half an hour apiece. Two books were chosen to be subjected to this intellectual *banzai* charge, both by Harvard authors.

[2] Perry, W. G., Jr. Examsmanship and the liberal arts: A study in educational epistemology. *In* Bramson, L., ed., Examining in Harvard College: A Collection of Essays by Members of the Harvard Faculty. Cambridge, Faculty of Arts and Sciences, Harvard University, 1963.

The first book is Lawrence Wylie's *Village in the Vaucluse,* a socio-logical account of life in a French village, and the second is *The Navaho* by Kluckhohn and Leighton, which approaches this American Indian tribe from the point of view of cultural anthropology.

This exercise begins by deliberately restricting the student's field of view. He is asked to spend eight minutes hunting in Wylie's book with a view to understanding the child-raising practices of the village, and nothing else. At the end of eight minutes, he is given three minutes to make notes on what he has found out, keeping the book shut as he makes them. At the next class, he is asked to find out what government is like for the Villagers, and to relate the child-rearing practices of the Village to its government as he goes.

He is allowed two more eight-minute passes at this book, one spent searching for economic behavior, another on a topic of his choice, trying to weave the topics together as he goes. When the second book is introduced, the student is told that he must compare the Navaho Indian and the French farmer along a series of axes of his own choosing, and is given four more eight-minute bursts in which to make his comparison. At the end of a total of 64 minutes of reading, he takes an examination question lifted from a Social Relations Course final exam dealing with similarities and differences in the two cultures. The results are often surprisingly good. It is not scholarship, any more than a painter's first charcoal lines on canvas are a work of art, but the purpose served is similar; it acts as a guide for more finished work and establishes an overall design.

The method used in this cramming exercise might be called the "principle of overlapping frames of reference." It can be illustrated geometrically, as follows: let the circles below represent the areas of the books concerned with child-rearing, government, and economics.

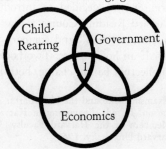

Where the circles overlap, the frames of reference represented by child-bearing, economics, and government have ideas, events, or clusters of data in common. For example, an event to be found in the area labeled "1" below would be a budget fight in the school committee. As anyone who has observed such a fight, or participated in one can attest, such an event may look trivial, but is intensely revealing about the structure of the society in which it takes place.

One of the greatest difficulties faced by a student new to a discipline is that he is not merely ignorant of subject material, he is unaware of the priorities to be observed in learning the material. The diagram suggests that what is to be learned in an academic subject as viewed from three frames of reference can be separated into categories in descending order of urgency, as follows:

1. *The Vital*: (area labeled "1") Material known by every professional in the field, and which the student must be able to produce whether he is asleep, drunk, or dead, ignorance of which is instantaneously disastrous.

2. *The Important*: (areas labeled "2") Material which can momentarily be neglected with no risk greater than humiliation and disgrace.

3. *The Relevant*: (areas labeled "3") Material which, if not mastered, will prove inconvenient.

4. *The Conditionally Superfluous*: (area labeled "4") Material not encompassed by the frames of reference of the observer. Therefore, material which can be neglected in relative safety, but also the greatest source of Unpleasant Surprises.

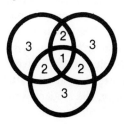

The fact that the "area of maximum overlap" is the area of highest priority in scholarly work should come as no surprise. Examples abound elsewhere. Whatever trouble registers on three of a pilot's instruments at the same time is the thing that the pilot must cope with first of all, if he is not to become a smoking hole in a cornfield. Whatever bothers the three vice presidents of marketing, finance, and production must cause the president of the corporation sleepless nights as well. Where many frames of reference find the same data important, *there* must the student head with his greatest urgency and attention.

Harvard, like any other educational institution, encapsulates the frames of reference it teaches in the examinations for its courses. A survey of old examinations makes historical changes clear.[3] Whereas examinations of fifty years ago frequently asked the student to pro-duce a datum ("What was the date of the death of Aurangzeeb?"), newer examinations are more likely to make use of the principle of overlapping frames of reference ("Trace the development of ration-alism in the pragmatist cosmogony.") For this reason, Harvard's examinations are dealt with in the reading course at some length. For many years, Harvard has kept files of old exams in various loca-tions about the University, in the offices of the Dean of Freshmen, the Bureau of Study Counsel, and in libraries. Not all students make use of these files. More of them should. The student, as the private in the trenches, knows that examinations are the payoff for study, for good or ill. Insofar as he cares about his grades, and most students do, he will find it necessary to do well here if he is to do well at all.

One problem which presents itself regularly to all departments offering counseling services to students is that of "exam panic." It is simply characterized: The student (whether or not he experiences the subjective sensation of panic) does markedly less well in exami-nations than he does in work performed under different conditions, such as papers, homework, class recitation, etc. Poor performance under exam conditions exists in varying degrees of severity. A mild form of the condition results in an extreme literalness and over-emphasis on "fact." Asked to compare the attitudes of Hamilton and Jefferson toward fiscal policy, the student writes down everything he knows about Jefferson, and all he can remember about the fiscal issues of their time. If the student's reading has been extensive and if the student is too tense to "think," he may be able to produce an impressive quantity of data without even a suggestion of an answer to the question, which requires comparison and analysis—not simply

---

3 Perry, W. G. Forms of Intellectual and Ethical Development in the College Years. New York, Holt, Rinehart and Winston, pp. 4–5, 1970.

a display of facts. Curiously, it is often this same student who complains that all his teachers ever want is "regurgitation."

In its more severe forms, the student may produce little or nothing in the pages of his bluebook. Sometimes he produces irrelevant essays, occasionally angry ones on the iniquities of the grading system and examinations in general. One Harvard student in an examination was observed to paper-clip two dollars to the pages of his bluebook, write briefly, and leave the examination room at the first opportunity. Suspicions of attempted bribery were dispelled when the student's message was read: "This is what I usually pay to get screwed."

Inability to perform on examinations may, of course, be a sign of a comparatively severe problem on the student's part. But as Jacques Barzun[4] has pointed out, "Exam-shy students are like fence-shy horses. They have been trained badly or not at all." A simple procedure exists which will discriminate most of the difficulties due to poor training from those due to more serious problems. It involves direct instructions given to the student, as follows:

1. A month before the end of the term, the student should prepare his own examination in a course which has him worried. This examination should be in finished form, as though the class were to take it on the following day. It should be the examination the student himself expects to receive as he can best anticipate it.
2. The student should check the files of old examinations and see whether the examination he has written bears any resemblance to the examinations actually posed by instructors in the course over the preceding five years. If not, the student is encouraged to wonder why.
3. The student should take an exam from a previous year to his room, and under examination conditions (three hours time, no notes or books used) should *take* the examination.
4. Immediately after taking the examination, the student should bring it to an independent source of judgment—teacher, tutor, advisor, etc. and ask to be graded. He should watch the grading done, and have a chance to discuss the results with the grader.
5. The student should repeat steps three and four *ad libitum* until at least one honor grade has been obtained. In severe cases, this number should be increased to three honor grades in a row.

The advantages of this procedure are easily apparent. Fear and trembling at the unfamiliar experience of the examination diminish.

---

[4] Barzun, J. Teacher in America. Boston, Little, Brown and Company, 1946.

The experience is no longer unfamiliar. The student's reading, in periods between the practice examinations becomes more purposeful and efficient. Finally, the procedure is a good diagnostic tool. Those who can use it and profit by it probably do not need professional help for exam panic. Those who cannot or will not use the procedure probably do.

This procedure has its greatest applicability in lower-level courses, especially introductory ones. Fortunately, this is where the problem of exam panic occurs most frequently. The reason for this is simple: students who panic on examinations are quick to fear the tyranny of their teachers. They often miss the point that the real tyranny in education is not the stick the teacher holds over the student, but the iron rod that the subject matter holds over student and teacher alike. In the very nature of things there are certain matters which teachers in introductory courses *must* therefore check. It is incumbent on any Physics 1 professor to see if $F=ma$ has registered somewhere. The teacher of American history *must* see if the student is aware of the existence of the Supreme Court. Questions on these matters do not appear on examinations at the whim of the instructor. They are simply inevitable.

But the student, who begins an introductory course in almost total innocence, does not know which parts of the course are essential and which are the teacher's side remarks, and this natural inability to discriminate gets him in trouble. He works as though everything were of equal importance, wastes his time on side issues, and slights the core of the subject. For this reason, inspection of final examinations at the very beginning of a course may have a prophylactic effect, especially if the student regards the old examinations as "overlapping frames of reference" and treats them as such. Any question which appears on the last three years' final examinations with only a change of names or numbers falls in the *vital* category, and should be treated as such. For example, inspection of the last ten years' final examinations in Mathematics 1a (the introductory calculus course) shows that seven questions, recurring again and again in slightly different form and wording, account for about 80 percent of the content. (Teachers reading this should not be alarmed at the propect of students reading it as well, discovering those seven questions, and studying them intensively in order to get a "B." If they did so, they would have achieved an excellent understanding of Math 1a.)

Above all, students should use the epistemological definitions inherent in examinations to direct the style of their reading. If the examinations reveal that Harvard teaches history as the effect of an interplay of ideas upon events, the student whose reading style is directed toward memorizing dates would do well to redirect his efforts. Final examinations give far better estimates of a course's ac- tual content and methods than its description in the catalogue, which is usually ten years out of date and was misleading when written. Students should be encouraged to pick courses with the aid of this material, and perhaps to pick their field of concentration in that way as well.

Another subject closely linked to reading is the making of notes. A glance at the student's notebook may often reveal important atti- tudes he bears toward his study, his instructor, and himself. For many a student note-taking forms a curious ritual, having much relevance to his emotional needs, but little to his educational ones.

Often, inspection of the student's notebook can be a field trip in educational paleontology. The student, at some point in his educa- tional career, was told to make notes in a certain format—as follows:

I. THE AMERICAN REVOLUTION
    A. *Apparent Causes*:
        1. Financial
            a. Stamp Act
            b. Tea. . . .etc.

This style of note-making may work if the lecturer's notes are simi- larly divided. If they are not, it is a bed of Procrustes for ideas which do not lend themselves to such organization. Rather than abandon this system, however, the student may cling to this ritual as the "right" way. If he does, the chances are strong that other meaningless rituals exist in his work as well.

Other students have gone to the trouble of learning shorthand, lest anything escape them in a lecture. Laudable as this might sound, it is seldom wise. The student, caught between listening to the sense of what the teacher is saying and the needs of stenography, often chooses to stick with stenography, thereby postponing the process of learning until he returns to his room to read the notes. Sometimes this postponement is permanent.

Overexuberant note-making can often be detrimental to the process of learning. One fourth-year graduate student of history sought help at the Bureau of Study Counsel for a system of making notes which had gotten completely out of control. This student would take down a lecture verbatim in Gregg, return to his room, type up the lecture, and then reduce the entire lecture to a single page. He would then further condense this page to one side of a 3 by 5 index card. After all this, he complained that he was unable to remember anything the lecturer had said.

Whatever else notes should be, they should be functional—aids to jog the student's memory. In style, notes should resemble an economical telegram sent to a moron. Time spent typing them is probably wasted.

Mildly compulsive behavior of the sort involved in useless note-making is common at Harvard, and most of the time is of no great significance. It often disappears spontaneously when the student realizes its absurdity. One student who was given to composing elaborate mnemonic slogans and jingles to remember physics formulas was cured by his roommate, as follows: the student greeted the roommate at the door with his latest effort. "What does *that* represent?" asked the roommate. There was a slight pause. ". . . I forget," said the student. "Oh," said his roommate. "A *pure* mnemonic!"

In spite of apparent irrelevance to the Harvard Reading Course's stated aims, the course frequently discusses methods of reading and study in dealing with courses in mathematics and the natural sciences. Here, pure speed of reading is clearly not possible, nor is "equations per hour" any better measure than "words per minute."

Study of this sort clearly involves special emotional problems for the student. It is not uncommon to hear someone say "I can't *do* math." The feeling of impotence when confronted by a mathematical problem is clear from the very grammatical structure of the disclaimer. To *do* mathematics is to solve mathematical problems. It should follow from this that the student of mathematics should place a primary emphasis on exactly that. Students having problems in a course in mathematics will often be found doing very different things, often having little resemblance to mathematical thought. They are not to be censured too harshly for this; the very structure of their textbooks suggests a different emphasis.

The usual mathematics textbook is arranged in chapters, each chapter being organized roughly as follows: first some paragraphs of theory, next an "example problem" (often in boldface type) and finally the problems for the student at the end of the chapter. Both historically and pedagogically, this format is upside down. Mathematicians did not begin with a theory and then devise problems from it in order to torment their students. They began with the problems and the theory was built to solve them. Therefore, at which end of the chapter should the sensible student begin? With the problems.

The student should not merely look at these problems, he should try to solve a couple. Because he lacks the theory, he is likely to fail in his attempts, but these very failures will tell him what he needs to know from the theory. At this point, he can address the theory with a sense of what he needs to know from it, and can read the beginning of the chapter with a sense of its purpose.

The most vexing problem for both student and teacher in the Harvard Reading Course concerns the reading of literature. Some resistance might be expected from the literary scholars of a university, should they suspect a reading instructor of trying to deprave their students by suggesting that *The Divine Comedy* be read in 45 minutes. Such objections have a great deal of merit. One does not bolt one's Christmas dinner, nor observe the paintings in the Louvre from the back of a speeding motorcycle. Yet a difficulty arises in the very nature of a scholarly approach to art. The requirement for breadth of reading is forever at war with the requirement for depth. Perhaps the first reading of *The Divine Comedy* should be rapid, for the same reason that one stands back from a painting before closer scrutiny of the little miracles of brushwork the artist has managed in the details.

But even overall views of an artistic work can be, and should be, taken for different purposes. What is Dante's moral position? What is he doing with language? Why is purgatory so much more interesting than heaven? How does *The Divine Comedy* relate to the

Bible historically? What were its political implications? What in hell (literally) is going on? And what in heaven's name is the student going to think about it?

Questions like these demand an overview of Dante's universe. More properly, they involve several such overviews. Answers cannot be found from considerations of feminine endings or verb tenses. An overall view of the work is necessary.

Nor is speed of reading entirely irrelevant. Slowness of reading restricts the student's range. To have "read" *The Divine Comedy* once will yield a certain type of understanding. To have read it five times from five different points of view will be something else again. But were the last two readings more instructive than an inspection of *Paradise Lost* would have been? It is hard to say. And yet, by the very fact that they "assign" certain works and do not assign others, literature teachers make this very sort of judgment every fall. Presumably, they do a great deal of soul searching before the reading list is final, and wish that they had more time for the limitless job. The students wish so too. Time, as the harsh master of realists, limits both student and teacher as they go about their work, and both must use good will and good judgment as they do it. The "right" way to read literature is likely to remain elusive, but mute reverence for a work of art is less appropriate while reading it than an active inquiry into how its beauty comes to pass. The problem for the reader remains the same, but with the added puzzle of aesthetic judgment.

Each year, the students do battle in Widener anew, and each year their ignorance retreats bitterly, yard by yard, into new redoubts of complexity and confusion. The spirit the students show is unquestionable: It is the sort of cheerful courage which would charge the main gate of hell with a bucket of soapy water. The task of the reading teacher is to caution them against breaking their strength uselessly, to add strategem to their strength and cunning to their valor. It is happy work.[5]

---

[5] This chapter is used by permission of the author, who holds its copyright.

13

The Return of the
College Dropout

David Sorenson

The literature on college readmissions is spotty. What has been published comes from research carried out at a small number of schools.
The readmission policies and experiences of most colleges have not
found their way into print. This chapter will review what literature
there is on the return of the dropout, then summarize the results of
a recent study that examined the psychological test variables associated with different styles of coping with Harvard after readmission,
will present some illustrative cases and, finally, will discuss the implications of this study and the earlier literature for administrative policies in the future.

Past Administrative Policies

What administrative guidelines are followed by colleges when
readmitting dropouts? Only a little literature answers this question.
As we read between the lines, we gain the impression that, in general, most dropouts who apply are permitted to return.

Yale, for example, has the general policy of giving any student
who drops out a second chance. However, few third chances are
given. It is felt that if a student leaves school twice, the Yale en-

vironment must be the source of significant and unknown stress and it would thus be better for the student to attend some other school. When a student has left on medical leave (psychiatric or physical disability) readmission is automatic once he has received medical clearance.[1]

Harvard follows a similar policy. No hard and fast rules are adhered to and each case is considered individually. A student who withdraws voluntarily is almost sure to get a second chance. Where the Administrative Board of Harvard College has required a student to withdraw for disciplinary or academic reasons certain requirements (which vary individually) must be met before he can return. The Board looks at the work and behavior record of the student as presented in letters from employers, commanding officers, etc. Students on psychiatric leave must usually undergo a psychological evaluation as part of the readmission process.

Giesecke and Hancock[2] report that at the University of Illinois an assistant dean interviews all students applying for readmission and on the basis of this interview and test data available makes "the decision." They note that this policy leaves a great deal to chance.

Some tough moral questions about readmissions have not been faced squarely by colleges. The question of whether a college ever should deny the opportunity of trying again to the student who desires readmission, even in view of good statistical evidence that he is likely to fail to obtain his degree, is a troublesome one. Many feel the student should be given the chance if he wants it, while others support the idea that a student should be expected to meet a set of criteria before being readmitted. The responsibility of the college towards the students whom it initially admits is another question not easily answered. How much and how long should we labor with the student having trouble meeting the stresses of college when there are thousands who desire to occupy the limited space which the school has?

---

[1] Peszke, M. A., and Arnstein, R. L. Readmission to college after psychiatric medical leave. In Pervin, L. A., Reik, L. E., and Dalrymple, W., eds., The College Dropout and the Utilization of Talent. Princeton, The Princeton University Press, 1966.
[2] Giesecke, G. E., and Hancock, J. W. Rehabilitation of academic failures. College and University, 26:72–178, 1950.

NUMBERS RETURNING AND GRADUATING

How many dropouts return to college? Eckland's[3] research at the University of Illinois provides a good starting point for answering this question. He went to great lengths to follow up on all students, including dropouts, in the class of 1956 and learn of their activities before and after leaving college. Ninety-four percent of the dropouts returned his questionnaire. Some data was also obtained on many of the remaining 6 percent. At some point during the next ten years, 70 percent of these dropouts returned to school and 55 percent graduated. Half of the graduates took their degrees from the University of Illinois and the remainder from other colleges.

Pervin[4] has established the number of dropouts returning to Princeton. Some caution must be exercised in viewing his data, however, as the return rate on his questionnaire was low. He had sent questionnaires to all students in the classes of 1940, 1951, and 1960. Of those reporting, 57 percent of the dropouts in the class of 1940, 82 percent in the 1951 class, and 87 percent of the class of 1960 had returned to some college. In the class of 1940, only 10 percent of the returnees returned to Princeton while 30 percent of those in the classes of 1951 and 1960 who returned to college went back to Princeton. Of those who returned to college, 30 percent in the class of 1940, 64 percent in the 1951 class, and 85 percent of the class of 1960 obtained their B.A. degrees. According to Pervin's figures, the percentage of entering students ultimately obtaining their B.A. degree is increasing quite significantly.

Figures on readmission at Maryland State Teachers College have been given by Tansil.[5] She does not give the percentage of dropouts returning but reports that, between 1951 and 1961, 336 dropouts reentered the college. Of these 336 students, 260 had withdrawn

---

[3] Eckland, B. E. College dropouts who come back. Harvard Educat. Rev., 34:402–420, 1964.

[4] Pervin, L. A. The later academic, vocational, and personal success of college dropouts. *In* Pervin, L. A., Reik, L. E., and Dalrymple, W., eds., The College Dropout and the Utilization of Talent. Princeton, The Princeton University Press, 1966.

[5] Tansil, R. Report on dropouts and readmission study made at Maryland State. Higher Education, 19(7):11, 1963.

voluntarily and 76 had been required to leave. Two hundred and one of the readmits have graduated and 38 were still enrolled at the time of the study. The remaining 97 withdrew a second time. Thus, between 60 and 70 percent of the readmits at Maryland State received their degree.

Three studies carried out at Harvard give some idea of the number of Harvard dropouts returning. Whitla[6] reports that 72 percent of the dropouts he studied sought to return and 95 percent of them were readmitted. Of those readmitted, 58 percent obtained their degree. Thus, 40 percent of the dropouts in his sample eventually obtained a degree at Harvard. Whitla's figures do not include those Harvard dropouts who attended and graduated from some other college.

Nicholi's[7] study gives data on both the dropouts who return to Harvard and those who go elsewhere. He reports that 49 percent of the dropouts leaving school over the 1955 to 1960 time period returned and graduated from Harvard. Of the remainder, 29 percent attended and graduated from another school.

Both authors give some data relating return rates to the original causes of withdrawal. In Whitla's sample, 73 percent of the academic dropouts applied for readmission and 20 percent of them were readmitted. For the nonacademic dropouts, 69 percent applied and 92 percent of these were readmitted. Looking at the cases classified as psychiatric and nonpsychiatric dropouts, Whitla found that the same percentage of each applied for readmission (72 percent) and the same percentage (95 percent) were readmitted. However, only 38 percent of the psychiatric readmits graduated. This would seem to indicate that the psychiatric dropout has a poor chance of ever obtaining a degree from Harvard. However, Nicholi's findings regarding psychiatric dropouts do not support this finding. He writes: "A comparison of the rate of return, attainment of academic honors and of eventual graduation from Harvard showed no significant dif-

6 Whitla, D. K. A study of college dropouts. Office of Tests, Harvard College, (duplicated), 1961.
7 Nicholi, A. M. Harvard dropouts—summary of main points of research. Paper presented at the research symposium of the Amer. College Health Assoc., Washington, D.C., March 31, 1967. Also see by the same author: Harvard dropouts: some psychiatric findings. Paper presented at the Amer. Psychiat. Assoc., Detroit, May, 1967.

ference between the psychiatric dropouts and those who drop out for all other reasons."[8]

To understand the reasons for the discrepant statements one must pay attention to the differences in the way the two investigators defined what they mean by "psychiatric dropouts" and also to the differences in sample selection. To some degree the differences in rates may be an artifact of the definitions used and methodology rather than real differential rates.

Whitla studied only those students whose cases had been presented before the Administrative Board before leaving (60 percent of the total dropout population). A dropout was classified "psychiatric" by Whitla if he had a University Health Service (UHS) rider attached to his record or if the Administrative Board had made official note of a deteriorated psychological condition. Nicholi, however, investigated all dropouts from Harvard during the period of his study and defined a psychiatric dropout as one "who consulted a psychiatrist one or more times before leaving and who was given a specific psychiatric diagnosis by the psychiatrist."[9] All students who seek psychiatric help at UHS do not have a rider attached to their records. Therefore, it is reasonable to believe that there were some dropouts in Whitla's nonpsychiatric group who were getting psychiatric help but nevertheless were not included in his psychiatric category.

One can even make the same comment about those dropouts Nicholi classified as nonpsychiatric. It is known from reports of other agencies in and around Boston that for various reasons numerout Harvard students seek psychiatric help from doctors or agencies not connected with Harvard. Similarly there were likely others who were in need of psychiatric help but did not seek out psychiatrists. Thus the 38 percent figure which Nicholi gives might possibly be low.

However, one must be cautious in saying this. There are good reasons why many he classified as psychiatric may not have dropped out because of an emotional disturbance. Nicholi's method of selecting students for his psychiatric sample was basically a method of

---

[8] Nicholi, A. M. Harvard dropouts: some psychiatric findings. Paper presented at the Amer. Psychiat. Assoc., Detroit, May, 1967, pp. 3–4.
[9] *Ibid.*, p. 2.

"self-selection." That is, to be included in the psychiatric category a student needed only to visit a university psychiatrist once and be diagnosed. The point was made that all people with emotional disorders do not seek out psychiatrists. The reverse of this is also true. Many who visit psychiatrists are not emotionally disturbed. Nicholi did try to account for this by including only those who were given a diagnosis by the psychiatrist. Yet, one must question the accuracy of these diagnoses. A diagnosis made on the basis of only a one-hour interview and without psychological testing can hardly in most instances, be described as well substantiated. "Tentative" and "open to revision" are more realistic adjectives. It is also possible that many in his psychiatric sample may have been suffering temporary disorders due to the stress of dropping out itself rather than a disorder which made withdrawal necessary. In short, the number of dropouts who leave due to an emotional disturbance is not easily determined. The accuracy of both Whitla's and Nicholi's percentages must be questioned.

Other studies have tried to determine the rate of return and success of the emotionally disturbed dropout. In an earlier study at Harvard, Blaine and McArthur[10] found that 40 percent of 160 students who dropped out because of emotional problems returned to Harvard and 79 percent of these were in good standing at the time of their report. Not enough is said about how they selected their sample, defined emotional problems, or obtained their data to make close comparisons with the Whitla and Nicholi reports.

Harrison[11] carried out a study similar to Blaine and McArthur's at Yale and reports that 48 percent of the students leaving for emotional reasons returned to Yale and 69 percent of those subsequently graduated.

Yale was also the setting for a study by Inman and Altemeyer.[12] They looked at students readmitted between 1952 and 1962 who withdrew sometime after their freshman year. Of those readmitted,

---

[10] Blaine, G. B., Jr., and McArthur, C. C. Problems connected with studying. *In* Blaine, G. B., Jr., and McArthur, C. C. eds., Emotional Problems of the Student. New York, Appleton-Century-Crofts, 1961.

[11] Harrison, R. W. Leaving college because of emotional problems. Student Medicine, 4:49–60, 1956.

[12] Inman, S., and Altemeyer, R. Readmission study: 1952–1962, Yale University (mimeo).

79 percent went on to graduate. This figure of 79 percent is higher than Harrison's 69 percent, a difference probaly caused by Inman and Altemeyer's exclusion of freshman dropouts from their sample. Freshman dropouts have been found to have a lower success rate upon readmission than upperclassmen.[13]

One might summarize the finding of this section by saying that in recent years a surprisingly large number of dropouts (70 to 87 percent) return to college with the majority of them (55 to 85 percent) successfully obtaining a degree. Studies at Harvard and Yale have focused primarily on "psychiatric dropouts." Little evidence exists which would support the view that students leaving for psychiatric reasons are less successful that others in eventually obtaining their degrees.

Successful and Unsuccessful Readmits

Research to determine which variables differentiate returning dropouts who later graduate from those who leave a second time is not yet extensive.

Hansmeier[14] and Whitla are the only writers who describe factors differentiating between successful and nonsuccessful readmits without restricting their findings to those leaving because of emotional problems. Hansmeier conducted his study at the University College of Michigan State University. He found no significant differences between academically successful and academically unsuccessful readmits in terms of sex, age, whether they were veterans or not, and socioeconomic status. The hypothesis that the two groups differed in terms of high school achievement was supported by some tests of significance but not by others. Scholastic aptitude measures gave conflicting results.

One other finding of Hansmeier's is worth noting. The grades of both the successful and unsuccessful readmits improved significantly after readmission. However, those in the successful group improved

---

13 Whitla, *op. cit.*
14 Hansmeier, T. W. Factors related to the success after readmission of college students academically dismissed. College and University, 40(2):194–202, 1963.

almost twice as much. The improvement in the case of the un-successful group was not great enough to overcome their previous poor record and their overall grades made it necessary for the university to dismiss them.

Whitla's finding relative to Scholastic Aptitude Test (SAT) scores agree with those of Hansmeier. These scores differentiated between dropouts and nondropouts but "whether a man petitions to return, is admitted or receives his degree" is not related to his SAT scores.[15] A student's Predictive Rank List (PRL) was likewise not related to success or failure upon readmission. This variable is defined in *A Handbook for Harvard Advisors*. To quote: "The PRL is derived from a weighted combination of a student's College Board test scores and his secondary school rank-in-class, in such a manner as to obtain the best prediction of his Rank List" (p.9). Rank List is Harvard's measure of grade level.

In Whitla's sample the number of semesters completed before leaving was related to success after readmission if a dropout had left during his freshman or sophomore years. After a student completed his sophomore year, the length of his initial stay in college was immaterial.

Whitla's research pointed out the meaning of the dropout's work record while he was out of college. Having more than two employers was negatively related to coming back and obtaining one's degree. Likewise, dropouts who worked as research assistants while out of school and did not follow a set daily schedule were less likely to obtain their degrees. There was a positive correlation between suc-cess and holding a responsible position in business or working in sales.

An unpublished study by Harvard's Dean, Delmar Leighton, showed that during the forties and fifties the success of returned dropouts was a function both of their job performance while out of school and of the length of time they stayed out of school. Few readmittees did well if they had been less than two semesters out in the cold world. Fewer did well if they had not demonstrated continuous and satisfactory performance in a socially meaningful role, whether in the military, as an unpaid but responsible social worker, in a good job, or just plain pumping gas in a service station.

---

15 Whitla, *op. cit.*, p. 23.

The remainder of the studies seeking to compare successful and unsuccessful readmitted students have confined their attention to those students who left school because of emotional difficulties.

Harrison[16] reports on research carried out with both graduate and undergraduate students at Yale who returned to college after a dropout period brought on by emotional problems. Graduate students did better upon return than did undergraduates. Students in academic trouble before leaving were more likely to withdraw a second time. Those students who had been diagnosed as being neurotic or psychotic before dropping out were more likely to graduate than those diagnosed as having a character disorder. Whether a returning dropout had had treatment or was getting treatment had no effect on his chances of graduation nor was the length of time he was out of school related to success.

The Inman and Altemeyer study looked at such variables as length of time out of school, completed terms before withdrawing, academic load upon return, secondary school attended, marital status, financial aid status, activities while out of school, where they roomed after readmission, and causes for leaving. They found a readmit's chances of graduating were greater if he was married. Also, the greater the number of terms completed before leaving, the greater were his chances of graduating. A heavy academic load did not seem to be too difficult for students who had left because of emotional difficulties alone but the same did not hold true for those who withdrew because of both emotional and academic difficulties. Students who remained out of school less than two semesters were likely to be less successful upon their return. Students who had left because of emotional difficulties were more likely to drop out a second time than were those not classified as dropouts with emotional problems. When activities while out of college were looked at, no statistically significant differences were found, but students who traveled while out of school and those who lived alone tended to do better after returning than those who lived at home and/or those who had not worked or traveled while out.

Peszke and Arnstein[17] studied 101 readmitted students who had

---

[16] Harrison, *op. cit.*

[17] Peszke and Arnstein, *op. cit.*

returned to Yale between 1956 and 1963 and had left for psychiatric reasons. The only significant difference between those readmits who graduated and those who did not was the number of semesters the student had completed before dropping out. The less credits he needed for graduation when he returned, the greater were his chances of graduating.

Peszke and Arnstein give a number of impressions about the probable success of a readmitted student based upon their clinical experiences rather than upon any statistically significant evidence they could obtain. They felt that a returning student's chances of graduating are better if he can show some accomplishment of an academic, vocational, or military nature. They comment that while the dropout period can be beneficial in a variety of ways the benefits generally fall into two catgories: "either a gain in general confidence or a settling of vocational direction" (pp. 148-149). They feel that the length of time a student remains out of school should not be subject to any hard and fast rules. Students whose problem is "immaturity" should generally remain out longer than those suffering from psychopathology. In the latter case they feel that whether or not they have had treatment is more important than the length of time away from school.

Using interview and test data on 50 Harvard psychiatric dropouts who returned, Powell[18] compared those who later graduated with those who did not. Comparisons were made on 59 variables. Attending a public secondary school, having a C+ average or better before leaving college, coming from a nonrural home, and remaining out of college one year or longer were all associated with success. Those having a B average or better were almost sure to graduate. The success rate was very low for those remaining out less than one semester.

What the student did with his time while out of school was also significantly related to the successful completion of school. Those who held jobs with a set routine to follow and who had to organize their time did better than those who did not work or who worked

18 Powell, D. H. The return of the dropout. J. Amer. College Health Assoc., 13(4):475–483, 1964.

as research assistants on a variable work schedule. A related finding was that, if the student went to work while he was out of college, the fewer employers he had while out, the greater his chances of graduating.

Rorschach tests data also differentiated between Powell's two groups. Those who graduated gave more responses and more of their responses involved color, animal movement, and human movement. They also tended to see whole organisms and fewer part of animals or humans. Powell interprets these Rorschach findings as indicating that the dropouts who go on to graduate are

. . . more open and reactive—more anxious and labile perhaps—but at any rate they are freer and more flexible. . . .The finding that the successful candidates more often are able to see a whole object indicates that anxiety is not impairing them in a specific way relative to their college experience. They are not defending by constriction as much. (p. 481)

The only significant difference between the two groups on the MMPI was a higher average score on the K scale for those who did not graduate. Intellectual ability, psychiatric diagnosis, and age at admission did not differentiate the two groups.

Although Nicholi[19] has not as yet published the full results of his study, he has pointed out one finding which is of interest in this section. Psychiatric diagnosis has tended to be related to a student's success upon readmission. Those dropouts diagnosed as schizophrenic do not return to college as often as do those in other diagnostic categories but if they do return they are not as likely to leave a second time. Those diagnosed as compulsive personality, psychotic depressive reaction, and manic depressive reaction are more likely to withdraw a second time.

We can now summarize. The two variables that differentiate most clearly between readmitted students who graduate and those who drop out a second time are the number of terms completed before withdrawal and the student's grades before leaving. Those who attended college the longest and obtained the best grades before leaving school do best when they return. The evidence on scholastic ability or intelligence is not quite as clear but it does not appear to be

---

[19] Nicholi, *op. cit.*

related to success after readmission. The Leighton,[20] Powell, and Inman-Altemeyer studies support the idea that students remaining out of school at least two semester are more likely to succeed but most of the writers reviewed would probably support Peszke's and Arnstein's statement that a university should not set any hard and fast rules in this area. How the student spends his time while out of school and what he accomplishes seems important. If he has demonstrated in work or other types of significant activities those qualities which lead to success in college, such as dependability, ability to organize his time, effectiveness in interpersonal relationships, etc., chances are greater that he can do well in school upon his return.

Powell's finding with Rorschach data suggests that those dropouts who show signs of openness and flexibility along with lower anxiety are more likely to succeed.

The evidence relating psychiatric diagnosis to success is very limited. Nicholi's finding that schizophrenics do better than other psychiatric groups and Harrison's comment that students with character disorders do less well are the only pieces of data bearing on this question. It is certainly not surprising that the acting out student (maybe one might say the nonconformist) does less well than others.

SCREENING BEFORE READMISSION

A few attempts to predict the achievement of returning dropouts have been made.

Giesecke and Hancock[21] report on a study at the Galesburg Undergraduate Division of the University of Illinois. They wanted to know when a student should be readmitted, whether counseling could help him decide for himself when he should return, and whether he could change his behavior sufficiently, with the aid of counseling, to make further schooling worthwhile.

Each dropout desiring to return was given testing and intensive counseling to help him understand himself better and thus be better able to decide when it would be in his best interests to return to

---

20 Leighton, D. Unpublished memorandum, Office of the Dean of Harvard College, 1956.
21 Giesecke and Hancock, *op. cit.*

school. The actual decision of when to return was to be reached jointly between the counselor and student. The authors write that they could have achieved a much higher rate of predictive success in the study if they had prevented all candidates for readmission from entering until they were "successful in meeting the terms agreed upon" (p. 74). In reality, only 50 percent met these terms.

Seventy-one students were readmitted. One-half made a satisfactory adjustment to school during the first semester after returning. Fifty percent of these, however, did not meet the minimum school standards during the second semester and left school. Thus after two semesters, 75 percent of the readmits had left. This is a rather low success rate and makes one wonder about the effectiveness of the counseling these students were given. The writers do not indicate how they sought to influence the student's behavior or the number of counseling sessions provided.

They reported that 27 of the 71 readmitted students were identified as clearly emotionally maladjusted and that a more thorough diagnosis would have revealed more such cases. They expressed the belief that subsequent failures of those readmitted were largely due to these emotional problems. Indeed, they "assumed that every academic failure is accompanied by unresolved emotional problems which may or may not be causative of the failure." (p. 78).

A similar piece of research was carried out at Ohio State by Warmen.[22] Only those readmission candidates referred to the University's Counseling and Testing Center for an evaluation were included in his sample. A total of 234 dropouts were seen by the counselors and after evaluation each was rated on a five-point scale. These ratings were given to the petitions committee which acted on the request for readmission. The committee did not always agree with the action proposed by counselors, however. The phi coefficient correlation between the ratings furnished by the counselors and those of the petitions committee was 0.47, indicating a fair amount of disagreement. Warmen reports that half of all those readmitted subsequently dropped out again.

The predictions of the counselors were made chiefly on the

basis of an Ohio State Psychological Examination, the student's academic record up to dismissal, and other materials such as letters from employers, parents, and the candidate himself. After the predictions had been made, the counselors noted that the students' scores on the test of scholastic ability correlated very hghly with their predictions of success and concluded that the ability scores were given too much weight by both the counselors and the committee.

The Peszke-Arnstein study already referred to was carried out to determine how well psychologists could predict the adjustment of the readmitted Yale student who had left on medical leave. Medical leaves are given at Yale when "the psychiatric condition is acute, incapacitating, and clearly diagnosable." (p. 133). Before returning, the student in this category must be seen for a psychiatric interview. The psychiatrist may or may not ask for psychological testing to be done. Most of the psychiatric interviews were conducted by the same doctor.

A total of 101 readmitted students were included in the investigator's sample. All returned after a medical leave between 1956 and 1963. Of these 101 students who were given permission to reenter school (and for whom success was predicted) 70 percent have graduated or were in good standing at Yale when the study was made. This figure of 70 percent compares with the success rate of 80 percent given by Inman and Altemeyer for all readmitted students at Yale.

The basis for recommending acceptance or rejection of the request for readmission was not clearly outlined. Apparently it was a decision reached by the psychiatrist who made clinical judgments in each case. It should be noted that practically all students were eventually admitted.

Peszke and Arnstein were interested in seeing whether the predictive success of the staff had improved over the years. It had. Of those students admitted between 1960 and 1963, 80 percent were successful. Of those readmitted over the last two years of this period (1961 to 1963), 87 percent were successful. They feel the higher rate of success was the result of more experience in interviewing, greater use of psychological tests, and "more careful clarification of the medical leave status and the requirements for readmission." (p. 148). Possibly the latter factor is the most important. The writers suspect that the medical leave dropouts have become aware of the standards of the psychiatrist and a great deal of self-selection takes place. Those that do not meet criterion for readmission probably do not apply until they qualify. As the authors themselves note, it would be highly useful to have data on those who do not apply for readmission.

Nevertheless the 70 to 87 percent rates for success of the readmitted are very high when compared with the 25 percent figure given by Giesecke, the figure of 50 percent by Warmen, and with the 58 percent given by Nicholi as the success rate for psychiatric readmits.

We see that, in general, guidelines to be used in deciding who should be readmitted and the timing of such a decision remain unclear. The major part of these decisions are left in the hands of the dropouts themselves. Of those who decide to return, only a very few are prevented from doing so and those are cases where it is quite clear that the student would not be successful. This is not to suggest that the student not have a crucial part in the question of readmission. Rather it merely indicates that in fact the student's decision is tantamount to readmission, a decision based on desire with little or no systematic evidence.

Needed Research

The psychology of the adolescent has not been well applied in readmission research. If many of the researchers quoted in this paper are correct in their belief that personality variables and emotional adjustments are of overriding importance in the success or failure of the readmit, then future attempts to understand the behavior of the returning student might also do well to concentrate their focus on psychodynamic variables. To a great extent, past efforts have put too much faith in intellectual variables in the case of the readmit. Scholastic aptitude and high schol records are not nearly as useful, which is unfortunate because they are much easier to measure.

Longitudinal studies which follow readmitted students until graduation or until they leave a second time would also be tremendously informative. What types of stress do they meet which prove difficult for them to handle? In what ways do they approach the demands of school differently? As Riesman asks, to what extent have successful readmits "learned a better casing of the academic joint so as to get by with less work . . . ?" Are they later successful because "they no longer were freshmen, exposed to the temptations of free-dom in their first experience away from home?"[23] Did they change to more realistic majors or succeed by taking easier courses? These and similar questions are worth exploring.

Similarly, more research using experimental programs designed to aid the readmit adjust to college would be instructive and worth-while. It is probably unrealistic to expect students who have failed before to make a relatively abrupt about face and find the going easy when they return. Programs which aid the adjustment of the readmit would "save" some talented youngsters who are now in a position to achieve.

A RECENT INVESTIGATION

The author[24] has done a short-term follow-up of returning Harvard dropouts. To be eligible for inclusion in his study, a dropout had to be a Harvard male, to have completed at least one year of college, to come from an intact family, to have left school for reasons other than a physical illness, "act of God," or any reason which could not be interpreted as an inability to deal with stresses associated with school, and to have been accepted for readmission by Harvard College to start with the fall, 1968 term. The series contained 34 students.

The psychological tests used in this study were the Rorschach, the Student TAT,[25] the Myers-Briggs Sufficiency Indices, and a self-report questionnaire used in the Harvard Student Study. This ques-

---

23 Riesman, D. Letter to the Editor. Harvard Educat. Rev., 34:582–584, 1964, p. 584.
24 Sorenson, D. Coping with college demands after readmission: A study of coping behaviors in dropouts from Harvard College who return. Doctoral dissertation, Harvard Graduate School of Education, 1969.
25 Coelho, G. V., Silber, E., and Hamburg, D. A. Use of the student T.A.T. to assess coping behavior in hospitalized, normal, and exceptionally competent college freshmen. Percept. Motor Skills, 14:355–365, 1962.

tionnaire (#8) contains scales on self-confidence, on psychological mindedness, etc. All tests were completed within the first three weeks of the semester. Once the testings were completed and the tests scored, each subject was interviewed.

A follow-up interview conducted the following March served to gain a picture of the student's activities, accomplishments, and functioning during his first six months back in school after readmission.

Predicting Grades after Readmission

We cannot predict the grades a boy will make after readmission so easily as we can predict an entering freshman's grades. For Harvard students as a whole, the correlation between the Admissions Committee's prediction and the grades actually earned by the entering class has been close to 0.70 for the last five years. For our readmitted group this correlation was only 0.53. If our series is typical, this finding suggests that the earlier aptitudes and achievements which are considered in predicting freshman grades do bear some weight in predicting scholastic performance for the readmit but not with the same predictive weight they have for the rest of the Harvard population.

For Harvard students as a whole, a positive relationship between Scholastic Aptitude Test scores and grades exists. The correlation coefficient is usually between $+0.30$ and $+0.40$. However, SAT scores did not predict the grades of our readmitted dropouts. The correlation between their grades and their Verbal SAT scores was $+0.13$. Their Mathematical SAT scores correlated -0.15 with their grades. The Achievement Test scores in their College Boards correlated $+0.16$ with their grades. All three of these correlations could have arisen by chance if the true correlation were zero.

None of the psychological tests used in this study predicted grades successfully. The Rorschach did show correlations of $+0.36$ between Response Number and academic overachieving after readmission as well as a correlation of $+0.39$ between number of small d and overachieving. (Both these correlations are significantly better than chance.) McArthur[26] noticed the same trends in his Harvard Student Study panel and suggests that some professors may indeed reward sheer verbosity, quite as the student legend goes.

One reason no other predictors were found may be the restriction in range of grades after readmision. When preleaving grades of the men were compared to postreturning grades, the group as a whole showed an increase in average grade. Only five men had grades lower than those they made before dropping out. The decline was not dramatic for any of the five. (Similar observations were cited in our review of the literature.) None of the readmitted men worked at a level which would warrant academic probation or put him in any immediate danger of flunking out. Those who had had academic difficulties before leaving, and therefore had to do better to stay in school after readmission, all showed the required improvement. All but one man averaged C or better.

In fact, only one man dropped out a second time during the (admittedly brief) follow-up period.

In light of how some students described their study habits, this general rise in grades is surprising. Last minute cramming was a saving act for many. The experience of one student we interviewed was extreme in this respect, but not by far. He reports:

Until January I did nothing. But I studied hard in January. I came close to a nervous breakdown. I studied three or four days without sleep. I was concerned for grades and I wanted desperately to show I could do some work. It was romantic and peaceful to work while others slept. But I haven't done much work since the spring semester started.

Another stated: "I feel good that what I did at the end was a consistent effort. It wasn't much in terms of length. I didn't get down to studying until almost the end."

Many students were surprised by their grades. One who had coped poorly with college after coming back reported:

Academically the semester went better than any I've had before, which was a surprise to me. I was really worried about flunking out.

26 McArthur, C. C., and King, S. Rorschach configurations associated with college achievement. J. Educat. Psychol., 45(8):492–498, 1954.

I didn't do much work and was expecting the worst. I had a real problem getting to it. I could always find an excuse not to do anything.

One can only conclude that, as bad as things were for some, things were generally better than before these men left school and, further, that sheer ability carried many through the academics of the semester. They could flounder in regard to most demands and be unhappy but manage to get grades good enough to stay in school.

PREDICTING COPING SKILL AFTER READMISSION

Grades are not the only or even the best criterion of how wise we have been to readmit a student or of how wise he has been to come back to our college. The importance of developing a way of rating the "coping behavior" of the returned dropout was suggested by the work of Haan[27] on "coping maneuvers" as distinguished from "defense maneuvers" and by Erikson's[28] theory of the growth tasks of the postadolescent years. Following their leads, a detailed rating schedule, based on behavior reported by the returnee during his six months back at school can be spelled out. This rating system can be made to lead in turn to one summary Criterion Rating that measures how well a man is handling college the second time around.

We need not give the whole rating schedule here but, in short, the student who is rated as coping well shows detachment and objectivity in his perceptions and in planning his activities, he is aware of social standards and the reasons for having them but he is not a slave to their dictates, he has an internalized value system that is uniquely his own and gives direction to his behavior, he is not compelled to order his actions or judge them primarily in terms of the values of his parents, the demands made by Harvard, or existing social standards, but neither does he feel it is necessary to flaunt these values,

[27] Haan, N. Proposed model of ego functioning: coping and defense mechanisms in relationship to I.Q. change. Psychol. Monogr., 77(8, whole no. 571), 1963. Also see by the same author: An investigation of the relationships of Rorschach scores, patterns and behavior to coping and defense mechanisms. J. Project. Techn., 28(4):429–441, 1964.

[28] Erikson, E. H. Identity and the Life Cycle. New York, International Universities Press, 1959.

demands, and standards. With respect to the changing demands made upon him he shows flexibility of response, yet his degree of flexibility is not such that he responds without planning and he can delay the gratification of his impulses and desires when such a tactic would work to his best advantage.

Ratings of coping behavior thus defined turned out to vary independently of college grades.

It was hypothesized that the way the heroes a student created in the stories he told in his Student TAT coped with the demands depicted in ten test pictures would predict how the student, himself, would cope with similar demands after readmission. This hypothesis was strongly supported by the data. When ratings from the student's reports of their own behavior during the follow-up semester were correlated with STAT ratings a correlation of 0.55 was obtained.

The two measures of self-confidence used in the investigation both predicted follow-up interview coping ratings well: the Self-Confidence scale from Questionnaire #8 correlating +0.58 with our Coping Criterion and the Self-Confidence scale from the Myers-Briggs correlating +0.57. The Myers-Briggs Stamina scale also correlated +0.57 with the Coping Criterion while, appropriately enough, the Myers-Briggs Strain scale correlated in reverse, at −0.27.

The author of the Myers-Briggs test[29] reports that a Stamina score below 8 together with a Strain score above 12 almost always indicates emotional disturbance. Three members of our readmitted group had such a pattern. All three were clearly coping poorly and emphasized in the follow-up interviews their unhappiness with both themselves and Harvard. Each man was conscious of and depressed by his inability to meet his own expectations for himself or the expectations of his father.

With two students a low Stamina score was accompanied by both a low Self-Confidence score and a low Strain score. The behavior of these subjects fits what the test theory would lead us to expect. They were not actively involved with the demands of school nor were they intensely unhappy. Interview excerpts will illustrate.

---

[29] Myers, I. B. Emotional difficulty as evidenced by the Reported Sufficiency Indices of the Myers-Briggs Type Indicator. Educational Testing Service (mimeo).

One remarked:

> I had a problem of getting to my studies and also a problem con-
> centrating. . . . Study is a frustrating experience. That's way I don't do
> it. . . . Another bad problem is that I didn't do much more than the class
> work. I had a couple better relationships with others but didn't get in-
> volved in any activities.

The second student, when asked how the semester went, reports:

> It was better and worse. There were a lot of ups and downs. I
> didn't like it here at times and I thought of quitting. . . . It seemed like
> a colossal waste of time to be spending all the time here. I feel I'll just
> try and last out the semester. I don't want to have to come back.

These two appear to have an emotional distaste for difficulties
(lack of Stamina) and a low Self-Confidence. It also sounds as if
they did not experience high Strain.

These three scores from the Myers-Briggs did not correlate
with grades for the semester. The correlations were all very close
to zero. Thus while these indices relate strongly to the Coping Criterion they do not predict classroom achievement. They relate best to
how one deals with "out-of-the-classroom" tasks and issues.

A summary rating of mental health as shown in the Rorschach
correlated +0.38 with the Coping Criterion ratings. While this
correlation is too large to have occurred by chance, it is disappointing.

Two case studies are given here to illustrate in detail some of
the primary differences in the behavior of readmits rated high on
coping and readmits with low ratings.

A Case Rated a "High Coper"

Steve spent his high school years in three different schools on
the West Coast. Like many Harvard students he earned honor grades
throughout the four high school years and was active in numerous
groups and projects. Writing for school publications, drama, and soccer
were his favorite activities.

His father, trained in law (Yale Law School), has been a politician
for many years. Mother is a Radcliffe graduate and has had an off and
on career in elementary education. Although he claims to have always
been close to both parents, he has more interests in common with his
mother.

Steve has both an older sister and an older brother and also a
sister and a brother who are younger than himself. His oldest sister is
the assistant to a United States Ambassador in a large foreign country.
The older brother is a high school athletic coach. One brother is still in

high school and the second sister married after one year of college. Steve and his older sister, who attended Radcliffe, are clearly the academic stars of the family and if any male is to do as well as or better than father it will have to be Steve.

According to Steve, he was never really happy at Harvard. His classwork was not interesting to him and he was not getting as much out of school as he hoped to. After two years he dropped out. He reports: "I thought I'd like to get a job. I didn't feel I was getting anything out of the college experience. I also thought it would be nice to concentrate on one thing for awhile."

He went to New York hoping to get a job in the entertainment business. Offers came but he was not pleased with them. After a few months he returned to Cambridge and worked at the Loeb Theater until school began in the fall. He then enrolled once again.

Although much more active with his time he remained unhappy. After another semester he left again (February, 1966). He states:

I'd turned my life upside down. I was up nights and slept days. I smoked too much and lacked any discipline. I wasn't doing any work for my courses. I'd been in a play and gave it most of my time. It got good reviews in the *Globe*. My grades were one B and the rest D's and E's.

He decided he wanted intensive psychotherapy and entered a private hospital for that purpose. After seven months he left to get a job and take some night courses. After another seven months his job appointment ended and he had two poor grades to show for his classroom efforts. He returned to Cambridge and applied for readmission. His House Master refused to support such a move. After an unsuccessful effort in summer school he again entered a mental hospital. Doing so was pretty much forced upon him by his parents. Steve had been refusing to see them and had moved several times in an effort to make it very difficult for them to find him.

He remained in intensive therapy and hospitalized until he returned to Harvard in September, 1968. In the later therapy relationship he responded well. He reports: "It was a very different experience. Before I was unhappy because I got little response out of the doctor. But this time we worked together." When asked how he was different he responded:

I'm more relaxed and less easily annoyed. I'm rolling with the punches more. I'm quite different now than then; perhaps the change was inevitable. I expect less out of other people in dealing with me. I expect people to be less singularly concentrated in me.

He was seen for a psychological evaluation before returning. From a slow and nonemotional response style he seemed a little depressed. But aside from this constriction and a desire not to reveal too much about himself, his test responses were quite healthy.

Excerpts from the psychological report written to the psychiatrist give more of the test picture:

This is obviously a bright fellow and he is able to use his intellectual resources at the present time. You think from watching him that he is moving too slowly to do well but he surprises you. . . . There is an air of mystery to this student. He doesn't permit you to get close to him or learn anymore about his thoughts and life than is absolutely necessary. . . . His test responses do show good impulse control and the presence of mind to answer the questions in such a way that he looks psychologically sound. . . . Although the psychometrist felt he lacked confidence in himself, on the intellectual tests Steve's self-ratings on the self-esteem questionnaire indicate that he feels he is up to making a good record if he returns.

I feel he is ready to return. His report on his development since leaving makes sense and shows noteworthy progress. I would feel more confident in this recommendation if I had gotten to know him better through tests. But he keeps his cards close to his vest. . . .

His STAT heroes show they are capable of coping with typical problems facing college students. They enjoy dating, can communicate with their parents, study in spite of distractions, enjoy extracurricular activities, etc. They do a little brooding but, as he puts it in one story, 'the broodings are broodings of all young men facing manhood.' Steve will probably function as well as his heroes.

When he returned for the follow-up interview in March, 1969, he reported that things had gone very well for him. The report can best be given in his words:

It's been a good experience. I'm very very happy with the return to Harvard. It's been richer and more meaningful than for a considerable time before I left. Events in my personal life have been quite satisfactoy. I've had good relationships with family, friends, and girls. I've enjoyed extracurricular activities.

I approached the semester with trepidation. I had a bad period at midterm when I wasn't sure I'd passed an exam. My final grades were C+, B—, and A—. I'm not disappointed but I would have liked better ones. I haven't considered the issue of the worth of grades. The grades were accurate. I was impressed with the sympathy and competence of the graders.

I studied quite a lot. I had some activities which interfered at times but I was consistent in getting to my studies. That's what I liked about it. I kept up with things and was generally relaxed. Before leaving I did nothing. I got too far behind to ever catch up.

(Did you have any study problems?) No real ones. But I took a course in philosophy that I had no background for. That made me uneasy. I was only able to give a pedestrian performance.

(Paper writing?) I took the maximum amount of time to do a paper. I would always take an extension if it were offered. I never went over the day where points would be deducted. They went well.

(Test anxiety?) No great anxiety. This has never been a problem for me. I don't like them but they aren't great problems. . . .

(Spend nonstudy time?) Too much time wasn't left. I went home (family has moved to East Coast) on vacations and some weekends to see parents. I saw girls and friends. I read a lot of material. I went to some movies, plays, symphonies, and art galleries. I was a member of _____(club) and did some writing which may be published.

(Dating?) I dated more on vacations and weekends when I was out of town. I had an appreciable number of dates. . . .

(Interpersonal relations?) Richer. More meaningful. More honest. Less role playing in them. . . . They are no different in the number of friends I have. A lot of people I knew before have left.

(Any change in self-image since returning?) I don't see any big change. I've always had a good opinion of myself. My only concern was whether I could reach what I'm capable of doing.

Not much more needs to be added. It seems likely that Steve will graduate and will have spent his time since readmission quite profitably.

Clearly he is much better controlled than before. One might even call him highly controlled. He is careful to keep up-to-date with his studies. Although he did not write out a schedule he had one in the back of his mind which he stuck to pretty closely. In this respect he differed from most subjects. His semester does not sound particularly exciting. Other "high copers" had a much more lively time. But Steve did what he hoped he could do.

A Case Rated a "Low Coper"

This case study was selected for presentation because it illustrates a large number of factors which in this study are associated with poor coping.

Ray comes from a suburb of Boston and attended a public high school. Although he did well in his classes, was captain of the track team, and was in various other groups, he did not have to work to keep up with everything.

His father graduated from Harvard College and has a law degree. But he has never practiced law. At present he is a "sportswear manager" in a department store. Ray describes him by saying. "He doesn't have a mean bone in his body. He's very quiet and locked up—ineffectual. I've had nothing to do with him. Never!"

Mother, a former nurse, is described by Ray as: "The opposite of father. The usual; a very domineering bitch—very active in the community—very concerned—very self-righteous—totally emasculating."

There are two older brothers and one younger than himself in the family. The oldest attended Harvard, won a Fulbright Fellowship, and is presently a lawyer working for the Poverty Program. The second is, according to Ray, "the brilliant radical in the family." He is a drama critic in New York. The younger brother is the "black sheep" of the family. Ray reports: "We were all little whiz kids but he turned from school. He's a whiz in electronics. He's been in therapy a long time and has come a long way."

In speaking of his relationship with his brothers Ray claimed a fondness for his younger brother but was not sure how he felt towards the others. He states: "Before I went to college I never spoke to either. That's how it was in our family. But since college I've gotten closer to them I guess." He feels he has been trying to compete with both but "they are always a little above me."

Like Steve, Ray was unhappy at college from the day he entered. He reports:

My courses in the first year all stunk. I was filling requirements for medical school and hated them. I wasn't self-motivated and was always behind. Two weeks before the last semester of my sophomore year I had six papers to write and all my exams to prepare for. I came to the Health Services to see Dr. —————. He told me it was a long-term thing so I left and went to ————— Hospital. I was in therapy there twice a week.

He had trouble in other areas besides the classroom. He goes on:

My roommate was pushy and insincere. He overdid it. I had no privacy. I also had problems with a girlfriend. The bad roommates, boring courses, and girl problems caused me to isolate myself more and more. I dropped premed after the fall semester of my sophomore year and took on too many reading courses. I was overloaded.

His problem with his girlfriend was quite central to his leaving. He described what happened this way: "She was the first girl I ever dated. She led me, opened my eyes to all sorts of things. I learned all about dating and girls. I was totally dependent on her. We spent a lot of time together." Then his girl began going out with other fellows and Ray could not accept this:

She was going out and I wanted her very much. I was very angry at losing her. Emotionally I'm six years old in a lot of ways. I withdrew. This is my way of handling anger. There was total paralysis. I couldn't laugh or anything. There was total demoralization. I couldn't talk for weeks.

Due to this turmoil Ray found himself even further behind in his work than was usual. Cramming got him through his exams and he tried to write the papers over the summer. He did not succeed and decided not to register the next fall.

While out of school he had various jobs. After a summer as a camp counselor he returned to Cambridge to work in a book store. Very shortly he quit and then worked as an orderly in an animal hospital. This job lasted two months. He reported: "I liked the work but couldn't stand the people. The atmosphere was crude, impersonal, and unfriendly."

For the next two months he worked as a salesman in a department store. This time he quit to stay with a sick friend while the friend's parents worked. In February he met the director of the camp he had worked for previous summers and talked the director into letting him work at camp making repairs in preparation for the new season. From then until June he lived with the director and his family. Ray reports: "It was the first time I had relaxed in 16 years. They were good people. There was good physical work which I needed."

In September he decided to return to Harvard even though he was not sure he was prepared to do so. He was referred to the author for psychological testing.

In commenting on whether or not he felt he should reenroll at that time Ray demonstrated uncertainty:

I planned to come back only when I knew what I wanted. But I realize now I won't know that for a good while. My therapist has been pushing me to tell him why I want to return. I can't give specific reasons. I just want to come back and see if I can learn something.

Excerpts from the testing report give more of the picture:

Although Ray is slowed down and was not functioning up to his potential on the tests he still came out with some pretty good scores. He demonstrated top-notch creative talent.

The most disturbing aspect of his intellectual performance is the fact that he is not asking a great deal of himself. He has more potential than he is using or willing to apply to a problem. Ray also suffers from strong feelings of inferiority relative to his ability. One of the main themes of his STAT stories is that 'his being intellectual is a bluff.' He figures that someday the ruse will be found out. . . . Ray is very definitely depressed.

The depression results from doubts about his ability to please others and doubts that he is an object worth notice. He speaks of never having been noticed by his parents as a child. The effects of this have stayed in his self-image.

The feelings which this boy has inside come out most clearly on the Rorschach. He saw numerous insects which were 'pinned down and unable to move.' His animals 'slink along' and his humans 'crawl.' On card four he seemed to identify strongly with a ragged giant who is 'just chomping along.'

An infantile search for a warm and understanding mother is the most important thing on Ray's mind. Were this problem to be solved he would be in a much better position to devote himself to other tasks including school. Emotionally he is a child in many respects. Dependency needs are so strong he cannot put them aside to meet other demands.

Can he make it through if readmitted? My answer would have to be that I doubt it very much. Too much of his case is built on hope.

I am impressed by the message given by three of his STAT stories. In story one he writes: "He had long been anticipating his first day of college. Thoughts of glory to be achieved, awards to be reaped in, flooded his mind like grape juice. Finally—here—arrived—this to be the site of all his triumphants. Suitcase gripped firmly, he resolutely began his search for his dorm. He came to a fork in the road. Smile fades, suitcase slips, hands seek out his head in confusion, body collapses."

Story six goes as follows: "She has studied diligently an entire semester, reasonably confident in her ability, until two days before the final. In a flurried panic she suddenly understood nothing and could not calm down. When the exam finally came she sat thoughtless and motionless for the first hour and a half watching the time appear and disappear, shrinking minute by minute."

We get a similar message on card 10: "Relaxing in his easy chair, arms stretched comfortably behind his head, he felt at peace. Twenty years of schooling finally over. He felt as if his life was finally his own to rule. Dreaming thoughts of knights, and princes, castles and kingdoms; unbounded but for the skies, dense blue, revelled in his freedom. He slept 30 days and 30 nights, dreaming beautiful visions but never awoke to implement them."

These do not seem to be the stories of one who feels up to dealing with school.

If he does come back it will be touch and go. As he admits, writing papers will be rough and it is not clear where the motivation to do the work will come from. If all the breaks are in his favor he would have a chance. But the odds are against it.

How did the semester go? Excerpts from Ray's own report tell the story well:

It went okay. It had its tense moments. In fact it was almost as bad as my sophomore year. But unlike sophomore year, I managed to finish many things.

I still didn't do much more than work. It's still a bad problem.

I had two finals and did okay on the first. I had a week to study for the second one. I had done 10 percent of the reading before hand. I had a lot of reading to do. I panicked in the final. I had an A— going in and came out with a B—. I must have done poorly on the exam.

I got an A, B+, B and B—. It was my best semester gradewise.

(Did it go as you thought it would?) It went exactly as I expected. I knew it would be rough. I knew I'd be nervous on exams and papers. I did expect I'd do more work however.

(Study habits?) Erratic, unstructured. There were three to four days at a time when I could study steadily and I did study some when I wasn't under pressure. I react poorly to pressure. My study habits are the same as before I left. I've always lacked steady discipline. I can get out of here without having learned to work at all. That worries me. I had a problem with getting to it and also a problem of concentrating. I read slowly and have a hard time remembering what I read. It's a frustrating experience. That's why I don't do it.

(Paper writing?) I missed most of my deadlines. Papers are a hassle but they get written eventually. They are the key part of my grade. They are put off as long as possible.

(Perform during tests?) I only had two exams, except the final where I panicked. I blew one of them. The other went okay. I learned I don't remember anything unless it's relevant.

(Extracurricular activities?) I do some running and ran in a cross-country meet. I did a little informal writing—diary stuff and poetry.

(How did you spend the bulk of your nonstudy time?) That's hard to say. It's hard to account for all my time. I spent a lot of time sleeping, but not as much as I did sophomore year. I listened to a lot of music. That blows a lot of time. Also talking with friends.

(Dating?) Pretty dry. I hate to start dating. It might be the same thing over again. I don't know if I can handle a girlfriend.

(Was it easy to make new friends?) I had no one to talk to sophomore year. It was a nice change that I did this year. I clashed with people before. Had a bad clash with my roommate. This year my roommate is inoffensive. But I'm close to a couple of guys downstairs. They are the most solid relationships I've had. I don't have many friends outside of my House.

(Parents?) My parents are just as distant and tense as ever.

(Career goals?) They have been put off. I have no idea what will happen. I think of teaching and counseling. It—if the war is going on it will almost have to be teaching after graduation. But I still haven't figured out what I want to do. But I feel I'm more capable.

(Prognosis for future?) I sort of figure I will stay in until graduation. But if I could figure out something else to do I'd leave again.

Ray's story illustrates the not uncommon action of returning to school because there is little else the student wants to do. Before returning Ray had trouble with everything he tried and was lost as to where to go next. His therapist felt he had to make his own decision, even if wrong, and let him do so. The university felt the same way evidently and in spite of evidence that he had not changed a great deal he was permitted to return.

This case also demonstrates what the talented readmit can do by way of earning good grades, at least for one semester, on the basis of a few hours of effective study through the semester, some last minute cramming, and his good ability. Ray would be the last person to say he had learned a great deal, used a large segment of his time productively, made a significant contribution to the Harvard community, or been happy. Yet he had excellent grades.

It should be noted that in one of his four courses each student graded himself. Although Ray did little he claimed an honor grade. In another course the instructor did not take grading seriously and gave everyone a B or better. Grades are not always a good measure of coping or of the excellence of one's education.

Ray's story also shows the defensive stance which the "low coper" is likely to take in areas which are particularly stressful to him. Ray stayed away from dating, not because he did not want to date but because he did not feel capable of functioning adequately in this area. It threatened him and he chose to "stay off the tennis court."

Ray did reach out to fellow students to a certain degree, but not very far. His friends were those who lived within a few doors of his room in the dorm. Time with them was spent in bull sessions, listening to records, etc. While it was to his credit that he did reach out to peers (and there are elements of coping in his efforts) the stance might still be interpreted as defensive. What he and friends did together was kill time and support each other's efforts to stay away from studies and other "out-in-the-Harvard-community" activities.

STUDENTS FACING UNUSUAL STRESS

These two case studies illustrate the possible effects on adaptation when a student faces stress not associated with "an average-expectable environment."

John has always looked upon his relationship with his father as being of extreme importance. He had always been close to his father, a surgeon, and wanted desperately to please him by also becoming a doctor. An older brother was already enrolled in medical school and rivalry between the brothers was intense. John saw it as imperative to attend a better medical school than his brother and earn better grades.

His obsession with marks good enough to win his acceptance to a top flight medical school made him extremely anxious on tests and his grades suffered. In John's senior year his applications were rejected by the medical schools to which he applied. There followed an attempt at suicide and hospitalization.

A factor which added complications was homosexuality. His sexual relations with other males led to severe guilt feelings and to the conclusion that he could never face his father again.

John remained out of school a year. Though hospitalized for much of this time he was able to reestablish communication with his father and gain some perspective on his ambitions.

He returned to Harvard planning to remain in medicine but willing to accept attendance at an "inferior" medical school. His STAT heroes demonstrated good coping skills and his test scores on the Self-Confidence and Stamina scales were high.

For two months everything went well. John had good grades on his midterm exams and was up-to-date with his work. He was dating a girl regularly and felt he had established a good relationship with her.

In November this all collapsed. During the Thanksgiving vacation his older brother (and rival) "dropped in" for a visit. His brother and John's girl "fell in love with each other" during the two day period and John was rejected. His brother and girlfriend were soon married.

John reported, "Everything fell apart. I put myself back in the hospital. My tutor fixed it up so I could withdraw again."

It is true that he may have experienced unusually great anxiety once again when the time for finals arrived. But John's story does point up how unusual stress can mean an end to what had, for a few months at least, been good coping behavior.

With Boyd unusual stress brought a different reaction.

He came to Harvard from a "rich and sheltered existence." The "hugeness" of the college overwhelmed him. Everyone else seemed to know what they were doing. In fear he established relationships of dependency with various roommates. After an unhappy three years and the failure of many in-college attempts to find himself, he felt it necessary to leave and "find some backbone." He also wanted to see a side of life to which he had never been exposed.

Boyd spent two years in Vista working with families in poverty. He reported: "I enjoyed the experience. I lived through a whole lot of things I'd never experienced before. I made a lot of close relationships with others."

Upon return he felt he had grown a great deal while out but yet rated himself very low on both measures of Self-Confidence. His STAT heroes adapted poorly to conflicts and his Stamina score was one of the lowest in the group.

A few weeks before he returned to school his knee began to pain him. In fact the pain was so great that he requested the interviewing for this study take place in his apartment. Walking was a nightmare. The pain and the drugs taken for the pain made it difficult to study and his classwork did not go well. Doctors at the college diagnosed his problem as "tendon trouble" and did a repair operation. But the pain persisted. While he was home for the Christmas vacation the family doctor, upon hearing of his pain, hospitalized Boyd and did an exploratory operation. Cancer was found and the leg was immediately amputated. The doctors warned that the operation may have come too late.

Boyd's parents made arrangements for him to move back with them and, even though in a depressed and upset state, this frightened him. In facing this threat of increased dependency he concluded that he should live as normal a life as possible and do it as soon as possible. He insisted on returning to Harvard directly from the hospital and did so. He set about making up the work he had missed.

Due to the fact that Boyd had not completed the semester's work and had been impaired as far as extracurricular activities, dating, etc., were concerned, he was not included in the sample of 34 whose test scores and coping ratings were handled statistically. Although he was unable to meet some of the criteria for good coping which were established for the study, he was clearly coping well with some very real difficulties and issues.

Admittedly the stresses faced by John and Boyd, although severe for both, were not equal in the meaning they held for the individual. The type of stress encountered undoubtedly had much to do with whether they could or could not cope with it. Yet these cases do serve to illustrate the merit of not ignoring the stress agents in any analysis of one's ability to cope well.

DISCUSSION OF FINDINGS

The investigation's primary value, relative to the readmission process, derives from the fact that a group of readmits, most of them not emotionally disturbed, were studied with clinical intensity. Emotionally disturbed dropouts have been studied with clinical methods and groups more representative of the total readmit population have been studied using questionnaires and objective tests. The results of the present study are more representative than those from past clinical studies in the area and, at the same time, give a more complete picture of the subjects than do questionnaire investigations. But the "ideal" investigation designed to study a representative group of readmits with real intensity remains to be done.

Our results pointed up the fact that coping success and academic performance are not closely related to one another. Men who adapted poorly in most areas earned grades which, when averaged, were almost as high as those of men who adapted well. Some information gained from the interviews is helpful in understanding the apparent lack of relationship between those variables. The majority of the subjects in the sample claimed that their grades were fairly unimportant to them. For some this claim might have been an easy rationalization but for most it was seen by the investigator as a simple statement of feelings. Many of these students felt it would have been possible for them to have earned better grades. But they quite consciously chose to devote much of their time to other goals. What must not be forgotten is that most of the subjects left school because of difficulty in coping with stress in general, stress not necessarily associated with less than acceptable grades. After readmission each was likely to focus his attention on the problem or problems which had previously forced him to leave. In a sense, too, it may be that readmits in general had developed some perspectives as to achievement at Harvard and were not so concerned about achievement at a highly specific level.

There is still another factor to consider. The ratings we made to evaluate coping skill emphasized the efficiency of a subject's study habits. How long he studies was not as important as his getting the work done, his making good use of his time, and his ability to handle the demands of papers, tests, and home assignments to his satisfaction. A few "low copers," because of study conflicts and the resulting inefficient study habits, had to put in more time to get grades equal to those of the "high coper." Although their grades were acceptable they had not benefited as greatly from the college experience.

This argument has been discussed by Silber et al.[30] They point out that two factors must be considered in evaluating coping skill. The first is the effectiveness with which each task is accomplished and second is the cost to the individual of this effectiveness. In coping, the task must be "accomplished according to standards that are tolerable both to the individual and to the group in which he lives" (p. 355). Thus, the "low coper" can obtain acceptable grades but it is frequently at a cost in anguish, lost opportunities, and lowered self-esteem which is excessive.

Clearly, then, the readmit is concerned with earning grades good enough to keep him in school. In many cases self-feelings require higher grades than this bare minimum. But the argument that the student should forget all else and concentrate on earning the highest honors which his abilities and efforts can achieve was not accepted here. It has also been shown that the Harvard College readmit rejects this argument. Academic performance may be a concrete measure but it is apparently too superficial an index to relate to coping or noncoping.

Results obtained with the predictive measures used support the proposition that a good way to determine how well a student will cope after readmission is to ask him, albeit sometimes indirectly. The scores which related most strongly to later ratings of coping skill were those derived from self-report instruments; the interviews and picture-story test.

In a real sense the STAT gathers material which is part of the individual's consciousness. While it is not a self-rating measure in the true sense of the term, it approaches one in practice. (In this it differs from the standard TAT, which often taps unconscious or unacknowledged emotions.) As the subject is shown pictures depicting some potentially troublesome situations inherent in college life he is undoubtedly aware of the fact that he will find himself in similar positions during the school year. As he writes his descriptions of what his hero will do he is more often than not trying to convey what he thinks he will do in the same situation. The high relationship found between the readmits' story outcomes and their actions

30 Silber, E., Hamburg, D. A., Coelho, G. V., Murphy, E. B., Rosenberg, M., and Pearlin, L. I. Adaptive behavior in competent adolescents. Arch. Gen. Psychiat., 5:354–365, 1961.

during the semester would suggest that the individual is a good judge of his own coping potentialities. It would also argue that the subjects possessed a good degree of self-insight. To describe accurately how he will behave the student must have a feel for his present level of adjustment and the resources at his command to deal with conflicts.

In previous studies[31] the STAT has quite clearly differentiated between highly competent adolescents, "normal" adolescents, and adolescents who had been judged emotionally disturbed. It was also successfully used by the same investigators as a screening instrument to discriminate between dropouts who return and cope with college on a broad front and those who continue to be troubled by stress and are unhappy. It is not known whether it will differentiate between those who will remain and obtain their degrees from those who leave again. Follow-up data are needed to learn how well it will perform this function.

Coelho and his associates[32] have not had great success when correlating STAT scores with interview ratings. Such correlations have always been positive and significant in order of magnitude but low. They have believed that the STAT scores would relate more strongly to interview ratings if the ratings reflected more closely the same content and emphasis as the STAT pictures. The correlation between STAT scores and the Coping Criterion obtained in this investigation is supportive of this contention.

The success of the Sufficiency Indices of the Myers-Briggs in differentiating between "high copers" and "low copers" is, in light of their length, sobering. The Self-Confidence scale has 16 questions, the Strain scale 18, and the Stamina scale 9. No more than 15 minutes would be needed ordinarily to answer the questions on these scales if they were to be separated out from the other questions of the Myers-Briggs test. (Of course this might well alter the task considerable as well as the "set" of the client.)

To our knowledge the Sufficiency Indices have only been used in the one study reported on in the manual and in the Harvard

---

[31] Coelho et al., *op. cit.*
[32] Coelho, G. V., Steinberg, A. G., Solomon, F., Wolff, C.T., and Hamburg, D. A. Predicting confidence in college-life situations: Prediagnostic use of the Student-TAT. Nat. Inst. Mental Health (mimeo).

258 / EMOTIONAL PROBLEMS OF THE STUDENT

Student Study. Thus, it is difficult to compare findings. Surely they deserve more attention in future investigations, elsewhere?

The Stamina scale is particularly interesting. The motivation for its development derived from the observation that a few capable members of a high school class taking part in a research investigation had a conspicuous tendency to quit or "lie down on the job" when faced with serious demands. The test author[33] is convinced that a low Stamina score also reflects "basic instability due to absence of judgment." She writes: "On empirical grounds, we have repeatedly found very low Stamina scores in people who have messed up their lives in spectacular ways." (p. 5). She also reports that a "very low stamina alone means a quite different and more damaging defect than either very low self-confidence alone or very high strain alone." (p. 4). This finding was gratifying to her because while other measures of self-confidence and strain exist, the Myers-Briggs is the only test to measure stamina.

One of the reasons why these indices could be expected to correlate well with the Coping Criterion is that both were determined from the subject's feelings about his own adequacy. As a determinant of behavior, how the individual feels both about himself and what he has done is, however, just as real, in some cases more real, than his actual accomplishments. One is as likely to drop out of school again because he feels unhappy and inadequate as he is to leave for some other reason.

The failure to find a significant relationship between Rorschach scores and the Coping Criterion was due to a number of factors. First of all, in theorizing how a "high coper" could be expected to perform on the Rorschach, the findings of McArthur[34] were given emphasis even though the index of success at Harvard in his studies had been "gradegetting."

The Rorschach scores which related most strongly with grades in our data were those determined most directly by productivity on the test (total R and O percent). Scores which try to assess the quality of one's perceptions (W percent, F+ percent, and O+

[33] Myers, *op. cit.*
[34] McArthur and King, *op. cit.*

percent) all correlated negatively with grades. (These correlations were not significant.) McArthur noticed the same trends in his "gradegetting" study. But coping varies independently of gradegetting, so we should not expect coping also to be predicted by these same Rorschach variables.

The Rorschach predicted coping most successfully in this study and in a previous study by Haan[35] when it was treated as a simple task or demand. The student who appeared to enjoy dealing with the Rorschach was likely to enjoy dealing with other demands and to deal with them well. But the relationship between our ratings on the student's "affective enjoyment" of the Rorschach task and the Coping Criterion was not as high as Haan's results had led us to expect. Two factors seemed to be responsible. Her descriptions of Rorschach behavior written to anchor the two ends of her rating scale were not clear. Where, using Haan's material, it was unclear in the investigator's mind how the Rorschach taking behavior of a particular subject should be rated, he relied upon his own judgment of how a good coper should respond to the test.

The second important factor was the behavior of "high copers" who were not "ego-involved" in taking the inkblot test. Their lack of enthusiasm resulted in low "affective enjoyment" ratings but they adapted well to school demands. This anomaly may well have arisen from the public school vs. private school dichotomy that cuts across so many psychological generalizations.[36] Private school men do not tackle the Rorschach in a gung-ho, Horatio Alger manner.

It is clear from the data that the time away from school had different effects on different readmits. But the process of becoming a "high coper" as a readmit did not begin the day the dropout left school. Most "high copers" were already better copers than the "low copers" before they left. This is evidenced in practically all behavioral areas explored in any depth in this study. This should

[35] Haan, N. An investigation of the relationships of Rorschach scores, patterns, and behavior to coping and defense mechanisms. J. Project. Techn., 28(4):194–202, 1964.
[36] McArthur, C. Personalities in public and private school boys. Harv. Educ. Rev., 24 (4):256–262, 1954. Reprinted In Lipset, S. and Smelser, N., eds., Sociology: The Progress of a Decade. Englewood Cliffs, N.J., Prentice-Hall, Inc., 1961, pp. 287–292.

not be too surprising. Human behavior can change and the amount of change occurring while these fellows were out of school is surprising, but behavior patterns and habits are, in general, quite stable. Few dropouts change drastically. Particular stresses are problematic for them and so they leave to reorient themselves or better develop particular coping skills. But they do not seek a "restructuring" of their entire personalities.

Better coping was already evidenced in the "high copers" by the fact that many of them left for their own reasons. They saw the "handwriting on the wall" and chose to leave rather than permit their performance to deteriorate to the point where the college would force them to leave. Making a decision to leave school on one's own because, in light of one's difficulties, it seems like a positive step to take shows better adaptiveness than does wanting to leave but waiting until poor grades, intolerable behavior, or an emotional crisis forces a leave. That more "high copers" choose to leave is additional evidence of their being better copers before leaving.

In looking at which "out of school" factors differentiated between "high copers" and low "copers" a small number of relevant variables were found. Of prime significance was the variable of structure in the environment. Leighton,[37] Powell,[38] and Whitla[39] all found that the subjects in their samples who had had only one or two employers while out were less likely to leave again. In the present study those who had been in the Armed Services or in a mental hospital were included in the same category as those who had held one nine-to-five job on a consistent basis.

One explanation for this finding is that those who were in a structured environment were used to a routine. This later proved useful in college. It had been required that they organize and perform their activities in a way that would meet the demands of some other person or organization.

What also seems important from their own remarks is that this group was more likely to have experienced visible success in what they did. They had stuck with one thing and had proven that they could handle the task assigned (work or Armed Services) or that

---

37 Leighton, *op. cit.*
38 Powell, *op. cit.*
39 Whitla, *op. cit.*

they had improved to the point where someone had confidence enough in them to recommend they return to school (mental hospital). As one student put it:

I'm more confident. I'm not sure of a lot of what I'm going to do but my confidence in myself has increased. I've proven a point. I wasn't sure I could do anything before. I feel now that I can do whatever I choose.

Most could point to an experience in their away-from-school period which had been successfully completed. Such an experience surely bolstered self-esteem. The student who tried many things while out was less likely to have demonstrated competence.

Those who were in overseas projects were, in a sense, among those who had tried various things while away from school. Their roles were unstructured. They were to accomplish certain things but how they went about it and when they worked was pretty much up to the person himself. Some were able to set a limited number of fairly clear goals and accomplish these ends. But others accepted many responsibilities. They failed in some things and succeeded in others. This mixture of successes and disappointments made it difficult for the subject involved to evaluate his overall effectiveness. He felt he had done well but was not sure.

Such a student also came to appreciate his freedom or a high degree of independence. He lived where he wanted in the town, came and went when he wanted, worked on what he wanted to do at the time, etc. Adapting to the demands of someone else was not one of the things he necessarily had to do; at least it was not central to the experience. But school does require that one adjust to such demands. The college student has more freedom and independence than the soldier, the eight-to-five employee, and the hospital patient but he is not entirely on his own.

The point I am making can be illustrated well by the remarks of a subject who had spent his time away from school in such a project. Upon return he made a request to the university that he be allowed to live off campus. The request was turned down. A running battle existed between the student and his senior tutor during the entire semester. The student commented as follows:

It was a very depressing semester. I did very little work. I was in the House but didn't like the House atmosphere or my roommates. The room stifled me. It's an unnatural atmosphere. I'm struck by the lack of contact students in a dorm have with the real world. It seemed pseudointellectual, unnatural, and perverted to have 400 men live together, especially during exam period. Everything happens at a fixed time. In Africa doing my own thing was accepted.

In short, the student demanded things be done his own way or not at all. The opportunity to do things his own way was there in the rainforest but not at Harvard. He could not cope well with the resulting conflict.

Another student from the same program had similar problems. He reported:

> I've had problems. I knew it would be difficult to get adjusted. It has. I'm not willing to adjust in some areas. . . . I pay little attention to deadlines. I read only what I feel like reading. . . . Before I was up tight about being inefficient. Now I'm happy to be inefficient. . . . I didn't write one paper which was assigned last semester. The papers will get done only when they have relevance to stuff I am interested in.

One might applaud the independence of such a student. But such a stance has put him consistently at odds with the university. While such a stance may be functional in such a setting as Malaysia, the Harvard College environment makes different demands.

An insight provided by King throws light on what is involved in the behavior pattern just described. He writes that his clinical work with students and impressions from the Harvard Student Study lead him to believe that:

> The unconscious conflict between impulses and anticipations of the demands of the adult male role is a frequent cause of apathy, negativism, and scholastic underachievement. Many students who drop out of college are struggling to solve the same issue.[40]

Poor impulse control and the general inability to live with restrictions on one's behavior appear as key themes in the interview protocols of these "independent students."

There is another view to consider. In a letter sent to most

---

[40] King, S. H. Personality stability: Early findings of the Harvard Student Study. Paper presented at the Amer. College Personnel Assoc. Conf., Dallas, March, 1967, p. 24.

dropouts the college administration states that staying with a job is something which is looked upon with favor when an application for readmission is being considered. "High copers" were more likely to take this advice, indicating either that they were better able to accept "words of wisdom," were more willing to conform to expecta-tions, or both.

Therapy also played a big role for some in later coping efforts. It has been difficult to offer objective evidence to support this state-ment since the "received therapy" variable did not differentiate be-tween "high copers" and "low copers." But using the case study method and clinical impressions support is found for the idea that therapy was a crucial factor with some.

Since all who had been in therapy felt treatment had been beneficial, it appears that therapy helped most, if not all, patients adjust better than they might otherwise have done. The experiences of the two patients who, on the basis of a preadmission evaluation did not seem prepared to return to college, suggest that treatment might have made it possible for them to remain in college longer than would otherwise have been the case. But treatment does not ensure graduation.

The role played by therapy can best be illustrated through two short case studies. The two students to be described left Harvard for similar reasons. Both were severely depressed when seen at the University Health Services before dropping out. An inability to relate satisfactorily with roommates and others was the major reason for their depression. Both were very dependent upon their parents and felt they were in competition with their fathers. Both had B averages.

One, who will be referred to as George, tried to commit suicide and left school because of his need to be hospitalized. The second, to be called Jerald, was caught stealing books and lab equipment from Har-vard to get back at the school for his loneliness. George has been in therapy since. Jerald has not. He was encouraged to obtain treatment but his parents will not accept this step.

George came back to Harvard with many insights into the causes of his previous troubles. The stress agents of the environment were recognized for what they were. Yet he did not feel capable of dealing with the particular stresses which had been identified and planned his semester accordingly. He did not date or attempt to make friends. Extracurricular activities were carefully chosen so he would not have to deal with others competitively. He recognized his dependency on his parents and accepted it. During the semester he lived at home.

Jerald returned with little insight into what had happened to him before leaving and while out. He had few plans relative to how he could better cope. He was ashamed of himself for stealing and had resolved not to "do that again." Thought had also convinced him that he had been working too hard for honor grades. By taking it easy he felt he could succeed. But he had no idea how to deal with felt interpersonal deficiencies, lack of involvement with anything at Harvard except the classroom, and concerns about what he wanted to do for a career. During the semester he spent the major share of his time either in his room or in the library. He did not steal but, and Freud would be interested in this, he spent hours every day "washing my hands and thinking how clean my things are."

Differences between the two, in behavioral terms, were not great. George did have more extracurricular interests. But there was a major difference in how they felt during the semester. Jerald was unhappy and lonely. He could only hope that things would improve and that his father would let him talk to a doctor at some point. George, however, felt secure in the knowledge that he had insights into his problems and was progressing towards behaving as he wanted. He could accept the present because he had evidence that the future would be better.

For a small group a key factor in their being able to handle school after returning was a close relationship with another person either through marriage or being sponsored by a professor or therapist. For others becoming more clear about one's career goals made the important difference. Having put some phychological distance between themselves and the college made coping possible for many.

Factors which proved to be almost sure signs that the readmit would not cope well with the semester (in addition to the "opposites" of the factors above) include: (1) a feeling that he was not coming back because he wanted to and (2) having left because of stress stemming from a "necessity" to compete academically with a parent or sibling. Evidently the stress associated with a competitive relationship was extremely difficult to control. The leave of absence gave students so troubled some perspective to the situation. Most had therapy while out. Yet they could not overcome a pressing need to view the college demands in competitive terms. The theme of competition seemed to focus on constant comparisons between themselves and other family members, not simply competition with their college peers. In this way their constant judging of themselves could become a continual self-fulfilling prophecy.

IMPLICATIONS FOR PSYCHOLOGISTS AND ADMINISTRATORS

It has been demonstrated that coping and self-esteem are concepts of relevance when one is interested in assessing how the re-admit will behave and/or in helping him adjust to college.

Taking a leave of absence is often a very adaptive response. It is regrettable that the present draft situation makes it more difficult for students to take a leave in order to restore damaged self-esteem by learning to cope better.

Further, it has shown that instruments exist which can be scored in a reasonably objective manner to evaluate the coping potential and self-esteem of the individual. How well his heroes cope in his "projections" and how he makes self-rating of his own sufficiency are relevant to in-school behavior. These tests do not take an unreasonably great amount of time to complete. They can be used profitably by the psychologist to provide an evaluation of a dropout's preparedness to tackle school once again.

Even the low scoring student can be a beneficiary. He can be told what his scores indicate and that it might not be in his best interests to return at the present time. A program might then be developed with this student which would better prepare him for school. If, on the other hand, the student chooses to return before he seems prepared to do so and the college is willing to allow readmission, then those in the counseling center could be alerted to his needs and provide specific support.

For those readmits whom the university does not require to undergo phychological testing before coming back, taking the tests might be made an optional procedure. Some in the group studied were interested in establishing contact with a counselor. Four students expressed the wish in interviews that steps be taken by Harvard to offer readmits counseling upon their return. When it was pointed out to the four that any student can talk over his concerns with a psychiatrist or psychologist they stated they had not been clear about the availability of counseling. A reluctance to visit the University Health Services because their concerns did not seem serious enough was also a factor. Others felt they would prefer talking with someone who "sort of specialized" in working with the readmitted student. As noted, five in the sample did seek counseling help during the semester. It is not clear whether the four who consulted the author would have sought counseling from another staff member had they not taken part in this study. Knowing someone on the psychology staff very likely made the step of obtaining help easier.

The above suggestions assume that policies on readmission will remain lenient. It is difficult to argue against a liberal policy because the behavior of those seeking to return cannot be predicted with absolute accuracy, because it is difficult for a dropout to be admitted at another college, and because most readmits do succeed in obtaining their degrees, it would seem that the college should open its doors to a dropout when he feels he is ready to return and any evidence that he will fail to succeed is not overwhelming. If for some reason a college chooses not to be so lenient, tests of coping potential should find their way into the procedure used to determine whether an applicant should be readmitted.

Almost all colleges have shown great interest in grade prediction. The reasons why are obvious. They want to admit applicants who will not fail in their courses. The student who does not pass is seen as a bad investment. But there is another reason why grades are given so much attention and it has been mentioned often in this paper. An admissions office appreciates a criterion of success which at least has the appearance of objectivity. Grades can easily be converted to numbers and used when calculating correlations against predictors. Trying to put the student's level of success at "being a good citizen" or scores on a variable similarly vague into the computer is much more difficult.

Justifying why one student is admitted and another rejected is crucial at many schools. For example, when a legislator wants to know why the son of two supporters did not get into a state supported college it is important to have a tangible reason as an answer. To say he had low SAT's and a low high school rank-in-class and is therefore less likely to pass his courses seems to do the job. We have learned to think grades are terribly important.

Coping measure can, if the results in this study have more general validity, be helpful to the admissions office as an aid in predicting who will survive and graduate. Whether or not one graduates is not merely a function of intellectual aptitude.

Another concern of a college is reflected in the question: What does the school do when it has 3,000 qualified and highly intelligent applicants for less than 3,000 openings in the freshman class? On what basis do you differentiate between the academically talented applicants?

Two areas stand out as one looks for the answer. They are: (1) the contributions the student can make to the college and to society and (2) his ability to profit from all or most of the offerings of the college; offerings in the classroom as well as those outside of it. The student who, when under stress, is not going to take a defensive stance and "stay off the tennis court" might be worth closer consideration. Coping tests may thus be part of the answer where a college wants evidence about one's adaptation potential which is more objective than that provided by interviews. Interviewing has carried the major assessment load in this area up to the present time.

14

The Movement

Charles C. McArthur

This chapter will be out of date by the time you read it. History goes fast. Especially on campuses. Who remembers beatniks now? We stretch to recall that whites were once upon a time welcome in the civil rights marches that now are not even marches but rather demonstrations. The time is at hand when there is no longer room in the Peace Corps for ideologues who aren't blacksmiths. That banyan tree, the SDS, has lately put· down three branches that have sprouted their own roots and by the next annual meeting is sure to sprout more. Radicalization has progressed so far that McCarthy's student supporters, the "clean Genes," seem at best Victorian. Pot has been made less illegal and bills are before legislatures that would legalize it. But, most of all, millions of young people "are quietly rejecting the conventional mores of American society . . . . and actively searching, sometimes in vain but often with success, for other character ideals that fit (their) conception of what manhood should be."[1] It all went by at a dizzying speed, as we whipped along one of those straightaways in the track of social history: the 1960s.

One paragraph is too short even to list the variety of great and small changes youth made in our society in that decade and will go on making in the 1970s. Organized or unorganized, social, political,

---

[1] Gerzon, M. The Whole World is Watching: A Young Man Looks at Youth's Dissent. New York, The Viking Press, Inc., 1969, p. 242. Reprinted by permission of The Viking Press, Inc., copyright by Mark Gerzon.

or very very private, a swarm of activities new to American life keeps appearing here, there, and everywhere that young people are doing their myriad "things." Ubiquitous, unrelated to each other, each event a tiny bud yet in sum totally changing our environment, these new things are rather like the coming of spring. Generically, they were all part of an undefined something students called the Movement.

What brought on the Movement?

A social psychological theory is offered to us by one of its members. Mark Gerzon, Harvard 1970, has written a compendium of the not very radicalized aspects of the Movement. After citing such obvious trends of modern history as urbanization, he goes on to remark[2] that "Between the time of our parents' childhood and our own, four spheres of life have witnessed great historical change." First, "To the postwar generation . . . prosperity was the normal state of affairs." Second, "This generation cannot derive meaning by blindly hating another nation, because it cannot hate men with whom it shares the confines of a powder keg." Third, "our world, sud- denly shrunk by mass-communication and transportation networks, no longer allows our young American the luxury of ignorance" about other residents in "the global village." Fourth, "The minds of this generation are the first which are ready to listen to the message of philosophers who, writing during the last credible war, have been disregarded by most members of adult society." (He is speaking of Marcuse, Adorno et al.) It is Gerzon's theory that "The goals of this generation could never have become so different from adult so- ciety's had it not been for the changes in these four historical spheres."

Likely so.

Still, the change was sudden. Cumulating historical forces don't explain sudden consensus. Gerzon (p. 23) observes, as we do, the passivity of the college students of the 1950s, followed by the activ- ism of the college students of the 1960s. In the 1950s (p. 242), "Members of that generation did not speak out; there were no audi- ences. They did not band together; there seemingly were not partners. Today's young people are convinced that only the fearful hide be-

---

[2] *Ibid.*, p. 15 et seq.

hind apathy and cynicism. Because of this, the tenor of youth culture is radically different." Our attention was drawn to this contrast in two college generations by one homely fact: it all took place between editions of this book!

Apathy and After

In our first edition, apathy as a clinical state was described by Dr. Coon as "not as definitive as the classical depressions . . . but quite as disabling and devastating to its victims" in Harvard College, while Dr. Binger reported (p. 176) "in the college girl," at Radcliffe, "a loss of zest, a feeling of apathy and fatigue" that was more common than true depression, and Dr. Walters devoted a whole chapter, which reappears in this edition, to student apathy. All three authors attribute apathy as a symptom to the same psychodynamics, epidemic among the student population of the 1950s. Then, apathy seemed to be a reaction to "realistically impending defeat" and "real confusion over the difference between competitiveness and injury, aggressiveness and aggression," with resulting inability to dare assertiveness and overuse of impulse control. The apathetic students could not clearly see people as love-hate objects.

Has there since been a change in young people's psychodynamics? Dr. Walters thinks so. In this edition's chapter on drug use, he describes students as having an altered emotional situation. The newer generation has found ways both to love and to hate. May it be, then, that the sudden focussing of forces that have long been building in history has a better psychodynamic than social psychological explanation?

The Kunen Document

Personality psychologists for a long time have used rich personal documents[2a] as a source for discovering psychodynamics. By good

---

[2a] See Allport, G. W. The use of personal documents in psychological science. New York, Social Science Research Council, Bulletin 49, 1942.

fortune, a neat armchair experiment of this kind is set up for us in a book called *The Strawberry Statement: Notes of a College Revolutionary* by James Kunen,[3] who was a leader in the riots at Columbia University. Kunen has written a book in the form of a diary, much edited, but still at bottom a "personal document" within the meaning of Allport. "This book was written on napkins and cigarette packs and hitchhiking signs," reports Kunen (p. 6). "It was spread all over, but so is my mind." Again (p. 7), "I didn't spend much time writing it. You will notice that a great deal of this book simply relates little things I've done and thought . . ." Ideal, for "personal document" purposes.

The Strawberry Statement also contains some material from the years before the Columbia riots and, indeed, before Kunen went to Columbia. Kunen lived as a prep school boy through the apathetic fifties into the activist sixties. Will Dr. Walters' suggestions about student apathy as the historical precedent of student revolt find analogies in the earlier parts of Kunen's biography as well as in his present-day psychodynamics?

CRYSTALLIZATION BY ACTION

The answer is "yes." The first thirteen pages of *The Strawberry Statement* offer about as good a description of apathy as you are likely to find this side of Russian fiction.[4] For Kunen and his contemporaries (pp. 11, 12) even private apathy games like those described below "become so tiresome that the whole endeavor moved from the 'Mildly Amusing' column into the 'Pain in the Ass' column. (My roommate classifies everything into one of these two categories.)" And small wonder, when (p. 11) "college years are exhausting, confusing, boring, troubled, frustrated and meaningless" —rather like the Denmark described in Hamlet's opening speech! And small wonder when nothing better to come is in sight? Small wonder that one escape was into games of fantasy:

---

[3] Kunen, J. The Strawberry Statement: Notes of a College Revolutionary. New York, Random House, Inc., 1968. Reprinted by permission, copyright Random House, Inc.
[4] Yoncharov. Ivan's Oblomov. New York, E. P. Dutton & Co., Inc., Everyman Paperback, 1960.

So we took adaptive measures which consisted chiefly of constructing an alternate world structure in which we felt a bit more comfortable. It was a world rife with dangers, but the forces active in it were clearly enough defined to be successfully dealt with by anyone with the exquisite finesse we all possessed in it. Actually, even we used to lose more often than we'd win, but at least the legions of evil bothered to attack us. (p. 11)

Just so. "At least the legions of evil bothered to attack us." Thus creating a world not so grey. A world offering what Gerzon likes to refer to as "a credible enemy."

But only in fantasy. And fantasy was not enough to solve the real problem. "Naturally this sort of life allowed very little time for classes, and it required a hell of a lot of sleep." Meanwhile, in real life Kunen had (p. 13) "the hugest sophomore slump you can imagine."

There are passages that make one wonder how Kunen and his friends escaped outright depression. His lyrical prose about New York City (pp. 3–6) ends forthrightly with "all of this makes us sad" but then foreshadows what is to come: "But sadness is not despair so long as you can get angry." Precisely. Anger turned out is a better choice than depression. Or than the halfway house of apathy.

Anger turning out was already available to Kunen, in sublimated form, in the competitive aspects of rowing, though perhaps it turned in again on himself in whatever masochism he could discharge by subjecting himself to the total discipline of the shell. Half-denied, anger went out in the sardonic humor of adolescents, a *lingua franca* for all who are that age. A teen-age language had come out of the more intellectual prep schools like Kunen's Andover to evolve into a vicious diction that used to be called, at least at the other Phillips Academy, "slashing." Examples of "slashing" can be found throughout Kunen's book; the patois of shared cynicism between pals (pp. 12 and 13) slips naturally into general "agin' the government" talk about "John's Little Drama" (p. 14) and thence into revolutionary truisms (p. 55) that Kunen may be expecting the reader to mistake for adult discourse. Finally his anger could take flight into somewhat intellectualized action in the form of a "rag."

Tuesday, May 30, 1967: I've been wanting to talk to somebody important about the war, and tonight, after a month, I finally got through on the phone to Ambassador Bunker in Saigon. I told him that I thought he was an ambassador from the U.S. government to a U.S. government. He couldn't go along with me on that, but he did say he'd write me a letter explaining what he was about. He admitted that he hadn't been on the streets to meet the people. (p. 10)

Such rags are, in British and Scottish universities, more institutionalized group events than they are here. But individual forays like Kunen's are admired in our cleverer adolescent circles, the number of prestige points earned being somewhat proportional to the impeccable, even ostentatious, propriety of the manifest content of the ragging behavior.

Yet, even all these tricks were not enough to discharge the rage under Kunen's apathy. By the end of his sophomore slump (pp. 13–14) "I finally just gave up and went around smashing things. My brother said . . . I was fighting even if I couldn't see what to fight. On the other hand, maybe . . . I had given up." These were his options. To fight, like Peer Gynt, an invisible opponent who said "Go round!" but never made itself visible, or to give up to apathy.

"Then Rudd did the thing."

Columbia became a battlefield. A grey world broke up into kaleidoscopic shards of black and white. Angers were supplied targets. Targets not really new, yet the more emotionally useful because from the old, less clear targets they represented only a slight displacement. Targets emotionally useful because nearby. (In President Kirk, a we-can-lay-hands-on-him form of President Johnson!) Targets that were emotionally useful because concrete. (That great ugly gash across the Harlem park—and even, deliciously, a fence around it. "I don't like fences anyway so I am one of the first to jump on it.") As a bonus, human figures to attach feelings onto. ("Columbia pays black maids less than they'd receive on welfare.") Gratefully accepting this largesse from new events, the student found himself bursting out of his apathy.

The shards of black and white, clearer, were still kaleidoscope. Events went by in an exhilarating whirl. Released feelings found polarization. What more focussing than a common enemy, a human enemy, rather than an issue, a physically assaulting enemy rather than a debater, an enemy who simplifies everything by drawing blood? At last, at long, long last, the legions of evil have bothered to attack us!

Anger-out has at last a here-and-now legitimation. The angry young man feels whole. His world is sharply illuminated now, in a sunrise of Black and White. At last he needs no intellectualizations. Simply (p. 44), "I resolve that nothing is going to get me off this campus tonight."

Honest emotions can follow. Fear. Courage. The dazzling new world universally experienced by men who have been under fire. "I'm thinking it's great," he says (p. 45) "that we're able to stand and joke with each other right after we almost got killed."

An end to apathy.

And as pretty a delineation of its psychodynamics as a psychologist could demand. The night fog of listlessness dissolves under the sunshine of dawning rage.

Not that apathy cannot return. After high drama, there are weeks of inaction. And persistent doldrums. Once "I almost gave up." One of the problems of starting with a spectacular is that the revolution must keep right on supplying Happenings. (This need was met later by little forays into Harlem that even Rudd saw as ideologically purposeless. The troops needed to exercise their emotions.) Kunen saw his own need.

And reacted against it. Though partly rhetoric, some proportion is honestly expressive (p. 94):

Friday, July 19: Reading over The Book I fear I'm giving the impression that I'm hanging loose and bemused and don't overly care about anything. Well, how's this:
   Leave me an my friends alone, bastards. . . .
(There follows the most Yippie tirade in the book.)

Lethargy must be self-consciously disciplined by regenerative raging.

THE COUNTERACTIVE THEME

One other theme accounts for many episodes in the experience of Kunen. He cannot make war until he's had a Pearl Harbor. In fact, he cannot even sell destroyers to Britain without first arranging all manner of "reasons." He cannot kick cold turkey the habit of telling himself that he is not a violent man.

Of course, all this is very American. The analogy of this rioter's rationalizations to the nation's in the time when Roosevelt had to cozy the American public into admitting to themselves that they wanted a war is quite just. Living with ourselves was a good deal simpler after Pearl Harbor. Today's Domino Theory appeals to the same American patterns in order to justify Vietnam. The New Left, by labeling the Domino Theory as a Fascist assault on Liberalism, is using the same very American way of coming to the opposite conclusion. Everyone feels justified by feeling attacked!

Kunen is not the only student radical who has trouble justifying his own aggression. Most of the New Left turn out to be the gentlest of men. Obsessive moralists and compulsive intellectualizers, they cannot even deal with the idea of violence in an obvious and common sense way.

For example, a simple task we use in assessing student personality is the Hand Test,[5] a small deck of cards on each of which there is a sketch of a hand. It is perfectly clear that they are hands; the point is that each hand is in a different position, so that the test question becomes: "What might a hand in this particular position be doing?" One of the hands is a fist. At least, "A fist" is the most popular response to this card. Or "Throwing a punch" or "a left hook" or "pow! right in the kisser!"

So far, none of the score of student radicals we have seen has reported a fist on this card. At least not without hedging and hedging:

This hand seems to be holding something tightly. It might be a fist if the thumb weren't in the wrong position; if he uses that as a fist he'll hurt himself.

This hand shows determination. Not anger, just firmness, a determination to get his point across.

This hand is doubled up; I don't know what it could be doing. It's an awkward position.

At the end of the Hand Test, the subject is asked to suggest some other hands we could have used. Often, these same respondents will then say things like:

[5] Bricklin, B., Piotrowski, Z., and Wagner, E. The Hand Test. Springfield, Ill., Charles C Thomas, Publisher, 1962. See also: Wagner, E. The Hand Test: Manual for Administration, Scoring, and Interpretation. Akron, Ohio, The Mark James Co., 1962.

What about the Strike emblem? I didn't see anything that looked like a fist.

Well, there's the sign (gesturing) that everyone is making nowadays. Just the sign; the idea of it.

Need one be a psychologist to realize that it was a "defensive" stance that evoked these emotionally distantiated but latently aggressive answers?

We have already seen Kunen's adolescent aggressiveness under the wraps of many intellectualizing and rationalizing defenses. And what Christian morals he expresses, even specifically recommending at one point the policy of turning the other cheek!

When a man needs to feel ringed by hostility in order to feel alive, he will find ways to see hostility all around him. The simplest way is to go where real hostility is. There is enough of it to be found. Another is to make oneself a visible target—which is half of Kunen's reason (p. 72) for growing long hair. Another is to prod people into expressing their rage—as by means of a demonstration. If worst comes to worst, another way is to project one's need onto an impersonal screen. ("I always hated fences . . .") Kunen does all these tricks.

His projecting is his most defensive activity—and so the most visibly distorted. The draft board mail is all signed "Mary Smith" so "who do they think they're kidding?" There is a stitch dropped somewhere in that bitter joke; it is not in Kunen's ken that a "they" could be doing nothing to him, that their purposes could be at 90 degrees to his. Yet another time he could see such a possibility being overlooked in the thinking of other students; when SDS thought *Life* magazine was trying to co-opt the Movement, journalist Kunen was able to remark that he "thought they were trying to sell magazines." More emotionally loaded topics preclude such clarity from him. Draft boards cannot be "just" doing something; malignancy must needs be imputed to Mary Smith.

Mary Smith might be a Biggee?

She is one of They. They who think they're kidding. They to whom, in his core confession of youth (p. 94) Kunen admits "We don't even know who you are . . ." Do most revolutions have invisible targets? The point is that an invisible assailant can justify rage.

"Anger and hatred is a place I go sometimes. You're making me live there."

Whoever you may be!

When in need of a target one can see, one can go find a Biggee to tease. So we see Kunen going to interview a succession of the bogeymen he has created (several of whom he had the perspective to admit were human when he met them face to face) just in order to goad them into statements he can quote with a sneer. Good journalism. But Kunen the author expects the reader to laugh. All the reader sees is Kunen picking a fight.

For example we have:

> I saw my only friend in Marlboro, a guy named Willy, who lives next door. I asked him what's he been doing, fooling around? "Playing," he said, preferring its more respectable connotations. I gave him a wild flower I had raped from the woods, and with that he decided I was indeed weird. The man's only three years old, but his openness is closing already. (p. 74)

Somehow the reader wonders if that three-year-old had all those sophistications or was just reacting to an intrusive and not recently familiar adult. Sure, the passage is half jocular—but only half? Something has slipped in Kunen's reality testing. He's used one of his modal psychological defense mechanisms: projecting his own need to rage onto improbable people who have unwittingly become his projective screen.

Passive aggression is another of his mechanisms. His most bitter-sweet triumph is to evoke hostility while ostensibly "doing nothing." Hitchhiking in long hair, a style that one adopts as a goad. (And wearing the uniform of the Movement?) "Just standing" on the scene of a demonstration. Merely "watching"—a favorite barb of journalist Kunen—but in the manner of Evil-Eye Fleegle, ostentatiously reading badge numbers. "Merely" sitting in a building. Setting the authorities up so he can yell "bad rap."

And so real enmity can always be engendered as when (p. 101) "the time came as it always does when the cops decide they've had enough. . . ." And then courage is stirred. In him, by counteractive feelings: "I had to be brave because all kinds of fright chemicals were coursing around in me." In his girl, Laura, because "she gets just upset enough."

One feels if one fingers the sore.

One is not, one says to oneself and the world, an aggressive person. One hates guns. One holds the bizarre theory that "children fight but young men seldom fight." Like the majority of the Movement, Kunen has been raised in a middle-class suburb and never seen the life of the Poor he creates in his mind—as another projective screen? Indeed, a poor speaker (p. 39) made him uncomfortable. He had to believe the Poor never fought until attacked, and so were always justified. And were encircled by the Enemy. That for them, as for him, it was true that to awaken oneself, one must project hostility everywhere. To provoke one's feelings.

SOLIDARITY OF *Fraternité*

Besides, one can then get close to those remaining people whom one does not project onto. That's the other half (p. 72) of the reason for hair: "Also, I like to have peace people wave me victory signs and I like to return them, and for that we've got to be able to recognize each other."

Nor is Kunen alone in this observation. Gerzon notes the importance of "partners" to the changed Movement of the sixties. One of the pioneer draft-burners remarked to me on the joy of "no longer being alone" in the Peace Movement as going well beyond the joy of being out of jail. Also, speaking of the Columbia riots, Alan Silver[6] remarks that "An intense communal life emerged, in which students at last enjoyed shared commitment and purpose. . . . This enjoyment became one of the chief purposes of the uprising, something that could not easily be bargained or negotiated away." Bettelheim,[7] who quotes these lines, cites a case of his own in support of the student rebels' needs "to escape their devastating isolation" and the "flatness in their personal relations."

Even if one has to go to the point of "thinking it's great that we're able to stand and joke with each other right after we almost

---

[6] Silver, A. Who cares for Columbia? The New York Review of Books, January 30, 1969.
[7] Bettelheim, B. Obsolete youth. Encounter, Sept. 1969, p. 37.

got killed." A veteran of the Vietnam War said much the same thing to me recently. "I almost got killed," he breathed in pleasurable awe. He was speaking not of the war he had fought but about Selma! About something that had come close to becoming a blood brotherhood.

But one needn't go that far to feel the sharing. There is a talk-brotherhood, too. After the first Harvard riot, there followed a seemingly endless series of meetings, each one generating hours of talk. These sessions were not just another proof that intellectuals are loquacious. (Though sometimes one felt how well Dostoievski caught the flavor of this stage of revolution in *The Possessed.*) The meetings generated a tingling excitement. Conscientious students would appear at a class and then excuse themselves with simple emotion. "I'd like to stay but I just can't; what's going on downstairs is too important. I just feel I *should* be there." What was going on downstairs was a prolonged ritual of people listening to each other. In those weeks a million hearkened sentences began, "I feel that . . ."

In short, getting away from being "useless and alienated," one can enter intense interpersonal relationships, affiliative or sado-masochistic, as they may be. In the absense of such activity, one falls back, like Kunen (p. 50), into feeling depressed.

RADICALIZATION

Handed this yeasty situation, the political activists set about its radicalization. Their problem was to catch the social conscience of men of good will. Their tactic had been made obvious by the moral victory of the Yippies at the Chicago Democratic convention. To elicit a show of force by police would ensure that other "downtrodden" young would identify with your group. For that matter, since this tactic brings us back once again to the American theme of the favored underdog, a little bloodletting would attract not-so-young and not-so-downtrodden sympathizers. One would grab middle-aged men of good will by their consciences. And so, whatever the psychodynamics of joy in risking getting one's head broken, the simple politics of it became its stated purpose.

But less planned demonstrations were already grabbing the consciences of the moderate young. Vietnam was already a moral issue. Long before SDS and YIP won big, there was the Dow sit-in at Harvard. Running through their pack of bursar's cards collected from Dow demonstrators, the Harvard deans kept finding the names of some surprising people. Intrigued, the deans called in and questioned these apparently middle-of-the-road students. Out of honest curiosity, the deans asked these young men what they had been doing in that besieged lecture hall. And got the same reply: "Well, I was just walking by on my way somewhere and I knew what was going on in Mallinckrodt and I just felt that I ought to be in there." Alternately, "It was a moral necessity. I'm not for SDS but this was different; I just knew I should."

"Should!"

What is the force of that word in that sentence? Perhaps it is not so hard to understand in the peacenik position. But Peace isn't the only issue that can be so exploited. Is there a more general explanation to this widespread feeling of moral compulsion? Gerzon (pp. 121 et seq.) explains the source of the moral compulsion blandly: these youngsters who "feel the pressures of society on them," knowing they have grown up absurd in an unjust world they never made, have two options: They can retreat from society into private lives of greater fullness and abandon any hope of changing society; or they can try to change society, so that they will be, as the tag has it, "part of the solution, not part of the problem." Of course a certain optimism must underlie that decision. One feels less constrained to take action that offers no hope. But the premise of the political, rather than the privately expressive, part of the Movement is that "All that needs to be done is to make people aware and active in fermenting this social change."

If you really believe those are the odds, how can you fail to feel guilty about remaining inactive? So long as the causes to which actions are tied continue to be chosen for being egregiously "just"?

No one feels this with more intimacy than today's young people. The difference between the social dropout and the politically active and dissident young man is this: the former emphasizes the fact that his personal psychological dissatisfaction reflects the disorder of the whole, and so decides to remove himself from the whole; while the latter emphasizes that his own dissatisfaction with the prevalent ways of life relates directly to the sickness of society itself, and so decides to establish himself in such a position that he may change the social whole.[8]

Or decides that, as a matter of conscience, he *should* establish himself in such a position.

And begins his politicization.

Which leads to radicalization by an ingenious means. All the SDS people are experts on the history of revolution. Not just on the story of their folk-hero, Che Guevara, the Jimmy Dean of revolutionary stars, but on older success stories as well. In the summer of 1969, it was the SDS moderates' view that they were in France in 1700. They looked forward to a lifetime of patiently radicalizing not just youth but the whole society, gradually, the way that drops of rainwater weather, crumble, and eventually split open a stone. The program was everywhere to encourage little lawless acts or even just unusual actions—so that people became more and more used to things going on that would have been outrageous to them before. Demonstrations, yes. Yes, violence in the streets. But not always. All manner of little happenings. Many of them not politically revolutionary. Indeed, SDS theoreticians pointed out, in 18th century France one index of the progressive crumbling of the cake of custom was that the crime rate went progressively up. Jean Valjean was no revolutionary—but he and thousands like him made people wonder just how wrong it was to steal a crust of bread. Acting out is a symptom that has great contagion. As happened in France then, today's Movement expects to get unintentional help from nonrevolutionaries who feel freer to do their "things." As intellectuals were in ferment in the 1700s, so are they now. In the end, unorganized crime, agrarian discontent, and disquieted intelligentsia melted into one giant disorder in 18th century France. In our 20th century, the mix may be different —though SDS clings to an idea that seems out of date in the 20th century: the alliance of intelligentsia and working class. But "a lot going on" is an atmosphere in which revolution thrives. "Fishing in troubled waters," is the political formula the Marxists know.

So will go the process of radicalization by ferment. We see its effectiveness already. The SDS moderates that summer were looking

---

[8] Gerzon, M., *op. cit.* p. 123.

to a lifetime's work to implement this program. They probably underestimated their own cleverness. By the next winter, demonstrations were doing more than making ferment. They were winning social changes. As one columnist observed, already "The majority has flinched."[9]

One focusses on SDS because they have formulated and publicly announced this program, but all radicalization programs are somewhat of this nature. Nothing the revolutionary does is an apolitical act. The Movement is one big sprawling charade: from long hair to Black Panther arsenals. The language of the revolution is gesture. And acting out.

Ironically, the very broadness of the farce seems to prevent its audience from getting the message. Puzzled middle-agers ask "Why do these kids do such crazy things?" They do no crazy things. Every little action has a meaning of its own. But a language barrier defeats the very purpose of communication. "What made Bobby Seale behave so strangely in that Chicago courtroom?" is a common question that would probably astonish Seale. Whatever else he was doing, he was talking to us all. As plainly as he knew how. What was he saying? Seale was saying what Kunen got to saying when he whipped up his rage with a conscious effort:

> Leave me and my friends alone, bastards . . . You're up against something here . . . We've had it up to here with you and you don't have much time left, man . . . You're playing with fire and fire burns, baby. I mean this. I mean it well. Hear me: you're going to get human or your stinking bodies are going up against the wall. (p. 94)

That's an important message. He's threatening to kill us. Maybe we had all better learn the language messages like that come in if we don't now understand it.

At any rate, the revolutionaries intend us to hear it so often that we'll get used to it. They choose to speak in the diction of extravagant acting out because they hope that, once we get with that diction, we may start using it ourselves. We would then, non-revolutionaries though we be, ourselves become part of a Brownian

---

[9] Alexander, H. Too many defeats for the majority. Boston Herald Traveler, November 24, 1969, p. 15.

movement in society, a random agitation of people, a molecular heating up of the social whole to unstable high temperatures.

ANARCHISM

And then what?

Then nothing. Anarchy is the end-game. This is something people over thirty seem to have great difficulty in understanding. "Suppose you destroy today's society," they repeatedly ask young-sters, "with what are you going to replace it?" Most young people duck that question or brush it aside as meaningless. (It is, for them.) A few mumble vaguely about "local socialism." None of them face the unfortunate fact that power abhors a vacuum—but the idealistic reason they can believe away that ugly rule is soon to be seen. For the truth is that they should answer, "Why, with nothing. The whole point is to free the individual, to lift from Man the burden of Society."

Of course special groups in the Movement have other goals. Black Power is realistic enough. The rank and file activist, however, has rediscovered the premises of philosophical anarchism. Apparently as an instance of multiple invention, though there is no lack of academic continuity with the past in thinking of the Movement's favorite radical philosophers. Anarchism is not used as a label for these youngsters' positions—though they put themselves near that position by repeatedly scorning the stuffiness of Marxism. But con-sider the identity of theirs and historical anarchism's goals and premises.

The most respectable anarchist theorist, Peter Kropotkin,[10] explains that the goals of anarchism are a society "conceived without government . . . harmony in such a society being obtained, not by obedience to any authority, but by free agreements . . ." As a result:

If, it is contended, society were organized on those principles, man would not be limited in the free exercise of his powers in productive

[10] Kropotkin, P. Anarchism. *In* The Encyclopaedia Britannica, 11th ed., Chicago, Encyclopaedia Britannica, Inc., p. 873. Reprinted by permission, copyright Encyclopaedia Britannica, Inc., 1929.

work by a capitalistic monopoly, maintained by the State; nor would he be limited in the exercise of his will by a fear of punishment, or by obedience towards individuals or metaphysical entities, which both lead to depression of initiative and servility of mind. He would be guided in his actions by his own understanding, which necessarily would bear the impression of a free action and reaction between his own self and the ethical conceptions of his surroundings. Man would thus be enabled to obtain the full development of all his faculties, intellectual, artistic and moral, without being hampered by overwork for the monopolists, or by the servility and inertia of mind of the great number. He would thus be able to reach full individualization, which is not possible either under the present system of *individualism,* or under any system of State Socialism in the so-called *Volkstaat* (popular State).

To hold such expectations, one must be an optimist about the goodness of Human Nature. The assumption is in the air, now, that Man is essentially good, and all one must do to see him behave well is unfetter his strengths. Not the least important modern source of that idea has been bowdlerized psychiatry—though the optimistic assumption has been the central one, anthropologists point out, in all the history of American culture. At any rate, philosophical an-archists, old and new, seem Utopian—though they will stoutly deny any charge of naïveté. Kropotkin continues:

The Anarchist writers consider, moreover, that their conception is not a Utopia, constructed on the a priori method after a few desiderata have been taken as postulates. It is derived, they maintain, from an *analysis of tendencies* that are at work already. . . .

So speaks the great anarchist philosopher—and so speaks the undergraduate Gerzon (p. 122): ". . . . most of them (students) have in the past felt that the unhealthy irrational parts of society that are detrimental to individual fulfillment should be weeded out; that each individual is striving for the same fullness in life that they are; . . . All that needs to be done is to make people aware and active in fermenting social change." Gerzon's position is stated blandly; most students in the Movement are far to the left of him.

Are they, then, Communists? A few are. (One recalls the son of a Communist organizer who was told by his father, "When you go to Harvard, do not get involved in student politics; it destroys the mind!") Most are something quite other and much more radical. Kropotkin says Anarchists have something "in common with all

Socialists, of whom they constitute the left wing." Yet he also sees that the two have never been able to form alliance for long. During the Russian Revolution, Trotsky wound up by turning his cannon on the anarchists. With nice irony:

> A wave of excitement in America in 1919 led to the deportation of certain well-known anarchists to Russia. Among these were Alexander Berkman and Emma Goldman, both of whom were well-known for their propaganda work. They found the new regime intolerable by reason of its sterile authoritarian character, and the constant imprisonment of their anarchist colleagues led them to leave Russia in disgust. Both published angry denunciations of the new system, of which *My Disillusionment in Russia* (1925), by Emma Goldman, is an interesting picture of the reaction of the Bolshevist state upon a mind strongly wedded to freedom.[10a]

Most students, even those who chant for Ho or quote Mao, could not stand Communist discipline for long. Theirs is a far more sweeping design for freeing up man to create a Moral Utopia.

THE PRIVATE SIDE

Meanwhile, members of the Movement are living "A Separate Peace" in their private lives. These students are usually not active members of The Resistance, as the politicized arm of the Movement is known, but remain sympathetic to it, while maintaining their individualism and privatism. (Again, we see very Amercan values being expressed.) Historically, the Hippies were the beginning of this side of the Movement, but nowadays one need not be a hippie to be an individual who is with the Thing. Indeed, hippie colonies, as such, have become suspect as too collective to express individual freedom of choice. The result is a confusion to squares (*Life,* March 11, 1970) who think that any individual with long hair or mod costume is necessarily part of any group. The whole point of privatization is that it is individual! Or at least, like Noah's ark, a state that is entered two by two.

[10a] Laski, H. J. Anarchism. *In* The Encyclopaedia Britannica, 14th ed., Chicago, Encyclopaedia Britannica, Inc. Reprinted by permission, copyright Encyclopaedia Britannica, Inc.

There are many aspects to the private side of the Movement. Drugs are one. Religion is another. Value judgments is a third—and perhaps the most intellectually respectable and to become, if we are not all victims of The Bomb, the most historically enduring. All in all, the individual members of the Movement warn us to respect an Apollonian[11] aspect of their activities: not every young person who rejects what his parents do is a political rebel at heart! Those readers who are themselves introverts may feel some sympathy for young people who live under an Atomic sword of Damocles and are trying to devise for themselves (and perhaps their sexual partners) A Separate Peace.

PRIVATIZATION: DRUGS

The Movement is a buzzing about of millions of young, each stirred into his own activity by the *Zeitgeist*. In all this buzzing, there are two kinds of natural directions of swarming: one toward politicization, one toward privatization. There are people who attempt to impose structure on both sides: on the political side, the radicals, on the private side, the drug peddlers. We have said something about radicalization, what about criminalization?

Make no mistake about the opportunism of organized criminals. The "reefer" salesman outside your high school during afternoons in the late thirties was an amateur compared to the intown wholesaler of the sixties who can count on the youngsters to come to him. To know a distributor can be a pride point in the suburban clique— much like knowing the bootlegger in the twenties. And it gives one the heehaw on local police. "The cops keep asking me where I get the stuff in Lexington," one teen-age addict laughed, "but of course that's not where the sources are. We all go into Boston."

But he was a hooked "head." Few amateurs are wholesale sources; presumably their professional competitors would soon put them out of business. On the other hand, hundreds of thousands of amateurs are the informal network of distribution to the ultimate consumer. To pass along a joint or a pill is a friendly act that con-

---

11 Benedict, R. Patterns of Culture. Boston, Houghton Mifflin Company, 1934.

firms brotherhood—rather like the sharing of a scarce cigarette during the Big War. "I can go down along the beach anytime," a youth at a summer resort patiently explains, "and get whatever I want." Of course, there is petty black-marketeering too. And wise guys appear in any crowd. "We wanted some bread so we went down to New York and sold joints of catnip." One trusts these two young men got out of New York fast! Or were exaggerating their story.

On the whole, all these phenomena are an old story to those of us who lived through prohibition. Yes, nowadays, there are also bathtub stills.

Like alcohol during prohibition, drugs cannot be controlled because the social consensus is that their use is acceptable behavior. Even nonusers abide by the rule that "turning on" is a private act: it would be an antisocial act to interfere with behavior that is the other fellow's own business. Moreover, arguments for the rightness of drug use are many and persuasive. What is emerging is a socially sanctioned position that hard drugs may be another matter but marijuana is less deleterious and more moral than that vice of one's parents: alcohol.

As with alcohol, all kinds of motives create users. Just the adolescent need "to be big," for a simple one. Not every tenth grader who brags about the trip he just made really dropped acid—or even possessed any!

And a party is a party: a pot party is first of all a social ritual; as a cocktail party is. True, the pot party is more exciting—so were cocktail parties when they were illegal, in the twenties. At a pot party more often than at a cocktail party, people find themselves performing the late adolescent growth task of ceasing to be ashamed of their bodies. (But this is a rare event at either.) Sex is allegedly stimulated by marijuana, though doctors write again and again that this rumor must be false, because the pharmacological effect is the reverse. (What the doctors are overlooking is the surround of social support.)

But sex needn't be in it: just to be "turned on" is enough. Somehow, in the favorable instance, one has that sensation of heightened awareness and mental power that occurs for that moment just before alcohol produces a thick tongue. ("My, I can clink thearly!" one inebriate whose mind has been so opened exclaimed.) With pot, this feeling of clinking thearly may endure. It leads to the mental activity known to psychologists as "primary process." Distant sensa' tions and ideas are juxtaposed—to the thinker's delight. "There is a kind of marijuana humor" which is a remote association process. Sensations also may be remotely linked. Synaesthesia occurs. "Have you ever listened to music with pot?" Even dropping acid may be so motivated. Scornful of erudite theories, one private school teacher pointed out that his tenth graders "do it just to see the pretty colors." And that is often so. Though the adverb "just" in that sentence may be invidious. Some of the overdetermination of seeking to see the pretty colors is discussed by Dr. Walters in another chapter. Perhaps our college people are intellectually and psychodynamically more complicated. Perhaps they have to intellectualize and fabulize everything they do. The various roles played by drugs in their searches for themselves, for truth and beauty, for warmth, or for *Weltanschauung* are every bit as various and complicated as Dr. Walters describes them—and by the students' own accounts. The types he describes range from ordinary inwardly directed members of the Movement to students caught up in the Movement who have already brought to it their own pathology, diagnosable as "border' line" in today's psychiatric nosology.

There is one type that is sicker than any so far named: the deteriorated hard-drug addict. College student or no, these young men show all the attributes described in the extensive literature of heroin addiction. The psychologist in his report describes how a young man is perpetually self-defeating, knows little and recks less of social consequences and lives in an endopsychic world that is empty, in a veritable affective Sahara. His oldest psychiatric colleague interrupts with, "Come on, now, we've always known addicts were like that!"

Perhaps all that is new is that addicts get admitted to good colleges.

PRIVATIZATION: OTHER FORMS

Drugs, whether for cosmic revelation or just to listen to music and joke by, are only one part of the inwardly turned aspects of the Movement. There is a whole second half of the change these stu'

dents mean to bring about. To destroy the power structure is not
enough. They mean also a moral house cleaning. Their intent is an
end to all hypocrisies, to all rigidities, to all the yokes that cause
good, warm expression behaviors to be squelched under the weight
of social forms. The moral revolution need not be pursued as part
of a mass movement. Apolitical young men make a separate peace:

> Because of this preoccupation with the workings of the mind, some
> young people try to minimize the control that social pressures exert
> upon them. They try to break the dichotomy between their public and
> their private selves by making their whole lives private. The student
> quits school, hops on a drug kick, manages to get a psychological draft
> deferment that exempts him from military service, works as a waiter
> in some little coffee shop on MacDougal Street in exchange for a room
> upstairs and meals, and enmeshes himself in a small underworld that
> can still manage to survive despite the omnipresent federal and metro-
> politan eyes. . . . He removes himself from the mainstream of social
> life and from the values that always flow with it . . .[12]

Or, academic demands being so moderate in the Ivy League in relation to academic potential, he need not drop out but can establish a
subworld within the college community! Our friend across the political world know this adjustment as the Inner Emigration.

There are many places the inner emigrant can go. Sex is one of
them; it is the aspect of the Movement's life-style that attracts the
older generation's attention. Freedom and frankness in sex matters
are, indeed, a major change that this student generation has brought
about. In the words of a veteran social worker, "Until 1960, when
students had sexualized a relationship they were at pains to tell me
so; now, they are at special pains to make clear to me if they have
not!" Sex is put in the service of the value of "a relationship" and
the old crude codes of possession have been supplanted by elaborate
new intellectualizations about interpersonal honesty. It may be as
dishonest to each other not to make love as to make it. For all the new-
ness and pervasiveness of this change, sex is not the only moral revolution nor perhaps the most important.

Music is another aspect. Music in an hypnotic function it has
not often had in the West. Music as message, too. Political or moral.

Religion is another. Again, the East supplies religion in modes
and functions it did not serve traditionally in the West:

---

[12] Gerzon, op. cit., pp. 121–122.

Chant the mantra, delectable Eastern lyric, four heartbeats to a measure . . . indelible. It's not something to read. It's to breathe and to sing. Try it, for the record.

> Hare Krishna
> Hare Krishna
> Krishna, Krishna
> Hare, Hare.

. . . . Someone who has Krishna Consciousness develops a luster in his face.[13]

The motivation here is somewhat nobler than that of the child who told me how she'd discovered that by not going to sleep for five nights she could "hallucinate."

Yet, in the end, most of these paths lead to something similar. These young people, at various levels of awareness, from the cynical teacher who just wanted to see the pretty colors, to the narcissistic seeker of any means to turn on, to the seekers of honesty in self-expression through human relationships, to the mystic seeking Karma, all seem to be facing in the same direction: toward the good latent in Being. It seems to me they have rediscovered an old religion: gnosticism. For this ancient sect, the key value was a spark that lay within each man: his gnosis. A man's gnosis needed to be set free. Its unveiling was the point of all religious exercises. It lay within him, under layer on layer of social and bodily calcification. To break its bonds—that would set the divine principle free.

Or the "collective unconscious?" In the 1920s we had a pseudo-Freudian revolution; in the 1960s perhaps a pseudo-Jungian one?

Gnosticism of the inner life, anarchism of the outer life, these two are parallel. Both are optimistic about the nature of man. Both expect to realize his ultimate goodness by setting it free. Both chose unconventional means to this idealistic end: orgiastic means for the gnostic, revolutionary means for the anarchist. Both views have been all but suppressed by Western civilizations as heresies. Both are, in the Movement, less the result of going back than of multiple re-invention. Dionysian[14] values have appeared and reappeared in Western civilization, at least since ancient Greece.

---

13 Reed, J. Hare Krishna, Hare Krishna. In Herald: The Magazine of the Sunday Herald Traveler, January 4, 1970, p. 9–10.
14 Benedict, op. cit.

Need I be right, then, in coupling these two world views as the quintessences of the Movement? No, I need not be. Yet I find some comfort in noting that these two labels have been used by their own people. A guerrilla writer, Robin Blackburn[15], writing in *Hard Times* last September, refers to the "anarchopopulism" of the political side of the Movement. (That is very good; this is a populist uprising, a hydra. That simple fact explains its baffling ubiquitousness and unsquelchableness and its many forms.) As to the inner emigrants among Movement students, they have been described as "gnostics" by no less a guru than Allan Ginzburg.

VALUE SYSTEMS: THE PREMISE GAP

At any rate, the very premises of the Movement are at odds with the premises of American culture. I don't mean just the values each espouses—success versus humanity, etc., I mean that the difference goes deeper, right down to each system's unspoken assumptions. At bottom:

The theory that seems most useful for formulating American subcultural personalities has been proposed by Dr. Florence Kluckhohn. Dr. Kluckhohn starts by assuming that: "The five common human problems which are tentatively singled out as those of key importance can be stated quite directly in the form of questions: (1) What are the innate predispositions of men? (2) What is the relation of man to nature? (3) What is the significant time dimension? (4) What type of personality is to be most valued? (5) What is the dominant modality of the relationship of man to other men?" These five problems, she argues, are everywhere immanent in the human situation.

Solutions to these problems are limited. If one's phrasing is general enough, one can state three logically possible answers to each. The innate predisposition of man may be good, it may be evil, or it may be a mixture of the two. Man's relation to nature may be dominating, or submissive, or simply one of being "in" the natural world. The important temporal emphasis may be on past, present or future. Man may emphasize his ties to his predecessors (and be said to possess a "Lineal" orientation) or he may emphasize his bonds with contemporaries ("Collateral" orientation) or he may emphasize the importance of the single person (and so be said to possess an "Individualistic" orientation). As to the preferred types of personalities, people may value a man for what he can accomplish ("Doing" orientation), for what he already is ("Being"

---

[15] Blackburn, R. Hard Times, September, 1969.

orientation), or for what he may, e.g., through spiritual growth, become ("Being-in-Becoming" orientation). There may be other possibilities, Dr. Kluckhohn realizes, but these sets of three offer "at least a testable conceptualization" of the range.

The dominant American orientation (the well-known middle-class value system often called "the American success culture" has the profile shown below. *Doing* orientation is most commonly viewed as the core of the value system, relating it to the predominant economic institutions and to the importance of the male wage-earner in the household. *Future* orientation comes next; the wage-earner plans to "get ahead." *Individualistic* orientation is strong; one "looks out for Number One." There is, however, secondary emphasis on the *Collateral.* One is loyal to one's peers, but rarely to other generations. Doers regard nature as something to conquer, valuing Man's potential position "over nature." These values are all facets of the dominant culture profile in America.[16]

The Movement begs different premises about every one of these questions. Consider the following lists:

Problem	Dominant Culture	The Movement
Man Innately	Evil	Good
Man—Nature	Man over Nature	Man in Nature
Time Valued	Future	Present
Preferred Personality	Doing	Being
Relationships Value	Individualistic	Collateral

Small wonder that members of the dominant culture and anticulture have trouble understanding each other!

As a footnote, we must add that there is another dimension that Professor Kluckhohn did not note: the interpersonal style preferred by a culture. There is a kind of interpersonal tolerance recommended by the students in the Movement, whether politicized or privatized, a style that is perhaps only an expression of Kluckhohn's Collateral orientation but deserves at least a comment. They express their value on an interpersonal web of accepting with fervor, well-nigh religious fervor. This desecularizing of togetherness was pre-

---

16 McArthur, C. Personality differences between middle and upper classes. J. Abnorm. Soc. Psychol., 50:247–254, 1955.

dicted by Margaret Lantis[17] twenty years ago. The interpersonal has not quite yet become a new religion, as she anticipated, but these young people seem to expect more than mere social contact can give. And minimally, they want interaction to be person to person in the sense of not being a mechanical use of human beings, especially not being determined by traditional social roles. Of course the result is a new set of roles.

REACTIONS: THE DICTION GAPS

The Movement has enjoyed a lively press. It keeps being news-worthy. Much of the reaction has been more editorializing than re-porting, but by 1969 a number of the better journalists were coming closer to "telling it like it is" than the radicalized students cared for —since for them the only satisfactory reporting would be Establish-ment propagandizing.

The most publicized reaction has been the "generation gap." The chasm between dominant culture and anticulture is indeed real and wide, as we have seen. Communication between people who share different assumptions is always hardest to establish. They talk past each other. Nor has either side been good at pinpointing their unshared assumptions. The youngsters have not always helped by talking in code. Unfortunately, part of one's gratification from being "in" in a cult is the privilege of talking the "in" lingo. Some of that jargon will soon be vulgate English—the word "bag" comes to mind —but then the in-group will have to invent new words to serve as recognition signals that give delight—and the co-opted word itself will slide over into a succession of new meanings or connotations; among its most *avant garde* users, the evolution of "camp" provides an analogy.

Nor have the radicals helped communication by talking stri-dently. Anyone over thirty has to agree with *Time* (Jan. 5, 1970, p. 58) that:

The fact is that New Leftese—a combination of evangelism, Ger-man sociology and Madison Avenue—does a marked disservice to itself

---

[17] Lantis, M. The symbol of a new religion. Psychiatry, 13:101–113, 1950.

and the ideas of the people who use it. . . . American radicalism is in danger of making itself voluble without making itself articulate.

But the other side of that is the unwillingness of elders to take at face value some simple statements. "Victory at MIT," a sidewalk pamphlet announces, explaining that, "Right now, this system of imperialism is being defeated in Vietnam by the National Liberation Front. . . . The actions at MIT were to support as strongly as we could, the NLF and the Vietnamese revolution, by trying to stop those projects which the U.S. uses against them and other peoples." This group, who refer to themselves as a Fifth Column of the Viet Cong, are not joking. When SDS spectators flash these marchers the V sign, the marchers may not return it, because "Do you suppose that a member of the Cong has time to do that?" No play; this is a guerrilla war. Adults' inability to grasp such forthright communication can have serious consequences.

The radicals have not helped communication by talking in charades. Acting out draws attention to itself. It buys television time and newspaper space. It does not get through the message. The charade scripts beg assumptions not yet in evidence in the minds of onlookers, (e.g., that cops are pigs). Though people's puzzled efforts to understand bizarre and incomprehensible events *can* lead to their learning. Slowly. Probably too late.

Meanwhile, the moral revolution goes on, partly by moral 'suasion, even by evangelism, but an evangelism that also suffers from the communication difficulties of begged assumptions and flaunted cant. Youngsters may teach their elders not to say things like "young and stupid," however little the association is meant as it sounds, but will youngsters teach their elders to believe that all of society is a bag?

Not soon.

REACTIONS: THE ALUMNI

As part of their 25th reunion activities, the Harvard Class of 1944 filled in a questionnaire that included one item that read: "How do you feel about Hippies and Student Activists?" Out of 600-plus men, 60 said they approved.

In The Grant Study, our panel of 250 men with whom we have been in touch more than 25 years were asked, "What do you think about today's student protests, drug users, hippies, etc.?" Given a chance to respond at length, our men's responses were complex. Understandably, they tended to divide the question. Their consensus was that hippies were useless, drugs were dubious, protesters had a point. (The Establishment has flinched!) A lot of these 40-year-old men showed that they have perceived what is going on. "There is a lot in our society that needs protesting," one of our men wrote. "Drug users and hippies are expressing their protest by withdrawing from society. For a while, there was some value in this because of its shock effect on the society." Even protest gets its blessings: "God bless the students, who have served to dramatize issues that middle-class society is prone to ignore."

But, save in those men already to the left of Liberalism, violence and totalitarian thinking were intolerable. This was especially so of the father who had Movement sons. "My oldest is headed for a major explosion and cannot be deterred by love or counsel," one father correctly perceived. A Peace Corps father sees the laudable independence of his boy, but as to protests: "I think they are pretty godawful! Protest is fine but don't disrupt." (One hears the organizers of protest greet this with a hollow laugh! Indeed their inimitably hollow laugh is their ritual response to comments like that, comments that miss the main premise—but does a ritual laugh communicate more than the laugher's feeling of moral superiority?) Again, "My oldest son is a protester and I look rather benignly; as long as they are not violent or provocative of violence, I admire them." Or the other limit to which elders are driven: "I'm sorry, I'm old-fashioned! If they knew what they were throwing out and had an alternative, I'd listen." They do have an alternative: they just don't really tell parents about it.

This is where there now is an unbridged communication gap.

REACTIONS: FACULTY

The same themes appear in faculty reactions—but there are extra pressures on the faculty because so much activity of the Movement is presented on an intellectual basis. Many intellectuals, but especially those in the humanities, as well as the social sciences, take as part of their job description the function of examining society to discover which of its aspects a thoughtful man must believe to be wrong. They must honor young people who seem to be undertaking the same intellectual task. Then, too, older faculty remember Hitler; they are in the jargon of today's learning theory "imprinted" with the expectation that totalitarians will appear from the Right, because that was their first experience of the free intellect's being melted down to a total society. Besides, they were themselves inclined to be liberals. The lesson that radicals are *not* "liberals, only more so," comes hard. Younger faculty have been brought up radical; they recognize no other form of intellectual respectability. The older teachers do not often see, the younger teachers do not ever regret that, if the rebels win, the countervailing power of thought will be consumed by "relevance."

Besides, there seems to be a real strain of masochism in the faculty; at Harvard, sane men have stood for "symbolic" indignities that went as far as physical humiliation. It is hard to imagine what the source of this willing self-abasement may be.

Yet there are two camps. Events at Harvard precipitated the loose federations of professors half jocularly dubbed "the liberal caucus" and "the conservative caucus." Age entered these alignments, as did previous political persuasions and faculty status. Elite universities are likely to have two faculties, the senior and the junior, marked by contrasts in value systems, attained kudos, needs, and ascribed statuses. The rapid flow of "up or out" young instructors past the rocks of tenured chair-holders froths up in perpetual agitation, in times of general peace as well as in times of crisis. The institutional arrangements by which rare junior men are selected to become seniors for the most part ensures that juniors and seniors are two breeds. Seniors are not just older, more successful juniors. (A nice description of these breeds at Harvard will come out of the Harvard Student Study.) As a result, one has to speak of the reactions to any event not of the Faculty but of the two faculties. In the matter of the Movement, these reactions range from a foot-dragging retreat from the moral obligation to support any group that appears from the Left to simple gutsy we-feeling with radicalism.

Only by misunderstanding intellectual history could we expect otherwise.

But one dilemma confronts the senior faculty: their concern for civil rights. If all good things are "known" to come from the Left, how can these student radicals be so authoritarian? How can they believe in their civil rights while violating the other man's? That is, of course, a question that could only be asked by someone so out of date as a liberal. Or a Full Professor.

In this conflict lies the only handle by which today's situation can be grabbed by administrations. (Of tomorrow's situation, who knows? Perhaps no tactic will remain viable.) Deans, presidents, trustees have shown their individual differences in responding to both privatized and radicalized student protest. Many have shown gross misunderstanding of their opponents' tactics: the usual mistake early on was to confuse a tactical issue (ROTC, housing, Negro reparations) with protest's goals. For an administrator to do his *mea culpa* over a sore the SDS has picked does not swerve SDS from its path. Winning a protest only forces the protestor to find another carious area to attack. Society will always have enough of them.

There is a formula of defensive (if probably only delaying) tactics for which there is much to be said. Even though masochistic confessions of a guilty social conscience will not deflect the Movement's juggernaut, the administrator does well to acknowledge a palpable hit when he feels it. Otherwise he cannot live with himself. Or be strong in the eyes of others when he begins to cry "foul." The position he can prepare for siege, expecting to be supported by his senior faculty, is that of demanding the civil rights of others. Not just of protestors, blacks, and young, but also of squares, whites, and the aged. To radicalized protesters, the idea of such nonpeople having civil rights will seem absurd, almost a nonidea, to be met with tolerant laughter. But the moderate community, properly approached, will not react that way. At Harvard, there has been created a form of administration and student "agreement" on the boundaries of breaches of civil liberties during protest. Only nonprotesters care that such a formality as student consent has been observed—but it is non-protesters with whom the administration must form an entente. Nonprotesters of good will, moreover. Those squares who were dragged hypnotically into the Dow sit-in by their social consciences.

The effect is that valid and half-valid social criticisms by protesters lead to administrative changes that men of good will can acknowledge were overdue—while, at the same time, protest that violated the persons or freedoms of others, whether deans, students or bystanders, leads to expulsion of the overzealous protester from the university.

There probably is no better formula. One foresees the consequence of this one: polarization. Polarization of issues, as protest has to go far out to return to its tradition of "nonnegotiable" demands. Polarization of personnel, as the storm troops of the American Cong are recruited more and more from exstudents and nonstudents. The defeat of any revolution is brought about by forcing its hand prematurely. By driving college administrations into a position where they have but one viable tactic, protest may have undone itself, even while an end of protest was *not* the purpose of the administrators. Or, even was not, in the eyes of the intellectual community, desirable.

Is that the outcome we can envisage? Probably not. Reactions to protest are too varied, too often unreasonable. Nor are protesters always as cute as they should be. The Weathermen may undo all the SDS has wrought. "Adventurism" is the besetting temptation to any revolutionary. The SDS had the formula that would have worked. Ours was a society whose crystal structure was ready for erosion. But kids are impatient.

Adventurism may spoil it all. It is hard, writing at a desk on the East Coast, to believe that out there on the other coast there is a danger of totalitarianism from the political Right. One meets a Business School student who represents the Young Americans for Freedom and one is fascinated by this strange species—but one recalls one's colleagues' warnings of reaction elsewhere. What seems certain in the future everywhere is polarization. To the Left.

A NEW BREED?

Meanwhile, since the writer is not a social historian but merely a psychologist, he finds interest in a last psychodynamic question. While America proceeds to its *Götterdammerung,* may we indulge ourselves, quaintly, in intellectual curiosity? The question, that has only theoretical interest, is: Are we in the presence of a new breed in this younger generation? Or do the laws of nature still apply?

The radical's answer is "No, sir! The kind of human nature you postulated is now dead. It was always a very inhuman sort of Nature, a set of social conventions you mistook for personhood. Perhaps, way underneath all these layers of socially prescribed shells, there was a real person, but like the barnacle, he never appeared out of his shell." The psychologist resents such an answer. He suspects that folks don't change that much. He remembers all that stuff his Soviet colleagues told him about "the New Man." Or Hitler had to say about Jugend.

But the psychologist could be mistaken. In the history of psychology, psychologists always have been, so far, mistaken.

To regard this student generation as new is the modal attitude of students, faculty, and administrators. Students say, with Gerzon, that they were the first generation raised in the mass culture and that what Benedict[18] as far back as 1938 described as "The Discontinuities of American Culture" first applied to them. Faculty pundits like Riesman describe with glee the disarray of the American upper class. Faculty members see a new kind of student (but never say this kind surpasses the extraordinary G.I. Bill gang in intellectual vigor) and Administration is so hung up on seeking bright, uneducated blacks and bright, uneducated white boondockers that they do not even formulate the question of whether they could get better pupils from the schools they once searched for admittable talent. As is usually so in the course of social process, no one does the critical experiment.

---

[18] Benedict, R. Continuities and discontinuities in cultural conditioning. Psychiatry, 1:161–167, 1938. Also published in Kluckhohn, C., and Murray, H., eds., Personality in Nature, Society and Culture. New York, Alfred A. Knopf, Inc., 1954, pp. 522–531.

So we'll never know whether today's undergraduate is different because today's generation is different or whether the social change we have seen since 1960 is a result of the Admissions Committees who picked this decade's undergraduates. The psychologist who thinks of himself as a scientist, rather than a humanist or political activist, has a professional bias towards examining the "null hypothesis."

Were this generation of high school graduates as a whole different from the high school generation we knew in the fifties or forties? The Movement members insist so. They blame the difference on this generation of parents, all of whom, these rebellious youngsters insist, were just like the fatuous pair in the opening scenes of the movie *The Graduate.* Somehow it is a little hard to believe that this can be so: the sympathy in parents' reactions to the Movement, albeit ambivalent sympathy, betokens a willingness to listen that does not jibe with the children's complaints that, "They never hear." As we have remarked, it is hard for anyone to "hear" across a *premise* gap. That universal problem doesn't indicate unwillingness to try. Studying this very parent generation these last 25 years has left me wondering who these "deaf" parents may be.

And yet this parent generation has had a unique history. They remember the Depression, they fought a war. And they have some trouble controlling their face when today's young men explain all about corruption and bestiality on "our" side, as though never before had social rules been broken down by "our" side when a war was being fought. Many parents went to college as a result of the war, never having dreamed they would become college men. Then they were put on the treadmill of affluence. It is hard to know who is affluent today; in an inflationary society "affluence" is a chimera. As one's salary goes up or capital gains roll in, it seems that one is about to win the bitter fight for economic survival, the old, old Darwinian struggle one began in the Depression, so one keeps striving, only to have victory crumble into defeat just when victory seems to be in one's grasp. Tantalization does command one's attention! Perhaps this parent generation have indeed pursued Mammon, but out of anxiety more than out of greed. They have been on a cruel treadmill. The cruelest in American history.

At any rate, their offspring as a whole may be different. A nationwide survey by the American Council on Education recently showed that 15 percent of high school seniors already had protested something, that a quarter of them expected to use drugs, etc. Of course, these are now culturally available behaviors.

One still wonders. In the 20th century, wave after wave of "new men" have inundated the colleges. The biggest surf was the G.I. Bill crowd—the best students the faculty now, in 1970, remembers ever having taught. It seemed as though after the G.I. Bill there would be no one left to be the first member of his extended kin to go to college. Of course that turned out not to be true: during the fifties and sixties personnel consultants watched a steady, silent tide of new men come to the colleges, mostly to the streetcar and the state colleges, mostly from ethnic groups that do not "protest," mostly from poor but honest families, newly raised just over the margin of subsistence. These new men have followed an historical succession of openings that have appeared in the opportunity structure: engineering having replaced chemistry as the forties succeeded the thirties, and with the flowering of all manner of minor business functions whose job titles contained the misnomer "engineer" characterizing the defense industry of the fifties, and now with the rash of clerical functions that in the sixties have surrounded the computers. These new men were singletons; they were never discussed by social scientists or journalists until the era of protest shone the light of journalism on them when SDS flourished at the Harvards and found tough going at the Northeasterns. A new wave has entered the Harvards and also many of the Northeasterns in the late sixties. This wave has washed over the now fading ground swell of middle-class students who have been tragically misled into believing that it still is a normal part of their life to go to a good college, and has caught up with the wave of the poor but honest opportunists. This newest wave is characterized by the protest minorities but also by nonminority entrants who would not in the course of usual social processes have gone to college but were "found" by the recruiting efforts of admissions committees: minority members and working class youngsters, often from long distances away from the college that tabbed them for membership.

Recruiting is a new role for admissions officers. Only coaches used to do it. Admissions recruiting came into fashion in the late fifties in the private schools—especially those that were by tradition "national high schools"—but by the late sixties even the most exclusive prep schools were doing it, as were the good colleges. The result was a man-made rerouting of what had been pretty much naturally caused social channels. And a student body like no other.

The most astonished reaction of all came from graduate students who had just been undergraduates. "I don't know this college generation at all," members of the Harvard Student Study class of 1964 would tell us in 1965—or even say about the freshmen when they, themselves, were seniors. "Our class has been a watershed. These kids are different."

Maybe the applicant pool suddenly was stocked with new fish. But maybe everyone all at once began fishing in new pools. There is no natural experiment available to show us which went on. (Though we do observe that youngsters in usual places during their secondary school years wound up in some bizarre college placements, so we know that the old pools, if shrinking, were far from dry.)

One good study highlights another shift in admissions emphasis. Dean Whitla[19] has been doing a factor analysis of Harvard admissions decisions year by year since 1954. Every year there turn out to be two principal dimensions underlying the complex process of getting into Harvard. Factor I is Personal Attributes. Factor II is Academic Ability.

There have been interesting changes in the importance of these two factors over the last decade and a half. For the entering class of 1958, Academic Ability has been weighted equally with Personal Attributes. Ever since, year after year after year, there has been a steady erosion of the weight given to Academic Ability until nowadays, it has almost none! True, extreme ineptitude (say, College Board scores of 200) may preclude admission to Harvard. The Dean of the College can still avow during Freshman Week, with his tongue only slightly displaced toward his cheek, that "There is no one here in this auditorium who cannot do the work!" But the fact is that, absurd extremes excepted, the sea of freshman faces raised to him as he speaks have almost entirely been washed up at his feet by the accident of their Personal Attributes. Nor is this true only at

---

19 Whitla, D. K. Testing and the freshman year. Cambridge, Office of Tests, 1968, pp. 23–25.

Harvard. Regard the break in confidence in College Boards at Bowdoin. One sees what Professor Huntington meant about the passing of the Academic Culture.

What are these heavily weighted Personal Attributes? Officially, they include items labeled: Alumni Interview Rating, Extracurricular Rating, Personal Rating, Principal or Counselor Rating, Staff Interview Rating, and Teacher Rating. In fine, any number of gatekeepers have agreed that this lad looked like the Right Sort. And, as the one objective criterion, he was also on his record demonstrated to be an Activities Boy. (Not, however, an Athlete. Athletic activity is a third and very minor factor. The athletes, like their peers, are also primarily selected for Factor I. The traditional "jock" need not apply!)

In short, admission to Harvard is almost entirely the consequence of one's "social stimulus value," using this term in its jargon intent. Examining Whitla's data, we may be struck by the fact that Alumni Interview Rating, done by members of local Harvard Clubs from Boston to Walla Walla to Honolulu, appears in the factor space cheek by jowl with the Personal Rating, done by the Admissions staff in Cambridge. That is to say, the local amateurs reach the same conclusions as the University administrators. Which do we believe, that the amateurs are somehow as insightful as professionals or that the administrators are reacting like laymen? That is to say, that "social stimulus value" is the almost exclusive basis of admission, at the expense of what a psychologist would call "personality" on the one hand, or academic ability, on the other?

A further inference is unproven but tenable: Social stimulus value is, in the literature of psychology and psychiatry, notoriously an asset of personalities with character disorders. And of immature adolescents. Of, in short, the "acting out" segment of the population. And *not* of scholars.

Again, this data happens to be available at one school, but admissions policies increasingly emphasize personality and politics at most schools. Maybe the colleges who have reaped the acting-out whirlwind have no one to blame but themselves. Good sociology ought to be done on this still ongoing process: it matters because the college admissions officers are the Personnel Directors of tomorrow's society. Are they sowing the seeds of Cadmus?

What of the Future?

What of the future, indeed? Speculations range from Robin Blackburn's[20] view that the Movement's anarchopopulism "is very useful because it is undermining the archaic institution of private property" and, the reader presumes, because the Movement will ripen to fall into Marxist hands, to the growly view held by fathers overworked by affluence, "Wait till they get out of college and have to survive!"

The test of the latter prediction is just now beginning. We are just starting to do executive assessments on young Movement men finally done with the preliminary educational and military phases of their lives. "Memories of college events sure get in the way," they tell us and many of them come seeking service functions, not profit-oriented ones, staff rather than line activities. But many don't come at all. The anticulture provides other ways to survive.

Will the cake of custom crumble? Very likely so. We will never again have the same society. But then, social arrangements have never survived as many as three generations. The presence of the Movement is already felt. So soon, it has wrought material changes, ranging from a diversionary emphasis on ecology to repeal of the prohibition of pot. Civil rights increasingly exist *de facto* as well as *de iure*. The parents who never listened have heard. And will hear more.

If only the young will speak to them. Perhaps it is the razor by which we distinguish the young reformer from the young revolutionary: the Revolutionary cannot afford to let the Establishment hear. He must preserve the Establishment at its worst so as to keep it there to overthrow.

Will that happen? It can happen here. The revolutionaries are not fuzzy little men with wild eyes: they are some of the best minds of the next generation. And good planners. Though their shibboleths may be the cancers that in the end destroy their thinking. Their practical tactics can be brilliant; their grand sociological theory is bizarre. One day, they may jump the wrong way because they believe

---

20 Blackburn, *op. cit.*

a German sociologist's textbook. And time violence too soon? And count on unnatural choices of allies? (In Paris, the workers were as little affiliated to students as they are in the United States.) Short of such self-defeat, the question is not whether the students will make a political revolution, but when?

And a moral revolution is already upon us. Probably for our own good.

15

Emotional Disturbances Among College Women

Carl A. L. Binger

The battle for the educational rights of American women has been
pretty well won. There are still, to be sure, occasional border skir-
mishes, but they do not seem to amount to much. In most liberal
arts colleges, men and women (or boys and girls, as they are now
called) do the same kind of work. The curriculum is not sex-linked.
Perhaps because of interest or native proclivity more girls will select
courses in child psychology or in art and more boys in mechanical
engineering, but this need not be true and has no bearing on academic requirements. Whether a student is at Vassar or at Yale, at
Princeton or at Smith, at Harvard or at Radcliffe, the number of
courses required for graduation and the subject matter will not, in
general, be related to the sex of the student. The kind of education
offered to both boys and girls is the same.

By emphasizing this fact I do not mean to decry it or to intimate
that it should be otherwise. I know there are many who hold that a
girl's education should prepare her specifically for the life she will
be called upon to lead—for homemaking and child-rearing—and a
boy's should prepare him for a job. Others believe that a liberal
education should not be primarily concerned with the practicalities
of living. This is an old quarrel among professional educators. My
own opinion is that the present system of disregarding sex differences
in the content of courses of instruction is the better.

Having said this, I must add the conviction that, in educational matters treating girls as if they were boys, or, at least, making no concessions to their different natures, puts an extra strain on them. In those colleges where they mingle daily in the classroom with the male students, they are conscious of competing with what they often regard as superior intelligences; when they recite they are most anxious to make a good impression. This is not to say, however, that competition with their own kind is not just as intense. In the exclusively female institutions, standards from the best men's colleges or universities are the accepted norm and so the same element of strain is apt to be present. This may be a fine stimulus to hard work, but there are undercurrents of tension in the situation to which many students react somewhat unfavorably.

In our culture, women still seem to regard themselves as inferior. Perhaps they want to; perhaps it is a genuine feeling, or perhaps it is imposed upon them by men. The new freedom has not done away with it—not the vote, nor bobbed hair, nor trousers, nor cigarettes, nor even somewhat similar standards of sexual behavior. Indeed, all of these indices of equality appear often as an uncertain effort to deny the confusion of roles in which modern society has placed them. But this aspect of their condition must be dealt with, if their education is to be fruitful and effective. I shall come to this again later.

Education is not acquired simply by taking courses, reading books, writing term papers, attending seminars, or even by drinking tea with a tutor, however brilliant, charming, and tweedy. What Whitehead said of religion could as well be said of education, namely, that what should emerge is individual "worth of character." This idea could be expanded and spelled out in greater detail. One can hope from a "liberal" education—that is, an education open to free men and not to slaves—for at least the beginnings of some intellectual discipline and honesty; some refinement in taste; some enthusiasm, if not passion, for things of the mind and spirit; some respect for the ways and opinions of others; and, as well, some self-knowledge and capacity for self-criticism.

All of these traits will contribute to individual worth of character, and they will contribute mightily to the prospects of living a good life, in spite of its visitations and chances and its infinite variations on the theme of loneliness, boredom, misery, and despair. Such an education, moreover, should give men and women a common meeting ground and provide in marriage one of its most cementing ingredients: a similarity in tastes and pleasures.

If the formal college curriculum does not recognize a difference between male and female students, this does not mean that their needs are identical. Far from it. I know that to generalize here is risky business and that what I shall say may be only partially true. But it seems obvious enough that, before long, as a boy approaches graduation he will have his weather eye out for a job or a career and a girl will have hers on marriage. This does not mean that college boys are indifferent to finding a wife or that girls are unconcerned about earning money soon after graduation. The many early collegiate marriages in which young wives today contribute to the family income, if indeed they don't pay for most of their husband's graduate tuition, would belie any such notion. Whether they are gainfully employed or not, however, or whether they have decided to go to graduate school and perhaps prepare themselves for one of the professions—architecture, business, city planning, engineering, medicine, the ministry, law, scientific research, social work, teaching, or others (all are now open to women)—they usually are interested, first and foremost, in finding a mate. They do not shout this from the housetops. They often spend a good deal of their time and energy in trying to conceal this from themselves and from others. There are exceptions, of course—among them some few dedicated female scholars who put their work ahead of everything else, often, to be sure, at great cost. But this is not true of the run of the mill. For them marriage is the paramount goal and the presiding wish. Sometimes they are willing to postpone it until they have achieved more proximal goals—this degree or that job, for example—but it is pretty constantly in the back of their minds.

In some women's college as many as 50 percent of the senior class continue their formal education in graduate school. Many of these young women prepare themselves for the professions or continue their studies from various motives other than a clear interest in scholarship—to postpone the evil day of going out into the world; to raise their market value in getting jobs; to remain in the relatively protected environment of an institution of learning; to continue to meet interesting people. "People," it should be said, is the current euphemism for men. (One must not call the devil by his name.) We know that the motive behind study may have determining influence both on the quality of the work and on the enthusiasm with which it is undertaken. When motives are too mixed they may result in confusion, conflict, and dissatisfaction. Graduate work in itself, however, need no longer be a deterrent to marriage. Many young women combine the two ventures with surprising skill and apparent equanimity.

Since the median age of girls when they marry is quite young (it is now about 20), the preoccupation with marriage becomes fairly persistent when this age is well past. One can observe this frequently among graduate students. Today a young lady of 21 who is still single is apt to think of herself as an old maid. She prefers, however, to see herself as well settled with the man of her choice, or of her dreams, who loves and cherishes her and by whom she will eventually have about four children. Once she has met him, she often appears to care little about how much money he will have, what side of the tracks he was born on, not much about his social or ethnic background or his religion. Love is what counts, or at least what seems to be love. And she thinks she wants a man whom she can look up to, who has been exposed to at least an equivalent formal education and is perhaps a little better in his studies than she is. This makes her feel more secure.

One hears a great deal about security. It has become the golden calf of today. When one stops to analyze what is meant by it, one soon learns that it has little to do with jobs, with income or social status, but it is a subjective feeling derived usually from a certain sense of approbation and depending more on self-approbation than on anything else. This is the rock on which many young college women founder. To have the affection and esteem of a young man whom they admire seems to many the safest bulwark against their self-doubt and their feelings of insufficiency. But the young man is often very young—far less ready for a real, rewarding, and growing relationship than is the girl. And so the bulwark often turns out to be but a slender reed, at least from the point of view of her needs.

Naturally enough, this may lead to trouble. The single most frequently encountered emotional disturbance among these young women is *depression*. Sometimes it is so sweeping that little seems left of the normally functioning personality and there may then be a real risk of suicide. Fortunately, this is relatively rare. What is common, however, in the college girl is a loss of zest, a feeling of apathy or fatigue and an apparent need for extra hours of sleep, a very much lowered self-esteem, with sensitivity to other people's opinions and reactions, and, above all, an inability to get work done. To hand in written material on time means somehow to commit oneself, to expose oneself to comment and criticism before which failing spirits falter. Often the printed page seems to lack meaning; attention, concentration, and comprehension are at a low level. Instead, there is brooding, day-dreaming, mounting dissatisfaction with self, and a feeling of guilt because of time and opportunities wasted— guilt tinctured with anxiety: "What will happen to me?"; "Will my scholarship be renewed?"; "I mustn't let my parents down; sending me to college has been a great sacrifice for them."; "I can't understand it. At high school I was third in my class of 250 and was President of Student Council."—and so it goes.

My first purpose here is to describe this phenomenon, which in greater or lesser degree is sufficiently common as to be called "normal," then to consider prevalent attitudes toward it, and finally to discuss what can be done to prevent its becoming so crippling that it vitiates the whole purpose and intent of being at college or indeed further gratifying development.

I have called it a depression; I do not insist on this as a clinical diagnosis. It has been described by some as an identity crisis, by others as adolescent turmoil. Behind it there are, of course, feelings of inadequacy, self-absorption, worry, and accompanying anxiety. The significant fact is the lowered self-esteem and the diminution in zest, energy, and capacity to function in a creative way. The depression seems to be a kind of *declaration of dependence*, of helplessness, and a muted cry for help as well. And it occurs at some time and in varying intensity in practically every girl during her career at college.

Now, the student who experiences this need not be severely neurotic; nor are these manifestations necessarily evidence of any profound or abnormal emotional disturbance. They may simply represent—in a freshman, for example—the first response of a sensitive, green, adolescent to a new, frighteningly complicated, and sophisticated environment. After all, some of these girls are only

16 or barely 17. They may have come from small towns and be the first ones from their high school to be accepted in one of the major women's colleges. All eyes are on them, and their parents are in-ordinately proud. The girls feel that they are in Heaven at last and blessed among women. But they soon find the atmosphere rarefied and the air heady. They may never before have had to work hard, even in order to lead their class. They are asked to write a paper not on the character of Silas Marner or on the most interesting experience they had during their summer vacations (in many high schools no written assignments are given), but, for example, on "The Relation of Leonardo's Writing to his Painting and to 15th Century Art in General." After chewing their pencils for a while and twirl-ing a lock of hair, they finally brazen it out and go to the library. Even after they have mastered the indexing system, they are appalled by the number of cards under the heading Leonardo; and they find nothing whatever on the assigned topic. Perhaps for the first time in their lives they are forced to read actively instead of passively and to do some quiet, hard thinking. This is not only a strange experience but almost akin to physical pain. And so there is a flight into solace; a little chat with the girl in the next room who may have been to one of those progressive schools where this kind of assignment was familiar enough; or perhaps their neighbor attended a high-powered, exclusive boarding school and has gained so much poise and self-assurance that nothing appears to daunt her.

Or maybe our young freshman is the daughter of a trustee and her mother was the college heroine of her day—not only Phi Beta Kappa but the belle of the ball as well. This puts added pressure on the student, who develops an egregious need to make good in spite of the awareness of her own ineptitude.

I have taken a simple situation by way of example. The reaction of depression is not confined to young freshmen, however, nor is it necessarily related to difficulties associated with study. The student may be in the graduate school—already past the first flush of youth —and perhaps a little *triste* or weary from the steady grind and worried by constant competition with a most gifted, accomplished, and brilliant galaxy of colleagues. At such times there may be a kind of tacit rebellion—an intellectual sit-down strike, so to speak—when the mind seems to refuse to do more work. Any one of many circumstances can bring this about—impending orals, a thesis due or over-due, an unhappy love relationship, or disquieting news from home. Even conspicuous success can bring on this reaction in some individuals.

Of course the common sense attitude would be to quit for a while, to do something else, to have some fun and then come back with renewed vigor. But this seldom occurs to them, partly because they have already lost some resilience and resourcefulness. The thought of absenting themselves from work is far too perilous. Instead, these students prefer to whip the tired horse. They stay up later and get up earlier, and they worry about all the ground they still have to cover. Sometimes fate takes over. They come down with the flu or "a virus" or they develop infectious mononucleosis. This seems a welcome and respectable respite, but it usually leaves them more exhausted than the illness itself could account for and still unable to work.

Many other devices are automatically resorted to as defensive maneuvers against the underlying depression. I will outline a few of them only. Instead of putting on an extra spurt of work, the student may stay in bed in the morning and sleep until noon. thereby missing her lectures or even hour exams. Her academic plight goes from bad to worse, her depression and feelings of guilt increase, and her self-esteem continues to plummet. She may adopt a kind of cynical, supersophisticated and supercilious attitude toward the whole academic community and cease to be a functioning part of it.

These, together with the other defenses I shall mention, are maladaptive in the sense that they are unrealistic and make matters worse rather than better.

Another common defense among young girls has to do with their eating habits. They try to allay their uneasiness and anxiety by eating too much. Some of them will stuff themselves with bread and butter at mealtime; others will fill up on ice cream and candy between meals; still others become night feeders and ransack the kitchen when they should be asleep. This extra feeding, which has little to do with hunger, may be episodic around examination time; it may be a reaction to having been jilted; or again it may have become a kind of chronic addiction. Of course it feeds as well the lowered self-esteem, puts an end to dating, and becomes a new source of discouragement. This phenomenon is seen almost exclusively in girls, seldom in boys.

Its obverse is more serious and indeed constitutes a major and malignant psychosomatic disturbance. I refer to the illness known as anorexia nervosa, in which there is a pathological refusal of food and a dangerous, sometimes fatal, loss of body weight. But this is fortunately not of frequent occurrence and, in any case, it is not my intention to write a medical treatise on the so-called psychosomatic illnesses of young women. Two of the commonest in which both emotional and physical factors play a part are acne and disorders of menstruation. About acne, the girl is seldom as concerned as is her mother, even though it may interfere with her success with boys. We know now that persistent absence of the menses or other chronic menstrual disturbances may be closely related to a girl's attitude toward her bodily functions and especially toward the acceptance of herself as a mature woman.

Rather than dwell on these more strictly medical topics I should like to discuss certain behavioral ones, especially those having to do with the relations between the sexes. This is a tender subject, seldom discussed between the generations. The contemporary sexual mores of young people are so different from those which governed their parents' or teachers' lives that a common meeting ground between them scarcely exists. (It is, of course, possible that the latter have forgotten some of the details of their own past experiences.) Girls seldom, if ever, discuss their sexual experiences with their parents, and when they do—unless they are facing a crisis—one cannot escape the impression that the parent-child relationship is a little unhealthy. To be sure, they often come to college with standards handed to them by their mothers and tacitly upheld by their fathers. Letting a boy kiss you good night, for example, is all right but preferably not on the first date. Here's where conflict often begins. If she is stand-offish and stiff, the chances are she will not see the boy again. But this is just what she wants to forestall unless he is a "jerk"; and so, partly to secure her aim and partly because she is moved and flattered, she accepts his kisses and soon after, if she hasn't already learned, she is taught to "kiss back." From this point on the boy takes over, unless he himself is very timid. He tries to impose his standards and rationalizations on her. He tries to convince her that it is both more honest and far healthier to have intercourse than to pet. He may be right. In any case, he is usually as idealistic as she is and not just out for fun or experience, but he is eager to prove himself. Since by this time she has been aroused—the more so because the boy is usually serious—and is, as the modern cliché has it, "emotionally involved" (as a fly is "involved" with a piece of fly-paper), she may accede to his wishes—often, to be sure, with serious misgivings and with a feeling of guilt. ("My mother would die, if she knew." The chances are that her mother wouldn't "die," at all; she might be quite understanding. It is fathers who need to be protected against the facts of life.)

The present arrangement in coeducational or quasicoeducational institutions facilitates these intimacies. Boys and girls are pretty constantly together in the classroom, in the library, at dances, at parties, at rehearsals. They drink their martinis and gin and tonics together. They light each others' cigarettes. And they study together, often in the boy's room, and sometimes they end up in bed. Roommates are an inconvenience but seldom a real hindrance. Much that is unspoken is understood. Only the curfew on females provides the rude awakening. The girl and boy become each other's property. At a dance they dance together all evening. To pursue another boy's date is to commit the unpardonable act of "bird-dogging." This is not acceptable behavior. Girls, as well, impose their proprietary rights on their dates. In spite of some sexual freedom, promiscuity, which is a symptom of a disordered personality, is not one of its manifestations.

The foregoing description is of one kind of behavior, but of one only. It is difficult to generalize here and not too satisfactory to try to create stereotypes. None of them is fixed or invariable. Behavior changes in response to outer impacts and inner needs and to those mores and conventions which the girl brings with her from school.

There are, of course, "popular" girls who have a different date every night and like to keep lots of boys on the string; idealistic, old-fashioned girls, perhaps with a religious upbringing, who want to keep themselves pure for the great love to come; shy, immature girls who do not date; and girls who manage to make themselves so unattractive by overeating or by their slovenly dress that they are seldom approached by boys. The boys themselves are often strikingly immature, adolescent, and dependent, and get much comfort and support from the steady affection of motherly young women.

One gets the impression that the relationship between the sexes is still in an experimental phase, that it is motivated partly by idealism, partly by a spirit of rebellion against parents or others in authority, partly by a desire to find out about themselves, partly by loneliness, partly by a kind of new conventionality and a wish not to miss out on anything, but above all, for the girls, by the feeling of approbation which the steady attention of one boy gives them. When he does not call up for two days, the girl's world begins to totter. The demands are often unequal and at variance. By the time the girl has said "yes" to herself and has stilled her doubts and her feeling of guilt, the boy may be on the way out of the relationship. This leads to quarrelling and a loss of dignity and self-esteem in the girl. She may feel bereft or, as they sometimes put it, "all empty inside." When she is then asked to do a paper on "Iambulos' Sun-State and Its Relations to the Pergamene Revolt under Aristonicos in 133 B.C." or on "Turkish Naval Power in the 16th Century," she may well be dismayed as she stares with a blank mind at a blank piece of paper.

I have surveyed all this—not because it is new or because anything need necessarily be done about it or perhaps can be. But it seems to me that parents and educators have at least the responsibility of looking facts in the face and not simply crying "my ducats, my daughter" when trouble arises. If they relax parietal rules sufficiently to permit girls to go to boys' rooms and remain there until late, then they should realize what the consequences are likely to be. They should realize, too, that these pressures on girls, even the most resilient and well balanced of them, will at times interfere with their work. It is all very well to say that this is part of life and that they must learn to take things in their stride. We seem to forget that life is fuller and moves faster for them than it did for us at their age. They have more "experiences" in a week than most of us had in a year.

Dean Briggs of Harvard used to say that college is a place to make mistakes, but mistakes today are far costlier than they once were. The price of academic failure or even mediocre performance may be great. It means that further graduate study is probably barred or that good jobs are not easily come by. The price of mistakes in relations with the opposite sex can be high indeed, sometimes nearly ruinous.

Young girls, one must remember, are vulnerable, sensitive, idealistic, often introspective and emotional, inclined to think ill of themselves and to compare themselves, to their own disadvantage, with men whose good opinion means so much to them. We should recognize them for what they are—wonderful young women in their own right—and build up this positive picture of them.

I have been greatly impressed with their candor and frankness, with their willingness to avow their feelings and to cut through much conventional cant and nonsense. Many of them have a gift for understanding themselves and others, and a need to talk out some of their perplexities and to find some ethical and aesthetic pattern for their lives. They are distressed by the formless chaos that surrounds them and sometimes recognize this for what it is— evil. They know intuitively that the unexamined life is not worth living. They are, of course, concerned with themselves and revel in their own freedom, but they are willing to prepare themselves emotionally, at least, for the eventual task of child-rearing, which they appear to do with so much competence and even joy.

A college which disregards their essential nature is doing only part of its job. If it wants girls to get the best out of their courses of instruction, then provision must be made for some easement and for some time for discussion with intelligent and reasonable mature adults who are not too quick to give advice but are willing to listen to them. I recall a young girl saying to me once that she could do her work all right but it did not leave her time to grow up. They need time for this and time to talk and to give expression to some of their perplexities. I realize that we have not found the ideal way to success in this enterprise, that each college will have to follow the plan that fits its own tradition. The problems are not essentially different in exclusively female institutions from those in coeducational ones, since they are both dependent upon pressures and upon the natural vulnerability which the girl brings with her. Everyone concerned with young people must be concerned with this aspect of their development. If not, what passes for education may be only a kind of "intellectual conditioning," without depth or meaning, or hope for the future.

I have no wish to end this chapter on a negative note, nor to leave the reader with the impression that nothing can be accomplished either by way of preventing these emotional disturbances in young college women, or of dealing with them, once they have arisen. Exactly the reverse is true. There is probably no segment of the population that appears to be more amenable to treatment than just this group of intelligent, sensitive, idealistic young women with their futures before them. From the therapist's point of view it is gratifying to try to help them, not only for the satisfaction of watching individuals grow up and live lives less dominated by automatically determined pejorative reactions, but also because one cannot escape the conviction that as they gain self-awareness and insight, these will eventually be passed on to their children. Thus one has struck a blow against the destructive and inexorable tendency for neurotic patterns to perpetuate themselves from generation to generation.

Professional treatment, when it is needed, consists of face-to-face interviews in which the student does most of the talking. The spacing of sessions is important. If they are too frequent, they may encourage excessive dependence; if too far apart, they may break the continuity of feeling, once it is established. In the presence of much anxiety or moody, taciturn depression not much will be accomplished by a therapist who assumes a sphinxlike, stony silence. He should be able to unbend, to laugh, to talk the student's lingo, even to curse at times. He may occasionally have to give some advice. For some younger therapists this may seem a crass contamination of their most cherished principles. And, without betraying confidences, he may have to confer with instructors, tutors, professors, and deans. With each of these, a skillful and seasoned psychiatrist can help build a healthier academic atmosphere without trespassing on their prerogatives.

Although some degree of difficulty such as I have described here can be expected in a great many young college women, it should not be assumed that I am recommending psychotherapy for all of them. Even if this were practicable, it is often quite unnecessary.

The indications for professional help depend on the severity of the disturbance and also on the apparently inexorable tendency for it to recur. Help can come from many other sources—from the spontaneous process of maturation and growth which does not move at a steady rate but rather in bursts. And help can come as well from new responsibilities and, above all, from meaningful encounters and experiences.

It is usually stated that about 10 percent of students require professional psychiatric assistance. This is a rough approximation but probably a fairly good one. It does not, however, mean that those who seek help are necessarily sicker than those who do not. They may simply recognize and acknowledge difficulties which others try to deny.

As for the prevention of emotional disturbance, here we are on still less certain ground. Thirty-five years ago the late Dr. Adolf Meyer, for a generation the intellectual leader of American psychiatry, said that there were two approaches to mental health: the utopian and the scientific. The utopian leads to moralizing, and the scientific to experimentation and action. It is the latter which concerns us most, but I am far from devaluing any statement of ideal goals, however remote or difficult to achieve. The definition of mental health remains somewhat vague, elusive, and ambiguous; and, in any case, definitions themselves do not solve problems.

We have no formula to prevent the kind of depression I have described in this article. We do not know how to instill humor where none exists. But we can encourage self-acceptance and a sense of identity; and, unless the student has been too much damaged in childhood by a lack of trust, we can provide an atmosphere, even a rigorously competitive one, in which courage does not too quickly flag. There is much to be said for confrontation with more mature persons, not only in the faculty but in the student body, too, where the inclusion of some older men and women, who are completing unfinished college work, can add much to the meaningfulness of study. The choice of new members of a faculty should be made with an eye to their concern for students as well as for their creative scholarship. When the two are combined, the stage is well set. There is much to be said for the salutary effect of good talk, not only of the "bull session" kind, but talk with sophisticated, critical persons who are concerned with the human situation. Out of this can come compelling and charismatic ideas, which may last a lifetime. Nothing we can do for this generation or the next can be more important than to help these young women toward a clearer image of themselves. This will give them the self-esteem they need and the vigor to lead satisfying and creative lives.

16

Special Problems of Graduate Students in the School of Arts and Sciences

Robert L. Nelson

Psychiatry has a special importance to the graduate schools of a university. In size of enrollment alone, the needs of graduate students are important. In addition, they are preparing for positions in society that often exert an important and formative influence on others.

It is traditional to think of the health needs of university students in terms of the average undergraduate student who is usually in his late teens or early twenties, fresh from home or from the protective atmosphere of a preparatory school, and whose health problems are usually typical of late adolescence and early adulthood. A high proportion of students requiring the services of a university's health unit, however, are graduate students. An increasing number of American universities offer opportunities for work at the graduate level. At Harvard University graduate students make up slightly over one-half of the total enrollment. Many universities have a similar graduate-undergraduate ratio.

Graduate students are, for the most part, well into their twenties. They have little in the way of adolescent turmoil and have usually had the opportunity to make many independent decisions.

The vocational decision has frequently been made. An increasing proportion are married and have children. Compared with the undergraduate, many needs of the graduate student receive less attention from the total administration of the university. Outstanding in this regard are housing needs, availability of funds to finance graduate work, and nearness to general university facilities such as the health center and recreational facilities.

In an effort to learn about the needs of this large and important part of total university enrollment, a study devoted to psychiatric needs of graduate students was made. The group chosen was made up of those from Harvard's Graduate School of Arts and Sciences who had been seen by University psychiatrists during the course of an academic year. These students represent many fields of graduate education, and the enrollment is large enough to allow significant findings. The areas of study in this school fall into three major divisions: natural sciences, social sciences, and humanities. The subdivisions in each of these fields include studies having a direct practical application and others of a more general and abstract nature.

The Graduate School of Arts and Sciences at Harvard has no specific medical unit but shares psychiatric facilities with the College and with the other graduate schools. Of the 1,500 students enrolled, 100 were seen by the psychiatric service during the year studied. No special effort is made to acquaint the students with the psychiatric facilities of the University other than what is contained in the general announcements concerning the availability of health services. All but 3 of the 100 students interviewed had symptoms that required further evaluation and eventual therapy. The 3 exceptions involved administrative matters related to a student's illness or a request for advice about another person.

Approximately one-quarter of the students did not have a well-established mental illness in the conventional sense and were placed in a "problem" category. This refers to a less severe psychiatric need, frequently related to specific and clearly seen circumstances rather than to established symptom patterns. The number of psychiatric appointments appropriate to students in this category varies greatly.

One student benefited from a single interview. His difficulty was diagnosed "family problem." He had divorced his wife after a number of years of marriage and the birth of several children. Shortly before seeking a psychiatric interview, he suddenly wanted his children with him, even though it was not an opportune time for them. He had formerly shown little interest in being with them and had arranged to see them for a very brief period each year. In the course of an hour's interview he gained insight into why he impulsively wanted his children. He was taking steps toward a new marriage that had increased feelings of guilt at being separated from them. Awareness of the relationship between his impending new marriage and his present need to be with his children enabled him to make plans to see them in keeping with their best interests.

Another student, whose difficulty was diagnosed "intrapersonal problem," was seen for twenty psychiatric interviews. He was making an excellent academic adjustment to graduate study but felt socially inadequate and very concerned at his hesitation to develop warm relationships with women. In the course of interviews he gained an understanding of his inappropriate fear that he was unattractive to women. This related to an unusually prolonged close tie to his mother. He improved socially, and throughout his period of treatment continued to do excellent academic work, unlike a number of students with problems who often have concurrent academic troubles.

In none of the problem cases was there evidence of long-standing symptoms or personality disturbances that were severely incapacitating to the student or threatening to his total adjustment. In contrast to this less severe form of psychiatric need, approximately one-half of the students interviewed had clearly established psychoneurotic symptoms. In this group, anxiety reaction was the largest single diagnostic category, with depressive reaction a close second.

The students were referred for psychiatric interviews in the following ways: 65 self-referred, 19 referred by the medical service, 11 by faculty or administrators, and 5 by a friend or family member. The proportion of students self-referred to those referred by others was essentially the same in all the major diagnostic categories. Regardless of the manner referred, most of the students were completely acceptant of psychiatric evaluation and moved into therapy with little difficulty.

Most of the students interviewed were found to have had their academic achievement affected in some way by their psychiatric problems. Nineteen were severely incapacitated, 26 moderately, and 36 minimally. There was no effect in 17, and on 2 there was insufficient information to make an estimate. There were no proportional differences in any of the diagnostic groups, other than the expected severe incapacity of those having a psychotic illness. When a problem interfered with studies, other areas of the student's life usually were also disturbed. A few students were able to continue studies without interference despite severe symptoms affecting other life adjustments.

One student had a very specific academic problem as his main symptom, and it was clearly related to his basic character problem. He had extreme difficulty in writing papers for his courses, but otherwise did well in his studies. He was hesitant to offer his thoughts to the criticism of those in authority. This was reflected in his first efforts to move into psychotherapy. He had extreme difficulty in talking about his problems and could express his concerns only in the most indirect way. In the course of eleven interviews he was able to gain sufficient superficial insight to accept a move into more intensive therapy outside the clinic. At the same time he became moderately relieved of his academic problem and was able to continue his studies.

It is difficult to give an accurate estimate of each student's benefit from treatment. Many were seen briefly, and adequate follow-up was not uniformly available. However, a general estimate of benefit was possible, especially as reflected in academic achievement. Eleven were considered to have had marked benefit from therapy, 57 moderate, 19 minimal, 9 none, and with 4 no estimate could be made.

Among those who received no benefit from treatment, a severe resistance to entering therapy was frequently apparent. One student, referred by the medical service, had a history of prolonged nonspecific somatic complaints. Thorough medical evaluation failed to reveal any physical disease entity. He was seen for four psychiatric interviews, and it was evident he had a psychiatric disorder. He was very resentful of having been referred for evaluation and was unable to appreciate his need for therapy. He refused to continue with interviews, persisted with his complaints, and a short time later withdrew from graduate school.

There was remarkably little variation in each diagnostic group as to degree of benefit from treatment.

One student with psychotic illness showed marked improvement. He had received thirteen psychiatric interviews during former years of study at Harvard for what was considered a psychoneurotic condition. During the year studied he suddenly developed psychotic symptoms, centering around suspicions that elaborate plots were being made against him. When first seen he presented a picture that, under most circumstances, would warrant immediate hospitalization. However, he had a comfortable relationship with the therapist who had seen him previously, and in the course of three interviews gained very rapid awareness of his disturbed state and its relationship to earlier sexual concerns. He was dramatically relieved of his symptoms. They did not recur, and he was able to complete graduate study.

Ten students were considered to have character disorders. This illness is usually refractory to short-term treatment and requires prolonged therapy. However, among the students having this disorder, the number who benefited from treatment was proportionate to that of the other diagnostic groups. One student, whose problem was called passive-aggressive personality, obtained marked improvement from nine psychiatric interviews. He had used passivity as a way of expressing angry feelings for many years and was severely limited in his relationships with persons in a position of authority. During psychiatric interviews he gained insights that allowed him to move successfully out of this long-established personality trend.

The average number of interviews for each student was five. Each of the diagnostic groups showed some difference from this mean number. The extreme averages were two visits for those having a psychotic illness and six visits for those with psychoneurotic symptoms. Those having a psychotic disturbance usually had only an evaluation followed by arrangements for appropriate treatment. Those with psychoneurotic symptoms required the greatest number of interviews for evaluation and therapy.

Seventeen of the 100 students studied required more psychiatric care than was available through the clinic. As would be expected, four of the five with a psychotic illness required special treatment, although only one actually required hospitalization. Ten of the students with psychoneurotic symptoms required more intensive treatment than could be offered. When outside psychiatric care was obtained, it was usually essential for the student's general welfare and his university adjustment. It was estimated that other students would have benefited from more intensive therapy. However, a number of factors made this difficult to arrange: the heavy load at the clinic, insufficient funds for private therapy, difficulty in placement in public psychiatric clinics, and lack of sufficient motivation for therapy.

A superfical look at the psychiatric need of graduate and undergraduate students indicates great similarity. The percent seen and the mean number of interviews per student are remarkably similar for the two groups. This similarity may be influenced by the number of available psychiatric hours, for during most of the year the staff was able to see only those most in need, and for a minimum number of interviews. It must be remembered that the findings of this study reflect the students' needs during one academic year. A more recent study has been made of the needs of students from freshman year in college through the years of graduate education. The basic finding of this study is that roughly one-fifth of the students seek psychiatric help or are advised to get it at some time during the course of their undergraduate and graduate years.

Data related to diagnosis and manner of being referred to treatment were also available for the undergraduate students seen in psychiatric interviews. Comparisons with the graduate group were made. No significant difference in the incidence of most of the diagnostic categories was found, and there was no difference in the percentage of those requiring hospitalization. However, there was a significant difference in the number of those diagnosed psychoneurotic and those seen for "administrative and information" reasons. The graduate group had 25 percent more psychoneurotic illnesses, and 21 percent fewer were seen for "administrative and information" reasons.

These differences indicate that when a student reaches the age of graduate study he is less apt to involve others, such as university administrators, in matters related to his psychiatric need. He is more apt to present a clearly established psychoneurotic symptom picture. The difference also points to a need for more therapeutic time to be allotted to graduate students than to undergraduates. Most interviews for "administrative or information" reasons require relatively little in the way of psychiatric time, important as they may be. Therapy for psychoneurotic conditions is at the other extreme, usually requiring many interviews, and at times protracted and intensive therapy.

Sixty-five percent of the graduate students were self-referred, in contrast to 33 percent of the college group. In keeping with this high rate of self-referral, the graduate group had proportionately fewer referrals from such sources as the medical department, faculty, and administrators. This difference again indicates that the graduate student has a greater awareness of psychiatric need and is more apt to take an appropriate step regarding treatment before symptoms make themselves evident to others in the university.

Many impressions are held by faculty members, administrators, and members of the general medical staff, as well as by psychiatrists, as to what characterizes students who have need for psychiatric care. Frequently such impressions originate from gross manifestations of a mental illness observed in a student who in some dramatic way is different from the "average" student. Such signs of illness may be observed in students coming from colleges that rarely send students to graduate school, or in students who pursue an unusual course of study.

The students in the graduate school represent a variety of undergraduate backgrounds. An effort was made to see whether any type of undergraduate background was associated with a greater or lesser incidence of psychiatric need. Many colleges send only one student to this school of graduate study, and other colleges send many students. The enrollment was divided into the following groups: students coming from colleges sending one representative, colleges sending two to four, colleges sending five to fifteen, and colleges sending over fifteen. The patient group in each of these categories was found to be directly proportional to the total student body. Thus, whether the student came from Colorado College, sending one student to the school, or from Harvard College sending over 250, there appeared to be no greater or lesser likelihood of psychiatric disturbance.

It is a frequently held impression that some fields of study attract students with psychiatric problems. To test the validity of this impression, the patient group was compared with total enrollment as to field of concentration. The number of patients in each of the major divisions of the school (natural sciences, social sciences, and humanities) was directly proportional to the total student body in these fields. Field of concentration was also considered in terms of popularity of various subfields of study. All areas of study were divided into those subfields which had fewer than 20 students, 20 to 50 students, and over 50 students. The number of patients in each of these divisions was directly proportional to the total student body also. These findings suggest that there is no general relationship between incidence of psychiatric difficulties and area of academic interest.

At the Graduate School there is opportunity for considerable variation in the amount of time taken by a student to complete his work. Extremes range from one or two years to eight years or more. It is often thought that students who greatly prolong their years of graduate study are inclined towards psychiatric disturbance. In the findings of the study, however, 10 percent of the patient group were in their fifth year or over, and the corresponding percentage for the total student body was identical, showing no higher incidence of psychiatric disorder in students who are slow in finishing their graduate studies. When such a student has a psychiatric problem, however, it frequently is related to his hesitancy to complete studies.

One student in his eighth year of graduate study referred himself for therapy after twice failing to pass his doctoral oral examinations, each effort being associated with increasingly severe anxiety. His failures were completely out of keeping with his past academic performance and the expectations of his examiners. Psychiatric evaluation revealed that he had been extremely hesitant to move into an area of adult responsibility. He had been married many years, had a dependent relationship with his wife, and insisted on a continual delay in having children. On gaining insights related to his dependent needs, he showed a great improvemedt and was able to complete his graduate studies.

The patient group was also compared to the total enrollment regarding withdrawals from the University. As might be anticipated, the patient group showed a higher percentage of withdrawals. Twelve percent of the patients withdrew for medical or personal reasons, compared to 4 percent of the total student body. That 88 percent of the patients stayed in school indicates that the great majority of those having psychiatric need can successfully continue their studies when therapy is available. Psychiatric disturbance, however, is related to a higher proportion of withdrawals and further stresses the importance of adequate therapy before severe incapacity appears. Occasionally, withdrawal from school is a part of a successful response to therapy. Often, in such instances, the student's choice of graduate study was motivated by his psychiatric problems and was not in keeping with his abilities or interests.

Fourteen percent of the Graduate School enrollment were students who had spent their formative years in a foreign country, and 18 percent of this group were seen in psychiatric interviews. An independent study of those foreign students was made, and in 19 of the 76 studied there was found to be some relationship between the foreign student status and the psychiatric problem. In 8 cases there was a direct relationship, and in 11 the relationship was more superficial and indirect. In the remaining 57 cases there was no indication that foreign student status related to the problem. The number of cases in which there was some degree of relationship between foreign student status and psychiatric need does not seem out of proportion to the number of domestic students whose problems relate to adjustments involved in coming to the University from communities within this country.

Among the eight students whose psychiatric problems in some degree related directly to their foreign student status, one had language difficulty and could understand only about half of his lectures; in addition, he was concerned about being separated from his wife and child, who were in his home country. He also had very real financial worries. With the aid of psychiatric interviews, he was able to finish the academic year and then return to his home country.

The political situation in the home countries of two students made it uncertain they could return. Faced with the prospect of staying in this country an indefinite period of time, they felt under special pressure to make an excellent adjustment in every way. One was extremely anxious to do well, felt competitive with other students, was frequently argumentative, and insisted on knowing many things about his department chairman that were not relevant to his work as a student. He gained considerable insight during interviews and improved his adjustment.

Two students had symptoms stemming from difficulties in establishing a satisfactory sexual adjustment in this country. One felt great sexual tension as he was unable to find the kind of easily available outlet for sexual drive that was available in his home country. An opportunity to discuss this in psychiatric interviews relieved his symptoms. Another who had difficulty understanding and adapting to American standards of monogamy showed similar improvement.

Among the 11 students whose problems bore a superficial relationship to the fact that they were foreign students, the connection was usually only in the way that initial symptoms were expressed, and psychiatric interviews quickly revealed the more basic difficulties. Five patients in this group had distress at being separated from close family members. They had many dependent needs, and it is probable that separation under any circumstances would have produced the same symptoms. One such student had symptoms of anxiety and concern about what he called "loss of identity" on being separated from his wife and child. He also had unresolved occupational difficulties in the home country and was concerned at not being able to take steps to correct them. He was seen for seven psychiatric interviews, showed moderate improvement, and was able to complete his studies before returning to his family. Another student complained of homesickness and in the course of nine psychiatric interviews gained help in adjusting to new authority figures. He had been late in moving away from a dependent relationship with his parents, and coming to this country to study had been his first independent step.

Two students, from different cultural backgrounds, fell in love for the first time after leaving home to study in this country. Both were planning marriage and were later rejected by the women concerned. Both developed depressive symptoms but showed significant improvement with psychiatric interviews.

A woman student had difficulty adapting to graduate courses that included a new cultural approach to the position of women in society. During the course of thirty-five psychiatric interviews she gained basic insight into her long-standing fears of aggressive expression and her anxiety associated with this. She showed marked improvement, and a follow-up inquiry indicated continued improvement in her native country.

Psychiatric diagnoses usually found in domestic students in this age group applied to all the foreign students. Not only was the proportion of those having problems the same, but there was a similar incidence in each diagnostic category. The mean number of psychiatric interviews for the two groups was identical. (This may partially be a reflection of the saturation point at which the psychiatric staff worked.) There were no significant differences in the way students were referred for therapy; more than half the students of each group appropriately referred themselves. As a group, the foreign students had the same response to therapy as the domestic students. A general estimate of benefit from treatment was made on each student, and approximately 70 percent of both groups had marked or moderate improvement. Less than 10 percent of each group withdrew from school before completing their studies. It was also found that a similar number in both groups required therapy in addition to that available at the clinic. The foreign students, however, tended to be less severely incapacitated in their academic work. Sixteen percent less had severe or moderate incapacity, and 24 percent more had no academic incapacity as compared with the cross section of domestic graduate students.

The various large geographical areas of this country at times have medical significance, showing differences in the incidence of many diseases. They also represent varying degrees of cultural difference. In a general way, these cultural differences are reflected in the educational institutions of each area. An attempt was made to see if this had significance regarding psychiatric need. The students from New England colleges were compared with those from the West Coast. The findings showed no difference in incidence of psychiatric need in the two groups.

During his first four months at the University, each student is given a complete medical evaluation by the health services. This includes a confidential medical history, and for the most part, students are at ease in giving full information. A physical examination is given by an internist who takes sufficent time for thorough evaluation of any medical problems found. The information obtained from this evaluation was summarized on all in the patient group, and, also, on an equal number of students who had never consulted the psychiatric service and were considered as controls. The latter group was picked at random from the total enrollment of the Graduate School of Arts and Sciences. The following is a comparison of the two groups in areas that might relate to psychiatric need.

The medical evaluation covers much general background information. Areas of ethnic origin were compared to consider further the possibility of cultural differences affecting psychiatric need. However, areas of origin of the patient group were directly proportional to those of the controls. Being an only child or a student's relationship to one or more siblings frequently has significance in the course of psychiatric therapy. The patient group and the controls were compared, and in all the findings relating to sibling position there were no significant differences. When the histories of the students were reviewed, it was found that the two groups showed no significant difference in the occurrence of death of one or both parents, divorce or separation of the parents, or history of mental illness in parents and/or siblings.

The interruption of study for service in the armed forces is at times associated with psychiatric need. Some describe it as a maturing experience, and others consider it a delay or escape. An equal number in the patient and control groups gave a history of military experience, indicating that it is not related to incidence of psychiatric need. When seen for medical evaluation, the student is asked about career plans. A slightly higher percentage of the patient group had indefinite or no career plans compared to the control group. The two groups showed no difference in the number of students who had had a severe physical illness. Marriage and divorce occurred proportionately in both groups.

A number of items included in the medical evaluation deal more specifically with psychiatric need, and comparisons of the two groups in the following areas showed significant differences. Ten percent of the patient group spontaneously requested psychiatric therapy at the time of their initial medical examination, as opposed to only 1 percent of the control group. Forty-one percent of the patient group expressed symptoms related to psychiatric disturbance as they answered questions in the medical history, compared to 9 percent of the control group. The symptoms included in this category were only those directly related to psychiatric symptomatology, such as depression and anxiety. Symptoms of a somatic nature, having a possible relationship to psychiatric disorder, were not included. There was no significant difference in the number of patients and controls who gave a history of having had a mental illness.

The physician conducting the physical examination evaluates the student's personality. This includes a rating of "social relations" and "basic personality integration." Twenty percent of those who later came for psychotherapy were considered below average in this personality appraisal as opposed to 7 percent of the control group.

The physician is also asked to give an estimate of the student's future medical needs, including possible psychiatric need. In the patient group, 20 percent were thought to definitely need psychiatric care, and 22 percent were considered to have a questionable need. In the control group, psychotherapy seemed indicated for 2 percent, and 3 percent were estimated to have a questionable need.

In reviewing the findings at the time of initial medical evaluation, only the following were found to give some evidence of need for psychiatric care: spontaneous request for psychotherapy, description of a symptom related to psychiatric disturbance, the physician's statement that psychiatric care was clearly or questionably indicated. When all of these factors were considered, 53 percent of the patient group showed evidence of possible psychiatric need as opposed to 9 percent of the controls.

The important finding of this study is that nothing in terms of general background information significantly predicts a need for psychiatric assistance. If students qualify for admission to a graduate school, no routine information will categorize the majority of those who will have therapeutic needs. The study indicated that a complete medical evaluation after the student has begun his course of graduate study can be of considerable value. It not only anticipates the psychiatric needs of a significant number of students, but can also be of value in helping them arrange for therapy with the least delay.

Compared with college students, the graduate student shows a greater awareness of his needs, usually seeks therapy on his own initiative, and is less apt to involve the faculty or administration in his problems. This means that the graduate student comes to the psychiatrist highly motivated and with few resistances to beginning appropriate therapy.

Over one-half of the students interviewed had little or no interference with their studies at the time they first asked for treatment. Much can be gained if appropriate therapy is begun before a student has severe incapacity. More than two-thirds of the students who came for psychiatric help received important benefits from treatment. This points to the effectiveness of doing more than diagnostic service, despite lack of sufficient time for giving optimum therapy to all in need.

Most of the students were at an early age of their illness, which was responsive to treatment, and very few had an illness of such long standing as to be intractable. It is important that those who require prolonged and intensive therapy be aided in obtaining it. The study revealed that a high percentage of those requiring therapy beyond that available at the University had psychoneurotic symptoms; and that, compared with the college, the graduate school has a higher incidence of this illness. This suggests that more therapeutic hours should be available for graduate students than for undergraduates.

Specific need for psychiatric care, expressed in terms of symptoms, occurs in a significant portion of university students. There are indications that, in ways short of disturbing symptoms, graduate students sense a need for greater self-understanding. In a recent annual report, Dean Elder of the Harvard Graduate School of Arts and Sciences referred to a questionnaire sent to recent graduates in an effort to get helpful criticism. Fifteen hundred answers were received. They gave the following general impression: "On the whole, through the pages of the answers comes repeatedly the theme of the graduate student's lack of self-confidence—all sorts of signs to suggest that we almost seem to have encouraged immaturity during the years spent here rather than to have fostered a growing self-dignity and ripe poise."

Admission to a school of graduate study is evidence of considerable ability; most graduate schools require applicants to have completed undergraduate work at a high academic level. The important future role of the graduate student emphasizes the need to administer graduate study in a way that encourages maturity and fosters "a growing self-dignity and ripe poise." Much can be done to augment this process by having psychiatric care readily available to the students with special needs for greater self-understanding.

17

Special Problems
Encountered at the
Graduate School of
Business Administration

Henry H. Babcock

At this graduate school of the University there are encountered a
wide variety of emotional disturbances and maladjustments. There
are few if any reactions among business school students which are
qualitatively different from those which are to be seen among any
university student population. The difference lies in the quantitative
representation of the various types of reactions and disorders. In general, the diversity as well as the intensity of the reactions tends to be
less than among undergraduate students. Reactions are less diverse
because the external factors tending to produce stress are more nearly
the same for all of the students due to the uniformity of the academic
program, less intense because one finds less marked psychobiological
swings in the adaptational processes of men in their early and middle
twenties than would be the case with those who are in the transi-
tional period between late adolescence and adulthood. Thus, for
example, the incidence of the so-called "turmoil states," borderline
states, and psychotic reactions among graduate business school students is less by far than among the college students. The great majority of disturbances fall within the category of emotional maladjustments which can best be understood in terms of the interaction

between the stress factors inherent in this particular competitive program and the varying personality make-up of the students who enter
such a program.

The Harvard Business School student population consists mainly
of those who are enrolled in a two-year program of study and instruction leading to the Master's degree in business administration.
There are approximately 1,200 altogether in this group. Students
selected for this program have almost invariably completed the requirements for the degree of Bachelor of Arts or of Science. They
have been selected in recent years from a group of applicants about
four times the size of the entering class. Their average age on entrance is between 25 and 26 and about two-thirds of them are married. The great majority has had military service and many, in addition, have had one or two years' experience in the business world.
Those who have come from foreign countries are given the benefit of
a special indoctrination course of several weeks' duration prior to
the beginning of classes. Unmarried students live in dormitories on
the school campus.

The principal method of instruction is that referred to as the
case method. There are no textbooks and practically no didactic
or formal lectures. On the contrary, the teaching material is provided from written cases adapted from real situations in the business world, which are studied in advance and then discussed in class.
In effect, the students are placed in the position of various company
officials faced with the necessity of analyzing a complex situation and
then recommending what action should be taken. The aim is to provide
these students with as wide as possible an acquaintance with the
multiplicity of factors involved in business, ranging from the analysis
of complicated sets of figures to an awareness of human motivation
and interpersonal relationships, and to promote in them a skill in
weighing the evidence, making the decision, and taking responsibility for action in a vicarious manner. Each class of 600 is sub-
divided into six sections of 100 each, which constitute the classroom
units. They meet regularly in large amphitheaterlike rooms which
have a shallow-tiered semicircular seating arrangement. The teaching
material, aside from that which is written about the case at hand, is
derived from the numerous contributions of opinions from the voluntarily participating students. For the most part, the instructors play

the role of moderator, guiding the discussion rather than taking charge of it, promoting independent thinking rather than giving out authoritative opinions or conclusions. Students are graded largely on the basis of the degree and quality of their participation in the classroom and on the evidence of their growth in maturity and judgment.

It can readily be seen that the student is immediately plunged into a system of teaching and study which is foreign to his previous academic experience. It is a system which, instead of offering an organized body of factual information, fosters the gradual development of a skilled technique in tackling a wide range of problems and a sound judgment in the art of making decisions. It is only after the first academic year is well under way that the average student begins to appreciate the rationale of the method and can feel a sense of maturing effectiveness in his participation and grasp. (He starts to "see the big picture," as the saying goes.) Until then he has little to compensate him for the fact that the only apparent measure of his progress lies in a few quiz grades, and the only tangible evidence of his having learned anything is in the form of an increasing stack of "used cases."

One might think that a system of this sort would lead to ruthless competitiveness. A powerful mitigating force however is to be found in the organization of each section into small study groups consisting of from five to eight students. These groups are informally and spontaneously created soon after registration, and there is a wide range of latitude in a student's ability to change from one to another if he finds himself in incompatible company. As a rule these groups center around several sets of roommates in a single entry, many of whom are likely to be "head-mates" as well. This term, borrowed from the Navy, seems in this adapted connotation to point up the fact that students who share the same "head," or bathroom, feel embarked together on the same perilous mission. Married students form study groups, as well, using the library for meetings or going to each other's home. The function of the study groups is to permit the students a kind of preliminary rehearsal on the night before the case is discussed in the main arena of the classroom. Just as important if not more so is the fact that, owing to this more intimate and informal structure, students come to feel a closer identification and team approach than is possible in the full section of 100 men.

Is there such a thing as a typical business school student or personality? Probably not. It is important to bear in mind that the 5 to
10 percent of the student body which comes to the health service
each year for psychiatric help constitutes not only a small but a distorted cross section of the student body as a whole; and yet it is from
this 5 to 10 percent that the psychiatrist derives his strongest impressions. Although he might be tempted to make unwarranted generalizations, full-time practice in a university health service permits one to
gain a fair impression of a good many "nonpatient" students in the
course of daily affairs and makes it possible to draw some conclusions
about the school at large.

A pattern which is encountered with more frequency among the
business students than in other parts of the university is a certain
quality of concreteness in thinking, a naturalness in expression and
action, and an orientation to a world of practicality. Our phycholo-
gists report, for example, that these men give performances on the
Rorschach test that "are the only ones in the University to show any
signs of common sense." Such characteristics equip these men well
for the administrative role-playing which is the keystone of the case
method of instruction. A capacity for organized thought and action,
an ease in verbal communication, and a willingness to participate in
collective teamwork are further attributes of those who tend to be
selected, as well as those who are molded by the learning experience
afforded by this graduate program. It is not surprising that the men
who achieve success most easily in this kind of program are the ones
who have already shown evidence of leadership or at least a potential
for the assertion of such leadership. As might be expected, those who
require help in making emotional adjustments to the program are for
the most part the students who deviate rather widely from this pattern of characteristics. Though many of them will be effective in and
make significant contributions to their chosen field, the people who
make up this minority group form a contrast to the above-mentioned
pattern because of their sensitivity, passivity, introspectiveness, and
lack of ease in interpersonal relationships.

An unmarried first-year student of 26 sought medical help during
his first semester because of insomnia and tension. Referral to the school
psychiatrist was easily accomplished as the student himself had recognized the probable psychological significance of his symptoms.

Coinciding with his entering the school he had developed a fear that he would not be able to meet the requirements and that his failure would be ruinous to his stepfather's health and reputation. He studied excessively and almost constantly, always maintaining his preparations for two days ahead of time so that he might feel that he had some lee-way on which to fall back if necessary. He also would lie awake for hours at night, anticipating and planning for every imaginable event that might occur on the following day.

He was the only child of parents who were divorced when he was 5 years old, and he never saw his own father again after that time. Later his mother remarried a man who was described as successful and self-made, never having gone to high school. Actually, this man was in rather poor health, was given to drinking too much in the home, and had no interests whatever aside from his work. The student had a rather distant relationship with his stepfather and was never quite sure how to please him or what was expected of him.

After a relatively few interviews this student was able to recognize the underlying feelings of resentment stemming from this insecure re-lationship to grasp the significance of his unconscious need to avenge (mostly his own father) by failure—a need previously masked by a con-scious fear of failure. A fortuitous and timely meeting with his step-father, in which the latter reassured him of his acceptance regardless of what he might or might not achieve at the Business School, served to consolidate the gains mentioned above. The result was a remarkable and sudden disappearance of the obsessive and compulsive symptoms, an im-proved efficiency in his work, and subsidence of his tension and insomnia.

Over and over again one is impressed by the frequency with which unstable or insecure family relationships may be found ac-countable in large measure for the emotional disturbances experi-enced by the products of those homes. Many other cases are seen in which the struggle may be related almost entirely to an absence of educational precedent in the preceding generation—when parents fail to recognize the nature of the ambitions of their children and fail to promote them by vicarious participation or by enthusiastic moral support.

During the initial part of the first academic year some begin to wonder if they are in the right place—if they are really cut out to be business executives. They go through a kind of vocational crisis. They feel the immediate impact of the highly competitive system upon their underlying insecurity, self-doubt, and uncertain motiva-tion. For every one who reports or is sent to the medical office or to the psychiatrist there are probably several others who quietly drop out. With a minimum of supportive help a great many of these can weather the blast and integrate themselves into the teaching-learning process, provided that their motivation and determination can be mobilized. An alert assistant dean may often turn the tide by helping one of these students to find his way into a more suitable study group or by suggesting certain techniques in the approach to case studies.

Among these early reactors are also to be found a few who have long been under pressure by a father to enter the field of business primarily to be groomed for the family company. The difficulty resides not only in the domineering, directive parent but also in the son who has either passively complied or has continued an unconscious rebellion against such an influence. In the latter instance corrective therapy is more hopeful, for after such a student has worked through his feelings relative to his father he is better able rationally to choose another objective *for himself* rather than for someone else.

Differentials in age, previous work experience, or academic training may be seized upon by certain students as a rationalization for their inability to compete, masking the reality of their lower aptitudes in relation to the rest of the class. Some who come directly from college, without intervening employment or military service, may feel at a disadvantage in holding their own with the more "seasoned men of the world" who are their seniors by several years. On the other hand, men who have attained the age of 30 or above before enrolling, many of them having served in the armed forces during the interim following their undergraduate work, may say that they have been away from college too long to adapt themselves to study habits and that their minds are no longer agile enough to keep up with the pace of their younger competitors.

By the time that the first year is well along into the second or third month, the inhibited personalities have been fairly clearly identified by the teaching faculty because of their failure to participate much if at all in the classroom discussions. Some are referred by their instructors or by the dean's office to the medical department, but even more come of their own accord to seek help. By far the commonest complaint of the first-year students who are seen by the psychiatrist is that they find it almost physically impossible to speak or, if they do speak, to organize their thoughts enough to express anything meaningful. Varying degrees of anxiety, with the whole gamut of its physiological manifestations, accompany this struggle. Here in the arena of the classroom, where the majority dissent to a ventured opinion may be expressed in terms ranging from polite contradiction to sarcasm, scorn, or mockery, it is not surprising that the unresolved childhood conflicts of the vulnerable student become acutely reactivated. Little wonder that his feelings tell him that he is in danger of being " torn to pieces," that if he "sticks his neck out" it will get "cut off." All but the most severely affected are usually able to continue to function with reasonable effectiveness as members of the smaller teaching or study units. In individual therapy the task is long and painstaking, especially if one attempts to deal with the more remote phases of personality development. Although group therapy has not yet been tried in this particular setting, it might well have something to offer these inhibited students.

A 25-year-old, unmarried, first-year student referred himself to the school psychiatrist in the early part of his first semester because of anxiety symptoms and aggressive tendencies toward his fellow students both in and out of the classroom. Notable in his background was a dominating, controlling, and arbitrary father toward whom the student had long been in a state of active rebellion. During his undergraduate days at college he had engaged in much bravado, and alcohol had often been used to excess.

The impact of the case method on this student was particularly strong, as might be anticipated. Passive tendencies within him were being vigorously countered by an aggressive front, but at the same time he feared retaliation for his behavior, which frequently impressed others as obnoxious in nature. His difficulty was that he could not (even normally) assert himself without at the same time feeling threatened and therefore injecting elements of sadistic defiance.

It was necessary to continue with psychotherapy at weekly and often at semiweekly intervals throughout the entire academic year. This not only provided a supportive framework without which he might well have been obliged to withdraw from the program, but it also served to effect a certain amount of working through of the underlying conflicts, with resultant reduction in the degree of his "acting out." Further progress along these lines can be anticipated during his second year, although some form of continued therapy for this deep-seated personality disorder may have to be projected beyond the time of this student's graduation from school.

Even though the academic program in a graduate school such as this is highly competitive and demanding, there are still possibilities for providing concurrent corrective measures within the realm of psychological medicine.

Aside from these pathological reactions, one sees at this point in the curriculum other attitudes and feelings to be quite wide-spread throughout the student body. Most students, before coming to the Business School, have been accustomed to an altogether different mode of teaching—that is, the didactic dissemination of factual material through lectures and assigned reading. With such a traditional method the students know about where they stand at any given moment in relation to the systematized material that has been covered. Not so with the case method where the student soon finds that there are no ready answers to hold on to, no notes to refer to, no source material in which to find that for which he is looking, no standards against which to measure his absolute or relative standing in the class. The price to be paid for the exercise of independent and original thinking may seem high indeed. A great many students seem bewildered and confused. They often express this confusion by critical attitudes and sometimes by boredom or withdrawal. They may turn against the instructor, accusing him of not giving them definitive answers or solutions. Others condemn the whole method of teaching, saying in effect, "How can we put ourselves in the position of this or that executive who is faced with making a decision? How can we assume the responsibility? This is just a lot of play acting." But the wise professor lets other segments of the class be spokesmen for the rebuttal, the justification, or the defense. And thus after many weeks or months of volatile discussion, ventilation of feelings, and free expression of these critical attitudes, the process begins to "work itself through." Until that point is reached, many waves of discouragement and mass demoralization may have swept over the student body. Those who still persist in these attitudes are often the passive-aggressive personalities and those who have varying degrees of underlying paranoid trends. They feel that they are fighting against the process of "being molded by the group" and maintain a kind of willful pseudoindependence. Some cling to a stubborn, defeatist attitude, never thinking of their oral or written contributions as being their own but rather what the system calls for. "If this is what they insist upon, this is what I will give them."

One sees a few obsessive or compulsive students for whom the case method may be a particular challenge in that decisions must be made from the raw data of seemingly endless variables which defy exact measurement or definition. When confronted with subject matter which requires an understanding or an appreciation of the psychology of human behavior, such as courses in administrative practices or human relations, their neurotic patterns may become sufficiently aggravated to prompt them to seek treatment. As a matter of fact, such courses as these are apt to create stumbling blocks for any who have not achieved a reasonably mature personality development. Among these are found the rigid, the overly defensive, the passive, and the inhibited as well as the obsessive personalities. Whether or not human relations can be successfully taught to graduate students in a business school has for some time been a controversial issue between certain segments of the faculty. Some professors maintain that "certain tricks can be taught only to old dogs" and that the young graduate student who has not been exposed to much experience in the real working world may be tempted to utilize these techniques of dealing with people as a neurotic means of manipulating people to his own ends. Others among the faculty strongly feel that such skills and understanding can and should be taught at this level, and that it is the few who misuse their inadequate understanding that cause the impression of unteachability.

Aside from any consideration of the impact of curricular content, there constantly takes place in the activities of the classroom a kind of living education in the dynamics of group and individual interaction. Despite the exercises which may at times seem rugged, there is a steady growth in most students of the capacity to understand and to have respect for the other fellow's point of view.

Toward the end of the year few new referrals are made to the office of the psychiatrist aside from those who are inadequate in their academic achievements. Some have difficulty in the organization of their thoughts in the classroom and are lacking in the ability to conceptualize rather broadly in the manner now exhibited by the class as a whole. As one student put it, "In the beginning it seemed all right to talk frequently because everyone was offering fragments, but later on it was too much of a risk to contribute something which might be rejected for being wrong or too elementary." And there are others who have a pathological fear of final examinations or who actually become "clutched up" in the process of taking exams. Blockage of thought in this kind of situation may represent a dissociative (conversion) mechanism. In both of these groups showing intellectual inhibition or dysfunction, one finds an underlying conflict in the area of activity-assertion as opposed to passivity-compliance. The use of their minds has come to have the same emotional meaning to them as the earlier childhood sexual curiosity and forbidden activities. One student found it almost impossible to be assertive in class without at the same time feeling like a show-off, a clown, or a fool. Another could make no assertion except in terms of an aggressive defiance. Still another, whose father and older brother had gone successfully through the school, when faced with the necessity of appearing before the scholarship board for academic deficiency, said that he felt "as though I have lost something—I was always much more like my mother anyway."

These descriptions may suffice to give a picture of the types of reactions most frequently encountered among students during their first year within the framework of the academic setting in which they are competing. It would be difficult, and perhaps somewhat artificial, to attempt to relate all maladjustments to this framework. One or two frankly psychotic reactions are unlikely to be seen during the course of the year. Recommendation for withdrawal from school in the case of the borderline or incipient psychosis is not always accepted by the student and by no means always imposed unless the situation seems obviously dangerous to himself or to others. It is surprising how a few of them, given a sufficient degree of psychiatric supportive help, may be kept afloat and be able to finish out the year. But the chances of their being hospitalized within a month or two after finishing the school year are quite great. Classical conversion symptoms, chiefly globus hystericus, are more frequent than one might expect in this population. (Indeed there are some who still do not associate such a condition with the male of the human species!) In one year this constituted 4 percent of the psychiatric diagnoses made. There are a considerable number of reactions to situations which have little or nothing to do with the program at the school and which by their very nature are transient.

A 24-year-old, single, second-year student, who had had no previous psychiatric treatment, suddenly developed an acute paranoid psychosis only two months before the time of his scheduled graduation. He felt that a communist-inspired plot was being engineered against him, primarily by the family of the girl who had recently broken her engagement to him. His personality was so acutely disorganized as to warrant immediate admission to a mental hospital. After several months he was well enough to be discharged but continued in psychotherapy for the next twelve months with the physician who had treated him in the hospital. His improvement was steady and he was able to develop a good deal of insight into the nature of his problem. He reapplied to the school after eight months and, having been seen and favorably endorsed by the school psychiatrist, as well as by his own physician, he was readmitted, successfully completed his final semester, and graduated with the class which followed his own. A number of his friends as well as some members of the faculty felt that he was now a much warmer and more open person and better integrated than he had been before the time of his psychotic break. He experienced no difficulty in completing the program (in terms of emotional adjustments) and was well motivated toward continuing with his therapy at regular intervals during the remainder of the academic year.

An enlightened university considers an episode of acute mental illness no automatic bar to the occasional student who falls ill in this way during his course of study, provided that adequate measures are taken to reassess the mental status prior to readmission and that psychiatric supervision or treatment be continued if deemed advisable. Many of these students have no recurrence of such acute episodes and go on to achieve records of which their alma mater may be justly proud.

In the second year the stresses and strains are considerably less. The student who meets the requirements at the end of the first year has, with very few exceptions, little fear academically in his second year. The pressure is off, to a certain extent, from the statistical point of view alone. Whereas the courses taken in the first year are all required and almost invariably taught by the case method, the second-year curriculum comprises elective courses in all but one instance and may be chosen from a great variety of subjects. Relatively speaking, it is a year of specialization in which each student may turn his efforts to the field in which he has the greatest interest. Because of the increased number of the courses available, the classes are for the most part a good deal smaller than those in the first year.

Though the case method is still the essential approach, a certain amount of didactic teaching is employed, and considerable emphasis is placed upon individual projects, field trips, short and long written reports. Furthermore, the second-year student, by virtue of his summer job experience, is more seasoned and has had an opportunity to test some of his learning in terms of actual business practice. One often can distinguish a first-year student from a second-year student in a casual encounter by sensing certain qualities of greater maturity in the latter.

Whether the second-year business student is more self-sufficient and effective because of his therapeutic maturing as a result of participating in the program, or whether the competitive aspects are mitigated by the nature of the second-year curriculum, the incidence of those who seek psychiatric help is far less in the second year than in the first. Except for the students who have entered long-term or definitive psychotherapy, few of those seen during the first year return for any psychiatric help during the second. In the academic year of 1956–1957, first-year students outnumbered the second by a ratio of 3:1. The problems encountered revolve chiefly around the issue of job selection and placement. From midyear until shortly before the termination of classes, representatives from many businesses throughout the country schedule interviews at the school for the students who are prospective candidates for employment. By the time that this procedure gets under way, some students are still undecided as to what field of business would be most to their liking or most appropriate to their aptitudes. Some who are in high academic standing are torn between the desire to continue in the academic field either as research assistants or as doctoral candidates in preparation for teaching, or instead to secure their independence and start to make a living in the world. This conflict, aside from its realistic considerations, may be in part a repercussion of insecurity based on dependency needs whch have yet to be worked out. To over-emphasize this point would be to do an injustice to the majority of brilliant and highly capable people who choose the academic life without a neurotic motivation.

It is amazing to realize that some students may have reached this point without yet being able to say what it is that they are interested in. They ask to have tests not only to find out wherein lie their natural aptitudes but also to discover what it is that might *interest* them the most. Their past histories reveal that in each successive stage of their educational development there has been a singular lack of drive, a kind of drifting with the masses without much sense of direction. They have come to business school more by the process of elimination of other career possibilities than because of any positive motivation, and now they are again eliminating all the possibilities. Aptitude testing and vocational counseling will not be of much avail to them. Usually they end up by drifting out into the world on a trial-and-error basis. It is not quite so hard to try to help those whose conflict in the vocational sense is narrowed to several possible choices.

Foreign students, despite the fact that they constitute approximately 15 percent of the business student body, make up less than 5 percent of all who are seen for psychiatric consultation or treatment. The few who have been seen in the past two years have all been from English-speaking countries—Canada, England, and Scotland—which collectively supply nearly half of the total number of foreign enrollees. These are the very ones who might be expected to have the least adjustment difficulties from the standpoint of language or cultural differences. The effective selection of the foreign-speaking students, as well as the preliminary indoctrination period through which they pass, may account for the low incidence of adjustment problems. On the other hand, emotional disorders might be just as common in this group but not considered to be grist for the psychiatric mill because of differences in the cultural attitude toward psychiatry.

From an overall point of view some of the factors which tend to lessen the possibility of adjustment difficulties among all students are a fairly close-knit social structure on the campus and special consideration of and arrangements for the married students who, only a decade or so ago, were more the exception than the rule. Better arrangements for married students are badly needed in all parts of a university. There is also an easy accessibility to students of a number of the senior and junior faculty members, as well as representatives from the dean's office, the "study group" arrangement as mentioned above, and the existence of substantial funds from which loans and grants-in-aid may be made to students without regard to high scholastic standing. The fact that the possibility of failure to meet the academic requirements, although an unwelcome stigma, does not disqualify a student from pursuing a career in his chosen field as it does in certain other graduate schools serves to ease considerably the academic pressure.

The Middle Management Program is a separate course of study which is described in the official register of Harvard University as a program which "makes available to companies a broad and intensive education in management for their promising young men. . . . These men are old enough and far enough along to know something about business. They are young enough so that the benefits of this education will be realized by their companies through a long future executive life. . . . Through the case method of instruction each man can build on his past experience and on the experience of others in the program. He will be working closely with men from other fields, other companies, other industries, various departments of the government, and from abroad."

These men are for the most part in their early or middle thirties. The course of instruction extends over a period of eight months. A high percentage of this group are married and live with their families in rented quarters in the vicinity rather than on the campus.

Psychiatric disorders are not frequently found in this group of men. They have already demonstrated their stability through steady progress, leadership, and responsibility, and their companies have selected them because of their great promise. There have been a few instances in which anxiety or depressive states have developed in relation to the circumstances underlying the selection. One man, who suffered from a severe reactive depression, had been sent to take the course because his philosophy of management was at variance with that of his older brothers in a family-owned company. Another was nearly incapacitated by anxiety symptoms because he felt that he had already climbed as high in the company as he wished to go but was afraid to turn down the suggestion that he enroll in the program. Many of these men who suffer reactions to a lesser degree feel an inordinate amount of pressure upon them because of the competition that exists in the middle ranks of executives in big businesses. They feel that they may be called upon to produce more than it is in their capacity to do when they return to their companies. Some have fears that their companies are actually giving them a polite "brush off" by sending them to the Business School. Those who have come of their own initiative, when the company was not enthusiastic about their coming, may not have the financial sponsorship of the company and may not even be sure that they will get their jobs back again upon completing the course. Thus the motivation of *both* the company and the enrollee is a highly important factor to be assessed in the process of selection and of dealing with the problems of the enrollees when they arrive.

The Advanced Management Program is a 12-week course of training for men ranging in age from the late thirties to the early fifties who have been selected from the top levels of the administrative hierarchy. In relation to their companies, these men are in firmly established positions and have much less to fear from the possibility of being competitively displaced. Because of the relative shortness of the program, it is seldom feasible for them to move their families with them. While thus separated for the three-month period, they live together in the school dormitories in an atmosphere which is somewhere between "the old college campus days" on the one hand and a prolonged convention on the other.

The course is intensive. Many long-established concepts are challenged and often substantially modified as the result of the intimate meeting of minds from many fields in public and private industry as well as in government. Some of these men may be deeply troubled by the attempt to reconcile their thinking with ideas that seem new or radical, and this disturbance may manifest itself in tension, insomnia, or various psychophysiological dysfunctions. Notable among the latter is an overconcern about the heart precipitated by tachycardia, palpitation, or shortness of breath. Others are preoccupied with moral or ethical issues having to do with business responsibilities to government or to society. Though they may mention these conflicts to the psychiatrist, they feel fundamentally that such problems can only be worked out by themselves in due course of time. One man, for instance, with a mildly suspicious and overly sensitive nature, felt that one of the instructors was attempting to tear down his beliefs and convictions by a kind of shock treatment without replacing them with anything concrete. For a short period of time he tended to withdraw from class participation and developed symptoms of tension in the form of headache and insomnia. Ventilation of his concerns and some supportive therapy allowed him to continue and to benefit from the course.

18

Psychiatric Problems of Medical Students

Samuel Bojar

The Harvard University Medical Center Health Service has had the benefit of six years' experience in the care of the students of the medical area. During this time the opportunity has been afforded to observe three classes of medical and dental students throughout their four years of schooling and three preceding classes for periods of one, two, and three years, respectively. Students of the School of Public Health generally attend for only one year, with a number staying longer, while students in the Division of Medical Services are often under the medical jurisdiction of the Health Service for longer periods. Our patient population has been drawn from a varied community which has, as a common factor, a medical or ancillary scientific interest and orientation. Areas of divergence, however, appear in the cultural backgrounds, for the members of this community may be drawn from all continents of the globe. Emotional problems related to the difficulty in adjustment to a new cultural environment have been seen, mainly among older students, such as those at the School of Public Health, rather than among the younger ones at the Schools of Medicine and Dental Medicine.

The psychiatric division of a health service operating in a medical area community sees the same general diagnostic categories as may be noted in any other academic community, perhaps even in the population at large. The dynamic factors pertinent to the development of the presenting emotional complaint, however, are often quite different. In certain cases, they are related to the age group involved, with the emotional stresses associated with it. In other cases, they are related to the nature of the interests of the individuals as well as to the nature of individuals with medical interests. In still other cases, they must be considered as related to the problems unique to and inherent in the intimate nature of the medical educational process. These problems frequently arouse latent conflicts as the individual reacts to the unconscious significance that the particular problem may have for him.

In considering the effect of the medical educational process on the individual students, we must first concern ourselves with the often emotionally traumatic and stressful process of preparation for medical school that antedates the actual exposure to this process. The selection policies of the admissions committees of the various medical schools are sufficiently vague and mysterious in the minds of premedical students to give rise to a great deal of speculation, and to the perpetuation of the superstitions, myths, and legends that are indigenous to most undergraduate campuses. The anlage for later incapacitating anxieties during medical school is manifested during undergraduate years in the excessive emphasis on certain science courses, often to the exclusion of the liberal arts courses. One frequently hears, for example, that if a student does not get an A in Organic Chemistry, he might just as well forget all about getting into medical school. Grades per se acquire a disproportionate and even frightening degree of importance, so that class ranking and grades to the tenth of a point become the goal rather than the learning and preparation for later professional training. Some students whose natural bent is not along the lines of the physical sciences find it necessary to cram for examinations in order to attain the fantasied necessary grades. They then enter medical school with a preexisting substrate of anxiety that is aroused by the prospect of an overwhelming scientific curriculum.

Despite the deliberate effort made by admissions committees to seek out the more rounded individuals in their search for the personalities best suited for the future practice of medicine, selection often does favor those students who are ranked first in the class. Some of these students are well chosen. There are, however, a number of such scholars whose attainment of "first" is an obsessive-compulsive necessity in their defense against their own anxiety. The Harvard Medical School draws from among the best premedical students in the country, so that it is, to some degree, to be expected that the problem of the anxious obsessive-compulsive scholar should present itself from time to time. The student enters the medical school with the realistic knowledge that the work load will be greater than that to which he has previously been accustomed. The anxiety aroused by the increased demands often leads him to self-doubts with resultant apprehension and an insecure approach to the curriculum. At Harvard Medical School the attempt is made to deemphasize grade consciousness and to stress the importance of learning for the sake of preparation for future practice. Theoretically, this approach should tend to alleviate the anxiety of these students. For many students, perhaps it does. For the rank-conscious obsessive-compulsive, however, it has sometimes backfired. In undergraduate college these students had found it necessary to prove themselves and needed the high grade and rank as a defense against the anxiety of insecurity and vulnerability. When confronted with numerous others who similarly had been first in the class, or whose intellectual levels were equally high, if not higher, their defenses no longer operated, and their anxiety became intolerable.

One such student had led his college class academically and had been a campus leader athletically and politically. His fears of inadequacy as a man had been controlled by the mechanism of attaining a position of leadership that was unassailable. When it appeared to him that the competition of his classmates would make it impossible for him to utilize again the mechanism of security through leadership, his anxiety broke through. His feelings of panic were so intense that he became "paralyzed" in his scholastic efforts. Contact with the health service was necessary several times a day over a period of months in order to enable him to keep functioning.

The course material in the medical curriculum is quantitatively extensive, and during the preclinical years may appear to be virtually overwhelming. Much of the material is strange and most of it seems important. The ability to discriminate between what is important and what is a minor "footnote to the footnote" is rather difficult for many first-year students to develop. The frequent reassurance of the instructors that one cannot possibly learn everything is of but transient value, for it seems to impose all the more the need to be able to discriminate and also seems to attack the obsessional need to know everything for the sake of security. When this need is great, being told that he cannot hope to learn everything is seen by the student as tantamount to being told that he cannot hope to defend himself against his anxieties, especially in view of the fact that this defense had previously been developed because it seemed to be the only effective one for him.

A reflection of the operation of grade-consciousness with its emphasis on full-time study has been seen in the occasional student who feels that time allotted for recreation must by definition be time lost from study.

One such student was seen in an acute anxiety reaction with guilt feelings because he had permitted several classmates to "seduce" him into going to the movies with them one weekend evening. He had attained a straight A average in undergraduate college by means of studying seven days and seven evenings a week for the full four years. He felt that the greater demands of medical school must certainly require at least as intensive study as he had thought college had. He also feared that if the school authorities learned that he had "goofed off" for a night, they might rescind his scholarship.

Perhaps the most generally disturbing event of the early part of the first year is the occasion of the first midsemester examination. Many students comment that they could approach the exams with considerably more equanimity if they had any idea of how they stood in relation to their classmates. Coming from many different colleges at which examination policy is so divergent, pretest guessing among the students usually leads to confusion with apprehension about the possible nature of the questions to be asked and about the possible penalty for not doing well. The undergraduate pressure for high grades persists despite the reality of having been accepted into a medical school and is seen in the expressed fear of discharge from the school if top grades are not won in every test situation.

Medical educators are well aware of the fact that the unconscious motivation of students entering medical school varies considerably from student to student, though their consciously expressed humanitarian interests often have a familiar ring. In each entering class, however, there are some students, usually few in number, whose motivational drive has been toward the goal of getting into medical school but not necessarily toward the goal of becoming physicians. Doubts appear in the minds of these students, and the question arises as to whether they do or do not belong in medical school. Inhibition of scholastic performance develops, and depression appears in the wake of the loss of any true goal. Some of these students have felt driven to stick it out, mainly because of the parental pressures which may initially have influenced the decision to seek entry into medical school. Their academic records later indicate a level of performance appreciably below their potential. During this time, many of them may come to the health service with sundry physical complaints which in time are recognized as elements of a depressive reaction, or they may come directly for psychiatric help because of feelings of anxiety and depression which they may have come to appreciate themselves. Other students have resolved the motivational problem by accepting the fact that some other field of endeavor might be more appropriate and withdrawing to seek that other calling. In our experience, these students have gone into the physical sciences, mainly as researchers, into law or the ministry, while a few have left the academic community completely to go into business.

As the curriculum moves into the study of disease processes, anxieties stemming from fears of vulnerability and defectiveness become evident, usually associated with hypochondriacal complaints. While fears of physical illness appear in conjunction with the study of anatomical pathology and pathophysiology, fears of mental illness appear later in the setting of close personal contact with mentally ill patients. The nature of the symptom, though perhaps precipitated by the subject matter under consideration, is most often related to the past life experiences of the student and frequently may be traced to a personal or family history of disease.

Thus, a student whose mother had been hospitalized repeatedly because of recurrences of her schizophrenic process became very disturbed, expressing anxiety lest he develop symptoms of the illness himself, especially as he is confronted with a frankly psychotic patient during his psychiatric case work.

Hypochondriasis as a symptom in depression in which guilt feelings over hostile wishes toward the lost object are prominent is well known. This has been observed on a number of occasions when a parent or other loved one had been lost. The basic dynamic factor is the denied hostility toward the lost loved one. The current reality of the study of pathology and disease, however, exercises an influ-ence on the organ choice, so that the neurotic reaction may involve the same organ system as that involved in the fatal illness or an organ system that might be related but with which the student might not otherwise be acquainted.

A fourth-year student was in the midst of his course in Clinical Neurology when his father, long ill with arterial hypertension, died fol-lowing a cerebrovascular accident. Shortly after his return to classes after his visit home for the funeral, the student developed headache, in-somnia, poor power of concentration, and ill-defined feelings of unclear thinking. He diagnosed these symptoms as indicative of some form of disease of the central nervous system, "maybe brain tumor." That these hypochondriacal symptoms were not merely part of the depressive grief reaction became clear when they persisted beyond the period of mourn-ing and disappeared only after working through the early hostile feelings toward the lost parent.

Being confronted with concrete evidence of injury and disease arouses severe anxiety in still a different setting. To some students, such injuries are seen as realistic proof and confirmation of retalia-tory castration fantasies. Other students may view the same injuries with the anxiety that may be associated with the fears of their own repressed sadistic impulses.

A case in point is that of an upperclassman who experienced epi-sodes of severe anxiety whenever a male patient with a leg injury was admitted to the emergency ward where he was on duty. During his child-hood and adolescence he had had strong feelings of rebelliousness toward his father. He had also feared his very masculine father and resented the fact that his father had not helped him to grow up to be "a real man." He had been a rather undersized youngster who was overly sheltered by his mother, with whom he developed an extremely close relation-ship. During the student's adolescence, his father was accidentally killed during the war, sustaining mangling injuries to his legs. The relation-ship with his mother then became even closer for a period of time, so that he himself came to realize that they were abnormally close to each other. During the course of psychotherapy, the Oepidal nature of the relationship with his mother, the feelings of hostility toward his father, and his own castration fears became manifest to him. The symbolism of the anxiety-provoking leg injuries which he witnessed also became evident, with a positive therapeutic result.

The initial period of clinical work, with the approach to and contact with a living patient now a reality, imposes a new adjustment demand that not all students are prepared to make. For some students, it is the beginning of the realization of the dream of becoming a doctor. These students may feel overwhelmed with pleasurable anticipation while yet feeling the anxiety of doubt as to whether they are properly equipped and competent enough to assume the new role. At this point in the curriculum, the first steps are taken that give the students the feeling that now they are about to become doctors in the clinical sense. Often, during this period, unconscious motivational factors begin to manifest themselves. Sibling rivalry and identification with a physician father both are fraught with fantasied danger in the event of successful accomplishment.

Unsatisfied unconscious sexual curiosity, often Oedipal in character, is well recognized as a dynamic factor in the motivational pattern of a number of entrants into the medical profession. For the students in whom this factor assumes prominent proportions, this approach to the patient brings him to the very brink of satisfying the need that carries with it the anxieties of unresolved Oedipal fears.

A third-year student who had prided himself on his excellent adjustment to the stresses of medical school developed acute anxiety when about to perform, for the first time, a pelvic examination on a gynecological patient. Prominent in his fantasies were memories of a punishing father who would unquestionably forbid any such explicitly sexual behavior.

The next peak of emotional concern during the medical student's career occurs during the final year when, as he searches about for appropriate internships for which to apply, he finds himself confronted with the need to make some sort of specialty choice. At this juncture, he again becomes aware of grade consciousness, feeling that class rank will determine the quality of the internship available to him. Many of the anxieties occasioned by other exigencies of medical school again arise. While previously the practice of medicine may unconsciously have been conceived as a means of satisfying scoptophilic desires or aggressive sadistic impulses or as an instrument for the further resolution of the Oedipus situation, the time has now come to add to these unconscious motives the realistic necessity for making a choice that could well determine the success and happiness of his future career. Reality problems may operate most powerfully at this time to reinforce or to conflict with deeper motives.

In discussing the emotional problems of the medical student, certain other factors must be considered which are related to the particular age group here involved. The medical student is, in effect, a graduate student. His college classmates who have not continued on into higher education may be out in the business world, establishing their own material independence and security. He, on the other hand, is forced by virtue of his persistent schoolboy status into a circumstance of dependence that is continued well beyond his supposedly successful adolescent emancipation, for which he had struggled throughout college years. The "perpetual student" of the graduate schools is looked down on by the medical student, who prefers to think of himself not so much in terms of one in continued education, but as one in professional training.

To be held in a state of dependence has proven to be for many a source of anxiety with depressive features, as they felt themselves drawn almost inexorably into feelings of inadequacy and doubt about their future competence as physicians. This doubt has been manifested by students just about to enter their clinical work but has most frequently been heard from fourth-year students as they neared graduation. The very prospect of being cut loose from the constant supervision to which perhaps they have been grudgingly accustomed now becomes rather threatening to them. Many a former student, as he acquired a sparkling new M.D. to add after his name, has wondered in what way he was any better prepared to care for the sick than he had been just a few minutes earlier as a student subjected to constant scrutiny and supervision.

Another aspect of the problem of being dependent has to do with the desire of many students of this age group to be married. It is not the purpose of this writer to discuss the relative merits of the married versus the unmarried state for the medical student. Positive aspects may be seen in either state, as may negative ones, depending on the point of view of the observer. Be that as it may, many students have consulted the health service psychiatrist with problems related to their respective married or unmarried state. Single students may find that, as more adult medical students, their sexual urges and desire for gratification come more and more into conflict with the controlling forces of morals and social convention which had been so effective during their younger undergraduate days but which now seem to have diminished in their inhibitory strength. Nevertheless, as occurred with two students, castration fears of such intensity may be aroused that loss of potency develops. In one student, this persisted for but a brief period until his anxieties were understood, while in the other, the impotence was related to such deeply seated unconscious fears that psychoanalysis was required. There is among medical students the same weekend preoccupation with the problem of what to do for recreation, whom to date, and the like, that is the plaint of students at almost any level. Only rarely, however, has this assumed such significance that it has been brought to the psychiatrist as a problem.

The married student has no such problem as where to seek his dates or how to satisfy his sexual desires, but other situations arise in connection with matrimony. A number of married students are supported financially by independent incomes or by subsidies from their parents. An appreciable proportion, however, find themselves in the position of having to rely on the income of their working wives for their everyday expenses of rent, food, clothing, and recreation. Here, the reaction to a prolonged state of dependence is further complicated by the fact that the man of the family is, in effect, still a schoolboy, while the woman is the breadwinner. For some students, feelings of inadequacy that may have been present previously are enhanced by this circumstance and at times are elaborated into questions of doubts about their masculinity.

Still another situation arises which has brought not the student, but the wife to consult the psychiatrist. This problem stems from her inability to compete with her husband's books for his affections. The young bride complains that she finds it difficult to have to spend evening after evening watching her husband occupied with his studies to the point of almost total exclusion of any appreciation of her presence, much less of her desire for some attention. During the clinical clerkship periods, the young wives find it rather distressing

not to have their husbands at home every other evening and sometimes not until rather late into the night. Several wives were brought
to the health service by their husbands, who failed to understand
why they seemed unduly moody, often appeared to be brooding and
nursing complaints which they could express only in terms of feeling
neglected. Only after several interviews were they able to verbalize
their feelings of rejection, comparing the relative lack of attention of
the husband with the romantically affectionate attentiveness of the
suitor, as they had known it before the wedding.

It has been the purpose of the writer thus far to indicate in
review the nature of the psychiatric problems which may arise in the
course of the medical educational process and to suggest the relationships that appear to exist between those problems and the several
stages of progress in that course. It appears that each step in the
process of educating a medical student, of producing a new physician, carries with it the potential of threatening the equanimity of
the student, depending on his emotional past history and personality
structure.

The origin of the referral for psychiatric help in our clinic has
been fourfold: self-referral, referral by fellow students who may
have had experience with the health service psychiatrist, referral by
other health service physicians, and referral by the dean's office. During the first two years after psychiatric services were made available
to the students, most of the referrals were made by other physicians
of the health service, whom students would consult for emotional
problems which were but poorly disguised by somatic complaints. As
more and more students were seen by the psychiatrist, their impressions became the topic of increasing interest to others who might
have been considering such consultation for themselves. Occasionally,
some students would convince others that they should come for help.
In fact, a few were actually accompanied to the clinic by their
friends when they came to make their appointments. With the passage of time, the percentage of self-referrals increased while the referrals by others diminished considerably. Remaining consistent are
the referrals by the dean's office. These have usually resulted from
conferences with students who, having been called in because of ineffectual academic performance, may have been recognized as undergoing some sort of emotional turmoil or inhibition.

360 / Emotional Problems of the Student

The acceptance and utilization of a psychiatric service that is easily and quickly available to the student is shown in the fact that during the past several years an average of 13 percent of the student body has consulted the psychiatrist in any one year. Variation of any significance has not been noted among the classes from which the initial contacts have been made. It has been noted, however, that the number of visits by fourth-year students overall has been less than those made by other students. This has been attributed to the lack of available time of these students during their clinical clerkships. This has been supported by the finding that, during one year when appointments for fourth-year students were made in the early evening after the close of the usual health service appointment hours, there was no difference in the number of visits compared to other classes.

The question may be raised as to why medical students should be so ready to seek psychiatric assistance. A number of factors are worthy of consideration here. The experience during these years has been such as to indicate the importance of understanding the pre-medical and medical students' conception of the psychiatrist as it is altered by their medical education and by their personal contact with psychiatrists on the faculty. It has been the policy of the Harvard University Medical Center Health Service to include, as part of the routine initial physical examination, a psychiatric interview. Many students have appeared for this interview in a state of anxiety, manifested as anxiety symptoms, as resentful defensiveness, or a frank hostility. Almost invariably, the anxiety has been found to be associated with the fantasy of the mind-reading psychiatrist whose probing questions might cause considerable emotional distress. Frequently, students have verbalized these fears, remarking that this was the first time they had ever seen a psychiatrist and that they were not quite sure what to expect. Ordinarily, these anxieties have subsided during the interview, so that before its termination a number have expressed their relief from the preexisting anxiety and stated that they were happy to know there is someone available to whom they might come with their personal problems. On subsequent occasions, students who came spontaneously with such problems cited the initial interview as having been responsible for the willingness to return. They felt as though they were now coming to someone who already knew them and not to a total stranger. They also felt reassured that the psychiatrist need not be a threatening figure.

The commonly held misconception of a schism between psychiatry and medicine in general is shared by many entering students. Another misconception is that psychiatrists deal only with psychotic patients and those with weak characters. The willingness of the medical students to seek psychiatric advice or therapy seems to increase as those misconceptions have been dispelled. It was felt that since the Medical School is trying to teach the highest caliber of medicine, then its health service should try to be an example of that high caliber of medicine in practice. It thus became incumbent upon the health service to assume this teaching function as part of every clinic contact. If it was to be taught that psychiatry is a part of medicine, then it should be presented as such. Consequently, the Harvard University Medical Center Health Service deliberated long on the problem of the location of the psychiatrist's office, and it was decided finally that it should be in the same suite as those of the internists, and use the same waiting room. Whenever a student expresses feelings of shame or anxiety about being seen by fellow students as he comes in or leaves the psychiatrist's office, this has been treated as an emotionally determined reaction to be understood. This has most often met with a positive attitude on the part of the student who would come to view that reaction as well as other reaction patterns in its proper perspective.

The curriculum of the Medical School, which includes academic teaching by the Department of Psychiatry through all four years, has contributed a great deal to the development in the student of a more mature attitude toward psychiatry. While it is true that each year there have been some students who have felt uneasy as they came to recognize in themselves neurotic traits about which they were learning in the psychiatric courses, most students have come to understand better the scope of the problem with which the psychiatrist has to deal.

The question also was raised as to whether the psychiatrist of the health service should participate in the instruction of the students for whom he might be caring. Arguments were presented with regard to the ease of mind of a student who must discuss his handling of a patient with his own therapist. What might happen to the therapeutic relationship between them, what might happen to the transference, and what about the influence of the counter-transference on the grading of a particular patient-student? In our own situation, it so happened that the psychiatrist had been cast in the role of teacher before he assumed the role of therapist. It was decided that this circumstance should not be altered and that, if anything, the situation should provide us with interesting information. Our experience has led us to a number of conclusions. Primary among these is the finding that medical students who learn through academic experience with an instructor to respect his clinical judgment will turn to that instructor with personal problems. This has been reported by clinical instructors in other fields as well as psychiatry. Beyond this, however, is the students' searching interest in whether their personal problems are being taken seriously. Their best yardstick of judgment is how the instructor considers and discusses the case which they present to him. If he shows sympathetic concern, if he shows humanitarian interest beyond cold scientific interest, then the students will feel encouraged to consult him. The psychiatrist-teacher, especially when dealing with small groups of students in informal case conference discussions, finds himself continually being tested by various mechanisms employed by students: challenging his point of view, disputing his conclusions, questioning his data, or accepting whatever he has to say with an outward display of complete and passive recipience. The reaction of the psychiatrist often becomes the determining factor in deciding whether the student will consult him. The one prominently negative feature has been the problem of grading. It has been our experience that, should the psychiatrist be placed in the position of having to pass judgment on the patient-student academically, he is then viewed by the student-patient as one who might be expected to pass judgment on him in the clinical therapeutic situation. For this reason, it is felt that the therapist-teacher should not be the one responsible for the grading of such students.

The duration of therapy done in the health service has been extremely variable, so that our statistical annual average of 6.7 visits per patient really has no significant value for this discussion. Students who presented themselves with character neuroses or with other emotional problems of long duration have required prolonged psychotherapy, while those whose problems are relatively acute and usually related to situations such as those discussed above, which were associated with the medical school curriculum, responded much more quickly to therapy. Mention should be made of the relatively quick grasp and understanding of the basic dynamics that is shown by these students who are seen at the time of greatest urgency and when their motivation for treatment is at its peak. While the expressed position of the health service is that short-term therapy aimed at the alleviation of acute incapacitating anxiety is all that can be offered, it has been found that medical students often are not satisfied with what to them is an incomplete resolution of their basic problem. They request that psychotherapy be continued, along psychoanalytically oriented lines, so that they can come to a better understanding of themselves and of the personality traits that have left them in a position vulnerable to the emotional stresses of medical education. Within the limits of the time available to the one psychiatrist at their service, this request has been granted. No ambitious program of trying to effect major alterations in personality traits has been proposed, even if such were possible under these circumstances, for medical educators have voiced the opinion that certain traits, such as a degree of obsessive-compulsive behavior, is of great value to the thorough medical student and physician.

In summary, our experience has pointed up that there is a relation between the personally oriented intimate character of medical education and the arousal of emotional reaction states in the students undergoing such medical training. The nature of the reaction reflects the previous background and the past life experience of the individual. Its content, however, is often colored by the subject matter under study at the time and the unconscious meanings of events in his education. For many of the acute problems, brief psychotherapy has proven to be sufficient for the alleviation of the disturbing symptomatology. As in other segments of the population, deeply rooted personality problems exist among the medical students independently of their professional work. Because of their contact with the concepts of psychiatry, these students come to recognize their difficulties and seek psychiatric help sooner than others. As the various medical problems of the medical students have been brought to the attention of the health service, it has become increasingly apparent that the services of a psychiatrist are essential for the general welfare of the medical school population.

19

Therapy

Graham B. Blaine, Jr.

Short-term psychotherapy is particularly effective with patients in the college-age group. Although it can be a useful method with adults and children, treatment at these ages usually must be long-term.

Child psychiatrists utilize a type of therapy that involves the therapist to a greater degree than the patient. Because of the language barrier, communication must be through the symbolism of play and direct expression of emotion instead of the more easily understood symbolism of speech. It takes a long time to understand fully what the child is trying to get across and even longer to establish a method by which the therapist can get ideas back to the patient.

Adults have firmly set patterns of behaving and thinking. Even though their behavior causes them distress and they come to the therapist for help in changing these patterns, the unconscious forces that make them behave in this neurotic and disliked pattern are well established and deeply set. It takes much time spent in therapy hours and the living through of many life experiences to effect a change in behavior for many of them. Here, unlike the child, the patient himself does the lion's share of the work of therapy, being expected not only to contribute significant material but also, for the most part, to make his own interpretations. If the therapist plays too active a part in adult therapy, he may stimulate resistance that cannot be overcome. Most adults cannot learn by being told what to do; they have to teach themselves by putting together isolated bits of material they bring into therapy and adding up individual episodes in their every-day lives to make a meaningful conclusion—meaningful not simply in the intellectual realm—for it is only truly emotional insight that can bring about changes in behavior and relief of symptoms. All this bringing together of masses of information, correlating it, living through experiences, and learning by them takes a long time and constant attention. With patients of college age, verbal communi-cation is possible—even easy—and neurotic patterns are not yet too firmly set. Short-term dynamic therapy can therefore be attempted. It need not be exclusively supportive therapy but can often be inter-pretive. Psychoanalytic theory forms the core of the treatment, but the techniques are modified.

While the psychiatrist is particularly well equipped through his special interest and training to utilize these methods, the coun-selor, faculty advisor, or in some instances, the dean may incorporate many of these principles both consciously and unconsciously into his handling of the student who comes to him for help. Knowledge of the mechanisms and techniques of psychotherapy can be helpful to those in advisory positions within a university, and it is rarely that this knowledge is used to ill effect. Certainly in academic areas where psychiatric help is available only to a very limited degree, the good which comes from the intelligent use of established psycho-therapeutic principles by all those who come in contact with students far outweighs the harm which is done through their occasional mis-interpretation or injudicious use.

The armamentarium of the short-term therapist includes a variety of effective weapons. First among them is environmental manipulation. This is a technique which we use sparingly but one which can be extremely effective when appropriately employed. In general, we do not believe in altering reality to suit the neurotic emotional needs of a student but rather hope to help the student adjust to the conditions which have been adapted to by the majority of his contemporaries. Making concessions often confuses the student further and encourages him to perpetuate his illness in order to achieve further special consideration.

Sometimes, however, it becomes clear that a certain circumstance which can be easily altered without changing or violating rules can make a great difference to a student—for instance, a change of roommates or the assignment of a single room to a student who needs to have time away from others for quiet contemplation. Also we have encountered students who find examinations unusually anxiety-producing at specific periods in their career, such as during freshman year or at the end of law school. We often allow these boys to take their exams in a room in the infirmary by themselves. This has often saved a boy's career and has helped him to fear examinations less so that on the next occasion rather than ask for special dispensation again he will go to the examination room without seeking help or advice from us at all.

Permission to drop a course is another way of helping a student through a stressful period, but again it is not something we believe should be automatically granted. Often trouble with academic work is better served by the granting of a leave of absence than by giving permission to eliminate a single course from the curriculum. A moratorium from the stress of a full course schedule may at times be therapeutic and a necessary aid for the achievement of sufficient calm to look at the deeper problems which caused the student trouble in the first place.

Another device, giving information, seems simple. Perhaps some think that it is not the psychiatrist's job to be a teacher, but education often turns out to be therapeutic. Sometimes, misinformation or misconceptions on the part of the patient are responsible for serious neurotic symptoms, which may appear at first glance to be far more complicated and to have deeper sources.

A college sophomore came to the clinic because he was shy about going out with girls. He knew that he was sufficiently attractive and was able to talk intelligently, but he never seemed able to take a girl out more than once. He had feelings of anxiety when he thought of calling up a girl a second time. In the course of working with him we found out, quite surprisingly, that he was under the misapprehension that his erection was different from everybody else's because it was vertical and not horizontal. He thought this would prevent him from having intercourse. This misconception was contributing greatly to his anxiety. Once it was relieved, simply by supplying the correct physiologic information, he began to be less afraid of girls and better able to carry out a long-term relationship.

Another simple technique is obtaining information on the expression of emotion. This has been described as ventilative treatment
or catharsis. Knight[1] uses the term "expressive therapy." The recollection of a childhood memory or the expression, in the therapeutic
hour, of hitherto unexpressed emotion against a parent or some other
person who has been a source of resentment for years can be dramatically alleviating at times. One must be careful, when using this
type of therapy, not to get into difficulties with a student whose
conception of psychotherapy is that it is a search for a key incident
in his life, which, when remembered and revealed, will immediately
cure his whole complicated neurosis. Many students, from their reading about psychiatry, have this idea. Sometimes, patients seem to
want to talk about nothing except their childhood. They become
frustrated and upset when they are unable to dredge up forgotten
memories during an interview. It often turns out that this is because
they think that they are supposed to search for a recollection of the
time they were kicked by a horse or stumbled into their parents' bed-
room. Often this kind of ruminating is a waste of time. There are
occasions, however, when the recollection of some unremembered
event will be an important turning point in treatment, as in the
following case.

A college junior who was in therapy at the clinic for several months
came to treatment because he had been having crying spells, when talking
to his instructors, for no reason he could think of. This happened also
with colleagues and contemporaries, particularly when he was out with
his fiancée. He was at a loss to explain this, and we worked for several
months trying to understand what the source of this distress could be.
It seemed clear that he felt very unworthy and guilty and that, at times,
he was overcome with these feelings of guilt and began to cry. But an
explanation of this did not seem to change his behavior. He continued
to feel tense, and once at 3:00 A.M., he called to say that he had to see
his doctor right away. He had just seen his fiancée and had an argument
with her about how far he should be allowed to go in their petting. She
told him that she thought she wanted to break the engagement. He said
that he had become so upset after leaving her that he pulled his car over
to the side of the road, started to scream as loudly as he could, and then
began beating the steering wheel with his fists. This behavior had frightened him so much that he thought he ought to talk to someone right

---

[1] Knight, R. P. Evaluation of psychotherapeutic techniques. Bull. Menninger
Clin., 16:113–124, 1952.

away about it. Toward the end of this emergency interview, he said, "I've suddenly thought of something that happened when I was 10 years old and I don't know why I think of it now." He went on to describe some sex play that had taken place with his younger sister. This was something that he had never been able to recollect in any interview before. His anxiety was immediately alleviated, and he felt perfectly able to return to his room and go to sleep.

This interview proved to be a real turning point in therapy. From then on this patient was really able to believe in and to understand the irrational feelings of worthlessness and guilt that had to do with his symptoms, and it was not long afterward that he was able to discontinue therapy because he was no longer troubled by crying spells. This experience differs from insight because, at the time of recall, the incident was not connected in the patient's mind with his symptoms. All he did was bring this incident up and talk about it. He received some reassurance, which immediately gave him relief and was therapeutically effective without the necessity of having the correlation between the incident and the symptom pointed out or understood.

Another factor, transference, has come to have many meanings. The original, classic definition referred to emotional feelings transferred from parental figures to the therapist. These irrational, positive or negative feelings were the only ones included in the definition. Recently, the term has been broadened in common usage, referring more generally to the total relationship between the patient and the therapist, and it is in this sense that we are using it here.

There are two principal ways in which transference can be therapeutic in short-term psychotherapy. One is through building trust in patients who have come to distrust the world at large because of various experiences that they may have had in childhood with unreliable, rejecting parents. A clinical relationship with a therapist may be a way to reestablish trust in the world at large, in that the patient knows that the therapist is interested and anxious to help. Because of this he can often begin then to trust. If the therapist remains a solid person who is predictable and nonpunitive, trust can be increased and transferred later from the therapist to other people in the patient's outside environment.

Another effective use of transference is replacement. The therapist actually plays an active part in the patient's life, replacing a father figure who has died or one who has no adequate role in the life of the patient. Replacement has to be done carefully. Several things can result in a negative way from this kind of role-playing. One of these is overdependence. The patient may become so demanding that the therapist has to set up limits. The patient may interpret this as a rejection, and the illness may be perpetuated instead of treated. Also, the assumption of a role by the therapist is sometimes more frightening than relieving to the patient, for he may be fearful of people who offer advice or represent authority figures. If the therapist behaves in a directive manner, the patient may become resentful and believe that he has to terminate treatment.

There is another pitfall in this type of therapy if a part of the illness is the acting out of rebellion. The therapist can get a certain enjoyment out of listening to the equivalent of *Till Eulenspiegel's Merry Pranks*. It is often hard not to be amused when a boy describes throwing a cherry bomb down the toilet and the furor that it caused, or stretching a wire across the threshold to trip up his roommate as he comes in. Of course, if the therapist chuckles and asks for more details about these pranks, he plays into them. He does what the authorities do by getting interested in and excited about bad behavior and ends up by encouraging more acting out.

Transference in the classic sense sometimes plays a part in the treatment program, but usually in short-term therapy the actual transference of childhood resentments against a parent is seldom experienced. Even when this does occur and it is obvious to the therapist, it is seldom possible to make the patient aware of what is happening. An interpretation of this sort usually cannot be accepted until after many months of therapy. It often works out, however, that the patient reacts to the therapist in a manner similar to that in which he reacts to his teachers or his colleagues—rejecting help when it is offered, for instance, or suspecting the motives behind an expressed interest in his welfare. This irrational behavior within the interview situation can often be interpreted with profit and is another valuable use of transference.

Insight is a very effective therapeutic tool and can be of more help in the deep-seated type of illness than any of the other factors discussed so far. Insight is a difficult thing to bring about, however, because there is a stubborn barrier between emotion and intellect in everyone, and quite often this barrier is reinforced by the intellectual values stressed in a college environment. For insight to be effective, it must penetrate that barrier and reach the patient on a feeling level.

A boy seen this year at the university health service represents an interesting example; he was helped to understand his problem on an emotional level by a dream.

He was an undergraduate who was disturbed because he was unable to establish a close relationship with a girl. He seemed to pick out girls who he knew were going to reject him. He would go out with them, take their abuse for a while, and finally be completely rejected and thrown over. In fact, he would stimulate the rejection himself. He could see this happening, was upset by it, and was afraid that it would keep him from getting married. He talked for a number of interviews about this and discovered that his mother had been a very seductive person herself. She had been extremely resentful of all his girls, and had warned him against women. She told him that they were deceivers and out to trap him. This contributed to his feeling that the only kind of girl who was safe was a girl who would throw him over. The girl with whom he could succeed was dangerous because she was bound to hurt him. He understood all this intellectually. He was a psychology student who had a good deal of knowledge of psychiatry and was pleased by all these intellectualisms that were discussed, but there was no change in his symptoms.

One day he came in and reported a dream that he thought was important. He had dreamt that he was at a night club, sitting at a table with his mother. They were eating peas and carrots, and across at another table was a beautiful chorus girl, who kept looking at the patient and beckoning to him. He felt panicky and unhappy and was unable to go over to her. This dream seemed to be a confirmation of what had been talked about. The patient understood this but he said, "There's something important about those peas and carrots. I don't know what they mean but they stood out awfully clear. I think we ought to find out what they mean." So he talked for the rest of the hour about peas and carrots. He discussed the significance of color green and the color orange. He talked about the fact that carrots were long and thin and that peas were round, but nothing seemed to have much meaning for him.

When he came in for his next interview a week later he said, "You know, something happened. I suddenly realized what those peas and carrots meant. Every time before I went out with a girl, my mother would say to me, 'mind your p's and q's.' Suddenly, when I remembered that, I *felt* as though what we've been talking about all these weeks had meaning for me in a different way."

Actually it did have new significance for him. The intellectual insights discussed for so many weeks had penetrated to an emotional level as a direct result of this dream. His symptoms improved and

he developed a warm relationship with a college girl who was accepting and appreciative. Here, intellectual insight gave way to emotional
insight after a dream, and symptoms were relieved through the attainment of this insight on a feeling level.

Reality testing is another valuable technique which, at first
glance, seems to be therapy in reverse. It is especially utilized in what
Knight[2] calls "suppressive therapy" and is effective in patients who
are delusional, have ideas of reference, and have not been entirely
relieved of their symptoms by other kinds of therapy such as psychoanalysis, shock tratment, or prolonged hospitalization. They still
function reasonably well except in limited areas, where they are
definitely out of touch with reality. They have a sort of encapsulated
psychosis. Sometimes, it is transient and best not treated by deep
probing. In fact, sometimes, attempts to interpret the symbolic significance of their "crazy" thoughts upset these students more than they
help them. They respond more satisfactorily to the therapist as a
reality tester. They come to talk about these delusions and ideas of
reference and to check with the therapist about them, often saying,
"Is this crazy, or isn't it?" They are able to talk frankly about it,
often gaining enough reassurance to maintain their adjustment at
home or in jobs because of this help in suppressing symptoms.

A senior in college who came to the clinic because of intermittent
depression revealed in the course of treatment that he had a plan for
reorganizing the economics of the world by having the population live
on the water, leaving the land for cultivation. He had worked this out
to the minutest detail and had invented many new words. He was convinced that this was *the* Great Plan to save the world from starvation.
His behavior, otherwise, was perfectly appropriate. He had many friends,
went skiing, played tennis, did well academically but still had this delusion, which he told to only a few people who were very close to him.

With a boy like this, a therapist, by being a reality tester who
helps him understand how farfetched his reasoning is but who at
the same time admits that the patient needs to reason this way at
the moment, can help keep this kind of thinking out of other parts
of the patient's life. Often, after he gains competence in other areas
and a greater confidence in himself, such a patient can abandon his
weird fantasy completely.

---

[2] Knight, *op. cit.,* p. 178.

Psychoanalysis as a method of treatment for those in the adolescent period is viewed with considerable caution by therapists and analysts alike. The barrier between the primitive impulse and fantasy life of the unconscious and the behavior and thought processes of the conscious is so easily permeated and so inconsistent in its protective ability at this age that the encouragement of unconscious expression and the discouragement of repression may lead to an overwhelming of the ego. It is argued that in some individuals this is inevitable and that no degree of active suppressive therapy can prevent the inevitable psychotic breakdown. If this is true, it is argued, then it is better that the episode occur under supervision and be controlled effectively through proper handling than to have it smoldering unwatched after being temporarily quieted by suppressive psychotherapy. Whether this is a valid approach or not, there still remain a number of students for whom psychoanalytically oriented psychotherapy is inadequate and for whom psychoanalysis is therapeutic. These individuals are not so fragile that they are in danger of being overwhelmed by the forces that lie within their unconscious but at the same time they are incapacitated to varying degrees by the operation of these same forces.

It is not easy for the college psychiatrist to predict who will profit from psychoanalysis. It is far easier to foretell who will suffer from it. However, after considerable experience in evaluation one comes to adopt certain principles regarding referral. One centers around the complaints of the patient. Deeply rooted symptoms such as long-standing phobias, obsessions or compulsions, sexual problems such as impotence or premature ejaculation, and frequent extreme swings of mood usually do not find permanent resolution after psychotherapy, although we are constantly being surprised at how many apparently resistant symptoms do yield to short-term treatment.

In addition to the nature of the symptoms, the personality structure of the individual is highly important when it comes to evaluating the advisability of a referral for analysis. Not only is strength of defenses necessary but also a capacity for insight, a psychological-mindedness which can absorb interpretations, weigh them, and then utilize them to modify neurotic behavior. Sizing up the amount of psychological sophistication present in an individual student requires some testing out on the part of the therapist. Symptoms speak at

several different levels. A headache may have many different implications to some students all at the same time or it may have only one.
Most important, it may have an increasing number of meanings to
the student with a healthy unfrightened sense of curiosity about
himself.

A freshman was sent to the psychiatric clinic by the internist who
had given him his routine admission physical examination because the
boy had a history of constant headaches over a period of ten years. Extensive laboratory tests had been done by neurologists, allergists, and a
specialist in circulatory disorders without any positive findings. The student came to see a psychiatrist only because he was told to and it cost
him nothing. He felt that emotions could have nothing to do with headaches. The therapist remarked that the symptoms began at the same
time that the patient started school and asked if there were any difference in their intensity during vacations. The student stated that he
hardly noticed them during vacations except when playing tennis or going to a party. The doctor then commented on the competitive aspects of
school, tennis, and big parties. The patient agreed that these were competitive situations but said that he did not feel under tension at these
times so that he could not be having headaches because of being tense
over competition. When the therapist pointed out that headaches often
take the place of feelings of tension, the patient simply said he did not
believe it. The doctor was then able with the help of the student to
delineate carefully the relationship between the headaches and other
times when the student was repressing emotional feelings, not only of
competitiveness but also of anger, love, and a need to be loved, but the
student was not able to comprehend in his matter-of-fact mind any relationship between a physical symptom and an emotional state of mind.
He failed to keep subsequent appointments and a year later had a
psychotic breakdown during which he was free from headaches. He now
is working again at his studies and undergoing intensive psychotherapy
for his continuing headaches.

This student represents one end of a continuum on the other end
of which we find the patient who accepts readily and enthusiastically
every theoretical explanation of his behavior no matter how outlandish it may be. He usually has read many of the psychoanalytic
writers from Freud through Bergler and enjoys the feeling of importance it gives him to believe that he is similar to the interesting
patients described there. Blanket acceptance of any and all interpretations means a superficial intellectual insight, which is not true
insight at all, and serves only to ward off meaningful self-understanding my making a mockery of psychotherapy.

In the middle of the continuum lies the patient who has a good capacity for utilizable emotional insight and who can profit from psychoanalysis provided that his illness is amenable to such treatment and he has sufficient strength of defenses.

A sophomore who came to the psychiatric clinic for treatment of a complicated phobia was being considered for referral to an analyst. The clinic psychiatrist, in order to determine the student's capacity for insight, picked on one isolated symptom and tested the patient's ability to conceive of the different meanings of this symptom as they might be seen at different levels of consciousness and experience. The student complained that his performance on the track team as a shot-putter had fallen off markedly. The therapist suggested that an explanation of this might lie in the student's increasing self-consciousness. The student agreed that this might be a factor, and the therapist asked if there were any unusual feelings present at the time he was putting the shot. The patient reported feeling tense, tight, and clumsy, attributing this to a fear of failure to meet the present challenge or of not equaling his past record in this event. The doctor then asked if there were any other feelings present, and the student, instead of being satisfied with what he had already mentioned, went on to say that he also had fantasies about hitting someone with the shot as he hurled it out into space. He went on to say that he was not always ashamed of this at the time but that he had conflicting feelings—a satisfying kind of pleasure on the one hand and guilt and fear on the other. When the therapist asked whether the patient thought that this experience on the athletic field might symbolize conflicting feelings about aggressiveness in other areas, the patient said that he was not sure but that it was something "worth thinking about."

Visits to the university psychiatric clinic not only serve evaluative and referral functions in relation to psychoanalytic therapy but also can offer psychotherapy as preparation for later analysis. Many patients who have deeply rooted problems are not aware of the true nature of their difficulty. They may see a symptom as something rather annoying or slightly handicapping and feel that it should be easily removed after brief therapy. Only after they have learned more about themselves and what inner complicated trouble the symptom represents will they be ready to undertake the kind of long-term, intensive treatment which is necessary not only to get rid of the symptom but also to prevent more serious trouble in the future.

A married college senior came to the psychiatric clinic because of sexual difficulties within his marriage which involved premature ejaculation and occasional impotence. History revealed that these problems had been present for many years and were related intimately to his early psychosexual development. His masturbation fantasies had been sadistic in nature, and he could achieve orgasm in early adolescence only when riding horseback at a gallop and whipping the horse at the same time with great violence. At the end of the first interview it was explained that his problem was a deep-seated one and probably would yield only to intensive psychotherapy—probably analysis. The patient was skeptical. He very much wanted help for he felt that his wife was unhappy in her frustration but he did not wish to commit himself to the time-consuming, expensive, and in other ways threatening process of long-term therapy.

This student was seen in regular weekly interviews for a period of four months. Emphasis was placed in his therapy on the long-standing nature of his illness, the various hypothetical causes for it, and the degree of incapacitation which it was causing him at present. He began to see his parents in a new light. Instead of being accepting, loving individuals, he now thought of them as demanding and domineering. He came to discover previously unknown and bitter wells of resentment against them and to begin to express this toward friends. He also began to realize that his efforts to control himself and to laugh off things that worried or annoyed him was actually a way to keep from committing himself. He began to express dissatisfaction with his uncommitted way of life and began to wonder whether or not his inadequacy in the sexual area was not indeed related to his much more general feeling of inadequacy in relation to the world at large. Finally, he realized that inability to follow through with a job in a strong, firm masculine way was a very basic problem with him. When he saw the extent and depth of his original symptom as a result of these weekly interviews, he was able to accept psychoanalysis as a logical and necessary step. He asked for referral to an analyst and has been significantly helped by subsequent analytic therapy.

Group therapy has not been used extensively in our clinic, but there are indications that it can be used effectively in a university setting. At first blush it would appear that a group therapy program would enable the staff to be of help to more students, for eight to ten students seen for one and a half or two hours adds up to more student treatment hours than one student seen by one psychiatrist for one hour. We have found, however, that this apparently greater coverage does not actually occur. In the first place, the taxing quality of group therapy tends to drain the therapist's energy so that he is able to carry on fewer individual interviews. In the second place, patients well enough to participate in groups are often well enough to function without treatment, and being part of a group tends to hold them longer in therapy. Also, a number of hours have to be spent individually with group members anyway.

There is a tendency when the staff is hard pressed to find time to meet the demands of the students for assignment to a group to be made without much thought about selection. Either recommendation is made arbitrarily when there is no room on an individual schedule or else the less severe cases or those "for whom it can do no harm" are sent into a group. This sort of heterogeneous non-selected gathering is unlikely to coalesce and form itself into a serious, self-aware group. It has been our experience that such groups tend to be arenas for the acting out of symptoms and the display of differences rather than a place to learn to control impulses, get along with contemporaries, and begin to understand the causes of behavior. Although there may be some therapeutic value in acting out and performing within a group, it does not seem to us to be as useful an expenditure of valuable staff time as individual therapy, but our experience has been limited to two incompletely evaluated projects.

The college student is glad to discuss general subjects in bull sessions with contemporaries and even to reveal fairly intimate and personal experiences and feelings, but when this discussion is labeled therapy with the implication of illness, he tends to be much more guarded in front of his fellow students. This defensiveness makes a group discussion vague, inconclusive, and nonproductive. If, however, there is a definite goal to start with, which is understood and accepted by all, then the chances of building a cohesive group where members can trust each other enough to help each other is far greater. A group of this sort was instituted at Harvard recently. Ten boys from the sophomore class were selected by the dean as being in such poor standing academically that their chances of survival following the final examinations in June were less than one in ten. The boys were told this by the dean and again by the therapist in a letter which also invited them to participate in a therapy group. Eight of the ten reported for the first meeting which took place in April. Meetings were held weekly until the examination period (nine meetings in all), and discussion which originally centered entirely around study habits shifted quickly to family pressures, then to intrafamilial relationships, and finally to the kinds of conflicts which were deep inside these troubled students. The kind of unrestrained silliness and superficiality which characterized the nongoal-centered groups was simply not present. Presumably as a result of the group discussions, each student reported an improvement in his studying ability, and six of the eight brought their actual grades up to the point where they were allowed to continue in college.

Tranquilizing drugs have gained a limited acceptance at our clinic. Results seem to be in keeping with those reported by clinicians working in office practice elsewhere. Acute examination panic, stubborn insomnia, and a few cases of chronic anxiety seem to have responded well to the usual maintenance doses of Equanil or Thorazine. In some instances no effect whatsoever has been reported, and in general we feel that about 70 percent of those students treated report some benefit. One of our staff has found Dexamyl to be as effective in the treatment of anxiety as any of the newer drugs, which makes us wonder whether the words and the evidence of interest that accompany the prescription are not the most important ingredients. No definitive study of drug therapy has been made by us but such an undertaking is in the planning stage and should yield interesting results.

The problem of who in the average college population deserves therapy is intimately tied up with the question of who benefits most. Both of these questions need answering, for the psychiatric clinic at any university must be discriminating. None is in the position to meet the demands of all those who come asking for help. Not only do therapists have to keep their list of patients within the limit of their own ability to do good treatment but also their schedules must be flexible enough to allow for the handling of acute emergency cases which appear at certain fairly predictable times of the year. No set rules are possible in dealing with the handling of the case load in a clinic, partly because it is hard to define patient needs in specific terms, and partly because doctors, particularly psychiatrists, do not take kindly to regimentation. There are some general principles, however, which we have found valuable.

One of the most important is not to underrate the value of short-term psychotherapy. In college students many problems which appear to be deeply rooted and amenable only to depth analysis over a long period turn out either to be far closer to the surface than anticipated or else the student has defenses which are in such a transparent state that new understanding of the basic issues is surprisingly easy. A few evaluative interviews and the administration of projective tests usually make this clear.

A college sophomore came for help in overcoming a specific phobia. Beginning two years previously while in his last year at prep school he had begun to be afraid of chalk dust. It had started during a class in which the teacher wrote a great deal on the blackboard. The patient began imagining that the chalk dust was poisoning and felt compelled to brush every possible speck off his clothing and to wash his hands thoroughly after each meeting of his class. His concern became greater as time went on and broadened so that it involved all classes and finally all the students who were with him in classes as he felt that some dust might be on their clothing or hands and spread to him. As the school year drew to a close he began to get depressed and finally to be afraid that he would attack one of his teachers. He wrote to his parents who were living in a foreign country about this and told them that he thought he was losing his mind. His mother came to be with him and he improved enough to graduate and enter college.

During his freshman year he was untroubled. He roomed with two boys from a foreign country. Together they made such good friends with the proctor of the dormitory that they were able to lead a very free and uninhibited Bohemian life. Upon returning home for the summer the patient had a return of symptoms but not in as severe a form as previously.

Back in Cambridge for his sophomore year he found himself rooming in an upper class dormitory where there were a good many more restrictions and sharing his room with two boys who were former classmates at prep school. Almost at once he began to fear that there was chalk dust around the room. He thought that these students must have brought some dust from the classroom at school on their clothing and that this was contaminating the furniture, glassware, and toilet fixtures. He began to wonder whether either of them had been sitting in the chairs at the lectures he attended and started cutting classes in order to avoid the possibility of sitting in such a chair. Then he began to think everyone knew about his phobia, was watching him, ridiculing him, and about to take him to task on account of it. In this state of panic he came to the clinic for help.

In evaluating the appropriateness of beginning short-term treatment his therapist took into consideration the comparatively short duration of any kind of symptom (two years), the excellent functioning of the student academically, socially, and in athletics despite his symptoms and the fact that he was able to discuss his feelings freely, frankly, and without undue distress. He also ordered a battery of psychological tests and was reassured by what was reported. The tester stated that the boy showed a wealth of common sense and powerful conscious control mechanisms which were working successfully. He also felt that although the symptoms indicated a diagnosis of deep-seated obsessive-compulsive neurosis the Rorschach showed enough freedom in responses to allow some originality in form and a use of color in a direct fashion quite uncharacteristic of the obsessive patient. What the tests did show was an "inchoate agitated mood with some developmental immaturity."

On the strength of this test report and his initial clinical impression, the therapist proceeded with cautiously interpretive psychotherapy.

The patient responded with eagerness. The blocks against the verbal expression of hostility soon dissolved and his former school, the college, and conservatism in general were freely criticized. Later a dream concerning an old man being eaten away in the lime pits of a Nazi concentation camp opened the way for a discussion of feelings of aggression toward his father and shortly after this, at the end of ten interviews, the patient discontinued therapy and was no longer incapacitated by his phobia. The therapeutic factors present at the time of his recovery at prep school had been repeated. His aggressive fantasies came to awareness and he had the interest and support of an accepting person—this time his therapist instead of his mother.

Not all cases respond in such a gratifying manner, but it should always be borne in mind that the college student has a special kind of resiliency which allows him to resume the shape of normalcy with surprising ease. He usually is a rewarding patient. Of course there are occasional students who ask for treatment without being entirely sincere and others who are mildly curious about themselves but not in real need. It is important that these students be dispatched as quickly as possible. We have devised a method for giving appoint-ments which seems to accomplish this. Every senior staff member allocates three hours each week for new patients. These are the same week in and week out so that the appointment secretary has a block of time consistently available to fill requests. Some students come with a specific question which can be promptly answered; others are simply looking for the names of psychiatrists in the com-munity; and still others want to ask about another student whose behavior may be alarming to his friends. One appointment with an experienced therapist usually takes care of these problems. Students who appear appropriate candidates for therapy are discussed at a weekly two-hour meeting of the full staff. Here assignments are made to junior staff members, and an opportunity is given everyone to express special interest in taking on a certain case. Also at these meetings the general principles of disposition and referral are formu-lated, reviewed, and adjusted in relation to case load at the clinic and individual therapeutic time available. We have found that while in general the time spent in short-term psychoanalytically oriented psychotherapy is the time most valuably spent, still it is important for each therapist to have a few long-term cases in treatment. This allows him some variety in case material and keeps the staff in general aware of all the kinds of problems which college students have.

In conclusion, we can say in regard to therapy in a university setting that the college student is at a stage of development that is both remarkably vulnerable and remarkably treatable. He is flexible, impressionable, elastic, and resilient, but also brittle when hit too hard. He often blends into bizarre forms but still is malleable enough to return to conventional appearance with gentle and patient handling. He is usually in a mood to talk—to discuss values, ethics, motivations, life, death, suicide, and so forth. He is often anxious for guidance—direct advice, too—from someone who he believes is bringing order out of his own chaos, not superimposing direction on him or trying to get him to conform to a family pattern. In other words, he wants help toward self-expression—toward being himself—not molding by someone who has preconceived ideas about how young men should behave. If therapy is offered in this spirit, the adolescent responds in a most gratifying manner. He accepts interpretations with interest and curiosity without resenting them and without being frightened by them. His behavior, his productiveness, and his degree of happiness often change markedly for the better in a short period.

Index

Acne, 313
Acting out, 12, 271–274
Administration, 6, 10
  attitudes needed from, 315–316
  reactions to The Movement, 297–299
  role of, 170–171
Admissions, 7, 8, 9, 32
  application forms, 8
  changes in, 301–303
  recruiting, 301–302
Adolescence, 52, et seq.
  apathy as a feature of, 141–142
  ego in, 64–65
  prolonged, 52–53
Adolescent rebellion, 54, 170–172, 172–173, 312
  failure of, 136
Advanced Management Program, 348
Affluence, 300
Age, as source of anxiety, 339
Agitation, neurotic, 65
Alumni, reactions of, 294–295
Anarchy of impulse, 98
Anorexia nervosa, 313
Anxiety, 65, 166 et seq., 186, 339–340, 347–348, 349
Apathy, 86–89, 129 et seq., 310
  baffling aspects, 130
  as a defense, 138–141
  dynamic theory, 134–140
  educator's role in treatment, 129–130, 143–145
  and The Movement, 269, 271
  onset, 129
  in prisoners of war, 131

Apathy (cont.)
  psychotherapy, 145–146
  unconscious anger in, 87
  unconscious rage in, 138–139
  in women, 310
Aptitude tests, 33–34, 44
Athletics, subsidization of, 12
Auditory discrimination, 195–197

Beards, 94
Being orientation, 291–293
"Big League Shock," 59–60, 310–311
Body
  devalued, 69
  image, 57
Brain damage, 31, 39–40
Bureau of Study Counsel, 208–210
Business School, 333 et seq.
  first year, 337–343
  men, contrasted to undergraduates, 333–334
  program, 334–335
  second year, 344–345
  typical personality, 341

Case load, psychiatric, 377, 379
Case method of teaching, 340–342
Castration complex, college as cause of, 62
Catharsis, 367
Cerebral Dominance, 190–191
Character disorders, 93–100
  therapy with, 100
  at Yale, 99

Coddling, 21
Coeducation, 306, 314–316
  strains of, 307 et seq.
College, image of, 6
College Board Examinations, 44
Columbia, 273, 278
Community resources, 10–11
Complex, 68
Confidentiality, 3–4, 23
Conscience, 54
  externalized, 63
Coping, 243–252
Counseling, 19, 45–46, 48–49, 317–
  319
Counseling teacher, role of, 23–24
Course load, 366

Deception, 81
Defense mechanisms, 63, 66–67, 312,
  376
Defenses, lack of, 69–70
Dependence, 357–358
  declaration of, 310
Depressions, 25, 81–85
  contrasted to apathy, 140–141
  endogenous, 82
  endogenous treatment of, 84
  homosexual, 105–106
  onset, 81–82
  reactive, 81
  reactive, treatment of, 82
  in suicide, 110–111, 120–122
  in women, 310–313
Diagnosis, 23–24
Digit Symbol Test, 186
Discipline, 2–4
"Doing" orientation, 52, 291–293
Dow sit-in, 280
Drop-outs, 6, 175 et seq., 225 et seq.,
  elsewhere, 179–180
  numbers, of, 178

Drop-outs (cont.)
  psychological tests of, 178 et seq.
  therapy and, 263–264
  work while out, 260–263
Drugs, 148–162
  adolescent dynamics, 155–160
  adult views, 150–151, 162
  in The Movement, 286–288
Dyslexia, 188, 190
  bibliography, 205
Dysmenorrhea, 313

Eating habits, 312–313
Education, 145–147
Educators, role of, 1
Elation, in schizophrenia, 75
Emotional disorders
  frequency, 318, 321
  predicting, 331, 332
  in suicides, 109
Emotional disturbance
  frequency, 17
  signs of, 18
Environmental manipulation, 364–365
Erikson, theory of, 19, 55, 98, 180
Examinations, trouble with, 26, 218–
  220
Excuse system, 14, 94–95, 164, 366

F scale, 38
Faculty, role of, 17
  reactions of, 295–297
Failure, need for, 170
  to establish identity, 171–172
Family, good, 177
Father, 54
Flying saucers, 96
Foreign students, 328–330
  at Business School, 346
Future orientation, 53

Gnosticism, 290–291
Grades, 191, 322–323
  predicting, 241–242
  on readmission, 231
Graduate students
  Arts and Sciences, 321 et seq.
  Business, 334
  compared with undergraduate, 320,
    325–326
  described from questionnaire, 333
  women, 312
Grant Study, 295
Group tests, 188
Group therapy, 374–376
Guidance, requests in identity crises,
  56

Hand Test, 275–276
Harvard Block Assembly Test, 34
Harvard, Class of '44, 294–297
Harvard Reading Course, 208–224
Harvard Student Study, 240, 242,
  257–258, 296
Health, education about, 13–14
Heart symptoms, 348
Home, good, 66–67
Homosexual panic, 104–105
Homosexuality, 100–108
  administrative attitude to, 107–108
  in America, 101
  causes not understood, 102–103
  and discretion, 108
  and heterosexuality, 106–107
  parents and, 101–102
  temporary, 102–103
  therapy in, 107–108
  vagueness of concepts, 101–102
Hospitalization
  of manics, 89
  possible effects of, 79
  in psychotic cases, 77–78
  of suicides, 126–127

Hypochondriasis, 354–355
Hypomania
  frequency, 91
  onset, 91
  therapy, 91–92
Hysteria, 343–344

Identification, 19–20
Identifying in adolescence, 54
Identity, 170–173, 356
Identity crisis, 55–57, 95, 179, 310,
  338–339
  female, 310
  male, 63, 136–137, 343
  in The Movement, 269–279
  role, 57–58
Impulsive expression, 66
Inferiority feelings, 172–173
Infirmary, in psychotic cases, 78–81
Information giving, 366
Inner Emigration, 289
Insight, 369–370
Intellectualizing, 64, 66–67
Intelligence
  in neuroses, 61–62, 68–69
  test, 33–34, 35, 43
Interpretation, avoiding, 21

Krishna, 290
Kuder Preference Record, 43

Language
  aptitude test, 204
  audio-visual teaching of, 194–199
  brain damage in disability, 200
  disability, 39–40, 164 et seq., 186–
    205
  emotional causes of disability, 199–
    200
  foreign languages, 191 et seq.

Language (cont.)
  medical literature, 188–189
  requirements, 59, 64, 185–188,
    192–193, 197–204, 201–205
  syndrome, 189–190
Laziness, 129
  student, 173
Library books, 12
Literature, reading of, 223–224
LSD, 151–152, 160

Major field and illness, 326–327
Male identity, 94
Manic disorders, 89–92
  frequency, 90–91
  onset of, 89–90
  thinking in, 89
  unconscious depression in, 90
Marijuana, 148–149, 153–154, 287–
    288
Married students, 358
Masturbation, in identity crisis, 58
Mathematics, studying, 222–223
Medical center, diversity in, 350
Medical examinations, 109, 329–330,
    359–360
Medical School
  clinical years, 356
  first year, 353–354
  pre-clinical years, 352–356
Medical students, 350 et seq.
  contrasted to others, 350–351
  disease, 354–355
  goals of, 353–354
  wives of, 358–359
Medicine, preventive, 11
Memory, screen, 134
Middle Management Program, 347–
    348
Miller Analogies Test, 43
Minnesota Multiphasic Personality In-
    ventory, 36, 235–236
MIT, 294

Mnemonics, 222
Mobility, in identity crisis, 58
Movement, The, 267–304
  admissions, 299–303
  administration, reactions to, 297–
    299
  aggression denied, 277–278
  alumni, reactions to, 294–295
  anarchism, 283–285
  apathy and, 269–271
  case study, 270–279
  causes of, 269–270
  Columbia, 278
  counterreaction, 274–278
  diction gap, 272–273, 293–294,
    295
  Dow sit-in, 280
  drugs in, 286–288
  faculty reactions to, 295–297
  flight into action, 271–274
  fraternité, 278–279, 286–287
  gnosticism, 290–291
  music, 289
  new breed, 299–301
  premise gap, 291–293, 300
  privatization, 285–291
  radicalization, 279–283
  religion, 289–290, 292–293
  sex, 289
  values, 286, 291–293
Music, 289
Myers-Briggs, 240, 244, 245, 257–
    258

Neuroses
  adolescent vs. adult, 55
  difficulty of categorizing, 61, 67
  frequencies of, 59
  quiet decent, 64–65
  student, 52
NLF, 294
Nonpsychiatric help, 19
Nonpsychiatrist, role of, 27

Normal vs. neurotic, 56
Numerical Speed Alpha, 34

Oblomov, 86, 130–131
Obsessive neuroses, 84, 342, 351–352, 353
Oediphal conflicts, 53, 69–70, 356
Ohio State Psychological Examination, 238
Oral aggression, 69
Orality, 69

Parents, 311, 339–340, 354, 356
    appreciation from, 169 et seq.
    attitudes needed from, 315–316
    role of, 77–78
    sacrifices, 60
Parietal rules, 315
Passive aggression, 277–278
Patient
    new, 379–380
    role of, 26
Peer group, 54
Physical illness, 312, 354
Physician
    psychotherapy by, 21, 22, 23
    role of, 21–22
Physicians, outside, 4
Polarization, 298
Police, use in emergencies, 80–81
Potency, 68
Prankster, 94 et seq.
Premedical students, 351–352
President, college, 12
Preventive psychiatry, 318–319
    business school, 346–347
Private school, 259
PRL, 232, 241
Problem diagnoses, 60–62, 321–322
Prognosis, 18, 55, 70, 71
    in apathy, 90
    character disorder, 99

Prognosis (cont.)
    of college students, 379–380
    in endogenous depression, 82
    in graduate school, 323–324
    graduate students, 332
    with psychoanalysis, 372–373
    in reactive depressions, 81
    in readmissions, 227–235
    in schizophrenia, 73
    in short term therapy, 378–379
    in women, 317
Projective tests, rationale, 43
Psychiatric personality, 100
Psychiatrist
    acceptance of, 360
    and community, 16
    contrasted to psychologist, 30
    as instructor, 361–362
    and medical education, 362–363
    role of, 1, 18, 23, 24, 76–77, 359–360, 372–373
    role in suicide prevention, 127
    special skills of, 30–31
    unlike usual physician, 26–27
Psychiatrists as educators, 15
    number needed, 71
    numbers of, 16
    scarcity, 29, 70
    skills needed, 71
Psychiatry
    role of, 19
    social, 15–16
Psychoanalysis, 372–374
Psychological tests, 27 et seq.
    used in college clinic, 32 et seq.
    interpretation of, 35, 42–43, 45, 46–47
    interpreting, 28
    norms for, 34
    use in planning therapy, 40–41
    use by psychiatrists, 29–30
    referral for, 27 et seq.
    referral method, 32
    referral sources, 32

Psychological tests (cont.)
  reporting results of, 37 et seq.
  used in study of dropouts, 240, 244
  time needed for, 39, 44
  use in vocational guidance, 42
Psychologist
  relieving psychiatric load, 29
  role of, 28
  testing loads of, 51
Psychoses, 73 et seq., 343
  disposal, 324
  frequency, 73
Psychosomatic treatment, 49
Psychotherapy, 364 et seq.
  with adults, 364–365
  as an aid to psychologist's other
    functions, 50–51
  with children, 364
  choice of, 18
  in college, 70–71, 71–72, 333
  counseling, 47–48
  fear of, 95
  ground rules of, 26–27
  harm in, 18
  length of, 72
  of medical students, 362
  with medical intervention, 25, 49
  by psychologist, 46 et seq.
  referral by psychologist, 48–49
  results of, 71
  short term, 365 et seq.
  standards in, 47
  time for entering, 26
  with women, 317–319
Psychotic behavior, 25–26
  studies, 24–25
Psychotic emergencies, management
  of, 79–80
Punishment, 10

Questionnaire #8, 240, 244

Radcliffe, 307 et seq.
Reading course, 208–223
Reading
  of notes, 221–223
  problems of, 39, 65–66, 68, 206–
    224
  speed of, 210–212, 223, 224
  teaching of, 212–223
Readmission, 31–32
  policies, 225–226, 226–227
  research needs, 239–240
  screening for, 236–239
  study of, 240–267
  success of, 227–235
Reality testing, 371–372
Referral problems
  at Bennington, 58–59
  at Brooklyn College, 58
  at Harvard, 59–60
  presenting complaint, 60–61, 168
  graduate students, 326
  medical students, 359
  psychiatrist, 322
Referral sources
  psychological tests, 27–32
Religion, 289–290
Repressed, return of, 64
Repression, 64, 65
Research
  on assets of students, 14–15
  by psychiatrist, 14
  by teams, 14
Reversals, 189–190, 194
Riots, 9–10
Rorschach test, 32, 36, 38, 40, 44,
    62, 177 et seq., 337
  in college neuroses, 64–65
  in dropout study, 235–236, 241,
    245, 258–259
Rules, administrative, 6, 10
Rustication, 89, 312, 327–328
  value of, 183, 184

Schizophrenia, 72–79
  management of, 77
  onset, 74
  thinking in, 74
Scholar, role of, 19
Scholarships, 12
SDS, 268, 281–282, 297, 298, 301
Security, 309
Sex, 53, 64, 65, 67, 287, 289, 313–316
Slackers, 163
Slashing, 272
Social tensions, 9
Sociological sources, 326
Sorting out, need for, 180
Specific reading disability, 188, 190
Speed Alphas, 34, 45
Strawberry Statement, The, 270–279
Strephosymbolia, 188, 191, 196
  case, 193–194
  incidence, 192
Strong Vocational Interest Blank, 35, 43
Student groups, consultation with, 11
Student TAT, 240, 244, 256, 257
Studies, as projected emotions, 20–21
Study
  as aggression, 174 et seq., 343
  as dangerous, 62
  groups, 336
  methods, as a defense, 64
  as potency, 67–68
  problems, 163 et seq.
  as sexual curiosity, 343, 356
Study block, 310, 315
  conscious, 164
  unconscious, 163–164
Studying
  as a defensive, 64
  defined, 62–63
  gains from not, 62
Suicidal personality, 109

Suicide, 25–26, 88, 109 et seq.
  contagion of, 115
  depression and, 121
  dynamic theories of, 118–119
  family background, 113
  grades and, 116
  locations, 116
  losses preceding, 113–114
  medical complaints and, 122–123
  methods, 114
  mood changes before, 120
  prediction of, 109–111
  preventive measures, 125–126
  psychiatric contact and, 119–120
  rate, 112
  religious background, 113
  seasons, 115–116
  social causes, 112–113
  wartime, 116
Suppression, 64

Teacher, role of, 18–19, 365
Teachers, helping, 14
Teaching, effective, 14
Tests, psychological (see Psychological tests)
Thematic apperception case, 182
Thematic Apperception Test, 36–37, 44, 98, 182
Therapy, 363–380
  for dropouts, 263
Theory, steps into, 25–26
They, 170–171
  as externalized conscience, 63
Thinking, hard, 311
Tranquilizers, 49, 92, 377
Transference, 368–369

Unconscious expressions of problem, 20
Underachiever, 163–174

Underdog theme, 279
Universe, 180

Values, 291–293
Vandalism, 12
Ventilation, 366–367
Verbal Speed Alpha, 34
Vocabulary, 34
Vocational guidance, 41 et seq., 56–
    57, 357
  at business school, 345–346
  as general education, 46
  reliable sources, 45

Vorhaus Theory, 64–65, 66–67

Wechsler-Bellevue Intelligence Scale,
    43, 186
Wechsler Memory Scale, 186
Weltanschauung, 182, 183
Women
  careers of, 308
  college, 307 et seq.
  graduate students, 309
  marriage, 309
Word blindness, 188
  case, 193–194
Work sample, 34, 181